...mas Keneally is married with two daughters
and two grandchildren, and lives most of the year
in Sydney, Australia. He has been shortlisted for
the Booker Prize three times, and won it in 1982
with *Schindler's Ark*, which was subsequently
made into the internationally acclaimed film
Schindler's List, directed by Steven Spielberg. His
non-fiction includes an entertaining book on the
American Civil War, *American Scoundrel*, and a
superb epic about the Irish diaspora, *The Great
Shame*.

ALSO BY THOMAS KENEALLY

THOMAS KENEALLY

The Commonwealth of Thieves

VINTAGE BOOKS
London

Published by Vintage 2007

10

Copyright © The Serpentine Publishing Co (Pty) Limited, 2005

Thomas Keneally has asserted his right under the Copyright, Designs
and Patents Act 1988 to be identified as the author of this work

First published in Great Britain in 2006 by
Chatto & Windus

Vintage
Random House, 20 Vauxhall Bridge Road,
London SW1V 2SA

www.vintage-books.co.uk

Addresses for companies within The Random House Group Limited
can be found at: www.randomhouse.co.uk/offices.htm

The Random House Group Limited Reg. No. 954009

A CIP catalogue record for this book
is available from the British Library

ISBN 9780099483748

The Random House Group Limited supports The Forest Stewardship
Council® (FSC®), the leading international forest-certification organisation.
Our books carrying the FSC label are printed on FSC®-certified paper.
FSC is the only forest-certification scheme supported by the leading
environmental organisations, including Greenpeace. Our
paper procurement policy can be found at
www.randomhouse.co.uk/environment

MIX
Paper from
responsible sources
FSC
www.fsc.org   FSC® C016897

Printed and bound in Great Britain by Clays Ltd, St Ives plc

Eora people asked the question,
Waube-rong orab,
Where is a better country?

The thief colony might hereafter become a great empire, whose nobles will probably, like the nobles of Rome, boast of their blood.

The Morning Post, London, 1 November 1786

Author's Note

I have taken the liberty in quotations from historic sources to standardise spelling, and in cases of misspellings left intact, to avoid the use of the mannerism (sic). Any insertions I have made for the sake of clarifying the intentions of the original writers are signalled by square brackets.

All Aboriginal personal and place names have variations with which generally I have avoided burdening the text, though some of the variant spellings can be found in the notes.

As the text makes frequent use of imperial measurement, a conversion table to metric has been provided at the end of the book.

T.K.

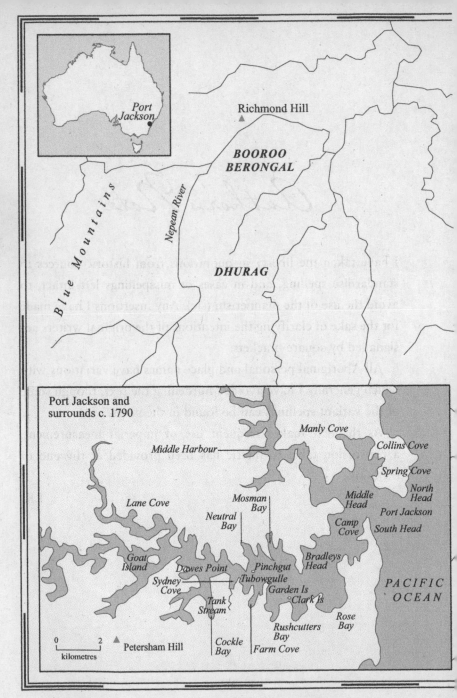

Probable distribution of some of the Aboriginal groups
in the Sydney region c. 1790

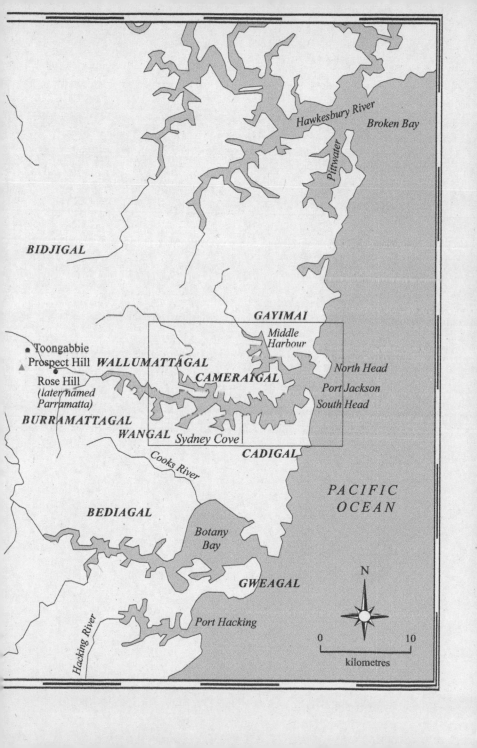

Book One

One

If, in the New Year of 1788, the eye of God had strayed from the main games of Europe, the Americas, Asia and Africa, and idled over the huge vacancy of sea to the south-east of Africa, it would have been surprised in this empty zone to see not one, but all of eleven ships being driven east on the screaming band of westerlies. This was many times more than the number that had ever been seen here, in a sea so huge and vacant that in today's conventional atlases no one map represents it. The people on the eleven ships were lost to the world. They had celebrated their New Year at 44 degrees South latitude with 'hard salt beef and a few musty pancakes'. Their passage was in waters turbulent with gales, roiling from an awful collision between melted ice from the Antarctic coast and warm currents from the Indian Ocean behind them, and the Pacific ahead. High and irregular seas broke over the decks continuously, knocking the cattle in their pens off their legs. The travellers knew they were past the rocks of sub-Antarctic Kerguelen Island and were reaching for the dangerous southern capes of Van Diemen's Land, which they intended to round on their way to their destination.

What would have intrigued the divine eye was the number of vessels – though they travelled in two sections, each division separated from the other by a few hundred miles. So far in the history of Europe, only six ships had come into this area named the Southern Ocean, which lay between the uncharted south coast of New Holland (later to be known as Australia) and Antarctica's massive ice pack. In 1642, a Dutchman, Abel Tasman, a vigorous captain of the Dutch East India Company, had crossed this stretch to discover the island he would name Van Diemen's Land after his Viceroy in Batavia (now Jakarta), but which would in the end be named Tasmania to honour him.

His ships, a high-sterned, long-bowed yacht named *Heemskerck* and a round-sterned vessel of the variety called a flute, the *Zeehaean*, were of such minuscule tonnage as to be overshadowed by HMS *Resolution* and HMS *Adventure*'s roughly 400 ton each. These last two, still tiny vessels by modern standards, less than one-third a football field in length, came through the Southern Ocean in 1774 under the overall command of the Yorkshireman James Cook. The *Resolution* travelled well to the south near the Antarctic ice mass, and rendezvoused with *Adventure* at the islands Tasman had named New Zealand. Then in 1776, the *Resolution* and the HMS *Discovery*, again under Cook, could have been seen in these waters. And that was all.

What were these eleven ships, as far from Britain as one could wisely get without encountering icebergs, that in 1788 followed the path of Cook and Tasman to the southern capes of Van Diemen's Land? One might expect them to be full of Georgian conquistadors, or a task force of scientists to suit the enlightened age. If not that, then they must have carried robust dissenters from the political or religious establishment of their day.

The startling fact was they carried prisoners, and the guardians of prisoners. They were the degraded of Britain's overstretched penal system, and the obscure guardians of the degraded. Any concepts of commerce and science on these ships were secondary to the ordained penal purpose. Few aboard had commercial capacities, though a number of the gentlemen were part-time scientists. Their destination was to be not a home of the chosen, or even a chosen home, but a place imposed by authority and devised specifically with its remoteness in mind. The chief order of business for all of them, prisoners and guardians, was to apply themselves to a unique penal experiment.

The merchant ships of the fleet, presently full of prisoners and penal stores, were to return to Britain after discharging their felons, picking up cargoes of cotton and tea in China and India on the return journey. But because this outward cargo was debased, some in Britain expected never to hear again from the fleet's passengers. It was believed they would become a cannibal kingdom on the coast they were bound for, and – one way or another – devour each other.

So what in the name of God, King, civilisation and all reason were they doing here, in this ocean prodigiously remote?

The idea of expelling convicts to distant places was not new. It had occurred to European powers from the fifteenth century onwards, once they began acquiring huge and distant spaces in the Americas, Africa and Asia. As a policy, it could solve many problems at the one time, including the problem which in modern days would be designated NIMBY, Not In My Backyard. The main differences of opinion soon emerged. As early as 1584, Hakluyt's *Discourse for Western Planting* proposed that 'sturdy vagabonds' should be sent away to the colonies so that 'the fry of the wandering beggars of England that grow up idly and burden us to this realm may there be unladen, better bred up, and may people waste countries'. Francis Bacon, however, debated the wisdom of unloading miscreants on far-off dominions in his essay, *Of Plantations*. 'It is a shameful and unblessed thing, to take the scum of people, and wicked and condemned men, to be the people with whom you plant . . .'

In reality, Hakluyt would win the debate with Bacon hands down. It *was* 'the scum of people, and wicked and condemned men' – and women – who made up the cargo of the criminal transports found in the Southern Ocean in the New Year of 1788. It would not have consoled the condemned on those wind-tossed mornings as they stirred and complained in their 18 inches of space on the convict decks that, uniquely placed as they were, they were also part of a long European tradition of transporting the unfortunate and the fallen, beginning with Cromwell's transportation of many Irish peasants, sent as labour to the plantations of the West Indies, and progressing to the 1656 order of the Council of State that lewd and dangerous persons should be hunted down 'for transporting them to the English plantations in America'.

The British were not alone in thinking of colonial penal arrangements. For example, the first two Europeans left ashore by the Portuguese in Brazil were convicts, or as the Portuguese graphically called them, *degradados*.

But in Britain it was a recourse governments thought of regularly. When prisoners were landed in the American colonies throughout the seventeenth and eighteenth centuries, settlers would buy this or that prisoner's labour – generally for seven years – at the auction block. The master took over the prisoner, and troubled the authorities only in the case of escape or major unruliness. Between 1650 and 1775, some tens of thousands of prisoners were sent on these terms to America, perhaps as many as 120,000. Sometimes vagrants and the poor – 'idle persons lurking in parts of London' – would voluntarily let themselves be transported and sold with the criminals.

The trade in convict or indentured servants was attractive to the British government because, unlike the prison system, it cost them little. Merchants would transport them cheaply, sometimes for nothing, in return for what could be earned through selling the convicts' labour. In fact, merchants often found this trade in white servants cheaper to engage in than that in African slaves. Between 1729 and 1745 the two chief contractors in London sent to America an average of 280 prisoners a year each, up towards 600 a year in total. Based on auction prices in Baltimore between 1767 and 1775, a convict's labour cost between £10 and £25, and it was possible for an affluent convict to bid for himself and do his time as, effectively, a free agent. But very few transported convicts could afford to buy their own labour, or return home from Virginia, Maryland or Georgia, even if they survived the 'seasoning period', the first few years of malaria and other diseases which killed two out of five inhabitants of Virginia, and so the convict engaged in field labour was likely to find an early grave in American soil.

In extolling the benefits of transportation for the home nation, the British government gave little attention to the impact it had on the region that received the felons. One North American colonist was left to complain that 'America has been made the very common sewer and dung yard to Britain.' 'Very surprising, one would think,' wrote another American colonist in 1756,

'that thieves, burglars, pickpockets and cut-purses, and a herd of
the most flagitious banditti upon earth, should be sent as agreeable companions to us!' Thomas Jefferson, the third president of
the United States, was faced with the same problem of post-
colonial denial as later generations of Australians, and wrote
unreliably that he did not think the entire number of convicts
sent out to the American colonies would amount to two
thousand, and 'being principally men eaten up with disease, they
married seldom and propagated little'.

The men and women surviving on flapjacks and desiccated salted
beef and pease – a porridge of compacted peas – in the great
Southern Ocean convict flotilla in 1788 owed their location to
the pressure on British prison populations. A new Transportation
Act in 1780 had sought to make transportation more obligatory
than it had been up to that point. The fact was that many
prisoners sentenced to transportation were in reality doing their
time in chaotic, overcrowded prisons while the government
waited for the American rebellion to end.

The offences for which a prisoner could be transported under
the accumulated Transportation Acts of Britain made up an
exotic catalogue. Quakers could be transported for denying any
oath to be lawful, or assembling themselves together under
pretence of joining in religious worship. Notorious thieves and
takers of spoil in the borderlands of Northumberland and
Cumberland, commonly called 'moss-troopers' and 'reivers',
were also subject to penalties of transportation; similarly,
persons found guilty of stealing cloth from the rack, or
embezzling His Majesty's stores to the value of twenty shillings;

persons convicted of wilfully burning ricks of corn, hay or barns in the night time (crimes generally associated with peasant protest against a landlord); persons convicted of larceny and other offences; persons imprisoned for exporting wool and not paying the excise on it; persons convicted of entering into any park and killing or wounding any deer without the consent of the owner; persons convicted of perjury and forgery; persons convicted of assaulting others with offensive weapons with the design to rob; vagrants or vagabonds escaping from a house of correction or from service in the army or navy; persons convicted of stealing any linen laid to be printed or bleached; ministers of the Episcopal Church of Scotland suspected of support for Bonnie Prince Charlie, exercising their functions in Scotland without having registered their letters of orders, taken all oaths, and prayed for His Majesty and the Royal Family by name; persons returning from transportation without licence; persons convicted of entering mines of black-lead with intent to steal; persons convicted of assaulting any magistrate or officer engaged in the salvage of ships or goods from wrecks; persons convicted of stealing fish in any water within a park, paddock, orchard or yard. Besides the penalty of transportation, between 1660 and 1819, 187 statutes providing for mandatory capital punishment were passed on the same principles to add to the nearly 50 already in existence. This was all a disordered and unfocused attempt to produce what would be called in modern times 'truth in sentencing'.

One sees in the long list a heavy emphasis on the sanctity of two institutions: property and the Crown in the guise of the Royal House of Hanover. The Irish and certain Scots were resistant to the Crown as it existed; and as for property matters,

William Blackstone, author of *Commentaries on the Laws of England*, thought with his eminent friends Dr Samuel Johnson and Oliver Goldsmith that 'theft should not be punished with death', but Parliament went on churning out statutes which did just that. The very lack of a British police force meant that legislators needed to impress the people with the terror of the law.

In theory, frequent public executions should have cut down on crowding in gaols. But even the lawmakers, members of the Commons, might mercifully take up the special cause of this or that prisoner, and the way the statutes were applied by magistrates, judges and juries was inconsistent and ill-coordinated, depending in a given courtroom and amongst the jury on feelings either of compassion for the accused – for example, terms commonly used to explain leniency included the prisoner being 'too young', or 'a poor unfortunate girl' – or else of sometimes gratuitous outrage at him or her.

Some of the women prisoners and many of the males on the great Southern Ocean fleet owed their presence on the prison decks to their youth or good looks. Many of them had had their sentences of death commuted, and in other cases juries had adjusted the official value of goods stolen to bring it below the level prescribed for hanging. Not that the prisoners, taking the air on the squally deck while their blankets dried out, called down blessings on the British criminal justice system. The accused prisoner generally came in front of the courts at quarter sessions or assizes without the judge or jury enquiring too closely into whether a confession had been beaten out of him, and generally without legal counsel. Curiously, a first offender in theft cases was entitled, by a legal technicality, to claim the grotesque medieval 'benefit of clergy'. The imputation was that the court could not prove the prisoner had not received divine orders, or the early rites prior to ordination which would make him a member of the clergy, and thus subject to special consideration by the civil courts.

Once that was out of the way, the trial proceeded more briskly than in modern times – the Georgian version of a day in court was a quarter of an hour. Major cases all ended with acquittal, transportation or the death penalty, also called the 'hearty choke with caper sauce', 'nothing more than a wry face and a watered patch of breeches' and 'dancing the Paddington frisk'. About one in eight of those committed for trial was sentenced to death, but (based on figures concentrated between 1761 and 1765) few more than half of those sentenced to death were executed. Between 1749 and 1799 in London and Middlesex, despite the frequently celebrated and written about eight hanging days at Tyburn Hill every year, and the fact that the heads of Jacobites (the Scottish supporters of Bonnie Prince Charlie) were stuck and exposed on spikes at Temple Bar until the late 1770s, the yearly average of those executed may have been only 34, with perhaps 200 hanged across the nation.

Yet the executions were a frightful public spectacle. From the mid-1780s they occurred outside Newgate prison itself. There, on a spring day in 1785, James Boswell, the Scottish writer and familiar of Dr Johnson, watched nineteen criminals, including thieves, a forger, a stamp counterfeiter and others who had illegally returned from transportation, 'depart Newgate to the other world'.

King George III attended to reprieves himself, sitting in council at St James's Palace, and receiving advice and lists of prisoners from judges and recorders. Though he was severe on forgers – indeed, it was still possible for women forgers to be burned at the stake – he generally accepted the advice of the trial judge, as did the Prince Regent, the future George IV, during his father's illness and lunacy, and remitted most of those recommended to his mercy to sentences of transportation.

The condition of the gaols of Britain in which the transportees and other prisoners accumulated in such numbers owed much to the neglect of government and the fact that these dingy buildings, ill-aired, ill-lit and epidemic-prone, were run under licence and as enterprises. To be a prison warder was not to be a servant of society but a franchise-holder, entitled to charge inmates a scale of fees of the warder's own devising. Many if not all prisons had taprooms run for profit by the keeper, and John Howard, a prison reformer, discovered in one London prison that the tap was sub-hired out to one of the prisoners. In another, Howard was told that as many as 600 pots of beer had been brought into cells from the taproom during one Sunday. From such sources as the taproom and those private apartments he could rent out to superior convicts, Richard Ackerman, keeper of Newgate for 38 years and a dining friend of James Boswell and an associate of the great Dr Johnson, left a fortune of £20,000 when he died in 1792.

In 1777 the first painstaking survey of conditions in English prisons, Howard's *The State of the Prisons*, was published, and gaol reform became a popular issue. Howard was a Bedfordshire squire who had been appointed to the sinecure of county sheriff some years before. To everyone's amazement he took his duties seriously, was shocked profoundly by his visits to sundry prisons including some in his own county, and became the most famous of prison reformers. In his tract, Howard depicted a cell, 17 feet by 6, crowded with more than two-dozen inmates and receiving light and air only through a few holes in the door. The 'clink' of a Devon prison was 17 feet by 8, with only 5 feet 6 inches of head room, and had light and air by one hole 7 inches long and 5 broad. In Canterbury, Howard found there were no beds but mats, unless the prisoners paid extra. In Clerkenwell prison, those who could not pay for beds lay on the floor, and in many other prisons inmates paid even for the privilege of not being chained while in the shared cells, or wards, as they were called. Howard claimed that after visits to Newgate the leaves of his notebook were so tainted and browned by the fearful atmosphere that on his arrival home he had to spread out the pages before a glowing fire for drying and disinfection.

The most infamous of prisons, old Newgate, was burned down by a mob in 1780. Prisoners were readmitted to the rebuilt prison by 1782. New Newgate prison was divided into two halves: the master's side where the inmates could rent lodging and services, and where those who had committed criminal libel, sedition or embezzlement were kept, and the more impoverished section called the common side. On the common side of the gaol, to the right as people looked at the newly built prison from the direction of the Old Bailey, were the criminal wards and the condemned cells. Earlier in the century, the writer Daniel Defoe, who himself had been thrown into Newgate for theft, described it through the eyes of his character Moll Flanders, in terms which seemed to be just as true of the post-1782 new Newgate: 'I was now fixed indeed; it is impossible to describe the terror of my mind when I was first brought in, and when I looked around upon all the horrors of that dismal place . . . The hellish noise, the roaring, the swearing and clamour, the stench and nastiness, and all the dreadful, afflicting things that I saw there, joined to make the place seem an emblem of hell itself.' Both in Moll Flanders's day and in the 1780s, tradesmen in Newgate Street were unable to take the air at their doors for fear of the stench of the prison.

Though prisoners and visitors had access to the taphouse where they could buy liquor, and there were several communal rooms, a chapel, a separate infirmary for men and women, and exercise yards, only the most basic medicine was given in the two infirmaries. Doctors often refused to enter the prison for fear their own health would suffer. Yet every day, ordinary people came to visit or sightsee, as we might now visit a zoo. Prostitutes worked their way around to service visitors and prisoners who had cash, and the turnkeys received a pay-off from this traffic as well. Meanwhile, unless the men and women in the common wards had relatives and friends to bring them food, they lived off a three-halfpenny loaf a week, supplemented by donations and a share of the cook's weekly meat supply. Their bedding was at the discretion of the keeper. One of the motivations for joining gangs, or criminal 'canting crews', was that if imprisoned, the individual criminal was not left to the bare mercies of the gaol authorities. For hunger hollowed out ordinary prisoners in the common wards in severe English winters like that of 1786–87.

In that last winter in England for many convicts who would soon find themselves on the departing fleet, one visitor noted that there were in Newgate many 'miserable objects' almost naked and without shoes and stockings. Women prisoners in the wards were 'of the very lowest and most wretched class of human beings, almost naked, with only a few filthy rags, almost alive and in motion with vermin, their bodies rotting with the bad distemper, and covered with itch, scorbutic and venereal ulcers'. Many insane prisoners added to the spectacle for the sightseers.

Despite all the criminal and capital statutes, the prison populations had gone on growing before, during and after the American War, and crimes abounded. The legendary Irish pickpocket Barrington could boast that 'in and about London more pickpockets succeed in making a comfortable living than in the whole of the rest of Europe'.

But the revolutionary war in America meant less and less transportation occurred even though more and more were sentenced to it. And so, the 1780 Act having failed to relieve the gaols, a further Act of Parliament passed in 1783 allowed the removal of convicts from the gaols on land to the dismasted hulks of old men-of-war moored in the Thames, and at Portsmouth and Plymouth, where they could spend time and do labour around the river pending their transportation. The British government, prevented by rebellious Virginians and vocal Nova Scotians from offloading its dross, was restricted to transporting fallen souls a few miles by rowboat rather than across the Atlantic. During their confinement on the prison decks of the hulks, prisoners were allowed to save their wages. The time of their detention here was to be deemed part of the term of transportation.

The hulks, an eyesore detested by respectable London and unpopular with convicts, were both a phenomenon and an enterprise. Duncan Campbell, the hulk-master, was a highly interesting Georgian figure, a reputable man and a good Presbyterian Scot. He had begun in the convict-transporting business in 1758, carrying felons to Virginia and Maryland. Since then Campbell had seen a great change in the penal-maritime business, and not only because of the war in America. In April and May 1776, even before the American colonies were lost, an end was enacted to the good old practice of placing 'the property and the service of the body of the convict' for sale on American auction blocks. Now the convict and his labour belonged wholly to the Crown. Nor could wealthy convicts buy themselves out of servitude anymore.

On top of that, the revolution in America threw the affairs of Campbell and others 'into dramatic disarray'. The amounts lost by British creditors in America, when Americans refused to pay British merchants' bills, meant that Campbell had a dizzying fortune of over £38,000 owing to him from gentlemen in Virginia and Maryland. But in modest ways the war in America also compensated Campbell. He continued to receive in his hulks more and more of the convicts sentenced to transportation. His initial contract, worth £3560 a year was for a dismasted hulk (he named it *Justitia*) of at least 240 tons to house 120 prisoners, mainly from Newgate, with necessary tools and six lighters for the convicts to work from, as well as medicines and vinegar as a scurvy cure, and the means to wash and fumigate the vessel. By 1780 he had accommodation for 510 convicts, and had purchased a French frigate, the *Censor*, and 'an old Indiaman' which he named *Justitia II*. He had a receiving ship, the *Reception*, and a hospital ship, the converted *Justitia I*. On Campbell's receiving ship, the prisoner was stripped of the vermin-infested clothes he had worn in Newgate or elsewhere in the kingdom, bathed, and held for four days while being inspected for infection. Campbell employed three efficient surgeons on a regular basis on his hospital ship, and they were busy assuring the healthiness of the hulks. The high death rate on Campbell's ships, and also on the less well-administered hulks moored in Portsmouth and Plymouth by other contractors, was partially the result of diseases prisoners had contracted originally in the common wards of city and county gaols, and brought from those prisons to the hulks with them. 'The ships at Woolwich are as sweet as any parlour in the kingdom,' Campbell asserted with some pride. Campbell himself lived near the hulks, at Blackheath just behind Greenwich.

Many of the prisoners aboard the flotilla in the distant Southern Ocean in 1788 had less enthusiastic memories of these river-bound prisons. Though Campbell himself had a reputation for decency, the Act of Parliament setting up the hulks called for prisoners to be 'fed and sustained with bread and any coarse and inferior food' as a symbol of their shame, with misbehaviour to be punished by 'whipping, or other moderate punishment'. There was on top of that the hulks' peculiar below-decks dimness, the frock of sewage and waste which adorned the water around them, and the horror of being locked down at night on the prison deck and abandoned to the worst instincts of the established cliques. The British thought of the hulks as a temporary expedient, but they would not be able to get rid of their floating prisons in the Thames and elsewhere until 1853 – indeed, the hulks made an appearance in Dickens's *Great Expectations*.

What Campbell could not control was the habitual brutality and extortion of some of the guards, or the savagery of locked-down prisoners towards the weak or naive.

Periodically reacting to complaints from their constituents, London's members of Parliament and city aldermen kept telling the government that the prisoners on the hulks should be transported anywhere convenient – to the East or West Indies, Canada or Nova Scotia, Florida or the Falklands. But the administration continued with the hulks. For except for the rebellious North American colonies, no one place seemed the right destination for transportees.

For a time, Parliament toyed with the idea of Africa. In 1780, a Commons Committee reported that 'transportation to unhealthy places, in place of sending better citizens, may be advisable'. Because they were put off by estimates of expense of transportation to New South Wales of £30 per felon, six times the cost of transportation to America, the committee considered the possibility of Gibraltar, or the Gambia and Senegal rivers in Africa. In the bureaucratic circles of Whitehall, New South Wales fell in and out of fashion as a destination throughout the mid-1780s. Everyone was aware a considerable maritime enterprise would need to be mounted to get prisoners there. New South Wales was still surely a region for small, well-planned expeditions, rather than for an unprecedented experiment in mass transportation and penology. So a draft letter from the Home Office to the Treasury, dated 9 February 1785, described the country upstream on the Gambia River in West Africa as abounding with timber for building, the land as extremely fertile and plentifully stocked with cattle, goats and sheep, a place where tropical food would grow readily and the natives were hospitable. The site suggested was Lemane, up the river some miles and distant from the malarial coast. Convicts could be left to themselves: 'They cannot get away from there for there is not a person who would harbour them.' By April 1785, Pitt's government seemed to have decided on this version of transportation. The only cost would be £8 per head for the journey out and the hiring of an armed vessel as a guard ship on the river during the trading season. Admittedly, 'upon the first settlement, a great many of the convicts would die'. But over time, as the land was better cultivated, 'they would grow more healthy'.

There was a violent parliamentary attack against this idea, led by Edmund Burke. Burke, the great Irish social and political philosopher, mistrusted grand schemes aimed at social reorganisation of the kind inherent in shipping miscreant Englishmen onto an unknown shore.

Botany Bay in New South Wales, on a coast Cook had visited in 1770, had an eloquent proponent, though for a different reason than the penal one. Mario Matra, an Italian-American from New York and loyal to the Crown, had sailed as a gentleman in Cook's company and claimed to be the first European to have set foot in Botany Bay. He had more recently visited New York during the American revolutionary war to recover what he could of the Matra family property, and disappointed, returned to London in 1781, where he found a great number of fellow American Empire Loyalist refugees living in some squalor. Britain was doing little for the loyalist Americans, and Matra drafted a pamphlet addressed to the British government, *A Proposal for Establishing a Settlement in New South Wales to Atone for the Loss of our American Colonies*. American Empire Loyalists should be sent as free settlers to New South Wales, and wives should be supplied to them if necessary from amongst the natives of New Caledonia or Tahiti. 'Settlement could be a centre for trade with East Asia or a wartime base for attack on the Dutch colonies of Malaya . . . And thus two objects of the most desirable and beautiful union will be permanently blended:

economy to the public, and humanity to the individual.' Without mentioning convicts, Matra nonetheless brought attention to New South Wales as a potential destination for awkward people other than loyalists.

Though Sir Joseph Banks promoted Matra's proposal to the government, the Tories fell and the Whigs came to power, and Lord Sydney, a recently ennobled political operator and Kentish squire in his early fifties, inherited the Home Office, including responsibility for prisons and colonial affairs. Even he, though sympathetic, was not as much interested in the fate of loyalists as he was in the pressingly urgent matter of the prisons and hulks. He was under pressure on that from all directions. On 9 December 1784, he had to write to the mayor of Hull, who had asked for the removal of his city's convicts to the hulks, saying that not a person more could be at present admitted to them. Sydney answered similarly to a request from Oxford.

Lord Sydney, later first Viscount Sydney, was a political operator whose real name was Thomas Townshend. He already had a solid political career, having been Secretary of War in a previous government and then Home Secretary both under Shelburne and Pitt. He was thought to be a good man who lived an orderly life at his house in Chiselhurst and avoided the extremes of drinking and sexual adventure which characterised people like Sir Joseph Banks and James Boswell. Oliver Goldsmith depicted him as the sort of lesser talent with whom great spirits such as Edmund Burke had to deign to negotiate. But he shared with Burke a passionate dislike of Lord North, the British Tory prime minister, and applied himself to the settlement of the American Revolution which had begun under North's government. His sympathies lay in particular with those loyal subjects who would lose their American lands, savings and standing, and he was involved in organising a new home for American loyalists in Nova Scotia, where there would grow a city named in his honour.

In 1779, the most significant witness to appear before the Commons Committee on colonies was Sir Joseph Banks himself, a great naturalist, commentator, sensualist and society figure. On Cook's *Endeavour*, as leader of a number of distinguished artists and scientists, the young Banks became so famous from his Botany Bay discoveries of new species that Linnaeus, the famous Swedish scientist, suggested that if New South Wales were proven to be part of a continent, the continent should be called Banksia. Even though in the journal of his voyage as a young scientist with Cook, Sir Joseph described Botany Bay on the New South Wales coast as barren, he urged the committee to consider that it might be suitable for transportation, and that there was sufficient fertile soil to sustain a European settlement. From there, too, escape would be difficult, he said. The climate was mild, there were no savage animals and the 'Indians' around Botany Bay, estimated at hardly more than 50, were not hostile.

Sir Joseph Banks was asked whether he thought land for settlement might be acquired from the Aborigines 'by Cession or Purchase'. Banks said he thought not, that there was nothing you could give the Aborigines, or Indians, in return for their soil. He told the committee that the blacks were of wandering habits and would 'speedily abandon whatever land was needed'. The Aboriginals were blithely nomadic; New South Wales was *terra nullius*, no man's land.

All very well for Sir Joseph, the potential transportees would have said had they noticed. All very well for a man in his early forties, the bloom of outrageous health and intellectual energy on his cheek, liberated by the rent of small tenants and the agricultural income of family estates at Revesby Abbey in Lincolnshire from all want, able to take a place as chief scientist on Cook's *Endeavour* and to bring along with him comforts unknown to the common voyager. All very well for the lustrous scholar to glibly nominate the netherworld, the southern Hades, for others.

In the end, this Commons Committee left the question of transportation destinations open, but also recommended the building of two penitentiaries, where the prisoners would be kept in solitary confinement with hard labour. By 1786, however, no progress had been made on the sites of the penitentiaries and the government had definitely decided to begin transportation again. Crime levels had jumped even more because of the sudden discharge of members of the army and navy after the war in America. Lord Sydney was left to write, 'The more I consider the matter, the greater difficulty I see in disposing of these people.'

So by the end of 1785, Prime Minister Pitt and Lord Sydney and his Undersecretary, a former naval purser named Evan Nepean, were still looking for a scheme. They considered Africa again, a tract of country on the west coast between 20 and 30 degrees South latitude, near the mouth of the river Das Voltas (now the Orange River) where there were copper deposits. Convicts could be shipped out in slaving vessels which could then proceed up the coast and pick up their more accustomed cargo of African slaves to take to America and the West Indies. The many American families who were still anxious to live under British rule could also be sent to Das Voltas and serve as the discipliners and employers of the convicts. In preparation, the government sloop *Nautilus* was sent out to survey the Atlantic coast of Africa up to about modern Angola, but its ultimate report was that the country was barren, waterless, hopeless.

The government also considered a settlement on the Caffre (Kaffir) coast around the Cape. But fears of aggrieving the Dutch in Cape Town made the British government pull back.

In March 1786, Londoners and their aldermen again petitioned against the unsatisfactory solution represented by the hulks. They reminded the government that demobilised and unemployed sailors would make a mob, and imbued with the fancy American ideas of the rights of man would set convicts free and burn the hulks. The hulks had brought the risk of mayhem and uprising as well as shipboard epidemics to within a long-boat's reach of shore.

At last, in August 1786, Cabinet finally plumped for New South Wales, the preposterously distant coast Cook had charted sixteen years past. Londoners rejoiced that a decision had been made to resume transportation. They believed it would mean an end to the river hulks.

A London alderman wrote to Jeremy Bentham, a young political philosopher with ideas about prisons who was then in St Petersburg in Russia, visiting his brother who had a contract building ships for Catherine the Great. Bentham was developing a plan for a panopticon penitentiary, a huge circular prison where every prisoner would be visible from the centre – an idea which Bentham had got from observing the way his brother had organised his office in the St Petersburg shipyard. The alderman told him the 'government has just decided to send off 700 convicts to New South Wales – where a fort is to be built – and that a man has been found who will take upon him the command of this rabble'. This meant that Bentham's new and revolutionary penitentiaries would not be built in Britain, not yet anyhow, and he would become increasingly disappointed by that fact.

From the alderman's letter it sounded as if contemporaries saw the task of leading the expedition to New South Wales as potentially destroying whomever was selected for command. The man the government chose was an old shipmate of former purser, now Home Office Undersecretary, Evan Nepean – a 49-year-old Royal Navy post-captain named Arthur Phillip, a man of solid but not glittering naval reputation, with some experience under fire. He had been at sea since the age of thirteen, and had no connection at all with the British penal system. But that did not worry the non-visionary Tommy Townshend, Lord Sydney. He just wanted a robust fellow to mount a flotilla and empty the hulks for him.

Two

To convicts, Phillip would later convey the very breath of civil magisterium, even though his early childhood might not have been much more socially elevated than some of theirs. Not only had he known British seamen, who came from the same class as the convicts, but he seems to have been a child of marginal London as well, the London where the lives of worthy strugglers like his mother were not immune from predatory crime. Arthur's mother, Elizabeth Breech, had been married to a sailor named Herbert. Some claim Herbert rose to captain's rank in the Royal Navy; others that he was a foredeck hand. Seaman or Captain Herbert died while still in his twenties of a fever caught during his duty on the Jamaica station. Indeed, it did not seem he had lived long enough to become a captain. Phillip's mother then married Jacob Phillip, a German, a 'native of Frankfurt' and a teacher of 'the languages'. If Jacob were, as his name implies, Jewish, this would have laid down another fascinating dimension to his child Arthur Phillip's brand of Britishness. Arthur was born in October 1738, a year or so after a sister, Rebecca. The family lived in Bread Street in the City of London. It was not necessarily an address of privilege, but many good houses and some fine churches, including St Mildred's, and St Paul's itself, characterised the area.

Arthur was admitted to the charity orphan school at the Royal Hospital for Seamen at Greenwich in 1751. The school was for the sons of poor seamen, 'training them up to a seafaring life'. Young Arthur's presence indicated that either Jacob Phillip gave up his language teaching to become a seaman and died as a British tar, or – far more likely – that Arthur was presented to the school as the child of the Englishman Herbert. Going to Greenwich was a deception which might have added further secretiveness to the boy's aloof manner. To his duty of transporting criminals, Phillip would bring his habits as a thoroughgoing British captain, but also a nature so complex and hidden behind official formality, for which he had an appetite, that it is hard to find the quivering human within.

His transportees are in many ways far more legible. At least half of them would be London convicts from areas north of the Thames River: Stepney, Poplar, Clerkenwell, St Giles's and Seven Dials, Soho. (Only a minority came from the South London dockside regions.) In the tenements around St Giles's parish in Soho – the famed Rookery of St Giles – and in Spitalfields to the east, in squalor unimaginable, lived all classes of criminals, speaking a special criminal argot and bonded together by devotion and oaths taken to the criminal deity, the Tawny Prince. The Tawny Prince was honoured by theft, chicanery and a brave death on the gallows. And, of course, by speaking his language, *flash* or *cant*. In flash talk, a *pal* was a pickpocket's assistant who received the *swag* as soon as the pickpocket had lifted it. A *kiddy* was the fast-running child to whom the pal passed the swag. A *beak* was a magistrate, a *pig* a Bow Street runner. *Tickling the peter* was opening a safe, and a *fence* was a receiver of stolen loot. All these terms mean something to us now through their entry into mainstream English, but at that time they were incomprehensible to respectable persons and officers of the courts.

'A leading distinction, which marked the convicts from the outset in the colony,' wrote a military officer named Watkin Tench much later, when a convict colony was at last established in New South Wales, 'was the use of what is called the *flash* or *kiddy* language. In some of our early courts of justice, an interpreter was frequently necessary to translate the deposition of the witness, and the defence of the prisoner. This language has many dialects. The sly dexterity of the pickpocket; the brutal ferocity of the footpad; the more elevated career of the highwayman; and the deadly purpose of the midnight ruffian, is each strictly appropriate in the terms that distinguish and characterise it. I have ever been of the opinion that an abolition of this unnatural jargon would open the path to reformation.'

The criminal classes availed themselves of the many public houses in the City and Spitalfields that were centres for prostitution, the fencing of stolen goods and the division of plunder. 'Hell Houses' was a common name for such places. They were to be found in a number of notorious locations: Chick Lane, Field Lane, Black Boy Alley. Over their half-doors fleeing criminals were free to toss whatever they had plundered and were on the run with.

There were special conditions which had driven many rural poor to the cities and towards crime. The English countryside was undergoing a revolutionary process known as Enclosure. Villages had previously been organised according to a system of scattered strips of open land variously owned by peasants and landlord, and shared common ground. This had been the way since feudal times. Under a series of Enclosure Acts passed by the

Parliament at Westminster, villages were reorganised by Enclosure commissioners according to new agricultural efficiencies, so that the ground of the chief landlord, of prosperous farmers and various smallholders was consolidated and fenced. In reality, Enclosure drove small farmers and agricultural workers off land their families had worked for centuries. Many smallholders not only found the expense of fencing with barriers of hawthorn and blackthorn beyond them, but discovered that the 'common land' traditionally shared by the community, on which they and even more marginal peasants had depended to run their livestock, was now fenced off too. The ancient right of the peasant to hunt and scavenge for game and produce from the landlord's ground also vanished as the crime of poaching came into being. And this process was occurring at a time when the cloth produced in cottages was required less and less, as great loom factories were established. Traditional village, church and family controls on the way men and women behaved broke down as families became itinerant and set off for cities.

Oliver Goldsmith's famed lament for the uprooting of rustic populations, the poem *The Deserted Village*, was written in 1770 when great numbers of people were seeking parish poor relief because of Enclosure, and the dispossessed pooled in big towns. In these times, says a historian, 'Everyone below the plateau of skilled craftsmen was undernourished.' And the rural poor became poorer still. Some became the scarecrow people of the countryside, but many more were forced towards the cities, creating a dangerous under-class, who saw crime as a better option than working an eighty-hour week as a servant, or toiling for the unregulated and dangerous gods of machine-based capital.

The precise extent to which the great Georgian dislocation

produced Phillip's bunch of convicts is still a matter of debate, but Goldsmith himself, until his death in 1774, had no doubt that Enclosure had become the great despoiler of rural virtue in the British. Addressing his rhetorical address to a fictional deserted British village, he declared:

> ... *a bold peasantry, their country's pride,*
> *When once destroy'd can never be supplied.*
> *A time there was, ere England's griefs began,*
> *When every rood of ground maintained its man;*
> *For him light labour spread her wholesome store,*
> *Just gave what life requir'd, but gave no more:*
> *His best companions innocence and health;*
> *And his best riches, ignorance of wealth.*

Times had changed for the worse, thought Goldsmith. Now, he said:

> ... *The man of wealth and pride*
> *Takes up a space that many poor supplied;*
> *Space for his lake, his park's extended bounds.*
> *Space for his horses, equipage and hounds;*
> *The robe that wraps his limbs in silken sloth*
> *Has robb'd the neighb'ring fields of half their growth.*

As a case in point for Goldsmith's thesis one might look at an adolescent convict like Sarah Bellamy, who came from an impoverished rural family frequently on parish relief in Belbroughton in Worcestershire. They were the sort of people who might once have been cottagers but since Enclosure lived in housing 'occupied by paupers of the said parish'. At the age of nine, Sarah began work for one of the parish overseers, and from the age of fifteen she was employed by Benjamin Haden, a weaver. At that age she was charged with theft for stealing from Mr Haden one linen purse, value tuppence, as well as £15 15s in coin and promissory notes. Whether she would have committed the crime if she had still been a cottager's daughter enjoying 'ignorance of wealth' can be debated, though people of like mind to Goldsmith would have said her days would have been blithe, habitual, crimeless village days. For it was true that before Enclosure her family had the right to graze livestock on the common, to take undergrowth, loppings, peat, fish from lakes and streams, sand and gravel, and acorns to feed pigs. Life was generally more viable.

In any case, Sarah ended in Worcester prison and heard from within her public ward there the beginning of the Worcester quarter sessions in the spring of 1785, the arrival of the touring judges being a festive event attended by the local gentry, farmers and other spectators. The judges, said a French commentator, 'enter a town with bells ringing and trumpets playing, preceded by the sheriff's men, to the number of twenty, in full dress, armed with javelins'. All this ritual of legal majesty must have greatly awed a country girl about to be tried.

There was something strange about Sarah's case. Her master, Benjamin Haden, was embarrassed about appearing as part of the prosecution, and it could be that the promissory notes she was accused of stealing were forgeries by him, for he soon appeared before the summer assizes on a bankruptcy charge. When sentenced to be transported beyond the seas for the term of seven years, Sarah 'guiltily prayed to be publicly whipped at afternoon at the next two market days', instead of being shipped away. But this pleading was not accepted.

The relative emphasis put upon property is shown by the fact that at the same assizes one of the listings reads: 'Richard Crump for killing Richard Bourn, found guilty of manslaughter, fined one shilling.' January 1788 would find Sarah Bellamy chilblained and pregnant aboard the *Lady Penrhyn* in the flotilla on its way to Botany Bay.

Humane spirits would have also read as one of 'England's griefs' the presence in the first compilation of felons for New South Wales of John Hudson. Hudson had been a child of nine years in October 1783 when with an accomplice he was said to have broken a narrow skylight above a window in a house in East Smithfield, the home of William Holdsworth, a chemist. The glass of the skylight was 'taken perfectly out'. Inside, Hudson and his accomplice collected one linen shirt, five silk stockings, one pistol and two aprons.

The English were proud of their lack of police officers, because police were associated with the French and thus with tyranny. Nonetheless, John was captured while visiting his loot in a nearby house. The Bow Street runners, London's deliberately token police force founded in 1749, arrested him, and told one witness it was 'the third time they had had him within ten days'. They claimed he confessed to them.

Brought to court, John Hudson found that Justice Wills and the jury wore nosegays of fresh herbs to counter the emanations of gaol fever – typhus – from the ragged prisoners of Newgate.

Court to prisoner: 'How old are you?'
'Going on nine.'
'What business were you bred up in?'
'None, sometimes a chimney sweeper.'
'Have you any father or mother?'

'Dead.'

'How long ago?'

'I do not know.'

Returning home, Mr Holdsworth the chemist testified to the court, he had found two toe marks on the glass of the skylight, and on a table, sooty feet marks. Holdsworth said, 'I took the impressions of foot and toes that were on the table with a piece of paper as minutely as I could.' One wonders how genuinely probative the impressions could have been.

The judge, Justice Wills, replied: 'I do not much like the confession of a boy of nine years old. I would rather do without it if I could.' But a woman witness had seen John Hudson at a water tub, sitting upon it to wash himself. 'I told him that it was water we made use of for drinking and I did not choose he should wash himself there.' Then, ascending the stairs by a nearby boarding house, she found the loot from Mr Holdsworth's bundled in a corner. A pawnbroker identified John Hudson as the boy who had pawned a shirt to him.

The judge instructed the jury that the only thing that fixed the boy with the robbery was a pistol found by the water tub. 'One would wish to snatch such a boy, if one possibly could, from destruction, for he will only return to the same kind of life which he has led before, and will be an instrument in the hands of very bad people, who make use of boys of that sort to rob houses.'

He was found guilty of the felony, but not of the burglary, and sentenced to transportation for seven years 'to some of His Majesty's Colonies and Plantations in America'. There was no separate child's prison for him pending transportation, and so he was thrown in with the adults at fearsome Newgate.

Lost children like Hudson had lately proliferated in the cities. Chimney-sweeps, commonly used by professional criminals to gain entry to houses, were a sign of the disordered times. They were orphans and the illegitimate children of paupers, often sold into service for seven years. Such a child 'is disposed of for twenty or thirty shillings, being a smaller price than the value of a terrier'. For boys like Hudson, there was no childhood. William Blake mourned their misuse in two separate poems, both entitled *The Chimney Sweeper*.

When my mother died, I was very young,
And my father sold me while yet my tongue
Could scarcely cry, 'Weep! Weep! Weep! Weep!'
So your chimneys I sweep, and in soot I sleep.

Blake's second chimney-sweep is also relevant to Hudson's caste of boys:

Because I was happy upon the heath,
And smiled among the winter's snow,
They clothed me in the clothes of death,
And taught me to sing the notes of woe.

Reforming evangelical groups were urging legislation to protect children from tyrannous masters, from the claustrophobia of the chimney, the lung damage, the death by suffocation and the criminal employment to which their trade often condemned them. But the first Act alleviating their lives would not be passed until the year Hudson was already part of a great new penal experiment at the earth's end.

Nine-year-old John Hudson, and James Grace, an eleven-year-old shoemaker, had both been put upon a ship, *Mercury*, which left the Thames for North America on 2 April 1784. Georgia was under no obligation to receive them, being no longer a British colony, but the captain intended if rebuffed to try Nova Scotia. On the morning of 8 April, the convicts seized the ship. John Hudson and James Grace were in one of two small boats that left the *Mercury* off Torbay, on Devon's south-east coast, on the morning of 14 April. They escaped the statutory death penalty for returning from transportation purely on the technicality that they had been intercepted by the crew of a naval vessel while still on the water.

Prisoners who had not left the *Mercury* but stayed on board were ultimately chained again and their labour sold off by the master of the ship, on the instructions of the ship-owners, in Honduras, along the Mosquito Coast of Central America.

At first kept in Exeter gaol, Hudson and Grace were tried for escape and transferred to the *Dunkirk*, a dismasted former warship moored off Plymouth as a floating prison. The Plymouth hulks were less carefully run than those on the Thames, and the prisoners laboured on fortification works in Plymouth Harbour. It was not until December 1784 that Hudson, Grace and the other male prisoners received an issue of clothing, including shoes. Dr Cowdry, the surgeon who attended the hulks for part of Hudson's time there, said that the men had 'almost every disease which vice and immorality could produce. Some of them had very bad venereal complaints.' Others had consumption. What might have befallen Hudson and Grace on the prison decks appals the imagination. Yet Hudson lasted nearly three years there, and with Grace was one of over 200 convicts, including

41 women, sent on 10 March 1787 from the dark *Dunkirk* to their transports in Phillip's convict fleet. The Philanthropic Society, which would later intervene in the case of transportees Hudson's age, was not founded until 1788.

Anyone reading the Old Bailey transcripts is struck by the imbalance between minor miscreancies and the ultimate, transglobal punishment of transportation. In modern terms, what happened with the Georgians was the equivalent of sending a shoplifter to some biosphere on another planet. The male prisoners were mostly small-time thieves, and as for the women, there is a repetitiveness and banality to the cases in which they, prostitutes or not, stole from men. Mary Marshall, sixteen years old, committed one of the characteristic small-order crimes of Georgian London. She was tried for feloniously assaulting a newly arrived Eastern European Jew, Daniel Levi, in the dwelling house of Mary Martin in Cross Lane, putting him in fear and danger of his life and of 'taking from his person and against his will 29 shillings . . . and 24 halfpence, value 12 pence, his property'. Levi, apologising to the court for his lack of English, testified he had heard that Mary Marshall had an overcoat to sell, and when he went to see it, she wanted 24 shillings for it. She declared she doubted whether he had such money, and so he showed her his money, and when he did she pushed him against the wall with great force, took the cash and locked herself up in a closet with it.

Marshall came out of the closet to face Levi and with another woman took hold of him and beat him, threw a pail of water over him and stole whatever else he had. 'A gentleman took my part,' said Levi, 'and fetched an officer.' The Bow Street runner claimed to have identified Mary Marshall from Levi's description and arrested her. 'I am innocent of it,' Mary Marshall told the court, and there was a chance she was. 'I have not a witness in the world.' On the jury's verdict, Justice Heath condemned her to death. She would be one of the women transported on the *Lady Penrhyn* when reprieved on condition of transportation for life.

Similarly Elizabeth Hippesley was brought to the Old Bailey for feloniously stealing a silver watch chain and other goods, the property of a master butcher. The butcher swore that he met the prisoner at the Fleet market and agreed to go home with her. Between one and two, he woke in Hippesley's room in a house in Port Pool Lane and found that he had been robbed, even of his garters. He fetched a constable the next morning who found Elizabeth, the garters on her legs.

In court, the prisoner Hippesley demanded of the butcher: 'Did you not tell me you had left all your money at cocking [gambling on a cock fight] and gave me the watch till you brought me some money?' Elizabeth was not believed and was found guilty and sentenced to transportation for seven years.

Some crimes were a little more novel. Hannah, or Anna, Mullens, an Irishwoman of St Giles, presented herself before the magistrates and swore that the last will and testament, partly printed and partly written, which she held in her hands, was that of a late seaman, who had wages due to him and owed her money. But the poor fellow had been blown to pieces in the East Indiaman, the *Duke of Arthur*. Hannah had taken a false oath that the document was authentic. Later, a probate official declared the document a forgery.

She was asked why she had taken eleven months to present the will.

'I was big with child, and I did not like to go till I was well.'

'How old are you now?'

'I am going on 26.'

She said that she came from Ireland but lived in St Giles with her child's father, a porter. The verdict was quickly brought down. She was guilty and sentenced to death, but humbly recommended to mercy by the jury 'because they supposed she had been drawn in', that is, that others had persuaded her to try for the sailor's estate. The judge, Justice Wills, revealed that this was not the first or second case of these fraudulent wills that Hannah had been concerned in. 'And if so, you would wish to withdraw your recommendation.' Mercy must have operated, however, for Hannah found herself in the end aboard the proposed convict fleet.

We read quite commonly in the Old Bailey papers that a woman prisoner 'pleaded her belly and a jury of matrons being sworn, returned their verdict: she was not with quick child'. Hannah also pleaded her belly – it could temporarily protect her against hanging and transportation – but was found to be 'not with quick child'.

A man in his twenties, Charles Peat, stood trial like young John Hudson for returning from transportation, a capital offence. The steward of the ship *Mercury*, the same ship Hudson had escaped from, recognised the prisoner as having been put on board the convict ship at Galleon's Reach, below Woolwich in the Thames. He had been found guilty of highway robbery and his death sentence had been commuted to transportation for life. He had been keen on his rights, and had argued with the ship's master about whether they were bound for Virginia or Nova Scotia. After the prisoners took over the ship on the morning of 8 April 1784, said the steward, 'I had then the pleasure of wearing what the gentleman here call darbies [irons]; until Peat went ashore in Devonshire.'

Peat was a forthright young man, and told the court that he had served His Majesty in the Royal Navy and had had the honour of bearing a commission, but while serving time on one of Campbell's hulks in the Thames, waiting to be boarded on the *Mercury*, 'I had the mortification of seeing my fellow sufferers die daily, to the amount of 250.' He was found guilty of return and given for the second time in his life a sentence of death, but though that meant he had to spend time in the condemned ward of Newgate, amidst its lamentations, screams, songs, brawls and riotousness, the sentence was in the end transmuted to transportation for life.

Indeed, the better part of one hundred prisoners on what would become known as the First Fleet were guilty of having returned from transportation. One of the prisoners destined for Phillip's convict fleet to Botany Bay, John Blatherhorn, originally a thief, had earned death twice in succession by being involved in the mutiny on the transport ship *Swift* in August 1782, and then in the mutiny aboard the *Mercury* in the spring of 1784. While the Nova Scotia-bound *Swift* was still in the English Channel, its 143 male and female convicts sent an extraordinary message from the prison deck to the captain, asking him whether he would take their irons off and telling him that if he would not, they would take them off themselves. When the captain refused, convict lock-pickers went to work, and the result was such a rush of convicts on the captain's cabin that the ship was taken. A number of prisoners, including Blatherhorn, then seized boats and landed in the Torbay area.

Negroes, emancipated slaves, were to join Phillip's fleet too –
ten of them. John Martin had stolen cloth coats, breeches,
waistcoats, a petticoat and a cotton gown from a dwelling house
where he may have been a servant. The son of the house saw
Martin decamping with the stuff. The jury valued the theft at
39 shillings, below the capital punishment threshold of 40
shillings, perhaps in an attempt to save Martin the gallows.
Martin's court appearance took all of ten minutes.

Britain was, through its institutions, telling all such people
and more, to begone.

Three

To saving Britain from epidemic petty crime considerable maritime expertise was applied. Lord Howe at the Admiralty had written to Lord Sydney at the Home Office on 3 September 1786: 'I cannot say the little knowledge I have of Captain Phillip would have led me to select him for a service of this complicated nature.' But Sydney liked and admired professional officers like Phillip, whom he rightly considered the journeymen of Empire. And then, what one officer would have had qualifications designed for such a service? This was a completely novel enterprise for the Crown, an unprecedented penal and society-making experiment, even if the Home Office, reacting to domestic pressure, did not necessarily see it in those terms. Being commodore not of two or three but of a flotilla of eleven ships, as well as captain-general of huge and unvisited territories, and gaoler-in-chief in the netherworld was a massive role for which normal naval service could only dimly prepare anyone.

Even so, Phillip – this obscurely gifted, secretive and earnest man – was, as he had been all his life, anxious for employment, and harboured enough respect for his own gifts to take on the immediate challenge offered by a convict fleet.

Arthur Phillip's seafaring apprenticeship had begun in 1753 in the squalid, grease-laden, profane atmosphere of the whaler *Fortune*, a 210-ton vessel built for the Greenland whale fishery. In winter, *Fortune* travelled to the Mediterranean to take part in the trade in herrings and oranges. But just after Phillip's seventeenth birthday, war was declared between France and Britain. During the conflict, later to be called the Seven Years War, he experienced the violence of cannonry in an inconclusive battle to save the British-garrisoned island of Minorca. Later, as a young officer off Havana in 1761, he survived both Spanish artillery and a wet season which, with its armoury of malaria, yellow fever, cholera and the usual typhus fevers spread by lice and rats, killed 7000 sailors and soldiers.

These experiences all prepared Phillip for further elevation within the officer class. It was just as well, since he lacked powerful connections. His character in his early twenties combined a dry humour with reserve, efficiency and intellectual hunger. To temper a tendency to be authoritarian, he possessed common sense and was not fast to anger. He lacked the raucousness and rambunctiousness of other sailors, and it is hard to imagine him on a loud stampede through foreign streets, looking for liquor or women.

On 19 July 1763, Lieutenant Phillip married Margaret Denison, the widow of a glove and wine merchant and fifteen to sixteen years older than he was, in St Augustine's, Watling Street. In separate portraits painted about then, he appears as a florid, cultivated-looking young man, and she a conventionally handsome woman with rather birdlike eyes. Whatever Arthur Phillip's sexual tendencies, he does not seem to have been a young man aflame with passion. The couple lived in Hampton Court for two years, but then went to rusticate at Lyndhurst in the New Forest in Dorset, on Margaret's estate of 22 acres, named Vernals. Phillip ran their property as a dairy farm, kept horses, and grew fruit and vegetables.

After a number of severe winters in the country, 'some circumstances occurred' which led to a formal indenture of separation, signed by the couple in April 1769. It stated that they had 'lately lived separate and apart'.

Phillip began to spend time in France as an agent – or spy – for the Home Office or Admiralty. With his gift for languages and his German colouration he was good at his work, but it was an ungrateful business and Phillip felt he needed to accelerate his naval career. The Portuguese Secretary of State for Marine Affairs and the Colonies approached Admiral Augustus Hervey asking for help in a fight with Spain on the Atlantic coast of South America. A disputed area known as the 'Debatable Lands', ran northward from the estuary of the River Plate, and was claimed both by Portuguese Brazil and Spanish Argentina. As token of their claim, the Portuguese had created their own colony at the Plate, across the estuary from Buenos Aires and west of Montevideo, and named it Colonia do Sacramento. They needed an experienced captain to help them defend it. Hervey recommended Lieutenant Phillip to his Portuguese friends. In a newly built, post-earthquake Lisbon, Phillip oversaw the business of fitting out his command, the *Nossa Senhora de Belém*, on the banks of the Tagus River, and quickly added Portuguese to the French and German he could already speak.

Phillip got on well with the Portuguese Viceroy in Rio de Janeiro, Marquis de Lavradio, and fought effectively against the Spanish. But in 1776, the Portuguese started to negotiate a truce. Lavradio had already reported to the Portuguese court that

Phillip's health was delicate but that he never complained, 'except when he had nothing special to do for the Royal Service'. It was true that many of Phillip's illnesses were associated with a kind of ardent waiting for action to occur, or else with circumstances in which he conducted dangerous work out of the direct gaze of the Admiralty. Ambition was his most restless appetite. Lavradio's opinion of him gives one of the most extended discourses on his character that we have: 'One of the officers of the most distinct merit that the Queen has in her service in the Navy . . . As regards his disposition, he is somewhat distressful; but as he is an officer of education and principle, he gives way to reason, and does not, before doing so, fall into those exaggerated and unbearable excesses of temper which the majority of his fellow countrymen do . . . an officer of great truth and very brave; and is no flatterer, saying what he thinks, but without temper or want of respect.' Phillip emerged from the Spanish–Portuguese War as a markedly solitary and self-sufficient man, awaiting only public recognition to complete him.

In 1779, the Treaty of San Ildefonso made the Debatable Lands largely Spanish. Phillip resigned his now futile Portuguese commission to seek fresh employment in the Royal Navy fighting the American War. After a stint as commander of a fire-ship, in 1781 the Admiralty at last gave him a better command, the frigate *Ariadne*. But in the River Elbe, when escorting transports of Hanoverian recruits for the British army, the onset of river ice forced him ingloriously to run his vessel into the mud of the Hamburg harbourside. It was not until the end of the following March that the *Ariadne* was able to leave.

During these frustrating months, Phillip came to place great reliance in Lieutenant Philip Gidley King, a sturdy young man of undistinguished background like himself, a draper's son who served him not only in the *Ariadne*, but also in his later command, the *Europe*, and eventually in the great convict fleet.

Amongst other friends Phillip met in these years, the most significant was Evan Nepean, a Cornish ship's purser aboard the *Victory* in 1779–80. The son of a Plymouth shipwright, in 1782 Nepean found himself by raw talent elevated to Undersecretary of State in the Home Office.

When that same year the Admiralty appointed Phillip captain of the *Europe*, a 64-gun, 600-man battleship, he was at last commander of a ship of the British battle line. He took Lieutenant Philip Gidley King aboard with him, and his clerk, a most eccentric man named Harry Brewer.

The American bosun on *Europe*, Edward Spain, would later write an ironic memoir of his time serving with Phillip, and of the relationship between Phillip and Harry Brewer. Brewer was an unmarried seaman of no particular rank, or else he could be counted at more than 50 years of age as the oldest midshipman in the Royal Navy. Brewer had for some years skilfully copied Phillip's diaries and journals for him, and worked up his watch lists and quarter bills. But Spain did not quite approve of the association between Harry and Arthur Phillip, remarking mysteriously that, 'Our captain was at that time in slender circumstances . . . and as they both [Phillip and Brewer] rowed in the one boat, no doubt they had their own reasons for wishing to make the voyage together.' Whatever else 'they both rowed in the one boat' might have meant, Spain certainly implied they were short of cash.

Bosun Spain was rather fascinated with Harry. He had some gift for architecture, said Spain, 'was bred a house carpenter, he was clerk at some great concern in the building line . . .' His coarse features and contracted brow 'bespoke him a man sour'd by disappointment'. Harry usually wore a rough-textured blue coat, a wool hat 'cocked with three sixpenny nails, a tolerable waistcoat, a pair of corduroy breeches, a purser's shirt not of the cleanest'.

At Cape Verde Islands, said Spain, Phillip 'was perfectly at home for he spoke Portuguese fluent and could shrug his shoulders with the best of them'. Spain would give us an insight into the only sexual infatuation Phillip would ever be accused of. The *Europe* put into the mid-Atlantic island of St Helena, and found four British sailors and their women stranded there, and allowed them to travel on board. 'But don't imagine that it was out of any partiality to any of them, except one, which one he had a sneaking kindness for and had he given permission to her alone the reason would have been obvious to the officers and the ship's company.' Her name was Deborah Brooks and Phillip's association with her would run a considerable time. She had eloped from England with a ship's bosun, Thomas Brooks, and for whatever reason they and the other sailors and women had fetched up on St Helena, waiting to be employed on a passing British ship. Spain seemed to see Thomas Brooks as a threat, and believed Phillip was trying to get rid of him, and to put Deborah's husband in his place. Deborah Brooks and her husband would also join Phillip on his ultimate journey to penal New South Wales.

Phillip's old friend Evan Nepean at the Home Office was responsible not only for prisons, but for espionage in France and Spain. It was as one of Evan Nepean's spies in the 1780s that Arthur Phillip, after his return from Madras on *Europe*, became known to Lord Sydney. Though Britain was not at war with France, something like a cold war persisted between the two nations. Late in 1784 Nepean called on Phillip to journey to Toulon and other ports 'for the purpose of ascertaining the naval force, and stores in the arsenals'.

In some roundabout way, this secret service, combined with Phillip's record as a 'discreet officer', a captain in both the Royal Navy and for the Portuguese, might have helped explain why the Admiralty and Home Office thought him adaptable enough to be the first governor of Britain's convict colony-to-be. A neighbour of Phillip's in the New Forest, Sir George Rose, Secretary of the Treasury, was involved in the costings of the enterprise, and he, too, supported Phillip's appointment, which Phillip does not seem to have hesitated in accepting. Many officers might have thought it potentially dangerous and unrewarding to voyage with a mass of felons to the far side of the globe.

The document that set out the *raison d'être* for the penal experiment, *The Heads of a Plan*, was prepared for the Lord Commissioners of the Treasury and others in Whitehall by Evan Nepean. It concentrated on the business of transportation to New South Wales rather than on any commercial benefit arising from the new place. New South Wales, it declared, was 'a country which, by the fertility and salubrity of the climate, connected with the remoteness of its situation (from whence it is hardly possible for persons to return without permission), seems peculiarly adapted . . . to providing a remedy for the evils likely to result from the late alarming and numerous increase of felons in this country, and more particularly in the metropolis'. The *Heads* dealt with the process of transportation, the taking on board of two companies of marines to form a military establishment, the provision of rations and the collection of supplies and livestock en route at Rio and the Cape of Good Hope. Towards the end of this

Plan, Nepean raised the issue of financial and strategic benefits which might arise from the New Zealand flax plant and the tall trees on Norfolk Island, an island Cook had discovered a thousand miles out in the Pacific from Botany Bay, where a proportion of the convicts were to be settled. 'Considerable advantage will arise from the cultivation of the New Zealand hemp or flax plant in the new intended settlement, the supply of which would be of great consequence to us as a naval power, as our manufacturers are of opinion that canvas made of it would be superior in strength and beauty to any canvas made from the European material and that a cable of the circumference of ten inches made from the former would be superior in strength to one of eighteen inches made of the latter.' Similarly, the *Heads* mentioned the procuring of New Zealand masts and ship timber for the fleets in India.

There has been a great deal of argument about whether this commercial thought was tacked on to the penal plan, or was the real purpose of the whole operation. But the document declares itself at its opening sentence: 'Heads of a plan for effectually disposing of convicts.' And if the proposed penal settlement in the south-west Pacific were to become a trading post, it would violate the chartered monopoly of the East India Company, and upset the Company's trade with Canton and in India. The East India Company's principal, Francis Baring, would quite early complain of 'the serpent we are nursing at Botany Bay'.

It seemed that His Majesty's government desired New South Wales far more as a prison than as a great port, or as an opening for British trade. Phillip was thus, in the strictest penal sense, to be a governor, and not an apostle of British commerce.

Four

Only one British ship, the HMS *Endeavour*, captained by a maritime prodigy, James Cook, had spent time on that most distant coast of New South Wales, in 1770. Now, under the vulgar urgings of domestic politics, Prime Minister Pitt and Lord Sydney of the Home Office were sending a reputable but not glittering fellow in command of many vessels stocked not with naturalists and artists but with Britain's sinners.

In his little office at the Admiralty, Phillip worked with his clerk, the unkempt Harry Brewer, and as if to focus his mind, wrote a document which represented his philosophy of convict transportation and penal settlement. It was a cultivated and informed essay, if not quite dazzling. Not as a visionary, but merely as someone acknowledging the state of British law, he wrote: 'The laws of this country will, of course, be introduced in New South Wales, and there is one that I would wish to take place from the moment His Majesty's forces take possession of the country – that there can be no slavery in a free land and consequently no slaves.'

His determination that convicts not be seen as a slave caste would have important results for many of the felons marked down for his convict transports. For one thing, he had respect for their right to as safe and healthy a journey as he could provide. But he did not see their status as fully equal to that of the free. 'As I would not wish convicts to lay the foundation of an Empire, I think they should ever remain separated from the garrison and other settlers that may come from Europe.'

Through secret caresses between free men and convict women, and other alliances forged on his ships, this would become a proposition already in doubt before the ships even sailed.

The Cabinet and the King having made their decisions and signed off on them, the gaolers thought only of emptying their cells and wards and hulks. Arthur Phillip was the one man in Britain thinking carefully of the transportation, and of ensuring the survival of the soldiers and felons he must ship. The early sight of convict vessels disappearing down the Thames estuary with sails set was the chief point for the Home Office, not how they fared from the instant of disappearance onwards.

The successful tenderer for the overall contract for the fleet was William Richards Jr, a prominent ship-broker of south London. There is a legend that contractors dumped their worst produce on Phillip, knowing he could not very conveniently complain. But two reliable young officers of marines, Watkin Tench and David Collins, no strangers to salt rations, would both independently agree that the provisions on the First Fleet provided by Richards were 'of a much superior quality to those usually supplied by contract'. We have no similar enthusiastic endorsement from any convict, though the low death rate during the flotilla's months of voyaging would suggest that Phillip, when visiting the vessels down the Thames at Deptford, and Richards himself must have been careful during their inspections of barrels of salt beef and pork and flour.

Richards had put a lot of thought into convicts and convict behaviour: their quarrels when they had to sleep together four to a berth – he unsuccessfully suggested individual hammocks; their jealousy when some dressed better than others – he thought there should be a standard uniform; the influence which the wicked exercised over the others – he suggested there should be three classes of felons sent on separate ships. Indeed Richards was conscientious to the point of crankiness.

He inspected and chartered five merchant vessels as transports – the *Alexander, Charlotte, Friendship*, the newly built *Lady Penrhyn* and *Scarborough* – and three store ships – *Borrowdale, Fishburn* and *Golden Grove*. His contracts with the ship-owners detailed the form of accommodation, rations, cooking equipment, bedding, fetters, ventilation equipment and so on to be supplied for the convicts, and the medicines and medical preventives to be aboard. They also specified the duties of the ship-owners and captains, and the number of crew required per tonnage. Ultimately, as the numbers loaded aboard grew, Richards would need to contract for a sixth convict transport, *Prince of Wales*. The transports were all relatively young vessels but not purpose-built prison ships, and they all needed to be specially fitted out by carpenters at the Deptford dockyard in order to receive prisoners on their normal cargo decks. All were three-masted and over 300 tons, except the *Friendship*, a two-masted vessel of 278 tons generally described as either a brig or a snow.

For Richards and the individual ship-owners the cream from this expedition would come after the ships finished the business of taking the convicts into the void. Some of them hoped to receive further charter from the East India Company, authorising them to go to China to load tea. Richards depended on Lord Sydney to apply pressure to the East India Company directors, who exercised monopoly over east Asian trade, but ultimately they would take up only three ships, *Charlotte*, *Scarborough* and *Lady Penrhyn* to bring a cargo of tea home from China.

Arthur Phillip could not be in Deptford all the time, but the navy had appointed an agent to represent him and it at the dock-yards to see that the necessary carpentering was done, and all arrangements were properly made for receiving prisoners. The convict prison on each of these ships was fitted out on the lowest cargo deck, where cradles – narrow sleeping bunks in sets of four or six – ran the length of the ship on either side of an aisle. Young Lieutenant Philip Gidley King, Phillip's protégé from *Europe*, was down at Deptford attached to *Sirius*, Phillip's flagship, and described the security being put in place on the transports. He saw that the carpenters were barricading an area on deck with a wooden barrier about 5 feet high, and topping it with pointed iron prongs, 'to prevent any connection between the marines and ship's company, with the convicts. Sentinels are placed at the different hatchways and a guard always under arms on the quarterdeck of each transport in order to prevent any improper behaviour of the convicts, as well as to guard against any sur-prise'. Below, to contain the prison deck, thick bulkheads had to be positioned, 'fitted with nails and run across from side to side [port to starboard] in the between decks above the mainmast, with loop holes to fire . . . in case of irregularities'. Forward of the prison space was the prison hospital, and the equally dark areas aft of the prison were often reserved for the marines, privates, non-commissioned officers and their families.

The hatches which gave onto the deck were 'well secured

down by cross bars, bolts and locks and are likewise nailed down from deck to deck with oak stanchions'.

The barricaded section on the open deck gave the authorities an area where even the most unruly convicts could be exercised, but many knew that in such close quarters the barriers might in some ways break down, and that there would be contact of various kinds, including sexual contact. For the transports were all very intimate in their dimensions. The largest of them was *Alexander*, 114 feet in length and 31 feet in breadth, barely more than the width of a decent parlour, and a mere 450 tons burthen. The lower decks had limited head room – the prison deck of *Scarborough*, for example, was only 4 feet 5 inches high. That meant that in prison and in the seamen's and soldiers' quarters, no one but a child could stand upright.

Phillip's flag ship, the part-victualler, part-frigate *Sirius*, 540 ton, named after 'the bright star in the southern constellation of the Great Dog', and with a crew of 160 men, was also at the Deptford dockyards, where an inadequate job was being done of fitting her up with what some called the 'refuse of the yards'. She would prove a bad sailer. Twenty guns were being hoisted aboard to give her the appurtenances and force of a warship. Her armed tender, the *Supply*, was a mere sloop of 170 tons. Lieutenant King could not see much sense in *Supply*, since she was not big enough to carry a significant amount of stores. But he would come to thank God for the existence of this tough and speedy little sloop.

Arthur Phillip would not be hustled. He had many requirements which he presented in letters to Nepean, Sydney, Sir George Rose, the Navy Board and Richards, the contracted broker. He would not budge from his small London office, unless it was to visit the expedition's ships in the Thames, until he was satisfied that the fleet was reasonably equipped in everything from scythes to undergarments. Phillip typically wrote to Undersecretary Nepean on 4 January 1787: 'I likewise beg leave to observe that the number of scythes (only 6), or razors (only 5 dozen), and the quantity of buck and small shot (only 200 pounds) now ordered is very insufficient.'

Already, in Whitehall in dismal winter, nameless clerks had begun work on the issue of who would be Botany Bay's first British inhabitants. There were no selection criteria for transportees based on health, suitability, trade or sturdiness. A convict of whatever age, strength and skill could go to Botany Bay. Time already served meant nothing, so convicts who had served five years of a seven-year sentence were included in the clerks' lists.

These lists were sent to Richard Ackerman, the keeper of Newgate, to the Clerk of Arraign at the Old Bailey, and to the hulk overseer Duncan Campbell. Estimates of when the embarkation would be complete were wildly amiss. In early December, it was thought by the Navy Office that it would take six weeks to get all convicts aboard. In fact, it took until the following May.

The fitting out of the transports finished, the ships moored at Woolwich, and the first convicts, men and women from the hulks and Newgate and from some county prisons, were rowed down the river to the *Alexander* and *Lady Penrhyn* on 6 January 1787. Many of them were sick and clothed in rags when received on board, and on the lower decks the cold and damp were intense. In the dimness of the prison decks, the convicts were often secured in place by chains which ran through an ankle shackle on each convict. Sometimes groups of convicts were shackled thus in lots of four, or even six, since six convicts made up a convict mess; but sometimes it was more. And some masters wanted the prisoners wristlet-ed as well. As yet the convict decks had empty spaces, but the allotted area per felon once a ship was fully loaded was eighteen inches width by six feet in length. Questions of elbow room would create many unrecorded conflicts. So did the waste arrangements – a series of buckets aft, topped by a plank with holes cut in it.

Even on *Lady Penrhyn*, reserved for women, the master kept the prisoners handcuffed and chained and below decks in those first days, purely out of fear. The poor country girl Sarah Bellamy, from Worcestershire, would most likely have found the cramped head room and narrow sleeping space claustrophobic. In the midst of the deck rose the great, groaning mainmast and the trunk of the foremast, like malign and barren trees. Security was uppermost in the masters' minds, and so ventilation was poor. On these lower decks oxygen could become so scarce that a candle would not light. Added to that was the noise of timbers and tide, and the raucousness and bullying of worldly, rebellious Newgate girls, their voices bouncing off the low head room. For young Bellamy the convict deck of the little *Lady Penrhyn* must have been a perfect hell, and when Joe Downey, a sweet-talking sailor soon to be appointed quartermaster, offered his attentions and protection, how grateful she must have been for what he could do to relieve the situation.

For love and lust would, by arrangement, influence and cunning, penetrate all the clever barricading of the ships, and seasoned seafarers knew that, and often turned a blind eye to everything except outright disorder.

In prison and on the convict decks of the fleet, experienced women tried to avoid pregnancy. They would delay weaning if they already had a child, they practised *coitus interruptus*, pleaded illness, including syphilis, and so on. Patent abortion medicines were advertised in newspapers, but the young women of the transports had no access to them. As for condoms, called by Casanova 'English overcoats', and 'armour' by James Boswell, they were available in London but were expensive, and a gentleman's device, designed more to avoid venereal disease than to prevent pregnancies.

On the *Alexander*'s prison deck, somehow, 195 male convicts would ultimately be placed, and elsewhere crew and marines, and marines' wives and children, and an extraordinary assortment of stores, beggaring modern belief that such modest space could accommodate so much human and maritime material.

Phillip came aboard his ships on 11 January to see the recently loaded men and women, and what impressed him most were not their criminal natures but their marginal health and their need of clothing and blankets. Clothing would always be a problem and was not standardised in quality or quantity. The navy did not want sailors and transportees to wear heavy wool – wool was worn on the hulks and in Newgate and infallibly attracted lice and typhus. So the male convicts were given woollen caps, but the jackets issued on board were of blue cotton cloth or the light, compacted woollen cloth called kersey. Shirts were of linen, trousers of duck, and stockings were of yarn.

Phillip complained to Evan Nepean that the clothes the women were sent down to the ships in 'stamp the magistrates with infamy'. He ordered that they be supplied with clothing from the naval stores of *Sirius*, and hoped the Navy Board would make up the loss. For 'nothing but clothing them would have prevented them from perishing, and which could not be done in time to prevent a fever, which is still on board that ship, and where there are many venereal complaints, that must spread in spite of every precaution'.

Phillip asked the authorities that the ships be moved out of the Thames and down the English coast to Spithead off Portsmouth, where, in the lee of the Isle of Wight, they could anchor on the broad Motherbank. Here, because of distance from shore, the inmates could be unchained and allowed fresh air. Indeed, the fleet would begin assembling there from mid-March.

For Phillip knew very well that the transports' masters would like the convicts to remain secured and immobilised for as long as possible, to keep the ships safe. But he also knew that for the sake of their health, the felons should be unchained once the transports were at sea, that in fact they would need to be unchained if their elected mess orderlies were to come on deck to collect their rations, and that all of them should be freely exercised on deck in good weather. As it was, with seasickness and diarrhoea, with dampness and the stink of bilges, with waves sloshing below and streams of water penetrating between ill-sealed timbers onto the sleeping platforms during storms, it would be hard enough to maintain the health of the felons half as well as an enlightened man of conscience would wish.

The busy Nepean responded to Phillip only as crises struck. Unlike Phillip, who had sat down to write out his philosophy of what was to happen, Nepean had the *Heads of a Plan*, but no overall concept for equipping the fleet. But the move to England's south coast was authorised.

Charlotte and *Friendship* headed off for Plymouth to collect prisoners from the hulks and gaols there. The two little vessels boarded between them 164 males and 41 females. One of the prisoners loaded from the hulk *Dunkirk* onto *Friendship* was a young, athletically built red-headed Norfolk man named Henry Kable. At the time of his sentencing to death in 1783 for burglary, he had been a lad of sixteen. Like his father and an accomplice, he was to be hanged on a gibbet outside Norwich Castle. At the scaffold, he was pardoned on condition of transportation, but saw his father and the accomplice executed.

In Norwich Castle prison, he had fallen in love with a slightly older woman, Susannah Holmes, guilty of burglary. Their prison child, Henry, born in the pen of Norwich Castle, had not been allowed to accompany his parents down to the dismal *Dunkirk*, and was being cared for by the Norwich gaoler, John Simpson. Now that Henry was on *Friendship*, and Susannah aboard *Charlotte*, the young family was utterly broken up. The efforts of Simpson to get Lord Sydney to let the baby be reunited with his mother would capture the public's imagination, which extended itself to romantic tales of doomed young felons but which, unlike the Victorian imagination, did not require that the lovers be virginal or married. Indeed, during their wait at Norwich Castle, Henry and Susannah had requested they be married but were refused permission. Soon, Simpson came down to Plymouth by coach with the infant. Baby Henry was presented to Susannah, and she and the child were transferred to *Friendship*. The family would not be broken up again by circumstance until late in the voyage.

Also boarded on the two ships were British marines from the Plymouth division. For the garrison in New South Wales, only 80 marines from Plymouth were wanted, though 130 had voluntarily offered their services under the incentive that a stint in the penal colony, should the fleet survive, would entail the option of honourable discharge and a land grant in New South Wales.

On 9 March 1787, Lieutenant Ralph Clark, a rather prim, neurotic officer who had volunteered in the hope of promotion, recorded, 'March with the detachment from the barracks to the dockyard and embark on board the *Friendship* transport with Captain Lieutenant Meredith and Second Lieutenant Faddy, two sergeants, three corporals, one drummer, 36 privates, nine women and children.'

At the same time the *Sirius*, its tender the *Supply*, *Prince of Wales*, *Scarborough* and the remainder of the ships were anchored on the robust tide of the Motherbank. Here further convicts and marines were rowed out to the transports from Portsmouth. *Scarborough* would receive over 200 male convicts, and cramped little *Prince of Wales* (318 tons) some 49 females and one male. Many of these convicts had been delivered to Portsmouth from other places, including London. A marine garrison of 89 men came from the Portsmouth division, and about the same number from the Chatham division had already boarded *Lady Penrhyn* and *Alexander* in the Thames.

Phillip was concerned to hear, however, that some of his marines were going ashore sick, and some of those sent ashore were dying. Part of the problem was that the marines were frequently quartered underneath the seamen's accommodation in the forecastle or aft of the prison, and were 'excluded from all air'. Their quarters on the transports were appropriate, Phillip wrote, only for stowing away provisions, and he began to look into ways of better accommodating them.

Though officers, for reasons unspecified but which everyone seemed to take for granted, were not permitted to bring their families on the fleet, some wives of private soldiers, about ten per company, were allowed to travel. A total of 246 marine personnel have been positively identified as having sailed in the First Fleet, and 32 wives and 15 children sailed with their marine husbands and fathers. Ten further children would be born to the families of marines at sea.

Movements of convicts from London to Portsmouth continued. One report of a gentleman's visit to Newgate showed convicts delighted to be slated for the fleet. Their merriment had a hint of the graveyard about it, of the vacancy yawning before them. One party left Newgate on the morning of 27 February, and a large contingent was moved in six heavily guarded wagons from a Woolwich hulk via Guildford. Following a night stop at Godalming, they reached Portsmouth in bitter weather. As the large body of felons was moved through the town, the windows and doors of houses and shops were closed, and the streets lined with troops 'while the wagons, I think thirty in number, passed to Point Beach, where the boats were ready to receive them; as soon as they were embarked, they gave three tremendous cheers, and were rowed off to the transport ready for their reception at Spithead'.

By the end of the loading process at Portsmouth and Plymouth, some 1500 people were spread amongst the eleven vessels, including 759 convicts, 191 of whom were women. They were issued further supplies from stores which had been originally set aside in Portsmouth for the late American campaign.

Bouncing around in the lee of the Isle of Wight, the convicts who had never sailed before became accustomed to the noises and motion of a ship and the claustrophobia of their low-beamed, cramped deck. Phillip was still in London but reactive to the reports of the naval agent and surgeons. The enterprising chief surgeon, John White, a veteran at 31 of a decade of surgical practice on naval vessels serving in the Atlantic and Indian Oceans, approached Captain Hunter, the Scots skipper of *Sirius*, and told him, 'I thought whitewashing with quicklime the parts of the ships where the convicts were confined would be the means of correcting and preventing the unwholesome dampness which usually appeared on the beams and sides of the ships, and was occasioned by the breath of the people.' So by late March at least some of the vessels were ordered back into dock at Portsmouth for the prison and soldiers' decks to be fumigated. The convicts were let up on the deck, a mixed blessing in March weather, while the whitewashing of the convict prison was attended to and gunpowder was exploded in small heaps to disperse the vapours associated with disease.

Early in May two late wagon loads arrived from Newgate, the prison decks were filled up, and the six months of the fleet's being in preparation were nearly over.

But there was now trouble with the sailors of *Sirius*. Lieutenant Bradley, the first mate, formerly a teacher at the Royal Naval Academy, Portsmouth, and going with the convict fleet chiefly for the chance to survey harbours in New South Wales and for scientific interest, said that when he came aboard in early spring, the seamen of the *Sirius* had been in employment upwards of seven months, during which time they had received no pay 'except their river pay and one month's advance'. Now they refused to work. Young Lieutenant King, no radical by nature, thought that in striking, 'the seamen had a little reason on their side'. A similar strike by some of the sailors in the *Alexander* transport led to able seamen from HMS *Hyena*, the naval vessel assigned to escort Phillip's fleet down-Channel, volunteering to take their place. Here were men who for pay or a willingness to gamble with life put up their hands on short notice to swap a Channel escort excursion for a voyage exponentially different.

A competent surgeon for the *Lady Penrhyn*, young Arthur Bowes Smyth, who did not join the fleet until late March 1787 and came to Portsmouth by mail coach, gives us a picture of the perils and shocks of being a journeyer in a changeable season. 'A corpse sewed up in a hammock floated alongside our ship. The cabin, lately occupied by the third mate Jenkinson, who died of a putrid fever the night before I came on board, and was buried at Ryde, was fresh painted and fumigated for me to sleep in.' When in a storm at the end of April the *Lady Penrhyn* dragged her anchors, Bowes Smyth noted: 'the women very sick with the motion of the ship'. He filled in his time waiting for the fleet to sail by landing and taking hikes – from Ryde to Wootton Bridge on the Isle of Wight, and from Stokes Bay to Gosport on the mainland. This was a luxury the convicts did not have, but at the insistence of Phillip and the surgeons, they *were* regularly permitted on deck to exercise, and officers and men, seamen and soldiers, spied out this or that pretty convict woman, and developed plans to associate.

Indeed, despite the guarded companionways and gates to the prison decks, and the lack of privacy, prostitution was a reality on *Lady Penrhyn*, *Friendship* and *Prince of Wales*. An unexpected roll-call on the night of 19 April revealed five of the *Penrhyn*'s women were in the crew's quarters. The women were put in heavy irons for it; three members of the crew were flogged.

On *Alexander*, eleven convict men, sick on loading, had worsened and died, and as April progressed morale was low even amongst officers of the fleet. Clark said, 'I am exceedingly sorry to say that the detachment on board here, and more so on board the other transports, do not go out with the spirit that was expected they would when they turned and volunteered for this service.' Private Easty, a Thames River marine attached to the *Scarborough*, who had watched the convicts come aboard, be inspected by a surgeon, go below and be chained up, had time to record such small things as the convict who was punished with a dozen lashes for secreting a knife in his shoe, the surgeon who 'left the ship for drunk', his own confinement to the brig in March for dropping his cutlass, and that of his fellow marine Luke Haines for disobedience. A token party of marines were gathered from every ship to go aboard the *Charlotte* to observe the punishment of Private Nash of the Plymouth division of marines, who received 150 lashes of a 200-lash sentence for 'un-soldierlike behaviour'.

Seventy-year-old Elizabeth Beckwith, guilty of shoplifting, and an 82-year-old peddlar, Dorothy Handlyn, sentenced for perjury, were minor celebrities aboard *Lady Penrhyn*, worth a visit from the gentlemen of the fleet. Beckwith would die at sea long before sighting the coast of New South Wales. Handlyn disappeared from the record, perhaps re-landed as absurdly too aged for such a journey.

The fleet was expected to leave in April but was still delayed both by contrary winds and Phillip's refusal to leave London until satisfied his ships were adequately provisioned. A Portsmouth local newspaper complained that the longer the sailing was delayed the more the port was thronged with thieves and robbers, those who had come down to see their old hulk- and prison-mates and fellow gang members ('rum culls') away. By now the idea of the departing fleet no longer attracted universal applause from Londoners. One citizen complained, 'Botany Bay has made the shoplifters and pickpockets more daring than ever. To be rewarded with the settlement in so fertile a country cannot fail of inducing every idle person to commit some depredation that may amount to a crime sufficient to send him there at the expense of the public.' A Tory declared, 'I beg leave to ask the advocates of colonisation whether the consequences of sending people to America were not eventually ruinous? And whether we have any rational prospect of more gratitude from the posterity of the transports we are about to settle in Botany Bay?'

Moralists still liked to remind the criminal classes, however, that in Botany Bay, 'no ale houses, no gin shops are to be found there. To work or starve will be the only alternative'. There was no question but that the coming expedition still teased at the public imagination. During most of April and May 1787 an opera entitled *Botany Bay*, 'partly moral and partly common, and upon the whole, a good thing', played to full houses at the Royal Circus, St George's Field, London.

During the long wait rumours came to the Admiralty that the Dutch had sent squadrons to Botany Bay to resist the landing of the British. The country, though named New South Wales by Cook, was still widely known as New Holland. The French had also made a gesture at claiming it; Captain Kerguelen, after whom the sub-Antarctic island is named, inscribed the French coat of arms on a piece of paper, put it in a bottle, and then cast it in the sea off the western Australian coast in the early 1770s, hoping it would wash ashore and create a title in law. The Duke of Dorset also informed the British government of a journey to the Pacific undertaken by a French nobleman, the Comte de La Pérouse. There were rumours that a race was on to claim the region, though no surmise about ownership of the place by its indigenous people broke the surface of this discourse. And none of these rumours and pieces of intelligence swayed Phillip's intentions as he worked inhuman hours in his office at the Admiralty.

The decks of Phillip's fleet were by now crowded with water casks and shacks and pens for animals. Phillip himself would bring pet greyhounds aboard *Sirius* to add to the noise and clutter. But there was other and more sophisticated freight. At the Board of Longitude's meeting in February 1787, the Astronomer Royal, Dr Neil Maskelyne, proposed adaptations for three telescopes and acquisition of a 10-inch Ramsden sextant to serve Lieutenant William Dawes, surveyor and astronomer, in making nautical and astronomical observations on the voyage to Botany Bay 'and on shore at that place'. Dawes was one of the Portsmouth division of marines, a very spiritual young man who had been wounded in a sea battle with the French in Chesapeake Bay during the war in America, and had volunteered for New South Wales out of scientific rather than military fervour.

On the crew deck the new Brodie stoves, big brick affairs, kept alight and guarded twenty-four hours a day, produced cooked food for sailors and marines, and if there were time or bad weather, for convicts as well. Often the prisoners' breakfast of gruel or pease porridge and their main midday meal – stews of bread and biscuit, pease and beef – were less satisfactorily cooked in coppers in a shack-galley on deck.

When on 7 May Arthur Phillip at last was able to reach Portsmouth from London with his servants, Henry Dodd and the

Frenchman Bernard de Maliez, and his clerk, Harry Brewer, he brought with him the Kendall timekeeper which would be used on board *Sirius* to calculate longitude. With the help of this chronometer, the calculations of Dawes and others on their journey to Australia would prove latitudes and longitudes 'to an astonishing nicety'.

Phillip had a final inspection of his fleet and looked into the availability of caps, porter, women's clothing and sauerkraut (which the convicts and sailors called 'sour grout' and were not keen on eating). Despite his earlier letters, not enough ammunition had arrived on board, so Phillip would need to buy from the Portuguese authorities some 10,000 rounds when the fleet reached Rio.

On board *Sirius*, greeted by the Scot master John Hunter, Phillip met a marine officer who would become a staunch friend of his, Captain David Collins, a stalwart fellow of not much more than thirty who was assigned to be the new colony's judge-advocate. In an age when boy officers sometimes commanded grown men, Collins had been a fifteen-year-old officer in command of the marines aboard HMS *Southampton* when in 1772 it was sent to rescue Queen Caroline Matilda of Denmark. The reckless sister of King George III, the queen had become involved in an affair and failed conspiracy with one of her subjects, and needed to be brought to safety in Hanover. Collins had also served on land, climbing the slope against defended American positions at the fierce battle at Bunker's Hill, at which American sharpshooters caused great casualties amongst British officers. Serving with the 21st Plymouth company of marines in Nova Scotia, in 1777 he married Maria Proctor, the daughter of a marine captain. At the end of the American War, he was placed on half-pay and settled uneasily at Rochester in Kent, for he hated being in reserve as much as Phillip had in his half-pay days. He was pleased to go back on full wages in December 1786, and willing for the sake of employment to be separated from Maria, who filled his absence by writing romances to enlarge their income. He would never put on record the same naked longing for Maria which Lieutenant Clark would express for his wife ashore in Portsmouth.

Collins's military superior, the leader of all the fleet's marines and Arthur Phillip's lieutenant-governor, was Major Robert Ross, a Scot whom some found hard to get on with, but who to his credit did not seem too shocked, mustering London convicts on board the transports at the Motherbank in March 1787, when some of them gave their names as 'Major', 'Dash Bone' and 'Blackjack'.

In John Hunter, captain of *Sirius*, Phillip was to find another companion spirit. The sea had claimed Hunter's ultimate affection over competing passions for music, the classics and the Church of Scotland. His first shipwreck, when sailing with his father, a ship's master, had been on a howling Norwegian coast at the age of eight. Once rescued, he had been saved from hypothermia by being clasped to a Norwegian woman in a warm bed, an experience which seems to have reinforced his suspicion that the sea was his true mother. Just over 50 and no ninny, he was the sort of officer others might describe as the navy's backbone.

And so the dispatch of the convict fleet was imminent. A Portsmouth verse expressed the compendium of anxieties and hopes which attended the event.

Old England farewell, since our tears are in vain,
The seas shall divide us and hear us complain;
. . . Our forfeited lives we accept at your hands,
And bless the condition, to till distant lands;
With a wish for our country we banish all sorrow,
For the wretched today may be happy tomorrow.

The sentiment in the last lines was a common one. At Botany Bay in the southern hemisphere, where south, not north, pointed to the polar region, reversal of destinies was possible.

A London broadside would more earthily proclaim:

Let us drink a good health to our schemers above,
Who at length have contrived from this land to remove
Thieves, robbers and villains, they'll send 'em away
To become a new people at Botany Bay.
. . . The hulks and the jails had some thousands in store,
But out of the jails are then thousand times more,
Who live by fraud, cheating, vile tricks, and foul play,
Should all be sent over to Botany Bay.

For such an exemplary officer, Arthur Phillip would sometimes hanker for tokens of respect, even for vanities. This tendency to press for distinction would remain into his old age. Before he left England, he tried to persuade the Admiralty to give him a specially designed pennant to fly from his ship. He was not permitted one.

Five

The fleet's prodigious journey began in darkness at 3 am on Sunday 3 May 1787. Phillip's instructions were to punctuate the voyage with calls at the Canary Islands, at Rio de Janeiro, his old Portuguese home base, and then at Cape Town. It was fear of that great eroder of human flesh and spirit, scurvy, almost inevitable on even shorter voyages than this, that was behind these orders.

The run down the Channel took three days, with great sickness amongst the women on the *Lady Penrhyn*, the new-built ship whose timbers were still howling and settling and whose master, William Sever, was unfamiliar with her. Uncontrollable seasickness filled the low-roofed prison deck with its acid, gut-unsettling stench, and spread rapidly down the crammed lines of women starboard and port. On top of that, the escort *Hyena* had to take the *Lady Penrhyn* in tow to keep her up to the other ships. In her cramped quarters the unrecorded but certain anguish of the country girl Sarah Bellamy was matched by that of the teenager Mary Brenham, who at the age of fourteen had stolen clothing while baby-sitting. No doubt the passionate interest of a sailor named William Crudis would become welcome to Mary too, as the torment progressed.

The fleet hove to some two hundred miles west of the Scilly Isles and *Hyena* departed, taking Phillip's last dispatches. By now, Phillip knew that there was a range of speed and performance between the various ships. Apart from the *Lady Penrhyn*, the transports *Charlotte* and the *Prince of Wales* were slowed by heavy seas, and their convicts suffered the worst discomfort and seasickness in storms. The deep-laden store ships, *Borrowdale*, *Golden Grove* and *Fishburn*, were susceptible to storm damage to masts and rigging. The handiest sailer was the little snub nosed tender, *Supply*, which could reconnoitre ahead and double back to round up stragglers, but could safely carry little sail in really big seas. The *Alexander*, *Scarborough* and *Friendship* were the three fastest transports.

By 3 June, the eleven ships reached Teneriffe in the Canary Islands, after a journey on which the irons of the convicts, except those under punishment, had been totally removed, and a routine for allowing the transportees on deck in fine weather had been established.

Sailors generally had two hammocks, which were regularly scrubbed and aired each day in nets hung in the rigging around the deck. In well run ships, like those of this fleet, convict bedding was also aired and dried in the nets. But despite all such care a number of males had died on the *Alexander*, which was the unhealthiest ship in the fleet. She had lost 21 convicts to fever, scurvy, pneumonia and the bloody flux (dysentery) in the few weeks since sailing and had a further 21 on the sick list under the care of a young, spiky Scottish surgeon by the name of William Balmain.

South of Teneriffe the weather was extremely hot and characterised by calms and rain storms. In the calms, amidst the cram of bodies, the air below decks reached fierce temperatures, and a skirt of stinking waste and garbage surrounded each ship. Wind sails were rigged like great fans, and swung across the deck to blow air below, and while the convicts exercised or slept on deck, gunpowder was exploded again in their prison to disperse evil vapours. The marine officers on *Friendship* found the ship infested with rats, cockroaches and lice, but the women convicts still needed to be battened down on their ill-ventilated deck at night, to prevent 'a promiscuous intercourse taking place with the marines'. By such a term, prostitution might have been meant, yet the rigour of separation between the sexes must have varied from ship to ship, to account for the pregnancies of convict women. Despite the ban on prostitution, there were so many alliances between convicts, male and female, and between marines and sailors and sundry women aboard, that perhaps Phillip and the Home Office, within the bounds of what they saw as proper discipline, were willing for such associations to occur. Some officers acquired housekeeper–lovers from amongst the convict women, and clearly on at least some of the ships, sailors were permitted to attach sea-wives to themselves. Thus girls like Bellamy and Brenham might have found themselves as much in the company of sailors in the forecastle as with their sisters below.

Lieutenant Clark on *Friendship* hated the disorderly women and ordered four of them to be put in irons for fighting, which must have been a hard punishment in that climate. 'They are a disgrace to their whole sex, bitches that they are. I wish all the women were out of the ships.' Clark was gratified that the corporal ordered to flog one London prostitute and *Mercury* escapee, Elizabeth Dudgeon, later in the voyage 'did not play with her but laid it home'. With the same ink and at the same hour he raised fervent thanks that God had sent him his wife: 'Oh gracious Jesus, in what manner shall I humble myself to make you a recompense for giving me so heavenly a gift?' Liz Barber, by contrast, abused Surgeon Arndell and invited Captain Meredith 'to come and kiss her cunt for he was nothing but a lousy rascal as were we all'.

But apart from the ten or twelve women who were always in trouble on the *Friendship*, the others behaved well, which might have meant in part that they were amenable to discipline but also to washing and sewing and other chores and demands.

Where the north-east trades blew, ships were capable of making good time, as on 17 June, when *Friendship* logged a refreshing 174 nautical miles to the *Sirius*'s 163. For the fast sailers to keep in touch with the slow ones was tedious, and Phillip was already contemplating splitting the flotilla into fast and slow divisions. Even on a good day for the whole fleet, 26 June, *Friendship* made 29 knots to *Sirius*'s 25.

Phillip knew from the stories of *Mercury* and *Swift* how endemic the dream of mutiny was amongst the convicts, the chief fantasy, and an attractive one in the northern part of the Atlantic from which, in the schemes of mutiny, the newly self-liberated American colonies, champions of men's rights, could most easily be reached. But Phillip seems to have accepted the presence of former escapees and mutineers on his ships with great sangfroid. One wonders did he ever look at Blatherhorn of the *Charlotte*, who had escaped from both *Swift* and *Mercury*, with special attention? Did he look twice at the highwayman Charles Peat of the *Scarborough* who had been sentenced to death for escaping *Mercury*? Peat was the sort of muscular, charismatic man who could handle a mutiny.

Lieutenant Clark and Captain Meredith on *Friendship* were very concerned; they asked the master, Captain Walton, to go on board *Sirius* and tell Phillip they doubted whether his order to unchain the convicts for their health's sake was wise. 'There are so many *Mercury*s on board of us,' Clark confided to his wife, Betsy Alicia, by letter. That same day, a convict came to the commanding marine officer on board the *Scarborough* and told him that two men were planning to take the ship over. Neither of them had been involved in earlier mutinies, but they were both sailors and knew how to work a ship. One of them, Farrell, had been transported for stealing a handkerchief – in his case, a handkerchief with a value of one shilling. The two men, Farrell and Griffiths, both in their twenties, were brought aboard the *Sirius* to have two-dozen lashes inflicted by the bosun's mate. Both men 'steadfastly denied the existence of any such design as was imputed to them'.

The two of them must have hoped that ultimately, when their time was served, their seamanship skills would earn them a journey back to Britain, and that in fact would turn out to be the case. It was little balm, however, for their junked and torn backs as they were transferred to yet another transport in the fleet, the *Prince of Wales*, and put under special watch.

A group baptism on the *Lady Penrhyn*, the Reverend Johnson, the chaplain appointed to New South Wales, performing the rite, was an event of 'great glee' with 'an additional allowance of grog being distributed to the crews of those ships where births took place'. But crossing the equator, the *Lady Penrhyn* and the *Charlotte* came close to colliding with each other, as the *Lady Penrhyn's* crew were distracted by the ceremonies of an officer or bosun dressed as King Neptune apparently rising from the sea to chastise and initiate those who had never crossed the line before.

On 5 July, Phillip felt it necessary to reduce the water ration to three pints per person per day, all of it going to consumption, leaving everyone to have recourse to salt water for washing clothes and bathing. Sometimes garments were washed by being dragged on a rope overboard, and one sailor lost a pair of breeches to a shark this way. A convict was washed overboard and lost when he went on deck to bring in the washing during the sudden onset of a storm.

On the *Prince of Wales* Jane Bonner, married, one child, guilty of stealing a coat, was hit on the head when a longboat fell from the booms where the ship's carpenter was caulking it. She died of brain injuries six days later. On matters of general health, Chief Surgeon John White and his three assistants were rowed around the fleet when weather permitted to consult with captains and such resident surgeons as Bowes Smyth of the *Lady Penrhyn*, and to inspect health arrangements or undertake care of the convicts.

The run was good to Rio, and on 5 August the fleet stood in the estuary off that city. Private Easty on *Scarborough* was impressed with the 13-gun salute from the fort, and the similar response from the *Sirius*. The total deaths since embarkation were 29 male and three female prisoners, which was considered an excellent result. The convoy had been able to keep in contact, although the journals of the gentlemen indicate that the *Lady Penrhyn* was continually lagging.

The Portuguese filled the first boat to return to the *Sirius* with fruit and vegetables 'sent as presents to the Commodore from some of his old friends and acquaintances'. On the second morning, when Phillip and his officers paid a courtesy call on the

Viceroy, a guard stepped forward and laid the national colours at Phillip's feet, 'than which nothing could have been a higher token of respect'. That night the town was illuminated in his honour. The English officers could go where they wanted within the city, without escorts. One evening a Portuguese soldier presented himself to Phillip and asked to be allowed to sail to New Holland with the expedition. Phillip would not hear of it and had him dropped off onshore, 'but with great humanity permitted him to be landed wherever he thought he might chance to escape unobserved, and have an opportunity of returning to his duty'.

Collins tells us that while in harbour in Rio, every convict was regularly given one and a half pounds of fresh meat, a pound of rice, a suitable portion of vegetables and several oranges. Sailors returning from jaunts ashore brought a great number of oranges and even pelted the convicts with them. The Viceroy set aside Enxadas Island to allow the expedition to set up tents for the sick and use as a shore base. Lieutenant Dawes of the marines also set up a temporary observatory there. The chief astronomical need was to check the Kendall chronometer of the *Sirius*. The correct local time could be found instrumentally from reading the sun and by fixing the exact time of an eclipse of Jupiter's third moon and comparing it with the astronomical tables which gave Greenwich time for such eclipses. By this means, Dawes found that there had been only an insignificant loss of clock time since leaving Portsmouth.

Many Portuguese astronomers made courtesy calls on the enthusiastic Dawes, and inspected his instruments and telescopes. His work here may have led to a correction in the until then agreed upon longitude of the city of Rio de Janeiro.

Also ashore, young Surgeon White watched religious

processions, and was astonished but titillated by the fact that there were many well-dressed women in the crowd, 'quite unattended' and trawling for lovers. He lingered by the balconies of convent novices and students, girls 'very agreeable in person and disposition', and felt a sentimental passion for one in particular. He also performed a demonstration leg amputation according to the controversial Allenson's method on the patient of an eminent Portuguese military surgeon, Dr Ildefonso. Ildefonso and his juniors were not impressed by the procedure but were happier about the quicker healing the method seemed to promise.

When the fleet departed after a fortnight, the Viceroy saluted Phillip with 21 guns, and could be forgiven for wondering whether such a varied and implausible expedition would be heard from again.

On the long stretch between Rio and Dutch-controlled Cape Town, rancour, ill temper, cabin fever and paranoia seemed to overtake many of the officers, not least on *Friendship*, and similar grievances must have filled the prison decks. And discomfort too. In late September, on the deck occupied by marines and women convicts, a sea broke which washed all parties out of their bunks. It must have been harder still for the men convicts on a lower deck. But the trip was relatively brisk. On one day *Friendship* logged 188 knots, and Cape Town, the Dutch headquarters in Africa, was reached on 11 November.

Here, a convict tambour maker or embroiderer named Eve Langley, sailing on the *Lady Penrhyn* with her small son, Phillip, gave birth to a daughter on a bed of clean straw in one of the shacks on deck. Phillip Scriven, a foremast hand, was listed as the father. By now the country girl Sarah Bellamy and the teenaged maid Mary Brenham were showing their pregnancies. There was a common Georgian belief, subscribed to by James Boswell, that sexual abstinence induced gout. The sailors of *Lady Penrhyn* were taking no risks.

There were no baby supplies or clothing aboard the fleet, and so as Surgeon Bowes Smyth of the *Lady Penrhyn* recorded, the women were reduced to 'plundering the sailors ... of their necessary cloths and cutting them up for some purpose of their own', a comment that casts interesting light on the subtleties of power aboard the *Lady Penrhyn*. The two leaders in this plunder were Anne Colpitts, a Durham woman whose own child, John, died on the voyage, and Sara Burdo, a young dressmaker guilty of having stolen from a Londoner who rejected her sexual advances. Both convict women would later be midwives in the colony, having helped the births of the *Lady Penrhyn*'s young. According to good midwifery methods, the mother's belly after birth was made moderately firm by the application of a table napkin, folded like a compress, and secured by pinning the broad bands of the skirt or petticoat over it. And though the midwives would have collaborated with the surgeon, the reality was that most convict women trusted their midwives more than any male. Because of their 'less exquisite feelings', wrote Bowes Smyth, 'the lower class of women have more easy and favourable births than those who live in affluence'.

The midwives must have been competent, for the *Lady Penrhyn* was the most healthy ship in the fleet. It also possessed more medical staff than any other – Surgeon Arthur Bowes Smyth and two assistants. Nonetheless, the elderly woman named Elizabeth Beckwith, long afflicted with dropsy, would perish aboard. Hugh Sandlyn, a convict woman's son born in Newgate, had died early in the voyage, aged eighteen months. Jane Parkinson, a milliner and thief, was already sickening for her death at sea, when she would leave a young son, Edward, for the other *Lady Penrhyn* women to look after.

Above decks was a babble of complaint from animals. In the fleet, said another surgeon, George Worgan, 'each ship is like another Noah's Ark'. Pet dogs roamed the decks. There were Captain Phillip's greyhounds and horses on *Sirius*, Reverend Johnson's kittens on the store ship *Golden Grove*, as well as on every ship a number of newly purchased sheep, pigs, cattle, goats, turkeys, geese, ducks, chickens, rabbits and pigeons penned in various structures on every deck. At the Cape of Good Hope, the women and some men aboard *Friendship* were transferred to other ships – again Henry Kable and Susannah Holmes were separated to make room for an additional intake of 35 sheep. Rural convicts and children took comfort from tending animals as they had learned to do from an early age.

After leaving Cape Town, and sniffing the westerlies below Africa, Phillip divided the flotilla into two divisions, the first division to be led by the little *Supply*, to which Phillip now transferred. Its leading group was made up of the *Alexander*, the *Friendship* and the *Scarborough*, now able to crowd on all the sail they had and travel as fast as they liked. On the convict decks it must have been miserable, with the sub-Antarctic cold and the heaving seas of the roaring forties. Visiting the *Prince of Wales* and *Friendship* by longboat, White found signs of scurvy amongst the women, particularly those who also suffered from dysentery. The symptoms were swelling and bleeding of the gums, a terrible breath which could make people wince even a considerable length away, pains in the joints leading ultimately to an inability to stand up, the appearance of large bruises on the flesh from the most glancing contact, an awful listlessness and a deadly depression, and finally the rupture of internal organs, internal bleeding and death.

He ordered the women dosed with essence of malt and good wine. Hail and snow came down, and officers like Clark were forced to wear a flannel waistcoat, two pairs of stockings and keep their greatcoats on continuously. But the convicts generally had only their light clothing and their one blanket, and welcomed what crowded warmth they could generate. Ahead, amidst the squalls, lay the south end of Van Diemen's Land, and its perilous coasts.

The second division of ships suffered the same turbulent weather. On 19 December 1787, Surgeon Bowes Smyth recorded that 'we spoke the *Golden Grove*, Captain Sharp, who informed us that Mrs Johnson, the parson's wife, was very ill, and also that the parson's clerk, Mr Barnes, was very ill'. A great wave which on 10 January in the New Year shook all the ships of the second division in turn and split the foresail and mizzen-topsail on *Golden Grove* and entered the Johnsons' cabin windows, tearing them away and washing Mr and Mrs Johnson out of their bunks. 'God of Oceans,' went one of Richard Johnson's prayers, 'when will you bring us to a safe harbour?'

The first division sighted the south-west of Van Diemen's Land and its South Cape on 5 January. It was summer in the southern hemisphere, but it did not feel like it there, and patches of snow could be seen on high ground. Surprisingly, it was less than two days after the first division worked its way around

South Cape that *Sirius*, with the help of its signal guns to attract the attention of other masters, and a large blackboard with the course chalked on it and hung over its stern, led the second division round and headed north. John White on *Sirius*, soon to be, aground, the surgeon with the most extensive medical practice in the universe, saw 'no hazard that attends making this land by day . . . as nature has been very particular in pointing out where it lies, by rocks which jut out into the sea, like so many beacons'. And he would see in a day or so that the New South Wales coast, though not without some shoals and perils, had a similarly frank coastline.

The fleet was now on the last leg towards fabled Botany Bay, using the charts made by Cook as their guarantee of safe arrival.

Six

They were close now, on 16 January in the New Year. *Supply*, *Scarborough*, *Friendship*, *Alexander*, the good sailers, were reaching northwards on the New South Wales coast. If the wind had favoured them and swung to the south, the first division might have made it into the longed-for port that very day.

The seas and handsome terrain they looked out on had been viewed by a mere handful of Europeans. The many beaches and bays were marked by bold headlands and backed by blue mountain ranges.

On the cluttered 70-foot deck of *Supply*, with 'a great sea running and cloudy dirty weather', Phillip witnessed the third squally dawn in a row, with heavy rain and lightning to the north. And yet the unprecedented nature of where they were did not seem to worry him or his officers, or the weather present them with an omen. These were all practical men, and when it was found that the chronometer in the main cabin of *Supply*, the almighty time-keeper by which longitude was calculated, had stopped here on the coast of the Antipodes, after working for the whole eight months of the voyage, they merely started it again and factored in the time during which they guessed it had not been working.

On the ships trailing *Supply* that day, and further south on ships around the *Sirius*, the convict mess orderlies, frowsy from sleep, so accustomed to the seas that memory of the solid earth and stone gaols had been washed out of them, were at the cook-shacks to collect the morning meal. Forward, on each vessel, from the heads by the bowsprit, two hunched sailors crapped into the sea. All was normal and vaguely hopeful, yet with the edginess of near arrival.

Though Prime Minister Pitt and Lord Sydney had authorised Phillip to look at this target coast as a vacancy, the people who had lived here since the last ice age had created their known earth, and whose ancestors had been in the hinterland for millennia longer still, had seen the scatter of ships and were sending reports ahead overland, clan to clan, of the astounding phenomenon they represented.

Modern dating methods show that the arrival of the first Australians occurred at least 60,000 years ago. The people who became the natives of the Australian continent had crossed from the prehistoric south-east Asian district named Wallacea between 60,000 and 18,000 years ago, when the Arafura Sea was an extensive plain, when sea levels were 30 metres below where they are now, and there was a solid land bridge 1600 kilometres wide between Australia and New Guinea. There was in that period a continent made up of Australia and New Guinea, their continental shelves and connecting lowlands, known to scholars as Sahul. Sahul's north-western coast received small numbers of individuals from Wallacea, possibly as few as 50 to 100 people over a decade.

Eighteen thousand years ago, when the east coast of Sahul still ran from New Guinea to the southern tip of Tasmania and beyond, the coast Phillip was now approaching was a region of cold steppes and sub-alpine woodland. Peaks higher than 1900 metres had glaciers descending them. When the ancestry of those who sighted Phillip's ships and sent word along the coast first explored the southern part of the continent, they may have encountered the 5-metre-long giant anaconda and the marsupial lion, the latter resembling a traditional cat, yet whose features also showed an obvious relationship to the kangaroo. The furs of marsupials would have been essential to the Aborigines of New South Wales at that stage. But now, for the uneasy observers ashore on this January day of 1788, ice existed only in tribal memory. The native coastline had stabilised in its present form about 7000 years before, when the glaciers melted. As elsewhere on Earth, innumerable camping places, stone quarries, burial grounds and sacred sites had been flooded by the sea. But in compensation, the coast had begun to mature and develop, providing sandstone plateaux, mangrove swamps and wetlands, rock platforms and beaches.

Now, as the fleet was delayed by northerlies off the coast, bushland and forest covered most of the eastern half of New South Wales. This was regularly set fire to by the lightning of the vigorous electric storms of the area, or by Aborigines using fire-stick farming – that is, using fire to flush animals out of the bush, but as a means of renewal as well. Cook had frequently seen fires during his journey up the long New South Wales shore in 1770, and columns of smoke would become a common sight for all who cruised here. The ancestral beings themselves, who had made the visible earth and its resources, expected the cleaning up and fertilisation wrought by the fire-stick. A number of Australian species of trees welcomed fire – the banksia, the melaleuca, the casuarina, the eucalyptus; and fire fertilised various food plants –

bracken, cycads, daisy yams and grasses. The fire-stick, in itself and as a hunting device, may have speeded the extinction of the giant marsupial kangaroo, the marsupial lion, the giant sloth and other species now vanished from the coast the flotilla was following.

For other food sources, the Eora, the indigenous people of the language-grouping in the Botany Bay area, were able to trace the small, stingless native bees to their caches of honey in hollow trees. Fish and shellfish were plentiful, but sharks and stingrays were taboo and could not be eaten. 'These people last summer would neither eat shark nor stingray,' Arthur Phillip reported to Lord Sydney. 'The Indians, probably from having felt the effects of their voracious fury testified the utmost horror on seeing these terrible fish,' said one officer. The shark and the stingray were clan totems of the coastal people, and besides that a subtle religious division into permitted and forbidden foods was apparent, and there were also prohibitions between individual men and women and their totem animals. One did not devour one's totem animal, whether bird, mammal, fish or serpent.

As sweet as life might be on that coast for hunter–gatherers, the conditions for the development of a sedentary life did not exist. Perhaps only one of the grasses which were the basis for farming elsewhere grew here, and the only semi-domesticated animal was the native dog or dingo, which hung around the people and helped them harry kangaroos, wallabies and smaller game in return for meat at the evening fire. The Aboriginal population of the entire landmass and islands, in that last undisrupted week, stood at perhaps 750,000.

This New South Wales coast, which was as far as government or the Royal Navy would venture short of the ice of Antarctica, was the centre of all things for the people who saw the phantasms of the fleet pass by. They would have been astounded that there were, somewhere else, in remote, northern, unholy mists, members of their own species who considered their country a netherworld, a legislated form of hell. And until now, they had not had any reason to think their horizons were about to collapse in upon them.

For the first division of the fleet, it was the morning of 18 January, when the wind shifted to the south-west and a hot breeze blew from an interior utterly unknown to any European, that they reached the neighbourhood of their landfall, Botany Bay. Twenty-nine-year-old Lieutenant King did not let any high emotion to do with historic beginnings enter his account of what happened on the afternoon of that day. He noticed the high chalk cliffs recede towards Red Point, named like many other topographic features by Captain Cook. Cook, who had come this way only once, had made such names both bywords for great distance and also a form of taming; he had reduced the coast to size with British tags. So there were comforting reference points for Phillip and his officers to look for. The officers took professional joy in seeing them come up. 'An eminence on the land . . . bore at this time W½ S 4 leagues which we take for a mountain resembling a hat which Captain Cook takes notice of.' Red Point was nine miles north of this, and then the southern point of Cook's Botany Bay, Cape Solander, named in honour of Sir Joseph Banks's Swedish assistant, was sighted. 'It is impossible to miss this place with Captain Cook's description before one.'

The *Supply* hauled in for the harbour at a quarter past two in the afternoon of the next day. Lieutenant Ball, who commanded *Supply* under the overall direction of Phillip, anchored in the northern arm of the bay, so that the three closest convict transports following, *Alexander*, *Scarborough*, and *Friendship*, and then all the ships of the second division, would be able to see them from the entrance and be guided in.

How could the place not fail to disappoint the travellers' long-sustained expectation? No one on the *Supply* made exuberant statements about it. It lay in its afternoon, sultry light, not much elevation to it, despite all the great sandstone cliffs and headlands they had passed further south. It was in part a land-scape of some shallow hills, eucalypt trees and cabbage tree palms spread as in a park, with the grass soon to be called 'kangaroo grass' growing between the trees. Otherwise, it was a country of low, indiscriminate earth, open ground in many places, with rank grass: the sort of country that promised there would be lagoons and swamps just behind the shore. Its sand beaches shone in the afternoon sun, but with an ambiguous welcome which hurt the eye.

As the *Supply* watched the earth, the inheritors of the earth watched the *Supply*. The Gweagal clan of the Eora language group occupied the south shore of the bay and watched and wondered why, after many years, the sky had ruptured again and the risky phenomenon of a craft as large as an island had returned. The Bediagal on the north-west side of Botany Bay were galvanised by the same question. Old men and women began to sing songs of expulsion, and the young repaired spears, not taking for granted the animal gut and yellow gum which held the points of stone or bone in place, and tested throwing sticks for solidity. A young Bediagal *carradhy*, a man of high degree and preternatural physical courage, Pemulwuy, if not actually present, was sent a message that the manifestation was back again. Mothers and aunts counselled children to be wary. The last time one of these phantasms had appeared, it had been an uneasy business, but they had been able to expel the alien presences in the long run.

Arthur Phillip knew from Cook's journals to be wary too, and conciliatory. Cook had not received an open welcome in Botany Bay eighteen years before. Phillip's task was harder – he did not need merely to be an investigator here. He was meant to make a penal town somewhere in this bay. Relationships with the 'Indians' needed to be as good as they could be for as long as possible. The instructions on this matter had been attached to his commission from the Crown and read: 'You are to endeavour by every means to open an intercourse with the natives, and to conciliate their affections, enjoining all our subjects to live in amity and kindness with them, and if any of our subjects shall wantonly destroy them, or give them any unnecessary interruption in the exercise of their several occupations, it is our will and pleasure that you do cause such offenders to be brought to punishment.'

At three o'clock the boats were hoisted out from the *Supply* and Arthur Phillip, Lieutenant King, Lieutenant Johnston, and Lieutenant Dawes all landed on the north side of the bay, 'and just looked at the face of the country, which is as Mr Cook remarks very much like the moors in England, except that there's a great deal of very good grass and some small timber trees'. A reliable young Cornish convict, James Ruse, had been moved to the *Supply* and would always claim he was the first ashore, wading in with Lieutenant Johnston riding scarlet and glittering on his back.

They searched that afternoon for a stream of fresh water, and could not find one. This must have concerned Arthur Phillip, though he was a man not easily daunted. Returning to the boat sweaty, Phillip spotted a group of natives on another beach and ordered the boats ashore at a point where two canoes lay. The natives immediately rose to their feet and called to the newcomers 'in a menacing tone and at the same time brandishing their spears or lances'. The usual testing rituals of arrival took place. Phillip showed them some beads, and ordered one of the seamen to tie them to the stern of a canoe, and made signs that they would be obliged if the natives could guide them to water. Arthur Phillip, as a founding act of goodwill, was carried ashore by a convict, and walked towards them alone and unarmed, and a male native advanced and made signs that he should lay the gifts on the ground. The native, edgy and trembling, came forward and took them, and then he and others came near enough to be given looking glasses and other wonders. Now or later, Phillip became aware that a missing front tooth of his own coincided with the tooth Aboriginal men lost in initiation, and this fact gave him a weight with the natives.

The Eora directed the visitors round the sand spit where a good stream of fresh water came down to the bay from the hinterland. Perhaps if the intruders were given water, they would depart.

Phillip was already doubtful about this bay, its shallow anchorages and fluky winds, and about its capacity to support an ill-supplied penal settlement. But he waited and kept his counsel. He was a man who would rather carry all of a burden than share it in easy conversation.

The next morning the other ships of the first division came round Cape Solander. They had made very good time. On

Friendship, Lieutenant Ralph Clark rejoiced in the fair wind after a lot of overnight lightning, thunder and downpour. He had his things ready for landing, having acquired from the carpenter a deal box to hold the butterflies he planned to collect 'for you my dear woman'. All night in his little hutch he had been haunted by dreams of his Betsy Alicia – that he was walking with her and that she was wearing a riding habit. At six o'clock that morning, the man at the masthead had called that he saw land on the port bow. Clark was pleased, since the sheep aboard, some of which he owned, had been living off flour and water and were in bad condition. Now he had the excitement of seeing the land very near, and a great many natives at Cape Solander.

When the *Friendship* anchored at last, a boat crew from the *Supply* brought aboard some mown grass, and that seemed to have resonated with Clark as an event as astounding as the sight of land. For 'I cannot say from the appearance of the shore that I will like it,' he noted.

We do not know what speculations occurred on the prison deck, but convicts were let up for exercise, and to help catch fish from the upper deck. January is good fishing time in New South Wales, and many were reeled in.

Major Robbie Ross, commander of the marines, was on the *Scarborough* with its big population of male convicts, and came ashore in time to take part in an expedition. Frustrated by shoals on the north side of Botany Bay and a brackish, boggy stream to the west, Ross and the others were sustained by sturdiness of soul, lack of imagination and uneroded belief in Cook's hopeful reports of the place from eighteen years before, and went into an inlet on the south-west side of the bay and 'ate salt beef and in a glass of porter drank the healths of our friends in England'.

There was a great shift of meaning commencing during those first hours of European permanency on the coast of New South Wales. This Botany Bay which the occupants of the ships, at the end of a journey as long as a human gestation, were beginning to suspect was a poor place had long since captured the imagination of the rest of the world. The animals Cook and Sir Joseph Banks found here or further north were nonpareils of the strange and exotic. On his journey through the Scottish Highlands in 1773, Dr Samuel Johnson had a party trick – 'imitating the newly discovered kangaroo: he stood erect, put out his hands like feelers, and gathering up the tails of his huge brown coat, so as to resemble the pouch of the animal, made two or three vigorous bounds across the room'. Hereafter, in the wider world, Botany Bay, renowned until now for the exotic, the furthest reach of human investigation and endeavour, famous for both botanic and zoologic conundra, would slowly become a name of scorn. As Robert Southey, sending up both the place and the proposed penal settlement at one hit, would write as doggerel during a pleasant evening with William Wordsworth,

Therefore, old George, by George we pray
Of thee forthwith to extend thy sway
Over the great botanic bay.

For the Gweagal and Bediagal clans of the Eora, a similar shift was in progress. It is as well to say here that the term *Eora* may have been merely a sample phrase from their language, and not necessarily what the region's natives called the language or themselves. Lieutenant King would mention that the people called themselves 'Eora – Men or People', and *Eora* or *Eorah* would be listed as a word for 'people' in a vocabulary put together by Phillip and Collins. Collins defined the word *Eo-ra* as the name common to the natives of the area the fleet would settle. It may, however, have been the local language's word for 'here' or 'the people about here'. In any case, for the indigenous people, the ghosts were abounding. One day: one ship, one floating island, one population of ghosts with mysterious outer skins. The next morning: four islands and four populations of strangers. They had not multiplied in this manner in their earlier visitation, eighteen years past. And on the morning of 20 January, when Captain Hunter on the *Sirius* led his second group of transports around Cape Solander, there were eleven of these floating phenomena with their huge and inhuman wings, their spider-web rigging, and infestations of questionable souls aboard. Some Gweagal and Bediagal, related by marriage, assembled on the southern point of the bay and yelled, '*Werre! Werre!*' across the water. They were speaking a language which the British did not understand, but this was their first, undeniable message to the men of the fleet, and it meant, 'Get out! Begone! Clear away.'

But the officers did not imagine themselves trespassers, and the private marines and especially the convicts would have found such a description whimsical.

A more poetic European vision had entered Botany Bay on the just-arrived transport *Charlotte*, in the person of the young captain of marines Watkin Tench. Captain Tench was in his late twenties, son of a successful and well-connected Chester boarding school proprietor. During the American War he had been made a prisoner in Maryland for three months when his ship, *Mermaid*, went aground. Like Collins and other officers, he had volunteered for service on the fleet to get off half-pay. In his striving, often elegant and curious-minded journal, Tench dared write rich prose for the arrival of this second division of ships. '"Heavily in clouds came on the day",' wrote Tench, quoting the English poet Joseph Addison, 'which ushered in our arrival. To us it was "a great, an important day".' Though I hope the foundation, not the fall, of an empire will be dated from it.' This sanguine and charming young Englishman rejoiced, not with absolute numeric accuracy, that 'of two hundred and twelve marines we lost only one; and of seven hundred and seventy-five convicts put aboard in England, but twenty-four perished en route'. He celebrated the fact that even though portable soup (blocks of compacted dried meat and vegetables), wheat and pickled vegetables had not been supplied to the fleet, and though a small supply of essence of malt had been the only anti-scurvy remedy put on board, such an extraordinary number of people had survived the voyage of what had been, for the second division of ships, exactly 36 weeks from Portsmouth, very nearly to the hour.

Watkin Tench thought that the low casualty rate amongst the fleet was the work of a beneficent government, and praised Mr William Richards Jr. But he knew too that a great deal of the success had depended on Phillip's demands for equipment and clothing, his organisational flexibility, his refusal to sail until they were properly supplied.

'The wind was now fair,' young Watkin wrote, 'the sky serene, though a little hazy, and the temperature of the air delightfully pleasant: joy sparkled in every countenance and congratulations issued from every mouth. Ithaca itself was scarcely more longed for by Ulysses, than Botany Bay by the adventurers who had traversed so many thousand miles to take possession of it.'

On the six ships in which the majority of the convicts were contained, we do not know to what extent joy stamped every countenance or with what feverish appetite for solidity men and women squinted across the glittering water and watched the strange earth and its people yelling 'Begone!' in the Eora tongue.

The convict women and nearly all the men were still kept aboard their vessels, and while they exercised on deck in a pleasant evening, their boisterousness echoed through the cove. To some the country obviously seemed enormous enough to offer room for escape, and some who did not understand that wildernesses were to provide the walls here already planned decamping. Wild elation, dread and depression competed for voice amongst these felons, some of them – despite Watkin Tench's sanguine view of their health – already pallid and doomed for the hospital tents Surgeons White and Balmain were erecting ashore. The wives of marines and their children also looked at the long dun foreshores of the bay with some surmise. They came from the same class as many of the convicts, and shared with them a capacity for stubborn acceptance.

To what could a woman turn her hands here? The 190 or so convict women of New South Wales had been either in service or 'single women of no trade'. They had few apparent skills to bring ashore. The one artificial flower-maker lacked tools and materials; the book-binder was in a country without publishers. Esther Abrahams, a Cockney Jewess, asserted, as did a number of others, that she was a mantua-maker – a maker of fashionable veils – but there was no society here to whom to sell such a refinement. As for Rebecca Bolton of *Prince of Wales*, she was what was then called an idiot, and had been in prison four years, which helped explain her mental desperation. She was in frail health and so was her little daughter of four or five. Both of them were chaff for the penal experiment. Tamasin Allen and Mary Allen, a prostitute and her accomplice in stealing a large haul of diamonds, jewellery and cash from one of Mary's upper-crust clients, by contrast had robust intentions of survival but little to offer except a questionable record. Tamasin was described in her trial papers as 'a lusty-ish woman with black hair . . . she seems to be a drunkard and unreliable'. She would be one of the women who would face the lash in the colony then in prospect, but had she known about that, she would have shrugged it off in defiance. Ann Fowles was another apparently incorrigible type. Officials had already recommended that her four-year-old daughter, who had come with her on the *Lady Penrhyn*, be taken from her as 'she was a woman of abandoned character', and sent to Norfolk Island as a 'public child'. It seemed that these women at least had not been chosen for their suitability as colonists.

Hunter and King and others surveyed the southern side of Botany Bay that same day, and, climbing a hill, found the soil an exceeding fine black mould, with some excellent timber trees and very rich grass. John Hunter, that characteristic Royal Navy officer, in effect the captain of Phillip's small navy, possessed the rigour and energy which often went with Presbyterianism. He was an accomplished organist, but far from any church organ here. He had served as a master, that is, navigator, since 1767, and then in the American War. Like Phillip, he was the sort of sailor whose career was rendered uncertain by lack of family connections, but he had become a post-captain through the influence of Lord Howe of the Admiralty, with whom he had served. And now he was bringing his talents and the template of his European mind imbued with his study of the classics and theology, up a hill in New South Wales, carrying with him too, as they all did, a word-for-word description of what had appeared in Cook's published journal, which influenced him to see the place in the best terms possible.

Encounters with the natives remained edgy. King and Dawes met natives who 'halloo'd and made signs for us to return to our boats . . . and one of them threw a lance wide of us to show how far they could do execution. The distance it was thrown was as near as I could guess about 40 yards'. King was alarmed enough to ask one of his marines to fire with powder only.

Lieutenant Bradley, Hunter's second-in-command, said that on the one hand boat crews 'amused themselves with dressing the natives with paper and other whimsical things to entertain them'. But the next day, after a landing party began clearing brush from a run of water on the south side of the bay, the natives became 'displeased and wanted them to be gone'.

By 22 January, when a seine net cast by a fishing party was hauled in and the natives saw the quantity of fish the sailors were dragging onshore with it, they 'were much astonished which they expressed by a loud and long shout'. They took some of the fish away, as a matter of right in their eyes, but as a form of primitive pilferage as far as the English were concerned. The sort of ownership the natives were asserting in raiding the net is clear when read now, but was invisible to the European eye then.

The next day the natives struck the fishers with spear shafts, took fish 'and ran off with them sensible that what they had done was wrong', wrote Lieutenant Bradley. It was not just that it suited the convenience of Phillip or the British government to ignore native ownership. Indeed, in other colonies, including Sierra Leone and the American colonies, and some years later in

New Zealand, treaties and land transfers were transacted. It was that the material possessions of the Botany Bay people seemed so slight, and their presence so flitting, that it was taken for granted that they had not yet left the state of innocence and childlikeness beyond which issues of title to fish, fowl, animals and land became important. Phillip found no grounds to take a different view. 'What they wanted most,' he reported, 'was the greatcoats and clothing, but hats was more particularised by them, their admiration of which they expressed in very loud shouts whenever one of us pulled our hats off'. An exchange of language went along with articles.

One day the Eora people indicated by very plain signs that they wanted to know the gender of the men in the boats, 'which they explained by pointing where it was distinguishable'. It became obvious to King that they thought the men were women, since they had no beards. 'I ordered one of the people to undeceive them in this particular, when they gave a great shout of admiration and pointing to the shore, which was but ten yards from us, we saw a great number of women and girls with infant children on their shoulders make their appearance on the beach, all in *puris naturalibus pas même la feuille de figeur* [completely naked, without even a leaf to cover themselves].' The natives had brought forth their women, thinking that the arrival of these pale spirits might have had something to do with a need of sex. The native males made it clear by their urgings that the men in the longboats could make free with the women onshore. 'I declined this mark of their hospitality,' said King. With a Low Church mixture of prudery and prurience, he urged a particular young woman to put her baby down and wade out to his boat, where she 'suffered me to apply the handkerchief where Eve did the fig leaf'.

Elders and tribesmen would have found the appearance of a flaccid ghost penis fascinating, but they would have been confused when the British refused a perfectly good opportunity to exercise these organs, to sate themselves, and withdraw to sea at last. As for the Aboriginal women, these figures to whom they offered themselves were more virtual than real. Since the great sexual sins of Aboriginal society were to have sex within forbidden blood limits – though adultery did bring its own private and public scorn and punishment – these pale people with their strange outer skins did not fit into the Eora world scheme. A dalliance with such phantasms had no moral or tribal meaning. That King should then invite a young woman out to his boat and affix a broad white bandanna over her thighs must have seemed a mystifying denial. It must have struck the Gweagal and Bediagal, and some of their visitors who might have gathered in from other areas along the coast, that these were people whose desires took considerable subtlety to discern. In any case the inducements so far offered – water, threat, and the offer of sex – had not worked.

Watkin Tench would initiate his own adventures ashore by landing from the *Charlotte* with a seven-year-old boy, the first child to disembark. Edward Munday, son of Private John Munday, certainly enchanted the natives. Tench undid the child's shirt and exposed his chest to show the natives his white flesh, and an old man came up and touched the child on the head and took an acute interest in him, trying to learn something about the newcomers from his demeanour. But in the end, it was '*Wer-re*' or '*War-re*' again. On his next landing Tench saw a scene that was always enacted early in imperial encounters with natives: an officer fired at a shield, placed as a target, with a pistol. 'The

Indians, though terrified at the report, did not run away, but their astonishment exceeded their alarm on looking at the shield, which the ball had penetrated.' Such shots were usually a demonstration in good faith, but in practice often served as a prelude to worse things. To reassure them that he did not intend to put a hole in them, the officer walked away whistling the then popular tune named Malbrook.

Later, in his glossary of Aboriginal words, Captain David Collins would also list the word Wo-roo-wo-roo to mean go away. The number of languages spoken on the continent of Australia in 1788 was about 250, but there were many dialects for each language. These indigenous languages tended to use the blade of the tongue against teeth and hard palate to create a far greater range of consonants than in English. Australian languages often had six corresponding nasal sounds, where English just has 'm' and 'n'. The sibilants, such as 's' and 'sh', were, however, totally absent in Australian languages. Later, Phillip's officers would chuckle at a visiting native's incapacity to say 'candle-snuffer'. Words showed case, tense and mood by the addition of meaningful segments, which created very long words and names. Woolawarre Boinda Bundabunda Wogetrowey Bennelong, for example, was the name of the native who would attract the officers' amusement over the candle-snuffer.

Just as the language had subtleties, Surgeon Bowes Smyth from the *Lady Penrhyn* admired the subtleties of the native lances, particularly the ones with the bone of stingray at one end and oyster shell at the other, and acquired one in return for a looking glass, each side being happy with the transaction. The bay was rich in stingrays which basked on its shallow, shelving waters, and indeed Cook had at first named the place Stingray Bay.

Generally though, for the officers, the expectation of finding Botany Bay the place of marvels which Cook and Banks declared it to be seemed challenged by the realities of their first reconnaissances. For example, a sentence in Cook's journal ran: 'We found also interspersed some of the finest meadows in the world; some places however were rocky, but these were comparatively few.' But what Cook really wrote had in fact been edited for the potential titillation and entertainment of readers who would never have to visit the place. The original entry in Cook's journal was this: 'I found in many places a deep dark soil which we thought was capable of producing any kind of grain, at present it produceth besides timber as fine meadow as ever was seen. However, we found it not all like this, some few places were very rocky, but this I believe to be uncommon.'

Phillip's landing parties could not find the 'finest meadows in the world' which made it to publication. Even Watkin Tench was typical of the general discontent about this place. 'Of the natural meadows which Mr Cook mentions near Botany Bay, we can give no account,' he would write after some months, recalling the disenchantment of those first Botany Bay hours. Surgeon White's final judgment would be: 'Botany Bay, I own, does not, in my opinion, by any means merit the commendations bestowed on it by the much lamented Cook.'

Virtually as soon as the storeship *Golden Grove* anchored in Botany Bay, the Reverend Johnson was rowed across to the *Lady Penrhyn* to christen a newborn child named Joshua Bentley. Perhaps Joshua could with hindsight be counted the first white Australian. His mother, Mary Moulton, had been tried at

Shrewsbury in March 1785 for burglary with a value of 61 shillings, and sentenced to transportation for seven years, having been originally sentenced to death. By the time she left England on the *Lady Penrhyn*, she had already served four years, and she was twenty-nine.

Joshua's parents, Joshua Bentley the sailor and Mary Moulton, must have known, like Mary Brenham and her sailor, Sarah Bellamy and hers, that a separation was inevitable, since the *Lady Penrhyn* was to return to England via China as soon as it was expeditious for the ship to leave. Some shipboard partners were ready for the separation, but some were bound to each other by desperate love.

When King got back to the *Supply* after one of his energetic reconnoitres of the bay on the afternoon of 21 January, he heard the news: Phillip intended the next day to go on an exploration of the far less famous inlets north along the coast, named in turn by Cook as Port Jackson and Broken Bay. It had taken Phillip just three days and a few insomniac nights to decide that, if at all possible, he would renounce the most famous inlet in the outer world. He did not, however, set out with an outright belief that shifting was inevitable. If he did not find anywhere better, he would set up house at Point Sutherland, just inside Cape Solander, the southern point of Botany Bay, where clearing work was already proceeding. But that was a place difficult of access from ships, and seemed far too small to support the envisaged town.

Three longboats were prepared with three days provisions for scouting up the coast. Arthur Phillip was to be accompanied by Captain Hunter and Captain Collins, by Lieutenant Bradley and a small party of marines spread throughout the three open boats. Putting out of the bay by dark on Monday morning, they found there was only a gentle swell as light came up on the aquamarine Pacific Ocean. It would be a witheringly hot day for the transports anchored in Botany Bay, but there was a sea breeze on the coast for Phillip's rowers. One of those who rowed the governor's longboat was the former American revolutionary soldier and now British seaman, Jacob Nagle. Able Seaman Nagle's father had been a colonel in the Revolutionary Army and in 1777 Jacob, fifteen years old, joined his father in the field. When he was eighteen, Jacob Nagle served in a number of American naval vessels and privateers, until captured by the Royal Navy with seventeen fellow American sailors and transferred to HMS *Royal Oak*. He and his comrades found themselves perforce somewhere between prisoners of war and pressed members of the Royal Navy. The end of the revolutionary war brought him to Plymouth and his journal implies that circumstances beyond his control kept him from returning at once to America. He formally joined the Royal Navy more or less as a means of working his way home, but it was a long process which he seemed pleased enough with and which had not been completed as he dug his oars into the spectacular azure sea off New South Wales.

Sandstone cliffs interspersed with beaches and headlands marked the way north. Several parties of Aboriginals cried out to the three open boats as they proceeded along the coast, yelling 'Wer-re! Wer-re! Wer-re!' in emphatic tones. That afternoon, Phillip entered the heads of Port Jackson, a dimple on Cook's map of this coastline, named to honour the judge-advocate of the Admiralty but not entered by Cook as he made his way up the coast in 1770. The great sandstone cliffs near the entrance decreased in size to become the weathered south head, whereas the north side displayed perpendicular heights. At some later and not too distant stage, these gates to Port Jackson would be capitalised as South and North Head.

Phillip's boats ran around the southern head, up the middle of the tide rushing in from the Pacific. They found themselves in a wide, bright blue bowl of sparkling water. It stretched away particularly on the south side. The foreshores of Port Jackson were cliffs of sandstone thickly covered with dun green forest, interspersed with yellow beaches. Phillip was already enthused, and the general sobriety of his prose would be swept aside when he later told Lord Sydney, 'We got into Port Jackson early in the afternoon, and had the satisfaction of finding the finest harbour in the world, in which a thousand sail of the line may ride in the most perfect security.' It was a sentiment which, coming from him, would certainly make his masters sit up. Not 'one of the most accommodating anchorages one could encounter'; not 'where some hundreds of ships might ride'. But absolutes: 'the finest harbour in the world'; 'a thousand sail'. The same number of sail Helen had launched in the war between Greeks and Trojans. The considered but exuberant sentiment would stand out unapologetically in the midst of Phillip's dutiful officialese, and it underpinned his decisiveness in declaring this, and not the great Cook's Botany Bay, as *the* destined place.

They circled to one of the north-side bays of this great, unexpected harbour, which Phillip then or later named Manly Cove, as a tribute to the general style and demeanour of natives who appeared on the beaches that afternoon. Then, in the evening, they headed southwards down the harbour and landed at a place within the south head which they inevitably named

Camp Cove, as a result of their pitching tents on a pleasant beach there. Nagle was impressed by the busyness of it all – marine sentries were put out and sailors were variously employed raising tents, making fires, throwing the seine into the harbour for fish. They had been the second set of Europeans into Botany Bay, but they were the very first people from the northern world to take their rest in Port Jackson.

At four o'clock in the morning, that keen taskmaster Arthur Phillip had them up again, on their oars, with one boat in the lead sounding the way from one bay of Port Jackson to another. 'We eat our breakfasts on our seats and pulled all day,' said the American, Nagle.

The broad sweep of Port Jackson ran away pleasingly southwards, with much better soundings than Botany Bay. By late afternoon they reached a cove some seven miles inside the harbour of Port Jackson. This place gave excellent soundings close to shore – in fact, its good anchorages had been gouged out by a vanished glacier. The official party landed on the west side of this inlet, under bushy platforms of rock. They walked around to the head of the cove where the ground was level. There were scattered large eucalypts, cabbage tree palms and low undergrowth, but more elevation and an utterly less swampy air than at Botany Bay. A good stream densely lined with ferns ran down the centre of the land and disgorged in the cove. It was pristine and plentiful even then, at the height of summer. The ridge on the eastern side struck Phillip and others as a potential site for the public farm.

Nagle, being the boat-keeper, had to remain aboard while the gentlemen made their reconnaissance, but he spent the time fishing and pulled up a bream. Returning, the governor and his party were in good form, Phillip very pleased with the cove. There was no need to go and look at Broken Bay to the north of Port Jackson. 'As a situation for a town, he was determined to settle in this cove.' He saw the bream and asked who had caught it – it lay silver in the stern like a good sign. Nagle admitted it was his.

According to Nagle, Phillip came up with the name for the inlet itself, saying, 'Recollect that you are the first white man that ever caught a fish in Sydney Cove where the town is to be built.' Perhaps the decision to name the cove to honour the Home Secretary was nearly as instantaneous as that. But it was a wise move for an uncertain expedition. A politician was perhaps less likely to forget a place named to honour him, a place whose deterioration might become a reflection on him. Phillip intended to name the township itself Albion, an ancient name for England, imbued with a certain holiness. But high-faluting Albion would never quite stick for the settlement, and the convicts and soldiers would use the name Sydney Cove, or Sydney Town, or simply Sydney for their penal municipality.

It already had a long-established Eora name – the Cadigal clan to whom it belonged called it Warrane. This whole country of vivid blue skies and water, sandstone headlands and ridges covered in vegetation, sandy bays and ocean beaches backed by marshland, tidal lagoons and mangrove swamps made the Eora a people united by salt water and a bounty of protein from the sea, from Port Jackson lying inside its heads Boree and Burrawara, from Kamay, their name for Botany Bay, and from the hinterland bush. By the standards of many of the Earth's other nomadic peoples and by comparison with the more exacting conditions faced by the desert tribes of the far interior, it was a sumptuous life. The Eora had no need to travel great distances in search of food and water.

But their good fortune had passed. For longer than any other population of *homo sapiens*, the ancestors of the Aboriginals were genetically and culturally cocooned from the rest of the world, and were right to suspect the freight of these ships. Phillip's sailors, soldiers and convicts were walking incubators for viruses and bacteria barely before present on this coast. These micro-organisms too were looking for a new landfall and had the power to descend upon and mar the planet as known and cherished by coastal clans.

Seven

Phillip, having reached the huge harbour named Port Jackson and found a cove within it which he named for Sydney, came back to the ships in Botany Bay, and told them they would be sailing a final small leg to take possession of it all.

Marine Captain Collins, who was to be the judge-advocate, was very relieved, even though some trees had been felled at Point Sutherland and a sawpit dug just in case a better place could not be found. But, 'had we been compelled to remain in Botany Bay, the swampy ground everywhere around it threatened us with unhealthy situations; neither could the shipping have ridden in perfect security when the wind blew from the south-east'.

At first light the next morning, 24 January, when on *Supply* the stock was being watered, and everyone exhilarated at news of the coming move, the watch saw two ships just off the coast, trying to work their way into the bay. On the *Charlotte*, Watkin Tench thought the look-out who first announced the two new vessels was having delusions. Amongst the officers visiting each other for breakfast, there were a number of wild surmises. 'Of what nation they could be, engaged the general wonder for some time, which at last gave way to a conjecture that they might be the French ships.'

At first Ralph Clark had hoped that they were ships from England; indeed, that idea ran through the fleet very quickly, and even the hope that they had been sent with a general pardon for all convicts and to order their return to England rocketed around the prison decks. Or else, it was surmised, the two might be back-up supply ships. But a white pennant similar in shape to that of a commodore in the Royal Navy – the sort of pennant the Admiralty had denied Phillip – confirmed that they were a party of whom Phillip had already heard something. They comprised the expedition of the Comte de La Pérouse, who had set out from France nearly three years earlier to explore the Pacific, and who had preposterously turned up here just as the British were ending their brief dalliance with Botany Bay.

Phillip knew of La Pérouse's reputation, that he had fought and been wounded in the Seven Years War, and then as part of naval operations in North America in 1782 had invaded Hudson Bay. This was a famous exploit which he had followed up by gallantly offering the English in the two forts he captured supplies to last them through the winter. His record with native peoples, however, would not do him as much credit.

The French government had decided in the mid-1780s that they would follow up the areas of obscurity left over from Cook's voyages. Louis XVI himself took a hand in drafting the plan and itinerary, and gave La Pérouse an audience before he sailed. By the time he appeared off Botany Bay, the Comte's two ships, La Boussole and L'Astrolabe, had doubled Cape Horn, refitted in Chile, sailed to Hawaii and then to Alaska, refitted again at Monterey, discovered a number of previously uncharted islands, surveyed the coast of Korea, and proved Sakhalin to be an island. Heading south again into the Pacific, La Pérouse lost a shore party in Samoa when natives killed his second-in-command and eleven others. He was still mourning his good companion Captain de Langle when he appeared off Botany Bay, and a French monk–scientist, Father le Receveur, one of two priests on the ships, fatally ill from wounds received in the Samoan imbroglio, would go to a grave on the shores of Botany Bay.

A ferocious nor-easter would keep La Pérouse waiting two days to enter the port safely, and tested the seamanship of *Supply* and the other ships as they tacked out from beneath La Pérouse's shadow. But the Frenchman's presence made Phillip a little uneasy. The French were the customary British enemy. 'Before they learn there is a God,' said a German of the Georgian English, 'they learn there are Frenchmen to be detested.' Was this French captain a mere expeditioner engaged in science, or did he too want to make a claim on this enormous coastline? The *Sirius* under John Hunter, outgunned by La Pérouse's two ships, nonetheless stayed on in Botany Bay another day to finalise the loading of equipment that had been taken ashore, while the little *Supply* led the convict fleet up the coast past the waiting French.

In the teeth of the nor-easter, *Charlotte* had great difficulty getting out of the bay, and the *Prince of Wales* and the *Friendship* had a collision, carrying away *Friendship*'s jib boom. Shaken, and concerned that they might have all been drowned in Botany Bay, melancholy Lieutenant Clark was revived by the sight of Port Jackson as his transport rounded the south head and the great sheet of blue harbour opened to sight. 'Port Jackson is a most beautiful place . . . The River Thames is not to be mentioned to it, and that I thought was the finest in the world.' Young Watkin Tench, too, had relished the short trip up the coast, and the entry into Port Jackson that bright summer evening, into a bay superior 'in extent and excellency to all we had seen before. We continued to run up the harbour about four miles, in a westerly direction, enjoying the luxuriant prospects of its shores, covered with trees to the water's edge, among which many of the Indians were frequently seen'.

This was the true arrival. The atmosphere of Sydney Cove was very different from that of shallow Botany Bay. Even so, on the convict decks, the hope had already formed that perhaps these two French ships a little way down the coast offered a means of escape, and that and other fantastical possibilities were discussed.

Back in Botany Bay, *Sirius* sent off a boat to help guide the French ships into port and away from its southern shoals. Phillip wanted there to be no misunderstanding about peaceful British intentions towards the new arrivals. As La Pérouse entered Botany Bay, the *Sirius* itself was departing. 'The two commanders had barely time to exchange civilities; and it must naturally have created some surprise in M. de La Pérouse to find our fleet abandoning the harbour at the very time he was preparing to anchor in it.' La Pérouse would later say that he had heard in Kamchatka of the intended British settlement at Cook's Botany Bay, and imagined that he might have found there an already built town and an established market.

If Major Robbie Ross, commander of marines and lieutenant-governor, looked on Port Jackson, Sydney Cove and its environs with a far more jaundiced eye than other officers, it was in part because he had found Phillip so annoyingly secretive about his intentions. Ross seemed lieutenant-governor in name only, and indeed, if Phillip died, he was, according to the Orders-in-Council, to be succeeded not by Ross but by Captain Hunter. Ross was a man who possessed principles, but who bore grievances easily against naval officers who took marines for granted. But the marines didn't much like him either. Of him Ralph Clark would express eventually a commonly held opinion that he was 'without exception the most disagreeable commanding officer I ever knew'. Ross was feverishly worried about his family in Britain, whom he described as 'very small, tho' numerous'. That was one of the reasons why on Captain Shea's death soon after landing he made his own son, John Ross, a child just about to turn ten, a volunteer lieutenant, a rank he hoped would be confirmed by the Admiralty with appropriate back-pay benefits.

By contrast with Ross, one historian has compared Phillip as a figure to the shark, a totemic animal of most coastal or island Pacific peoples, a master of life and bestower of death, inscrutable but reliable in all instincts, an enforcer of nature's rules, ruthlessly just to the level of blood sacrifice and secretive by necessity. Phillip was as mysterious a creature to Ross as he was to the convicts.

If the Gweagal and Bediagal of Botany Bay had been delighted to see the ships depart, they must have been equally confused when they were replaced by the French vessels, and the overland report of various visiting members of the Cadigal clan to the north that the original ships had merely gone on to infest Warrane, Sydney Cove, that choice inlet in the great harbour only seven miles to the north, must have been puzzling.

Before leaving Botany Bay, a number of marines and reliable convicts had been transferred to the *Supply* so that as soon as it came to anchor in Sydney Cove, work parties could be sent ashore. Amongst the convicts so trusted was a young farmer named James Ruse, who had stolen two watches and stood trial on the edge of his native Cornish moors at Bodmin. Like many of the men he carried a profound grief for his transportation, but he had a gift for negotiating it better than some.

The first night at Sydney Cove was spent on board the ships, but the next day, 26 January, there were scenes of unprecedented activity in the little inlet. In one place, said Tench, was a party cutting down the woods, while elsewhere another group set up a blacksmith's forge. Soldiers pitched officers' marquees, while a detachment of troops paraded in bright sunlight and cooks lit fires. Sydney Cove faced north, and the general delineation of the future town was created by its geography. The officers and military were stationed around the banks of the stream, and some ground to the west was to be allotted to officers to grow corn for their animals.

On the very point of the west side Lieutenant William Dawes intended to set up his astronomical instruments for an unprecedented long-term study of the southern sky. He called the place Point Maskelyne, to honour the Astronomer Royal. On that west side too, on level ground beneath the sandstone rock ledges, Surgeon White's marquee-hospital was to be set up, near an area Phillip had already assigned to be the convict women's camp, the men's camp being closer to the military tents. The good stream which divided the cove would before any great passage of time come to be known as the Tank Stream, since reservoir tanks would be sunk along its banks to preserve its waters against drought.

On the east side the ground was more open and suited for the public farm and the residences of the governor and his officials.

Arthur Phillip's portable canvas house, provided by Messrs Smith of St George's Field at the cost of £125, was accordingly erected there, about 50 yards from the water, and a number of tents for trustworthy convicts and those considered not terminally corrupted were put up there too.

In a matter of mere days Sydney Cove would be altered, in Phillip's mind, and to an extent on the ground, from a garden of nomads to a municipality. To celebrate that shift, in the afternoon of 26 January, most of the crew of the *Supply* assembled at the point where they had first landed on the west side of Sydney Cove. The first flagstaff had been fashioned already from a sappy pole of eucalyptus, and the British flag being run up, the governor and the officers drank the healths of His Majesty and the royal family, and drank success to the new colony while the marines fired several volleys. It was a spirited but obscure gesture of empire. But after this rite, something of great significance to the watching Eora occurred – many of the white spirits slept ashore, and the night became theirs as well.

On that first day, 26 January, the governor found the time to sign a warrant giving his old friend, that ancient midshipman Harry Brewer, a new identity as provost-marshal of the colony, that is, the official who would bring charged offenders before the courts. So New South Wales began its long career as a place where men of no description could achieve a label, a post, a self-definition.

Lieutenant Clark was domiciled in a tent ashore with his livestock, consisting of two hens and one pig. He shared the tent with Tom Davey, the son of a Devon mill-owner who had used a lot of influence to get his son a commission in the marines. Lieutenant Davey, a toper, had been invalided out of America in

1780, and he and the sometimes prissily abstemious Clark made uneasy tent-mates. They let Lieutenant Timmins put his cot down there the first night as he had not yet got his tent up. Clark lay uneasy on his bedding. 'In all the course of my life I never slept worse, my dear wife, than I did last night – what with the hard cold ground, and spiders, ants and every vermin that you can think of crawling over me, I was glad when sleep came. My poor pouch was my pillow.' He had come all this way in the hope of promotion to full lieutenant and perhaps captain, but he made a querulous occupant.

Yet when he shot a parrot the next day, he found it 'the most beautiful bird that I ever saw'. Both ashore and on the ships, the gentlemen were dining off fish, a beneficent influence on their digestive systems after the gut-abrading salt diet of the long journey.

The disembarkation of the bulk of the troops and some male convicts occurred the next day, on feet unsteady after such long periods aboard. 'The confusion that ensued will not be wondered at, when it is considered that every man stepped from the boat literally into the wood.'

On the basis of a few days tentative exploration in the bush around Sydney Cove, a cultivated young midshipman, Daniel Southwell, declared that there was nothing deserving of the name of fruit in this new southern homeland. And with some injustice he declared that the country's quadrupeds were scarcely to be classed above vermin. But he was also resourceful enough to discover that there were many 'salutary shrubs', that balm could be milked from trees, and that a native spinach, parsley and broad bean could be found. Many of the productions of the country, he said, were aromatic, and had medicinal properties, and could be used as *fomenta*, poultices on sores. A surgeon, an Irishman named Denis Considen, a graduate of Trinity College, Dublin, also found various gums and leaves suitable for brewing a form of native tea.

The next morning, after their last breakfast on the ships, the remaining male convicts, except those who were too sick to walk, gathered up their clothing and bedding and were taken ashore. How strange to leave the familiar convict deck where they had been for so long, the narrow bed space, the penal womb, to be reborn ashore. Not that they were reborn entirely, since they brought their habits of mind and the Tawny Prince, the deity of the London canting crews, with them.

The talkers of cant, and the country fellows as well, had the urgent business of clearing ground and building themselves shelters, for there were no tenements or even tents for them. Whitehall had decided, in the spirit of the age, that it would be good exercise for them to have to construct their own habitations. Under instruction from country felons like James Ruse, they began putting together structures of wattle and daub – plaited panels of branches providing the walls and the cracks being filled in with daubed clay, of which there was a plentiful supply on the foreshore of Sydney Cove. Longboats were regularly sent to the north side of Port Jackson in quest of tall straight trunks of cabbage tree which were used for the corner poles of huts. Roofs were of bark, thatch of cabbage tree fronds, or rushes plastered over with clay, or else with a limited supply of canvas from *Sirius*, which all made, said Collins, 'a very good hovel'. There were many economic but flimsy structures standing within a few days. Many, however, would be destroyed on 2 February in a characteristically violent Sydney thunderstorm.

As for any dream of log cabins, those cutting the tall trees found the timber incorrigible – resistant to adze and plane, knotty and with a mind of its own, a wood indifferent to European purposes. Hunter had hoped to use local eucalypts for repairs to *Sirius*, but found them unsuitable. 'We were here in the middle of a wood in which were trees from the size of a man's arm to 28-feet in circumference, but they were either so very crooked, so rent or so rotten in the heart that we could scarcely get one sound or serviceable in a dozen.' Surgeon White, who had sufficient patients to attend to, would have time to declare of this wood that 'repeated trials have only served to convince me that immediately on immersion it sinks to the bottom like a stone'. Clearly, it was not amenable.

Something else momentous but without ceremony occurred: public stock, including one bull, four cows, one bull-calf, one stallion, three mares and three colts, largely acquired in Cape Town, was landed on the east side of the cove. A range of Western Europe's useful beasts was herded for the first time on this shore, the cattle under the care of a convict named Edward Corbett. The Eora had not presented themselves in any numbers at Sydney Cove yet, but to those natives who observed the inlet, these must have seemed drastically new items in zoology.

On 29 January 1788, when Phillip landed at Spring Cove just inside North Head, twelve natives crowded round the boats, anxious to inspect the the newcomers, these owners of fabulous beasts and floating islands. It was the first contact between the races within Port Jackson. The sailors mixed with the native men who were 'quite sociable, dancing, and otherwise amusing', but who kept their women well away. The whites could not persuade any of the natives to return with them to the settlement at Sydney

Cove, but John Hunter found the Port Jackson inhabitants a 'very lively and inquisitive race', straight, thin, well-made, small-limbed, active and very curious.

Phillip was anxious to get the male convicts to work as soon as possible. In his ideal settlement, the convicts would work for the government from seven in the morning until three in the afternoon, with a half-day on Saturdays, and then have spare time to grow vegetables or pursue some other useful task thereafter. By 30 January, the first official work party of convicts was put to breaking ground for a garden and farm on the slope of the east side of the cove and just over the hill, in what became known as Farm Cove. As the tools were handed out by the conscientious and always stressed storekeeper, Andrew Miller, the convicts, directed amongst others by Phillip's manservant, Henry Dodd, showed little enthusiasm. The first breaking of sod by some anonymous shoveller in Sydney Cove was unattended by ceremony, or by any sense that in this immense continent they few were the first European delvers. There was not even wry comment on the fact that the earth furthest from Europe was being broken by Europe's lowest, most reviled hands. The urban convicts immediately proved themselves to be the worst, resistant to the cries of Dodd and the convict supervisors to put their bodies into what was to them the alien task of digging and farming. Even men as likeable as James Ruse became the enemy to the other convicts once they were put in a supervisory role. The phrase 'Kiss my arse!' was a popular one in Sydney Cove – it appears in the records of the judge-advocate's court as standard badinage, and may well have been uttered that penultimate January day in Farm Cove.

Even so, that first slovenly attempt at making a government garden had been a moment much looked forward to by Arthur

Phillip, and was significant in that it was an early instance in which the realities of the new society were forced upon him. The earth proved rocky, full of lumps of sandstone. Officers, and the occasional convict stonemason, thought that the yellowish sandstone was comparable to Portland stone and very suitable for working. But in the bush around the cove there were no limestone deposits for cement.

The lime trees, the lemons, the oranges, the figs and grapes which had been picked up in the Cape were slowly planted out in the government farm, but marsupial rats emerged at night and devoured them. Phillip's sleep beneath the canvas of his temporary residence was restless, since he suffered from these truths as much as from the chronic renal pain familiar to many of those subjected to the traditional salt-rich seagoing diet.

'The officers who composed the detachment are not only few in number,' Phillip would write to Lord Sydney, 'but most of them have declined any interference with the convicts, except when they are employed for their own particular service.' He had imagined them willingly taking at least a monitoring and encouraging role in the work of convicts, but the officers believed 'that they were not sent out to do more than the duties of soldiers'. So Phillip was obliged to put trustworthy convicts, such as the young, good-looking, well-liked Henry Kable, into supervisory roles. Kable would become a superintendent of the women prisoners.

In the tents placed for the sick on the west side of the cove, beneath the rocky, bush-embowered sandstone ledges, Surgeon White admitted with some concern that, after the preventive medical success of the fleet, the numbers of sick were increasing. Scurvy, dormant on the ships, suddenly seemed to manifest itself in some of the convicts now they had landed, and dysentery as well. This phenomenon of voyagers becoming ill when ashore after long journeys had been commonly noted. In that late January heat Surgeon White's sicker patients sat out on blankets in the sun and raised their mouths to bite off the air of this place beyond places. White complained that 'not a comfort or convenience could be got' for the sick in those first days, and his frustration was compounded by a quarrel with his querulous young Scottish assistant, William Balmain, a long-standing temperamental conflict that had begun with a professional argument in Portsmouth months before.

Lest the sailors on the two naval vessels – *Sirius* and *Supply* – begin to eat into the public stores not yet landed, and in preparation for any future travels, Phillip appointed for the use of *Sirius* an island not far from the public farm, a 'Garden Island' as it soon became known, on which to grow vegetables for the crew's consumption. Soon Ralph Clark would start using another island, Clark Island, in Port Jackson as a vegetable garden, and despite its relative distance down-harbour from Sydney Cove, it would sometimes be plundered by boat crews, and by hungry convicts swimming out there.

There was no priority to build a prison stockade in Sydney Cove. It had always been the plan that the environs would serve as walls to a great outdoor prison. The strange hinterland would be the chief guard and overseer. The First Fleet convicts were in the ultimate panopticon, where strangeness hemmed them in, and the sky aimed its huge blank blue eye at them. And yet from the day of landing onwards, a number of male prisoners walked the seven miles along a native track down to Botany Bay to bespeak the Frenchmen, and to plead political asylum or offer services as sailors.

Lieutenant Bradley, the teacher from the Naval Academy at Portsmouth, had been out surveying the shoreline of Port Jackson, and found on the north side twelve miles of snug coves, and – as in Sydney Cove – good depths of water and freshwater streams entering many of the harbour's inlets. At his task, working in sounding from a longboat, he became aware that the northern shore of Port Jackson, and the southern shore too, down-harbour, carried a considerable population of Eora, 'Indians . . . painted very whimsically with pipe clay and red ochre'. He came to notice that all the women they met had two joints at the little finger on the left hand missing. 'It was supposed by some to be the pledge on the marriage ceremony, or of their having children.' Most of the men had lost a front incisor tooth and were highly scarred. Their spears were twelve to sixteen feet in length, and they walked very upright.

On one of those early days, 1 February, Governor Phillip took his friend King aside by the door of his canvas house to discuss in detail the sending of a few people and some livestock in the *Supply* to settle Norfolk Island, the landfall 1000 miles out in the Pacific which Cook had found and whose pines and flax plants seemed to offer the resource both of masts and of flax – 'strategic commodities' as one historian would call them, as crucial as oil would be to later states. The recent problems of the Royal Navy in acquiring masts and canvas from the Baltic, and under the French blockade of the American colonies during the recent revolution in America, might be solved by Norfolk Island. Thus a potentially exciting opportunity to adjust the balance of the navy's resources seemed to lie ahead for young Mr King.

But Phillip asked King, before he went away, to slip down south to Botany Bay and visit the illustrious Frenchman La Pérouse.

The excursion was no doubt partly a spying expedition. Phillip wanted King to fool La Pérouse about the scale of the supplies the British in Sydney Cove possessed by offering him 'whatever he might have occasion for'.

So at three o'clock in the morning of 2 February, King and the astronomer, Dawes, set out by longboat with some marines for Botany Bay. King would report that they were received aboard the French flagship by the Comte with the greatest politeness. After King had delivered Phillip's message, La Pérouse sent his thanks to the governor and made the same formal offers of help, La Perouse playing the game Phillip had set up by saying exaggeratedly that he would be in France in fifteen months time and had three years stores aboard, and so would be happy to oblige Mr Phillip with anything *he* might want. He reported that a number of the male convicts had already visited and offered to serve aboard the French ships, or had pleaded for asylum, but that he had dismissed them all with threats and a day's provisions to get them back to Sydney Cove. If convict women, once landed at Sydney Cove, should present themselves, they would be treated in the same manner. Indeed, La Pérouse would write that '*les déserteurs nous causèrent d'beaucoup d'ennui et d' embarrass* [the deserters caused us a lot of trouble and embarrassment].'

Yet a French-born convict named Peter Paris went missing and *was* hidden by sympathetic Frenchmen in La Pérouse's vessels. Paris had originally been sentenced to death in Exeter in 1783 for burglary. Having disappeared from Sydney Cove in February 1788, he would have later been lost in the New Hebrides (Vanuatu) with La Pérouse himself and all the other members of the French expedition.

Before that happened, however, Monsieur de Clonnard, the

captain of the *Astrolabe*, made a return visit to Sydney Cove and again told Collins and others he was frequently visited by convicts. Abbé Monges, a scientific priest, accompanied de Clonnard on the visit and Clark entertained the *abbé* by letting him look at the butterflies and other insects he was collecting for his wife, Betsy Alicia.

The stiff politeness between English and French had never been so remotely played out as here, in Warrane, Sydney Cove. The same could be said of the death in Botany Bay of the Franciscan monk-cum-scientist, Fr. Receveur, who would be buried on the foreshore and whose grave would be periodically tended by the British.

Eight

And now society in New South Wales really began. The convict women came up from the prison decks to be landed on 6 February. On *Lady Penrhyn*, Surgeon Bowes Smyth was happy to see them taken off in the ship's longboats, beginning at five o'clock in the morning. Those with goods, portmanteaux or duffel bags full of clothing, decorations and hats, which had been carried in the holds, were handed their property and toted or wore it ashore, in combination with their well-worn penal clothes. 'Some few among them,' said Bowes Smyth, 'might be said to be well dressed.'

How silent the ships must have suddenly seemed to the sailors, as if a soul had gone out of them. The women were landed on the western side of Sydney Cove where bedraggled canvas and some huts of wattle and bark delineated their camp. The last of them landed at six o'clock on what would prove to be a typical summer evening, still and hot, but promising a southerly squall. 'The men convicts got to them very soon after they landed,' said Bowes Smyth. At the same time a number of suddenly lonely sailors from the transports also came ashore, bringing grog with them, and the marines were unable or unwilling to keep the women separate. *Lady Penrhyn*'s crew, in particular, joined in one mass outdoor party, Sydney's first fête of hedonism.

'It is beyond my abilities to give a just description of the scene of debauchery and riot which continued through the night,' wrote Bowes Smyth. The evening had turned humid and thunderous, the sentinel in front of Major Ross's marquee being so intimidated by lightning that he abandoned his post and ran in to join the gentlemen, Major Ross and Lieutenant Clark, as they were eating a wild duck Clark had shot that day. While the night proceeded, one potent stroke of lightning would kill six sheep, two lambs and a pig, all belonging to Major Ross.

The great Sydney bacchanalia went on despite the thunderstorm which so unsettled Ross's sentry. Fists were raised to God's lightning; in the name of the Tawny Prince and in defiance of British justice, the downpour was cursed and challenged, and survival and utter displacement were celebrated in lunges and caresses. 'The scene which presented itself at the time, and during the greater part of the night, beggars every description. Some swearing, others quarrelling, others singing, not in the least regarding the tempest, though so great that the thunder shook the ship . . .'

It is hard to put this idea of wild drinking and orgy together with what we know of at least some of the women. There is little doubt either that some of them were by dark safely with mentors. The forceful young Cockney Jewish convict Esther Abrahams was the passion of 23-year-old Lieutenant George Johnston, a Scot very severely wounded by the French as a fifteen-year-old in 1780 but now returned to manhood's bloom. The alliance between Scot and Jewish girl would ultimately lead to marriage. Jewish immigrants had begun arriving in England from Eastern Europe and Tsarist pogroms from the seventeenth century onwards, and settled in such London areas as Wapping and Spitalfields. Esther had been aged about twenty at the time of her seven years transportation for stealing lace to the value of 50 shillings, and at the time Lieutenant Johnston became interested in her, she had already given birth to a daughter in Newgate and brought her on board the *Lady Penrhyn* with her.

The Reverend Johnson and his wife had already that day gathered in as their young servant Elizabeth Hayward, an apprentice clog-maker and at fourteen the youngest female on the fleet. Margaret Dawson from the *Lady Penrhyn*, a seventeen year old Lancashire girl who had stolen clothing and jewellery to the death-earning value of £22 18s from her master and taken it away with her on the Liverpool coach, joined her lover, Assistant Surgeon Balmain, a 26-year-old Scot. Dawson must have been very pretty, since the Old Bailey trial documents explicitly note her youth and beauty as reasons for her being saved from the scaffold.

It is also hard to imagine that Sarah Bellamy, about to come to term, was an active rioter that night. If her lover, the sailor Joe Downey, came ashore from the *Lady Penrhyn* it must have been in part to protect her. But the generality of convict women and girls were, willy-nilly, participants in this event which so shocked Arthur Bowes Smyth.

There were grounds for a riotous, desperate party of some sort. The women had been on their ships a deranging eight months. Their sentences were now terminal – they had arrived inextricably in this outlandish and humid summer place; this was the unfamiliar and inscrutable region that would contain their bones. They would be buried in sandstone-strewn earth amongst the angular and tortuous eucalyptus trees. Their frenzy was that of people ejected from the known world and making a rough, brutal bed in the unknown one. Antipodean licentiousness had its beginning here and almost certainly Antipodean rape.

Surgeon Bowes Smyth was an evangelical Christian, and so easier to render aghast than some, though he had been surgeon on the *Lady Penrhyn* for the past ten months. 'While they were on board ship,' wrote (inaccurately), the less outraged Watkin Tench, 'the two sexes had been kept most rigorously apart; but, when landed, their separation became impracticable and would have been, perhaps, wrong. Licentiousness was the unavoidable consequence and their old habits of depravity were beginning to recur. What was to be attempted? To prevent their intercourse was impossible, and to palliate its evils only remained. Marriage was recommended.'

That was the voice of the Enlightenment, not of the fervent. Social good might arise from a regulated mingling of the sexes, and licentiousness was to be abhorred not so much as an abomination in God's eyes but as a threat to reason and good order.

Surgeon White, who had every reason to condemn an orgy for its capacity to spread sexually transmitted diseases, did not even mention the event in his journal.

But before Reverend Johnson was to perform the first marriages, civil governance had to be officially commenced. The orgy prevailed until the dripping, thundery small hours of 7 February, but by noon that same day civic formalities took hold. All the marine officers, their metal gorgets glistening at their throats, took post before their companies, which marched off the allocated, rough-hewn parade ground to adjoining ground cleared for the occasion, 'whereon the convicts were assembled to hear His Majesty's commission read'.

Bowes Smyth and Collins describe a scene that seems

Pythonesque if abstracted from its symbols and rituals, and the inherent beliefs of its more significant participants. Phillip, having dressed in his full uniform of post-captain and wearing his British and Portuguese awards on his breast, emerged from his palazzo of canvas and proceeded to the ceremonial ground at the head of the cove. Upon arrival, he took off his hat and 'complimented' the marine officers, and the marines lowered their colours to him and paid him respect as governor. The marines then formed a circle around the whole of the convicts, men and women, who were ordered to sit down like so many school children on the ground. A camp table had been set up with two red leather cases laid on it; they contained the commissions and letters-patent, ready to be unsealed and opened in the sight of everyone present and read by Judge-Advocate Captain Collins.

As Phillip stood by, Captain Collins read aloud the documents signed by King George III and his Cabinet which empowered Phillip in New South Wales. Waves of august language rose and perched like birds in the trees: George III by the Grace of God, King of Britain, France and Ireland 'to our trusty and well-beloved Arthur Phillip, Esquire'. Never had a more exceptional claim of territory been uttered than in this commission now read amongst the eucalypts and cabbage tree palms, and heard without comprehension by the no doubt observant Cadigal and Wangal clans of the area. Arthur Phillip was to be Captain-General and Governor-in-Chief over New South Wales, which was an area declared to run from the northern extremity of the coast, Cape York, to the southern extremity of South Cape – from 10 degrees South to 43 degrees South, that is, or the Southern Hemisphere equivalent of from the Tagus River in

Portugal to Trondheim in Norway. The claim also extended to all the country inland westward as far as 135 degrees East. Whatever was out there, 1500 miles west of Sydney Cove, a greater distance than London to Moscow, in this document now being read aloud by a captain of marines the Crown claimed it. A massive stretch of earth had been mysteriously transformed. It had become, for the first time, estate and realm.

This claim of George III, released into the sky and certified by Phillip's presence, did not run all the way to what would prove to be the west coast of Australia. Phillip, listening to Captain Collins that humid and hung-over day, with the sun already sucking up the water of the glittering harbour to make the coming evening's thunderstorm, knew well enough that the extent of the claim, the fact that it did not go even further than 135 degrees East, made room for the claims of other nations – especially of the Dutch, who had made many landings in what is now called Western Australia. Even though they despised it as a desert coast and had not yet claimed it, their sensitivities had to be respected. And the Portuguese had a long-standing claim on Timor, with which George III and his ministers saw no reason to quarrel, particularly given England's friendly relationship with Portugal. Just the same, it was a massive claim, close to three-fifths of what would later prove a continent of three million square miles, and it was uttered in front of such humble and debased and ragtag company and amidst canvas, wattle-and-daub and eucalypts.

The name *Australia*, meaning Southland, was not mentioned. In 1569 and 1570 respectively, Mercator and Ortellius used the terms *continens australis* and *australia continens*. Discovering Vanuatu in 1606, Pedro Fernandez de Quiros had posited a southern continent named *Australia de Espiritu Santo* or *Australia Incognita*. Throughout the sixteenth and seventeenth centuries the terms *Australia* and *Australis* appeared on maps as an ill-defined given. Cook, finding this eastern coast in 1770, thought of it as part of New Holland but did not know if it was a continent or an archipelago stretching away to the west. So he named this east coast New Wales and New South Wales. As a result, in Phillip's commission, the name New South Wales was used, not Australia, which would not then have had international meaning. But the terms New Holland, Botany Bay and New South Wales soon became interchangeable in the mind of the British public.

Arthur Phillip was, by the commissions and letters-patent, to have the power to appoint officials and administer oaths – he would administer one to Collins before that gentleman began his work as judge-advocate. Phillip had the power to pardon and reprieve, punish offenders and make land grants to civilians. He was empowered also to create a criminal court, a civil court, an admiralty court and so on.

The commission read, the marines fired three volleys to seal this extraordinary advent of authority. The light did not change and the air held its humidity, and somewhere in the huge harbour, native women fished from the insecure platforms of their bark canoes. The vast, mute, electric-blue sky hung sceptically over the giant claims of the British. Wise gods would have laid odds that this exercise could not succeed.

All those who were ill in Surgeon White's tent, and perhaps ten other convicts, missed the ceremony. Those not sick had gone to see the French or were otherwise putting the environment to the test. Could they live freely out there in the bush? The tales told by convicts who soon surrendered themselves indicated they could not. The earth lacked European-style sustenance, and the escaped convict had no place in the schemes of the natives.

The volleys fired off, Phillip now spoke to his charges – Bowes Smyth used the word 'harangued'. He was probably not in the mood for eloquence, and suffered from a certain post-landing depression and the onset of the gritty task. So he offered them no golden promise. He told them he had observed them to see how they were disposed. By now, he knew that many among them were incorrigible and he said that he was persuaded that nothing but severity would have any effect on them. If they attempted to get into women's tents at night, the soldiers had orders to fire upon them. (This would prove an unenforceable threat.) He had observed that they had been very idle – not more than two hundred out of six hundred of them were at work. Phillip told his people that labour in Sydney Cove would not be as severe as that of a husbandman in England who had a wife and family to provide for. They would never be worked beyond their abilities, but every individual should contribute his share 'to render himself and community at large happy and comfortable as soon as the nature of the settlement will admit of'. In England stealing poultry was not punished with death, he said, but here that sort of loss could not be supplied and it was of extreme consequence to the settlement that chickens and other livestock be preserved for breeding. Stealing the most trifling item of stock or provisions therefore would be punished with death. This severity, he said, was contrary to his humanity and feelings for his fellow creatures, but justice demanded such rigid execution of the laws, and if they stole food, the convicts might implicitly rely on justice taking place.

This extraordinary executive decision would ultimately scythe down a number of those felons sitting listening to him. On landing, Phillip had implemented his plan to provide full rations from the two years of supplies the ships had brought. Convicts were to receive an equal share to men and officers – 7 pounds of salt beef or four of pork, 3 pints of dried peas, 7 pounds of flour, 6 ounces of butter, half a pound of rice or, if it were not available, an extra pound of flour weekly. Females, whether marines' or parsons' wives or fallen creatures, received two-thirds of that ration. Phillip had no doubt at all – neither did any officer express an opposite view – that those rations needed to be protected from bullies and thieves by the sanction of death.

But some officials disapproved of the democracy of rations. Talkative Major Robbie Ross thought it appalling to give a lazy or malingering convict the same ration as an industrious one, or as one of His Majesty's marines, or, for that matter, as the governor himself. He complained that the convicts were unduly 'sustained by the humanity (I might have said folly)' of the government. Personal industriousness should be encouraged by imposed hunger, and industry should also be rewarded. While Phillip saw whatever the convicts produced other than in their own vegetable gardens as the property of the Crown, Ross would one day tell two convict sawyers working at the public sawpit that any timber they prepared during their breakfast or dinner time 'they ought not to part with any without they were well paid for it'.

Phillip knew that chaos and a wild unofficial market in food would result from an inequity in the rations. He was also aware from long naval experience of inspecting opened barrels of rations that the contents were never as copious in reality as they were on paper. The weight of beef and pork was enhanced in many cases by bone and fluid, and the meat, so mummified that sailors and convicts called it 'mahogany', shrank to a much lower weight when cooked. The butter was inevitably rancid and the weight of flour and rice included plentiful weevils. Phillip also knew that rations would soon need to be reduced unless the hinterland and the harbour proved unexpectedly to be bounteous sources of food. Indeed, the first reduction of twelve pounds per every 100 pounds of beef, and eight pounds in every 100 pounds of pork would be ordered within seven weeks.

And on top of that, convicts and marines, officials and perhaps even Arthur Phillip were aware that the aura of Sydney Cove was the aura of a place forgotten by God and government. Phillip could look at the dun forests and imagine realistically that a minor ineptitude on the part of either Lord Sydney or Evan Nepean, or some disaster overtaking a store ship at sea, could lead to a scene of famine, of white cadavers amongst the eucalypts, and even of that most feared and unclean phenomenon, cannibalism.

After his plain speech to the convicts, the governor retired to a cold collation in a large tent set to one side, to which the general officers of the colony only were invited, and, said affronted Bowes Smyth, 'not the least attention whatever was paid to any other person who came out from England'. For example, the masters of the different ships had attended the reading of the commission, but now they were left to return to their ships 'with no more accommodation for them than for the convicts themselves'. The military clique had established itself in Sydney Cove.

It was assumed that for further follies committed in Sydney Cove, some convicts would soon need to appear before the Court of Criminal Judicature, headed by Judge-Advocate David Collins. The court consisted of whatever panel of six officers or officials – the Reverend Johnson was eligible – David Collins could assemble. It had the power to impose the death penalty by a majority of five votes.

As much as Ralph Clark expected to be bringing down judgment on the heads of the convicts, he was in fact first summoned to sit in a judicial capacity in a tent near the military lines to hear relatively minor charges against some marines. To begin with, a misdemeanour endemic to soldiery the world over: a Private Green had been drunk on guard and though sentenced to 100 lashes by the court was put on probation.

The second case before the court-martial was a more significant and peculiarly Sydney Cove one. Private Bramwell had struck the convict woman Elizabeth Needham, 'an infamous hussy', according to Lieutenant Clark. She had once tried to shoplift stockings from a West End business, and had already been married when sent to Newgate. Aboard *Penrhyn*, she had become Private Bramwell's lover for part of her time at sea, but when Bramwell now asked her to accompany him into the woods behind the camp, she would not go. Since the male convicts had been landed she had met with a man and she intended to 'marry' him.

The hectic partner-swapping amongst some women appalled Lieutenant Clark. 'Good God, what a scene of whoredom is going on there in the women's camp – no sooner has one man gone in with a woman than another goes in with her. I hope the Almighty will keep me free from them as he has hitherto done, but I need not be afraid as I promised you, my tender Betsy, I will keep my word with you.'

Bramwell was sentenced to 200 lashes for assaulting Needham. Thus, Green being let off by Phillip, a marine disappointed in lust was the first in Sydney Cove to feel the lash on his back. He received 100 strokes on the parade ground at the steel triangle to which he was strapped, and after that was sent to hospital to recover. The marines were conscious that this was a case of a free man being punished for an offence against a convict. There was murmuring later, but it was all according to Sydney's and Phillip's plan that convict and free be equal before the common law and authority.

Nine

The Sunday before the women were landed, the Reverend Johnson had conducted a service ashore, 'on the grass', for the first time in all this immensity. The sermon that first Sunday, when only a proportion of marines and male convicts had been landed, had been based on Psalm 116, Verse 12: 'What shall I render unto the Lord for all the benefits toward me?' It was a question for which some of the male convicts might have had whimsical answers.

On the next Sunday, however, everyone but the sailors was ashore (and indeed, half of them were too) and the Reverend Johnson held service again gamely on the east side of the cove 'under a great tree', probably what would become known as a Moreton Bay fig tree.

Johnson was the son of a wealthy Yorkshire farmer. He would become a farmer here, since he had worked at that trade throughout his twenties, and at teaching as well, until he entered Cambridge in 1780. He had been ordained an Anglican priest in 1786.

He was a member of the Eclectic Society, a movement of evangelical priests and laymen who were influenced by Wesley, but not to the extent that they abandoned the Established Church and became Methodists. Young men had to be 'subscribing

Anglicans', that is, to vow themselves to the Anglican Church as the Church underlying the Crown, before they could graduate from English universities. In his youth, however, Johnson had tended towards the Methodist view of the Established Anglican Church as a corrupted entity. Phillip himself was not a great lover of the Church except as an arm of government, and convicts, when they thought of the Church at all, saw it similarly as an engine of state run for profit. Rectors and vicars all had 'livings', which meant they received income from tithes and from farming the glebe, the area of land set aside in every parish for their use. Vicars were known for the quality of their 'hospitable tables' rather than for their hours of prayer. Many favoured parsons did not live in their parishes at all, and held a number of them simultaneously, putting hard-up curates in place to perform their duties. The Eclectic Society was a reaction to the Church's general lack of fervour. Its members sought to give prayer and study priority over money. But their social program included a desire to reform prisons and to end slavery.

Before coming to New South Wales, Johnson had gone down to one of the Woolwich hulks run by Duncan Campbell. 'He was of delicate health, of sensitive nature, of retiring habit', and found the hulks worse than his imaginings of hell. If there had been any reforming zeal about prisons in Johnson when he was first appointed, meeting the profane convicts made him tend to the belief that the degradation to which they were subjected was their own doing.

Before he joined the fleet, his sponsors in the Eclectic Society found him a resolute wife, a sturdy, devout spinster, Mary Burton, and married him to her, since the Archbishop of Canterbury had already told Johnson he would not be permitted to administer the rite of matrimony to himself once he arrived in New South Wales.

When he first preached from a shipboard quarterdeck in Portsmouth, waiting for the fleet to sail, to convicts who had been brought up from below, he tried to interest them in the major theological debates of the day, questions of the nature of free will and grace which lay at the centre of his own consciousness but which were arcane to pickpockets. An unsympathetic and agnostic Phillip requested him to begin with and to stick with practical moral subjects. Phillip was not interested in his theology, but only in Johnson's capacity as a social regulator.

When Johnson and his wife came aboard the store ship *Golden Grove* they brought with them a considerable library, generally rather mocked by Australian historians, of 100 Bibles, 100 prayer books, 400 New Testaments, 500 psalters, 200 *Church Catechisms*, 100 copies of *Necessity for Reading the Scriptures*, 200 copies of the *Sermon on the Mount*, 25 plain *Exhortations to Prisoners*, 12 copies of *Instructions for the Indians*, 50 copies of *Caution to Swearers*, 100 copies of *Exhortations to Chastity*, 600 copies of a book named *Administrations*; and, indicating that he might have already given up on the present generation and be planning to evangelise their children, 200 copies each of *The Child's First Book* and *The Child's Second Book*. Johnson intended to run this collection as a circulating library amongst the convicts, who were permitted to take six of them at a time. The uses to which they put the pages of these books were often profane.

So, in the tale of the First Fleet, Johnson has always held the place of irrelevant and unworldly ninny. But he was respected as a spiritual adviser by Lieutenant Dawes and others. On the journey out, he had moved from one ship to another, preaching and baptising children, and he and Mary occupied their little cabin without complaint, though suffering from cruel dysentery and the bleeding from the anus caused by abrasive salt rations.

Now, after his second service on 10 February, read according to the rite of the Anglican Church, children were christened, fruits of the penal experiment and the eight-month voyage. The daughter of Private Bacon and his wife, Jane, was christened with the infants of bondage: John Matthew, son of Catherine Prior, a West Country highway robber; and Joseph Downey, child of the adolescent felon Sarah Bellamy. Both latter children were sickly from the voyage and suffering in the high summer heat, which might explain their mothers' touching and orthodox desire to see them baptised. John Matthew would indeed die the next month, but Joseph Downey would vanish first, on 29 February, desolating young Sarah, and as far as we know the first European child to be received into Sydney's soil.

After the baptisms, five convict couples were edifyingly married by the Reverend Johnson. Ralph Clark was sure some of them already had husbands or wives in England.

Had Phillip known of the pre-existing marriages, he would probably not have stood in the way of these new alliances. For here the affianced were in a new earth under a new heaven. Their British marriages had been annulled by distance and were of no help in moderating their behaviour here. The question worried the Reverend Johnson, however, and he does not leave a record of how he reconciled the issue in his mind.

The first couple to appear before Johnson that day were a literate Lancashire man named William Parr, who had cheated a shopkeeper, and his bride, Mary McCormick. Parr must have had a local fame in Liverpool, since court records described him as 'the noted swindler'. His wife was Liverpool Irish, tried in 1784 for receiving stolen goods. She had travelled on the *Friendship*, he on the *Alexander*, so perhaps their marriage had been negotiated since the landing, or perhaps they had known each other in county prison. At about 33 years of age at the time of the fleet's departure, Mary made a mature bride by the standards of the day.

David Collins thought that some of those who married were influenced by the idea that married people would be treated to various little comforts and privileges that were otherwise denied, 'and some, on not finding those expectations realised, repented, wished and actually applied to be restored to their former situations . . .' We do not know if William Parr and Mary McCormick married for such hopeful reasons. In any case, they made a solid pair, and William would prove reliable amongst the convicts and would later be entrusted with the issue of spirits from the stores.

The next groom, Simon Byrne, an Irish highway robber from Devon and a former stocking-weaver, had been noted aboard the notorious Plymouth hulk *Dunkirk* as 'troublesome at times', but Tench would find him admirable, though his colonial career would be marred by a fondness for spirits. He married Frances Anderson, a woman in her early thirties, also ultimately described as 'too fond of spiritous liquors to be very industrious'.

The third couple on the list were the young Norwich Castle pair whose destiny had so affected the English public: Henry Kable and Susannah Holmes. This union, between two marginal people in a place forgotten by God, would prove abiding, and end only with Susannah's death as a matriarch nearly 40 years later. It was the sort of alliance both Johnson and Phillip required – marriage as a moral rudder. It is in a sense a pity they were not the first order of business that day, for they would have brought great honour to the role of Antipodean Adam and Eve.

Next, William Haynes, a cabinet-maker highwayman in his mid-thirties, trusted enough to be transferred to the *Supply* off Cape Town as likely to be of help from the beginning of the settlement, married Hannah Green. He had been involved in the *Mercury* mutiny and the report of him from the *Dunkirk* hulk was that he behaved 'remarkably well'. Hannah was a mature woman of 31 at the time she was shipped, and in the spirit of the banal miscreancies of many of the New South Wales prisoners had originally stolen clothing with a value of four shillings. But then she, too, had returned from transportation following the *Mercury* mutiny, and the report from the *Dunkirk* was that she had behaved 'better than formerly'.

The last couple to bespeak Parson Johnson that day were as exceptional as the Kables. They already had a child between them. Or at least Mary Braund or Broad, a handsome Cornish girl in her early twenties, had given birth to a daughter whom she named Charlotte, the same name as the transport she and her new husband Will Bryant travelled on, and it was presumed Charlotte was Will's child. Mary had been guilty, along with two other girls, of ambushing a Plymouth spinster and robbing her of a silk bonnet and goods to the value of £11 11s. As they stood before the Exeter assizes on 20 March 1786, all three girls were sentenced to hang. Their sentences were reduced to seven years transportation.

On the *Dunkirk* hulk, Mary had met Will Bryant, a Cornish fisherman about 27 years of age, convicted exactly two years earlier than Mary at the Launceston assizes for 'resisting the revenue officers who attempted to seize some smuggled property he had'. He was sentenced to seven years transportation as well, so that he had served over four years in the *Dunkirk* at the time he was put aboard the convict transport *Charlotte*. Smuggling, Will's crime, was considered almost respectable, particularly in Cornwall. Anyone who had anything to do with the sea was involved in illegal import. It was known that the famous Robert Walpole, prime minister of Great Britain, used an Admiralty barge to run his smuggled wine up the Thames. Fishermen down-loaded tax-free wine, brandy and tea from French ships, or from British ones nearing port whose captains wanted to avoid paying tax, and brought the goods ashore, where the distribution networks ran deep inland. Good tables of squires and bishops could not be supplied without men like Bryant. In eastern counties like Sussex, smuggling wool *out* of England without paying tax on it was a common seafaring activity, and bitterness over the excise men, the customs police, would come close to causing civil rebellion. As one eighteenth-century observer wrote, there arose 'an organised resistance to the government, in which towns were besieged, battles fought, customs houses burned down, and the greatest atrocities committed'. Perhaps the excise officers who took Bryant were lucky or numerous or both, for it was not considered a grave sin to kill 'these cruel narks' who wanted to impose their excise on the supply of goods from France.

The Bryant who married on 10 February in Sydney Cove was the sort of man in whom a native independence and a dark sense of having been used hard were at work. They created in him a determination to return to the known world, and he was very frank, even with Mary, that he did not see a New South Wales marriage as binding should he escape. Yet, uttering her vows before Johnson on the strange southern shore, Mary would come to pay such a phenomenal price of loyalty to her spouse as would make the normal respectable marriage of better folk in other places look pallid indeed.

By the time he took his marriage vows, Will had been appointed the colony's fisherman with special privileges of residency on the east side of the cove, and the management of other convicts assigned to the government fishing boats. Of necessity, Phillip blessed him for his skills.

There was a rule by mid-February, very hard to police, that sailors were not to be admitted to the women's camp. The male convicts, however, were happy as soon as the women were landed to see it enforced against those sailors who had lorded over them at sea. The day after the weddings, a carpenter and a boy belonging to the *Prince of Wales* were caught in the women's tents. They were drummed out with a marine fifer and drummer playing the *Rogue's March* and marching before them, and the boy dressed in petticoats. Similarly, it was proving difficult to keep the male convicts out. Surgeon Bowes Smyth wrote, 'The anarchy and confusion which prevails throughout the camp and the audacity of the convicts, both men and women, is arrived to such a pitch as is not to be equal, I believe, by any set of villains in any other spot upon the globe.'

Yet there was purer, more admirable and singular love. A sailor named John Fisher, from the *Lady Penrhyn*, gave way to his longing to see his convict woman, Catherine Hart, and their infant son, John. Catherine Hart had been nineteen when tried at the Old Bailey in 1784 for some undistinguished act of theft. The prosecutor addressed the judge in these terms about the goods she had stolen: 'My Lord, I value them at thirty shillings in order to save her life, because the wretch's life is no value to me.' The child, John, had been one of the children baptised at the Cape of Good Hope, and now his father, the seaman Fisher, swam ashore a number of nights to see his mother and him. He would sicken and die at Sydney Cove on 25 March 1788 of chest infection and dysentery, Surgeon Bowes Smyth attributing his death to his 'imprudence' in swimming ashore naked. 'He would lie about with her in the woods all night in the dews and return on board again a little before daylight, thereby he caught a most violent cold and made his disorder infinitely more putrid than it would otherwise have been.'

The women of Sydney Cove would often be as practical about marriage as Phillip was. For after John Fisher died, Catherine became the lover of Lieutenant Robert Kellow, who would leave her with two of his children when he left the colony.

At Judge-Advocate David Collins's judicial marquee, on a warm hour in mid-afternoon, the first criminal court of three naval officers and three military officers, dressed in their uniforms and carrying side-arms, assembled on the day after the weddings to address the emergence of criminal unruliness in New South Wales. Harry Brewer in his raggedy naval jacket was put to work to bring along the first three accused of crimes in Sydney Cove. They were not very remarkable crimes. An angry young West Country thief, Sam Barsby, had been working at making barrel staves on the east side of the stream and had broken his adze. Unable to find a new adze at the store tent, and fired by rum sailors had given him in return for pointing out the women's camp to them, he was ordered back to work by Drum-Major Benjamin Cook. Barsby struck the drum-major with the broken adze and a melee began which ended with the soldiers guarding Phillip's canvas government house taking Barsby prisoner. During the evening of his arrest, Barsby raged in his bonds and was ultimately gagged. He was found guilty and sentenced to 150 lashes, harsh enough but less than Private Bramwell got for assaulting a convict woman.

By the time of this first criminal trial, Albion/Sydney had established itself as the Southern Hemisphere's London, since the same dodges, lurks and ruses characterised both places. Similar too was the justice system, which proceeded functionally to administer the punishment to Barsby as soon as the court had finished sitting. As with Bramwell, he was tied to an iron triangular frame and the lashes counted out. We do not know who laid on the whip – in the case of Barsby it was probably a nominated convict; in the case of Bramwell a marine NCO.

Flogging was considered unremarkable, and was passed off as normal in the journals of Hunter, Collins and Clark. Historians are quick to point out to modern readers that supervisors were permitted to flog children working in mills and mines, and masters their apprentices, servants and wives. As the case of Private Bramwell shows, it was not exclusively a punishment for prisoners, and both in their cases and those of the armed forces, the inflicting of lashes was attended with ritual and controls such as the presence of a surgeon.

The former revolutionary soldier, Jacob Nagle, observed that the cat-o'-nine-tails was feared until its first use, after which a deterioration could be observed in the sailor's or convict's character. For those who had not been flogged with a cat – its multiple knotted ends each encasing a lump of lead – flogging was unimaginable; in their profoundest soul, they hoped it would not happen to them. For men who did not consider themselves professional criminals – Will Bryant, the smuggler, for example – the triangle was an entry to a new, angry world in which they would have less power over their own souls and over the furies of their temperament, and thus over the progress of their imprisonment.

But those to whom it was happening a second or third time often 'endured it in a solemn silence, no cry, no groan, no prayer for mercy'. Only an occasional threat came from the prisoner: 'But damn my eyes if I don't have satisfaction one way or another, if I get hanged for it.'

The second person to be tried that afternoon was Thomas Hill, who had forcibly taken a quantity of bread from a weaker convict. It must have been a mere morsel for him to have been saved the gallows, but the crime suggests that for some in Sydney Cove hunger was already biting, not least because it was almost impossible for Phillip to prevent the convicts trading or gambling their rations, and being left voracious for days. Hill was sentenced to be kept in irons for one week, fed on bread and water, on the little sandstone knob of an island off the eastern end of Sydney Cove. A breeches-maker from Dorset who had as his founding criminal offence stolen a silver watch, Hill became the first man to occupy that rock which would acquire the name Pinchgut.

To round out the early cycle of punishments, and to show that

New South Wales was of full British weight, on 14 February two women received 25 lashes each 'at the cart's tail' – tethered to a cart as it moved around the camp – for theft. Private Easty mentioned so remarkable an event to modern sensibilities quite offhandedly in his journal.

Ten

To the bemusement of the Cadigal and other clans of Port Jackson, when Will Bryant and his assistants drew fish from the water, or when officers shot birds and game, no permission was sought by the newcomers before they made free of the earth and of the sea. Similar high-handedness, culturally comprehensible but legally reprehensible, characterised the French, who as soon as the British ships left Botany Bay built on its north side a palisade fortification to enable new boats or longboats to be constructed in safety. 'This precaution was necessary,' wrote La Pérouse, 'against the Indians of New Holland, who though very weak and few in number, like all savages are extremely mischievous . . . for they even threw darts at us immediately after receiving our presents and our caresses.' Expecting conflict, La Pérouse was not disappointed. In an ill-defined event on the shores of Gamay, Botany Bay, a number of Cadigal (Sydney), Bediagal (north shore Botany Bay), and Gweagal (south shore Botany Bay) natives were shot and wounded. 'We also have the mortification to learn,' wrote Collins, 'that M. de La Pérouse had been compelled to fire upon the natives at Botany Bay, where they frequently annoyed his people who were employed on shore.' Though this brought a general deterioration in the relationship between the natives and all Europeans, 'we were however firstly convinced that nothing short of the greatest necessity could have induced M. de La Pérouse to take such a step'.

Whatever native mischief La Pérouse experienced, it was notable that the new people in Warrane, Sydney Cove, seemed to require no fortification, nor was the judicious Phillip tempted to erect any. Some wisdom told him that a new society could not be created from within a state of siege. Not that the people in Sydney Cove had been pestered by natives, who seemed to stay away from the area in the early weeks. But on the second Saturday of February, two natives came down close to the camp to within a small distance of the governor's canvas house. They were 'both men pretty much advanced in life' and bore long spears. The governor, determined to be courteous, put on his coat and went out to meet them with a number of officers, and gave one of them a hatchet 'and bound some red bunting about their heads with some yellow tinfoil'. The two visitors sat beneath a tree but refused to go any further into the new town. One of them spent the time sharpening the point of his spear with an oyster shell, perhaps in the hope of showing the force he had to hand and thus moderating the behaviour of the newcomers.

When a black African boy from one of the ships came up to look at these elders, they opened his shirt and examined his chest, then felt his hair, and by signs begged for a lock of it. Surgeon Bowes Smyth cut off a tress. They put the boy's hair aside in a wreath of grass, and were quite willing to let Bowes Smyth take some of their own. Perhaps they intended to work some ritual of expulsion by using the boy's hair. Perhaps they thought he was one of them, lost.

Whatever their purpose, one could be sure it was unlikely to be idle, and worthy of a better response than bunting and tinfoil. In fact Phillip would soon hear rumours that some of his people had been involved in the rape and plunder of natives, and ultimately of murder, though there was no direct evidence of any of this. Almost certainly the two elders had come, amongst other motives, to observe the people who were so casual in violating the world set up by the hero ancestors, the beings who created the local environment of each clan and language group in the great period of generation known as the Dreaming.

For the individual native, the knowledge, ritual and mystery attached to maintaining the local earth were enlarged at initiation, and further secrets were acquired through a lifetime, sometimes by means of dreams. A network of dreaming tracks existed, criss-crossing the continent, certainly densely criss-crossing the Sydney basin, connecting one well of water or place of nourishment or shelter with another. The eastern coastline of New South Wales, built up of Hawkesbury sandstone, standing above the sea in great platforms and easily eroded to make caves, was full of such holy sites. As a visible symbol of that, there exists a huge number of pecked and abraded engravings of humans, ancestors, sharks and kangaroos on open and sheltered rock surfaces around Sydney, as the sandstone proved a good medium for that work.

Natives at particular ceremonial sites re-enacted the journey and acts of creation of a particular hero ancestor, and by doing that they sustained the earth. As in other places the priest became Christ at the climax of the liturgy, during their re-enactment they became the hero ancestor. It was certainly as custodians of the world made by the ancestor heroes that these two old men had come now to town.

Even though these people were early called *ab origines* – people who had been here since the beginning of the earth – Phillip had no way of knowing how ancient was their occupation of the land he had just claimed for George III. In what is now western New South Wales, near Lake Nitchie, some 6800 years ago, a number of men very much resembling these two elders, and members of the species *homo sapiens*, worked for the better part of a week cutting a pit into hard sediments and making it large enough to take the body of an important man. He was a tall man at 182 centimetres. He had died in his late thirties from a dental abscess. In 1969 the body was found, still seated after millennia, legs bent and head and shoulders forced down to fit him into the grave pit and bury him before he putrefied. He was daubed with red ochre, and interred with solemn ornamentation: scraps of pearl shell which had somehow reached this distant inland location, a lump of fused silica from a meteor, and a necklace of 178 Tasmanian devil's teeth. The Tasmanian devil became extinct in mainland Australia nearly 7000 years ago. This man was a figure of significance and power – his necklace and the care taken to inter him showed that. And although in some cultural aspects of his life he would have differed from these two elders who visited Phillip in February 1788, and although they spoke a different language from that spoken by the ancient tall man, the essentials of his life – ceremonial, hunting and social – would have been totally understandable to them. This was not to say that location or the passage of time had done nothing over 7000 years to alter behaviour and customs – that would be ridiculous. But in important respects, the issues of blood-ties, initiation, ceremonial duties, priorities and daily routine of the ancient 'important man' would have made perfect sense to these men. Whereas to Phillip they were, and would be despite his best intentions, an utter puzzle.

Not that the man of Lake Nitchie is the oldest of rediscovered burials in Australia. A female cremation–burial that occurred 26,000 years ago has been uncovered at Lake Mungo in western New South Wales. The light-boned woman's body was not totally consumed by flames when it was cremated on the beach of Lake Mungo, and the remaining bones were broken up and placed in a pit. Half a kilometre distant, but some 2000 years earlier, another body, almost certainly a woman's, her right shoulder badly afflicted with osteoarthritis, had been buried, ornamented with red ochre. Both these women were *homo sapiens* and it is likely that their cosmology too coincided in essentials with that of the elders who came to visit Sydney Town.

Other contacts made early in that remarkable month of February seemed to confirm the idea that the natives were very interested in the new people but were distressed by their unauthorised taking of fish and game. A pernicious trade in native souvenirs had also started between the convicts on land, and even some of the marines, and the sailors of the transports. The sailors knew they would soon be departing and were willing to buy stolen spears, throwing sticks and native nets as mementos. The fishing lines used by the native women were difficult for them to replace, being arduously spun from the inner bark of the kurrajong tree. Women would roll long strips of the bark on the inside of their thighs, twisting it together to make the lines. They used the sap of the red bloodwood tree to prevent the line from fraying. They also used bark fibre to make fishing nets, *carrahjun maugromaa*, and net bags, which they hung from their necks or foreheads and used to carry their fishing lines and other possessions.

Burra, fishhooks, made either of hardwood or of the spiral vortex of shells, were also stolen. The Eora forebears had fished with hooks and handlines and the multi-point spears the Europeans called fizgigs – from the Spanish *fisga*, harpoon – for at least two millennia. The men used canoes chiefly to cross from one bay to another, but always fished in the shallows. One European declared that a native had been seen to catch more than twenty fish in an afternoon by standing up in the canoe and striking at fish with his fizgig made of the flowering stem of the grass tree, or of wattle acacia, its four barbs fastened in place by gum. The wooden prongs were honed in the fire and headed with animal-bone points, sharp fishbones or teeth, or viciously cutting stingray spurs.

Collins says that at convict musters and morning military parades, every person in the colony had been forbidden from depriving the natives of their spears, adhesive yellow gum, or other articles. But there were obvious violations, and the bad conduct of a particular boat crew led to a landing party in one of the coves in the lower part of the harbour being driven off with spears.

Tit-for-tat, a game the natives played with the same vigour as the Europeans, was now established. A party of Aboriginal men, perhaps sixteen or eighteen, landed on the Garden Island of the *Sirius* and carried off a shovel, spade and pick-axe. One of the sailors there picked up a musket and got a shot away. A wounded native dropped the pick-axe. Was the attempt to take this item straight theft, was it the unknowing and accustomed picking up of whatever lay in nature, or was it an attempt at an adjustment of the books? It was, in any case, interpreted on the newcomers' side only as predictable native thievery. Captain Collins lamented, 'To such circumstances as these must be attributed the termination of that good understanding that had hitherto subsisted between us and them, and which Governor Phillip laboured to improve wherever he had the opportunity.' Collins was fair enough to acknowledge that the loss of their fishing lines and other implements must have created 'many inconveniences' for the Eora.

Nagle the sailor, however, like most of the other new arrivals, saw the Aborigines' assertions of ownership to be pure mischief. 'When we would be shooting the seine and came across a school of fish, and the natives see us, they would come down with spear in hand and take what fish they thought fit until we got them [the fish] into the boat, and push off. A few days after we had been robbed of our fish, we were shooting the seine in a large cove opposite the cove we had been robbed of our fish. One of the natives came over in his bark canoe and seemed very friendly. We knew him to be one of them that robbed us on the other side.' Nagle got this native to accept into his hand the powder from a cartridge, and then have fire put to it. 'Which he did, but the flame, smoke and the powder flying in his face, and the burning of his hand, he gave a spring and a hollow that I never saw equalled and run to his canoe and put off, sometimes paddling with one hand and then the other until he got to the other side.' Such little games expressed the annoyance that ordinary seamen and soldiers felt at the natives' intrusions on their activities, and carried inherent in them the seed of the interracial tragedy that was taking shape in Sydney Cove.

By the end of February 1788, the indigenous people began to shun the settlement. But contact between the two races was a daily occurrence on the water. The natives were scared of the red-coated marines, the 200 men of the four companies. 'From the first, they carefully avoided a soldier, or any person wearing a red coat,' wrote an observer. The natives called the musket the *gerubber*, or *gerebar*, fire-stick. Before long they would experience further demonstrations of its power.

Eleven

On 12 February, Lieutenant King came to Phillip's tented mansion to take the oath as superintendent and commanding officer of Norfolk Island. Phillip seemed to see King's occupation of Norfolk Island above all as a penal rather than a commercial expedition. Nonetheless, once King had 'taken the necessary measures for securing yourself and people, and for the preservation of the stores and provisions, you are immediately to proceed with the cultivation of the flax plant, which you will find growing spontaneously on the island'. Potentially, for an ambitious young Cornishman just shy of 30 years like King, a man of great endurance and average talents of command, the settlement on Norfolk Island offered great opportunity. In a far clearer sense than the creation of Sydney, which was merely an expansion of convict holding capacity, the occupation of Norfolk Island was explicitly to be the expansion of empire. The party sent thither was 'to secure the same to us and prevent it being occupied by the subjects of any other European power'. The corn, the flax, the cotton and other grains produced on the island were to be the property of the Crown, as was the produce of the public farm Phillip had the convicts tilling and planting in Sydney.

King was particularly warned not to permit the building of any vessel whose length of keel exceeded 20 feet. If any ship of that or greater length were to be driven onto the island, thereby opening up the possibility of sea escape, King was to scuttle it immediately or otherwise render it unserviceable. Norfolk Island was to depend passively on regular visits from *Supply*.

King had gone aboard the *Lady Penrhyn* in the earliest days of February to ask Surgeon Bowes Smyth about suitable women to take to Norfolk Island. Amongst those whose attitude Bowes Smyth praised to King was Ann Innett, a mature Worcestershire woman, a former mantua-maker. On the island she would become King's housekeeper and lover. A Yorkshire girl, Ann or Nancy Yeates, who was heavily pregnant with the child of one of the *Lady Penrhyn*'s sailors, was also recommended by Bowes Smyth, along with a number of others.

So the coming settlement on the island was designed for the moment to be a haven for relative innocents. The chief attraction for these women would be in getting away from what they might have considered more dangerous elements in the chaotic, fortnight-old convict camp. For all of them volunteered to go.

The little *Supply* departed Sydney Cove in mid-February on a rather cool summer's morning and beneath thundery clouds, with King and his six women and eight men, his surgeon and two marines, his carpenter and his weaver. On their journey they encountered arising from the sea a previously unseen, splendid and lonely pinnacle of rock, which would be named Ball's Pyramid to honour *Supply*'s master, and next they found an unknown island, unoccupied by Aborigines, with many plump giant turtles on its beaches. They hunted the turtles for their meat and named the island to honour Lord Howe of the Admiralty.

These Englishmen seemed to operate on a prompt instinct like Cook's – that what was named was tamed; what was addressed was possessed.

On arrival, *Supply* having taken more than two weeks of violent gales to reach Norfolk Island, they were greeted by a furious surf. Eighteen years past, Cook had landed on the north side, but King searched the coastline for a week before finding a halfway safe landing place along that coast. At a place he named Duncombe Bay to honour the Member for Yorkshire in the House of Commons, the first landing party was put ashore. The bay was found to be enclosed by reef, as was most of the island. Landed, King was enthusiastic about what he saw while exploring the central valley and the pine-clad hills with his surgeon, Thomas Jamison. King's journal shows he was quick to name geographic points after possible sponsors – not only was there Duncombe Bay, but also Anson Bay to honour the Member for Litchfield. He noted with some astonishment: 'We have not seen a leaf of flax or any herbal grass whatever, the ground being quite bare, which is rather extraordinary as Captain Cook says that flax is more luxuriant here than in New Zealand.' Banks and Cook had misled everyone about Botany Bay, and now about Norfolk Island! What was a young officer to think?

Norfolk Island could have been considered a lonely place by a more introspective young man. King was his own Aborigine here, for he was beginning from the beginning, and no natives inhabited the island. (Its later record for drownings and shipwrecks might explain why.) His charges having been selected for good behaviour, once ashore they pitched tents on open ground on the south side of the island, where there was a gap in the reef in the area he named Sydney Bay, but soon to become

Kingstown, to honour George III. The first Sunday ashore, King called the settlement together for divine service in his tent and read Phillip's commission to him. He took formal possession of the island and drank the toasts to the royal family. His subsequent speech was very much in the spirit of a middling officer in the Royal Navy, and rather like Phillip's in Sydney Cove – he told his charges that every encouragement would be given them to behave with propriety and industry, and that those who lacked those qualities would be punished 'as useless and destructive members of society'. He told them something Phillip had not told his charges in Sydney Cove – that if they behaved well, he would see to their repatriation. He then settled down to manage the community along the lines set by Phillip, as if it were a large farm and the convicts his farmhands. They did all that the people in Sydney Cove were doing, except the timber was kinder. They split and sawed pines to build storerooms and shelters. They sowed the ground and hauled away the branches of felled pines. And it all seemed to go better here. Could this become the penal utopia?

There were the usual earthly arrangements. Thomas Jamison, King's surgeon, a Trinity College man whom Lieutenant Clark called 'a cunning villain', formed an association with Elizabeth Colley of *Lady Penrhyn*, and produced two illegitimate sons for whom he would provide. But there was also the idyll: one of the young women, Olivia Gascoigne, would soon marry Nathaniel Lucas, a carpenter and cloth thief, by whom she would have thirteen colonial children.

As fresh gales combed the great pines and thunderheads hung low, King was delighted to find turtles on a sandy beach on the eastern side of the island. Huge turtles would supply many excellent meals for the people of Norfolk Island. After first planting some vegetables, he went in company with his people, free and convict, to Turtle Bay and there collectively, officer, man and convict, they caught three of the enormous creatures. But on 3 March, John Jay, one of the *Supply*'s quartermasters, insisted on trying to catch a turtle in the surf 'although desired to desist', and drowned. He would not be the last to suffer death in Norfolk Island's turbulent surf.

At last, later in the month, indeed on St Patrick's Day, 'I discovered,' wrote King, 'that the flax plant which Captain Cook takes notice, is of no other than that plant which I have hitherto called the larger kind of iris with which this isle abounds, but it in no manner resembles the flax of Europe.' A bundle of it was tied up and put into a pool of water to soak, with the intention of drying it after the European method of preparing flax, but the finished product was useless.

Here, as in Sydney Cove, it was the soldiers who committed the first sin. In April, King detected Private John Batchelor, one of his two marines, stealing rum out of the flask in which it was kept in King's tent. He did not doubt what must be done. 'In the afternoon I assembled the people together and punished him with one dozen lashes for quitting his work, one dozen lashes for breaking into the King's stores and one dozen for theft.' In a few months Batchelor too would drown when a huge surf broached a longboat he was travelling in.

The lash had made its entry into Norfolk Island like the entry of the serpent into Eden. It would from then on frequently distinguish the governance of the place. Charles McClennan, a fourteen-year-old, tried to steal rum out of the surgeon's tent and was punished with three dozen lashes. McClennan, from Durham, had been sentenced at the age of ten for stealing goods to the value of ten pence. However provoked, and for whatever cause, he had brought down the convictry of Norfolk Island to the level of those on the mainland. King determined he would have to make an even more severe example of the next person found stealing.

Now unpromising incidents abounded. Hail destroyed corn, barley and wheat, and grubs all the potatoes. The sawyers were poisoned by trying some native beans, and Charles McClennan was again lashed for uttering 'some very seditious and threatening words'.

What exchanges occurred between King and his housekeeper, the convict Ann Innett, in his primitive cottage of pine-wood, go unrecorded, as does the process by which she became his lover. She was to become pregnant with Norfolk Island's first child early in the Australian autumn. And after nine months had passed King still celebrated divine service with a gentlemanly lack of embarrassment, and baptised the newborn infant by the name of Norfolk, 'he being the first born on the island'.

Back in Sydney, as foreshadowed during the ceremonial of 7 February, Phillip had taken before David Collins the oaths of abjuration and assurance, made politically necessary by the Scottish uprising in favour of the House of Stuart's Bonnie Prince Charlie 40 years earlier. 'I, Arthur Phillip, do truly and sincerely acknowledge, profess, testify and declare, in my conscience, before God and World, that our sovereign Lord King George is lawful and rightful King of this realm . . .' The oaths asserted before God the claim of the House of Hanover to the Crown and denounced any claim of 'the pretended Prince of Wales and his open and secret abettors'. Phillip was also to make the declaration contained in the Act for Preventing Dangers which might arise from Popish Recusants, basically those who would try to restore the Catholic Pretender, the Bonnie Prince. By the time the oaths were taken in Sydney Cove, the Pretender had already made a sad, liquor-bloated corpse, having perished at the Palazzo Muti in Rome on 31 January 1788.

In any case, Phillip was a good supporter of the Hanoverian Crown. He would early emphasise how seriously he took the Crown's ownership of all things in New South Wales. A convict sold an animal 'of the squirrel kind' to the steward of *Lady Penrhyn* for liquor. The governor summoned Captain Marshall of the *Lady Penrhyn* and told him 'that all the convicts got was the property of government', demanded the animal back and subjected the steward to 50 lashes.

Equally the government's property were those areas up-harbour where the waters ultimately narrowed to become a river flowing down into Port Jackson from the hinterland. Officers and men still marvelled at the capaciousness both of the river and the port itself. 'In my belief,' wrote Jacob Nagle, 'I should suppose Port Jackson to hold nearly all the ships in England.' Phillip would soon investigate the upper reaches of the river, and the area to the north to see if they could be adapted to the colony's use.

Meanwhile, in Sydney Cove, no sooner had the commissary Mr Andrew Miller done his calculations over the supplying of rations, than four young men were caught with stolen butter, pease and pork from the tented storehouse. They were all young men with robust appetites. Thomas Barrett had long been a prisoner, having stolen from a spinster when he was as young as eleven or twelve. He had been condemned to death but reprieved to be transported on *Mercury*, from which he landed in England after convicts took the ship over. Like others, he was condemned to death again for return from transportation, but once more was reprieved. On board the *Charlotte* a few months out of England, young Barrett had been caught trying to pass counterfeit quarter-dollars made out of old belt buckles and pewter spoons, and Surgeon White had been impressed by his ingenuity in manufacturing the coins when a sentry had been on guard all the time over the hatchway, and hardly ten minutes elapsed without someone going down among the convicts.

Barrett, now aged about eighteen years, faced the death penalty for a third time under the terms laid down by Arthur Phillip in his first speech to the convicts. Henry Lovell, a London ivory-turner in his mid-twenties, and Joseph Hall, another graduate of the *Mercury*, also appeared before Judge-Advocate Collins and his bench of officers in the tented court at one o'clock in the afternoon. John Ryan, a London silk-weaver, the fourth man involved, also faced the bench. The first three were briskly and unanimously condemned to death, but Ryan was sentenced to 300 lashes, being adjudged more a receiver than thief.

Sydney Cove was now to achieve its first executions '*in terrorem*, testimony to the Majesty of the Law, a Dreadful and Awful Example to Others'. At five in the afternoon of a late February day, with the summer sun falling down the sky behind them, the marine garrison marched to the place of punishment, a tree between the men's and women's camp on the western side of Sydney Cove. All the convict population were compulsorily gathered to see this demonstration of the fact that their rations were considered sacrosanct. All three men appeared beneath the tree's long branches – it was probably a Moreton Bay fig tree like the one beneath which the Reverend Johnson had given his first sermons. Barrett asked to speak to one of the convicts, a *Mercury* crony, Robert Sideway, who on the *Friendship* had incurred a flogging and chaining and had a risky reputation. This request was granted and a confidential hugger-mugger passed between them. Then Barrett requested the chance to talk with one of the women but was refused, and mounted his ladder under the tree, as did Lovell and Hall theirs, the nooses hanging level with their necks. But as all three men stood there, Major Ross was approached by a sentry who came running from the governor's tent with a 24-hour stay of execution for Lovell and Hall. They came down their ladders and it was time for the final rites for Barrett. 'The Reverend Mr Johnson prayed very fervently with the culprit before he was turned off, and performed every office appertaining to his function with great decorum.' Barrett, of 'a most vile nature', expressed not the least signs of fear until he mounted the ladder, 'and then he turned very pale and seemed very much shocked'.

He was not the only victim of the hanging tree. A young convict named James Freeman, sixteen when he was sentenced to death at Hartford and reprieved in 1784, had been given the task of being the penal colony's hangman. In the next few days, he too had been sentenced to death for stealing flour from another convict, but there was evidence that he had merely stumbled on the flour cached in the woods. Governor Phillip pardoned him on condition he became the public executioner, and Surgeon

Worgan noted that 'here was an opportunity of establishing a Jack Ketch who should in all future executions either hang or be hanged' (Jack Ketch being a renowned criminal–hangman from Newgate). Freeman, like the unnamed convict who had been ordered to be hangman in Barrett's case, believed it would make him a pariah. In the case of Barrett, the convict assigned the task had delayed fixing the rope and taking Barrett's ladder away for so long that Major Ross threatened to have the marines shoot him. He had to be severely threatened also by Provost-Marshal Brewer, who disliked the scene anyhow and did not want to have it dragged out. Mr Brewer, said Surgeon Worgan, 'was under the disagreeable necessity of mounting the ladder himself in order to fix the halter'.

Having called on the convicts all to take warning from his fate, Barrett was 'turned off'. Freeman was in an unhappy position: 'All grandeur, all power, all subordination rests on the executioner,' wrote an eighteenth-century commentator. 'Remove this incomprehensible agent from the world, and at that very moment, order gives way to chaos, thrones topple and society disappears.' And in the spirit of that principle, Freeman had to be forced to exercise the office every time someone hanged from then on.

The First Fleet children saw Barrett asphyxiate and piss his pants and were thereby educated in the power of authority. What the Cadigal, drawn by the sound of drums and observing from the bush, thought of this strange ritual would be recorded later. They were astonished and appalled. Strangulation was not one of their punishments. They measured retribution in the more calculable currency of blood.

As thunder clouds came up from the south, the body hung an hour and was then buried in a grave dug very near the gallows.

Thus an acre of Eora ground was rendered unholy. Throughout the century, surgeons and physicians, helped by robust beadles and porters, had stolen the bodies of the hanged either from Tyburn Hill, where the London executions took place until 1783, or even from the new scaffold outside Newgate. But here, science had not advanced enough to threaten the eternal rest of Barrett. Overnight a thunderous downpour fell on his grave. Rain gushed in at the canvas and thatched cornices of convict huts. Convicts darted from camp site to camp site with a petition to the great central presence, Phillip, who would find himself presented the next morning with an appeal from the mass of the felons begging that the sentences of Lovell and Hall be commuted. The people who signed it knew well enough that the court system was a lottery, that the condemned had probably been worked at by hefty marines and temporary constable convicts before they confessed, guilty as they may well have been.

Phillip made no immediate reply to the petition. He let the preparatory rites go ahead. Prim Ralph Clark, leading a guard, collected the two men from Harry Brewer's keeping and marched them to the execution site. Johnson prayed with them as they mounted the ladder and Freeman prepared the nooses. But then the judge-advocate arrived with the commutation of sentence. Lovell was to go to Norfolk Island for life, and Hall to be stuck indefinitely on the little island just off Sydney Cove named Pinchgut.

Phillip, the source of these pardons, was to the convicts as well as to the later imaginations of Australians and others more an iconic than real figure. He is seen still as entirely a public figure, not as a man sitting in fraying shirtsleeves in his marquee and fearing for the future. Not as a man who may or may not have still loved his housekeeper, Deborah Brooks, made jokes in French with his servant, Maliez, patted his greyhounds whom he was reduced to feeding with the inedible sections of the weekly rations and kangaroo gristle, and who fed rice by the grain to his pet Sydney Cove fruit bat.

One of his multitude of disappointments was that there were no limestone deposits around the cove, which made it uncertain whether permanent habitations for himself and his officers, the people and the stores could ever be raised. The sandstone which stonemasons would later craft into splendid honeycomb-coloured public buildings did not answer Phillip's needs now. An adaptable building contractor from Kingston-on-Thames, James Bloodworth, who under financial pressure had committed some felony to do with the endorsement of cheques or the rigging of books, had taken a reconnaissance into the bush south of Sydney Cove and found good deposits of red clay highly suitable for brick-making. That February opened up possibilities for Bloodworth. Known to have a wife in England, he was embarking on a tender and passionate association with the grief-stricken Sarah Bellamy, who had just lost her shipboard-conceived son, and would soon lose his father, Joe Downey, when he sailed with the *Lady Penrhyn* to China. He also drew the attention of Harry Brewer to these potential brick-making deposits and thus, with Harry, assumed the position of chief of construction and superintendent of bricks. Phillip set some of the women to collecting seashells for Bloodworth to burn for mortar. It was urgent work, not just because a government house needed building, and a barracks for officers and marines, but so that the all-important storehouses could be constructed, the precious rations presently standing vulnerably in guarded tents.

Convicts employed in digging up clay and forming it into bricks with brickbats under Bloodworth's direction were met at the clay field, soon named Brickfield Hill, by natives of the Cadigal clan who threw stones at them then ran away. Perhaps some unconscious impulse told the Cadigal to resist the creation of permanent structures. But to Phillip the brick-makers were performing a founding act of good order. Bricks and seashell lime would turn Sydney Cove from a camp to a town.

It was 25 March before all the stores were landed from the *Lady Penrhyn*, *Scarborough* and *Charlotte*, and those ships were discharged from government service. They were the three going on to China for tea, and their carpenters had made the necessary adjustments in the hold to convert them from convict transports to normal freight carriers. Lieutenant George Shortland, the agent for the transports, confirmed *Lady Penrhyn's* discharge after she landed her government stores of beef, pork, bread, flour, pease, butter and rice in their various measurements – tierces, puncheons, barrels, firkins and brams. The ship had also landed a loom for weaving canvas; mill spindles, mill brushes, mill bills and picks; handcuffs with instruments; nearly 600 petticoats, 600 jackets, 121 caps, 327 pairs of stockings and 381 shifts; 40 tents and six bundles of ridge poles; a transport jack for repairing wagons; hoses, wind sails, some prefabricated cabins, bulkheads, beds, hammocks and marine clothing. Who would have thought that in addition to 103 women convicts and sundry marines, all that would have fitted in the 103 feet length and less than 30 feet width.

A new assessment of the rations to be issued was now

studiously drawn up by the anxious commissary, Andrew Miller. An immediate reduction of 12 pounds for every 100-pound ration of beef, and 8 pounds for every 100-pound ration of pork was made. But the marine wives that day, Sergeant James Scott was at least happy to report, were ordered their usual allowance of liquor, 'with the proviso that their husbands will repay it again'. The ration reduction was not the only bad news, since the same day the governor met the officers on the subject of grants of land, and told them that it was not in his authority to grant *them* land, although he had been authorised to grant land to privates and non-commissioned officers when they had completed their service in the marines. The best he could offer the officers was the use of pieces of ground for gardens or for feeding their stock, but they could not receive permanent grants. In his lieutenant-governor's tent, Major Ross was vocal to his closest friend, Captain Campbell, about what he saw as a carping, letter-of-the-law decision by Phillip. Indeed, had officers been given grants, said Ross with some point, it was likely they could have contributed significantly to the common welfare.

Major Ross was in a hard situation. He had not won the affection of his officers even though he had made it clear to Phillip they would not work as convict supervisors. For he grew spiky about small issues concerning the rebelliousness of some of his officers, and his misgivings about the governor and the country in general began to grate on those forced to listen to his complaints.

One matter that had begun plainly enough, but rapidly escalated into tension and conflict, demonstrates Ross's prickliness and lack of the adaptability needed if the colony were to succeed. When at the communal cooking fires and coppers where most of the convicts seemed to want to prepare their rations, as they had at sea, a good-looking Irish convict sentenced in Bristol, Jane Fitzgerald, spoke pleasantly to Private William Dempsey, a series of troublesome events began. When Dempsey answered, a Private Hunt came over and asked Dempsey how dared he speak to a woman from Hunt's ship, *Scarborough*, and so, in Hunt's mind, part of the sexual property of *Scarborough* marines. A convict tried to intervene and Private Hunt called him a 'Portsmouth rascal'. Hunt confessed to hitting Dempsey, but denied using any insulting words.

Captain Watkin Tench presided over Hunt's court-martial, taking evidence from Jane Fitzgerald and others. The sentence brought down was that Private Hunt should either ask William Dempsey's pardon, publicly, in front of the battalion, or else he could receive 100 lashes. Within an hour of the sentence coming down, Major Ross sent the case back to the court martial claiming that they were wrong to bring down alternative punishments. He instructed the court to impose one sentence only.

At four o'clock that afternoon, the five officers signed their reply to Ross, saying that they were unable to reconsider the sentence. Ross wrote to the officers again, and at seven o'clock that evening they wrote back saying that they considered it impossible to alter their decision. Thus rancour went whizzing from tent to tent around Sydney Cove. The members of the court certainly felt that their honour as officers was being impugned, but Ross's personality added a certain tincture of pleasure to their refusing what he demanded. As Private Easty said in his journal, 'The court sat four times when Major Ross would not accept the court-martial upon which the court confined themselves . . . and said that [rather than give way] they would go home to England.' Ross immediately placed them all under house arrest.

The officers of the court wrote to Phillip, and so did Major Ross, but Phillip had to overturn Ross's suspension of the five officers – the colony needed their services. Ross insisted they remain under technical arrest with their ranks frozen.

Now, with the ration reduction, a level of hunger and a great yearning for the lost delicacies of Britain became the lot of all the settlement. Fresh meat from marsupials like the kangaroo and wallaby, and fresh fish from Port Jackson were in inadequate supply, and much of what was caught went to the hospital. Men and women remembered with passionate fondness the food pedlars of the English towns, the sellers of watercress, asparagus and chestnuts, cakes, mutton and pork pies and steaming sausages, oysters, fish and fruit in season. How richly they must have talked about the horse-drawn early-breakfast stalls which would set up on some corner or by the approaches of a bridge and sell scalding tea and coffee and hot, fresh bread soaked in butter, all for a halfpenny. The people of Sydney Cove had wronged the cities which had presented them with such delights, and they were being punished in a shire naked of such pleasures.

Now scorbutic – scurvy-prone – women and children were nursed with infusions of the leaves of the bush named *Smilax glyciphylla* which grew around the cove and contained ascorbic acid. It was prepared like tea and widely drunk not only in the hospital but as a tea substitute in the tents and shelters of Sydney Cove. Such enterprising surgeons as Bowes Smyth and John White set groups of women searching also for the blue berries of *Leptomeria aceda*, of which a cupful was said to be sufficient to keep scurvy at bay. 'Our little camp now began to wear the aspect of distress, from the great number of scorbutic patients that were daily seen creeping to and from the hospital tents.' Every carpenter from the transports and store ships still in the harbour of Port Jackson, every half-skilled artisan amongst the convicts was sent to assist in building huts. The longboats of the ships still brought up the cabbage tree fronds for thatching from the lower part of the harbour, and a range of huts was begun on the western side for some of the female convicts. The *Supply*, returning to Sydney from dropping King at Norfolk Island, had brought a beneficial supply of fresh turtle with it, and White suggested it should be sent out to fetch more. Collins was worried by the general condition of the people, because 'the winter of this hemisphere was approaching'. Venereal disease was also in the camp, even though many of the sufferers had tried to conceal it. Typically, Arthur Phillip decided on drastic and community-wide preventive health measures. 'To stop this evil, it was ordered by the governor that any man or woman having and concealing this disorder should receive corporal punishment, and be put upon a short allowance of provisions for six months.' Surgeon White could treat the infection with mercury drops and salve, but in many bloodstreams it lay dormant.

Twelve

The American sailor Nagle, a member of the governor's boat crew, seemed very fond of Phillip, even though he had refused the boat crews permission to carry firearms. Nagle was aware that the governor liked particularly to escape the cares of Sydney Cove and travel with other gentlemen to explore the region. In early March Phillip was rowed out of the heads and along the coast in his cutter, accompanied by a longboat, to investigate the inlet next northwards from Port Jackson, named by Cook Broken Bay. Rounding its great, bushy headland, Phillip found that on the north side there were shoals and swamps, but on the south side, 'the finest piece of water I ever saw', which he named Pittwater after the prime minister. The hills of Pittwater, however, covered in thick foliage, fell straight to the beach or petered away into tidal mud, and did not offer lowlands of alluvium. Phillip began to see that he had been lucky to find Port Jackson with its deep anchorages.

Exploring a dozen or more miles up the river, he encountered new clans of natives and spoke to them and traded, not always successfully. His party was fascinated to see that not all the Broken Bay women had the first two sections of their left little finger missing, as did the Sydney women. As for future settlement here, where the river had created floodplains, he concluded, 'There are some good situations where the land might be culti- vated.' This river for thousands of years had borne the name Deerubbin. Phillip named it the Hawkesbury, in honour of the Earl of Liverpool, Baron Hawkesbury, head man at the Board of Trade in London.

Exploring the foreshores, encountering occasional Aboriginal corpses laid out in a sort of open-air burial, the party heard for the first time that Aboriginal cry, *Coo-ee*, which would become for the whites also a means of finding friends in deep bush.

Nagle gives us a picture of the gentlemen removed from the fretfulness of Sydney Cove, dining on mullet on the north side of Broken Bay within hearing distance of the seamen and soldiers. According to Nagle, Dr White said to the governor, 'I am amazing fond of those mullet.' The governor being in what Nagle called 'jocus youmer' answered, 'So I perceive, for you have eaten six of them as you say, and you must allow that the least of them weigh 3 pound, and by calculation, the whole must weigh 18 pounds.' This created an atmosphere of what Nagle called 'sport and diversion'.

Phillip returned to Port Jackson after a nearly ten-day journey. He had intended to march back to Sydney Harbour overland, but had caught what he called 'a cold in his side', with resultant pain. His kidney and urinary pain had become a chronic problem.

Phillip found the land near his house on the east side of Sydney Cove to be aesthetically pleasing with its park-like spacing of trees and gentle slopes from which he could look down on the ferny tangle around the Tank Stream. As the site of government gardens and farms, however, it was serviceable but not wonderful. Phillip was driven by a desire to find superlative farming land, adequate to sustain his people – the sort of Eden new worlds were supposed to deliver up as a matter of course. The Hawkesbury floodplains were too far away, so he decided to take another trip, this time up the broad river which entered Port Jackson from the west and which could be considered a continuation of the great harbour. The river was a magnificent complexity of bays, inlets and entering streams, and the first night out, having taken a southward-leading tributary, they came to mangrove swamps and had to camp 'near some stagnant water' amidst a typical Sydney thunderstorm. At about eleven o'clock, sleeping on drenched ground, the governor fell ill again; he 'was suddenly attacked with the most violent complaint in his side and loins, brought on by cold and fatigue'. Surgeon White, who was with him, thought correctly he had not got over his journey to Broken Bay. But Phillip insisted on going on, up the main artery of water, and passed bushy tiers of sandstone, beaches and bays of mangrove, and then found grass 'tolerably rich and succulent . . . interspersed with a plant much resembling the indigo'. The second night White fed the sick Phillip by hand with an excellent soup made out of a white cockatoo and two crows. The evening thunderstorm came, and again the governor suffered.

Next day, at last, they came to an expanse of large broad sandstone, a natural weir over which the by-now freshwater river ran. There was a native quarry of slate nearby. And amidst the trees, which were spaced with very little underbrush, the beautiful rainbow lorikeets flashed like hurled clots of colour. Here too ducks and teal were plentiful, and during their migration season from brackish water downriver to the fresh water via the natural rock weir, masses of eels would be found writhing and tumbling in the river, in great knots of potential food. The local Aborigines for that reason called the place *Burramatta*, eels, and themselves the Burramattagal, the people of the eel country.

Phillip's party continued on foot, approving the open ground as they went. The hill at the southern end of this stretch of promising riverbank, fourteen miles from the heads of Port Jackson, was named Rose Hill by Phillip to honour his former neighbour at Lyndhurst, Sir George Rose, who had spoken up to get Phillip this job. But the usage *Parramatta* became gradually more common. In any case, Phillip felt a weight lifted from his body. This new world was not as recalcitrant as everyone, especially Major Ross, his lieutenant-governor, feared. Writing to Lord Sydney, Phillip was relieved to report, 'There is good country near us and it shall be settled and cultivated early in the spring.'

It was time for some of the transports to leave Sydney and go home. The departure of the *Charlotte*, the *Lady Penrhyn* and the *Scarborough* on 1 May brought an end not only to many a long association between seamen and women ashore, but to the companionable crowdedness of Sydney Cove, and was a token that within weeks the last ship would go. The authorities were anxious that convicts, soldiers and even sailors associated with the remaining ships, *Sirius* and *Supply*, would stow away, and searches of the vessels both by the masters and by the military were thorough. Nonetheless, the *Charlotte* carried away a naval rating belonging to the *Supply* and a young sailor who was an apprentice to the boatswain of the *Sirius*.

In Sydney, the enthusiastic expeditions by the settlement's fishermen and the 'rage of curiosity' involving official and unofficial trafficking in souvenirs and curios to give to everyone from King George III downwards would produce a reaction from the Eora later in the month. On 21 May 1788, William Ayres, a young convict recovering from scurvy, wandered with another recuperating convict, a young Irishman named Peter Burn, to the cove beyond the farm, Woolloomooloo, to pick greens and sweet tea or sarsaparilla (*Smilax glyciphylla* or *Smilax australis*). That evening Ayres stumbled back into camp with a broken-off spear protruding from his back. Burn had been with him, but had run away when Ayres had been speared, and the natives had pursued him. It would be a few days before a soldier found a shirt, hat and a piece of Burns's jacket pierced by spear-holes in a native shelter in the bush.

The natives used different weapons to administer different degrees of discipline. The spear used on the convict Ayres was designed to stick fast amidst bone and musculature and to be difficult to extract. White wrote, 'The weapon was barbed and stuck so very fast that it would permit no motion. After dilating the wound to a considerable length and depth, with some difficulty I extracted the spear, which had penetrated the flesh nearly three inches.' One wonders how William Ayres was made to sit still for this operation. Ayres, recovered, told the officers what had happened. The Aborigines had tried to drive them away from the place with rocks, and he and Burn had thrown rocks back. Then the Aborigines had proceeded to throwing spears. As Ayres had been taking the spear in his back, Burn had been pursued by another party of Aboriginals who then hauled him away with his head bleeding 'and seemingly in great distress'. Peter Burn was in fact dragged off and speared to death, an excruciating process.

The wounding of Ayres and murder of Burn produced a spate of comments about the treachery of the natives, although Tench said their skill in throwing spears was 'far from despicable'. And the reaction of Phillip was not as vengeful as some would have wished. The governor suspected with virtual certainty, but without firm evidence, that there had been earlier attacks on and misuse of Aborigines, and rapes of native women by convicts, let alone theft of their tools, nets, shields and spears.

Mutual murders did not end, despite Phillip's regular warnings to the convict population at morning muster. Some male convicts had been set to work cutting rushes to thatch cottages. Two of them were killed at the end of May 1788, and there is some debate about the place – it could have been at Rushcutters Bay, near Sydney Cove to the east, but the indications are that it was to the west of Sydney Cove in what is now called Cockle Bay. Captain James Campbell of the marines – a man who had been scandalised by what he had thought of as chaos in the camp under Phillip's direction, and who doubted that the 'three kingdoms could produce another man, in my opinion, so totally unqualified for the business he had taken in hand, as this man is' – had visited the rush-cutters in their camp. Finding some splashes of blood near the tent, Campbell followed them into the mangrove bushes and found both cutters, William Oakey and Samuel Davis, two cellmates from Gloucester prison and shipmates from the *Alexander*, lying dead some distance from each other. White wrote, 'Oakey was transfixed through the breast with one of their spears, which with great difficulty and force was pulled out. He had two other spears sticking in him, to a depth which must have proved mortal. His skull was divided and comminuted so much that his brains easily found a passage through. His eyes were out, but these might have been picked away by birds.' Davis mysteriously had few marks on him, 'and his body, lying amongst the mangroves in which he had sought shelter, was warm'. White concluded that while the natives were dispatching Oakey, Davis had crept into the trees where he was found, 'and that fear, united with cold and wet, in a great degree, contributed to his death'.

Again, there was a curious reaction to these two deaths. John Hunter of the *Sirius* said of the deceased: 'As they had hatchets and bill-hooks with them, it is believed they might have been rash enough to use violence with some of the natives.' There was also the sense, not shared by many convict males, however, that the murders of Oakey and Davis were payback killings. There was a story the two men had stolen a native canoe, an alternative form of an Eora man's soul, and the authorities tended to believe it. Surgeon White thought 'that from the civility shewn on all occasions to the officers by the natives . . . I am strongly inclined to think that they must have been provoked and injured by the convicts'. (Typically, he then went on to describe a new bird, a yellow-eared flycatcher that had been caught that day.)

Nonetheless, Phillip felt that the killers needed to be identified so that there could be at least a parley and a mending of grievances. Phillip, White, some marine officers, six marines and two armed convicts visited the murder site and then followed a native path running from there to the north-west arm of Botany Bay, where they found 49 canoes drawn up on a beach. Keeping an eye out for the murdered men's tools, they had a friendly meeting with more than 200 Eora men, women and children gathered for some ritual occasion. Each man was armed with spear, woomera, shield and hardwood club. When Phillip approached them, unarmed and offering fishhooks, beads and other presents, one man stepped forward to show him a wound in his shoulder apparently caused by an axe, and another claimed by mime that the rush-cutters had killed a native by slashing him across the stomach. Returned to Sydney, Phillip gave an order that no group with less than six armed men was to go into the bush 'on account of the natives being so numerous'. Phillip said of the Aborigines in a letter home to the Marquess of Lansdowne, the former British prime minister in whose honour he had named the western mountains beyond Rose Hill, 'I think better of them having been among them.'

One of the chief rilers of natives was the governor's head huntsman, John McEntire. He came from amongst those Irish harvesters who sailed to England as deck cargo each year to work for the summer, while, back home, their wives minded the small holding and potato crop. During his time in Durham, McEntire had been found guilty of robbery and sentenced to death, the sentence being commuted to transportation. No one could predict how profoundly ran the rivers of loss and grievance in such a man, but he was a good shot and brought kangaroos and other marsupials to Phillip's table. He also had a certain charm and quickness, since many of the gentlemen were happy to include him in their parties of hunting and expeditions into the interior. He was necessary not only as a provider of protein to the settlement, but was an essential aide to the naturalists of the fleet. For he shot birds, kangaroos, possums and an emu as natural history items, supplying subjects, for example, for the excellent plates which would one day adorn Surgeon White's memoirs of his time here.

His rancour and bitterness would emerge full face in his dealings with the Eora, amongst whom he became, without Phillip's initial knowledge, a detested person. It may even have been in part as a vengeance against McEntire that Burn, his fellow Irishman, died, and Ayres was wounded so severely.

In Australia, April is the beginning of autumn but a benign month, characterised in Sydney by daytime temperatures in the early to mid-twenties (20 degrees Celsius), with evening temperatures in the late teens. May brings little more threat of ice to the Sydney autumn, which found Henry Kable and his wife, Susannah, like McEntire, young convicts in a favoured position, dwelling in a hut on the east, less boisterous, side of the stream. Kable wrote, 'I am, thank God, very easily situated, never worked one day since I have been here; some officers have been so pleased with my conduct that they continue me in the office of an overseer over the women.' The young couple lived in confidence that some £20 worth of clothes and personal goods bought for them by public subscription in England, and placed on *Alexander* by a Mrs Jackson of Somerset Street, would be unloaded eventually and given to them. Mrs Jackson had been an official of the fund-raising committee founded after the story of the two young convicts and their child became a *cause célèbre* in the London press. But repeated requests to Captain Duncan Sinclair of the *Alexander* throughout early 1788 failed to uncover anything of theirs except a few books. Though English law theoretically regarded felons as 'already dead in law', the handsome young couple were both great favourites of the officers and very useful to the governance of the colony, and David Collins let Kable, the convict, take a civil case, the first in the history of the place. Eventually, on 5 July 1788, before the *Alexander* left Sydney Cove, the case would be heard by a civil court summoned by Judge-Advocate Collins, and Provost-Marshal Harry Brewer now had sufficient eminence to ensure the appearance before it of Captain Sinclair. Sinclair being unable to produce the goods collected for the Kables, they received a judgment in their favour to the value of £15. Reverend Johnson was delighted, since Mrs Jackson had had him place the goods on *Alexander* and he was abashed that they had been pilfered by sailors during the voyage. The young couple seemed to incarnate Johnson's belief in redemption in general, and in redemption here, in this un-churched place, in particular.

For young Henry, that court case was a new experience, the first time he saw the law as *his* lever, *his* weapon of equity, and it would never afterwards be far from his hand. Many years later, in 1807, Governor Bligh of New South Wales could claim that Kable and his partners ruined competitors in the nascent New South Wales shipping business 'with constant litigation and infamous prosecutions in the courts'. That first of all civil actions in 1788 had given Henry ideas.

Another convict who, like McEntire and the Kable family, lived in as privileged a position as the netherworld could offer a felon, in a society where there were not enough public officials to attend to all tasks, was Will Bryant, the former smuggler and attacker of excise men, and now government fisherman. Being a realist, Phillip knew that Bryant would be under pressure from other convicts to create a black market in fish. It was quite possible that one or other of the London convicts might see power and possibility for great leverage in unofficially cornering the fish market in a society where food was the ultimate commodity. To keep Bryant partially insulated from these pressures, a special hut was built for him and for his wife, Mary Broad, on the east side, away from the convict camp, and he was always presented with a portion of the fish he caught. In fact he may have become the first private employer of Sydney Cove, since he had a convict working in his vegetable garden in return for fish. Collins thought him fairly fortunate: 'He wanted for nothing that was necessary, or that was suitable to a person of his description and situation.'

He was, however, proud, and considered himself no criminal. He cherished freedom not just as a concept but as a reality, and was aggrieved he did not possess it. Thus he had a raw political sense, and the darkness in Bryant probably reduced the extent to which he was willing to consider himself lucky.

Through another relatively trusted convict, the first European cattle were about to go wild and become strays on the thin topsoils of New South Wales. The convict cow-herder, Edward Corbett, had confessed to a sailor that he had staved off hunger by stealing goods and giving them to another sailor, Kelly, in return for food. Collins committed Kelly in a hearing to trial by a criminal court. Corbett now knew his turn would be next, and ran away into the bush. So far all this was the penny-ante nicking and fencing which had got people here in the first place, but Corbett's running off had significant results. The same day Corbett ran away, the cattle – four cows and two bulls – strayed from the government farm, a far more grievous loss in the eyes of the administration than was Corbett himself.

Amongst the ark of the First Fleet, these were the first European creatures to go loose in Australia, the first of the hard-hoofed, hard-mouthed beasts in which Europe measured wealth to go out pawing and ripping at the ancient Gondwana soil. Corbett similarly was one of the first Europeans to attempt to live off the land and with the Aborigines, but though the Aboriginal groups he ran in with did not treat him with hostility, they did not welcome him either, or adopt him. While wandering in one of the bays near Sydney Cove, looking for his place amongst the Eora, he saw a convict's head which seemed to have been burned, but which he identified as that of Burn, the young man who had run away on the day Ayres was speared while picking native tea and berries. Absconding convicts often made discoveries, horrid or useful, which they stored away to present to the gentlemen if they should have to return.

The worrying disappearance of the cattle occurred on the eve of George III's birthday, 4 June. It would be celebrated that year in places both distant and tenuously retained by the Crown – in Martinique, for example, at Cape Castle in southern Africa, in Canada and in remote princedoms in India. But Phillip, being such an enthusiast for the constitutional monarchy, ensured that nowhere would it be better celebrated than in this most unsubstantial and grotesque of all the King's possessions. Nowhere more unlikely than Sydney Cove would the subjects' cheers resonate with their varying layers of predictable devotion and all too imaginable ambiguity.

At Phillip's canvas house on the day, healths were drunk to the person of the King, certainly, but above all to the Protestant liberties of mind and property for which he stood. Phillip's housekeeper, Mrs Deborah Brooks, staged a dinner during which the marines' band played patriotic tunes. It was a feast by Sydney Cove standards – Surgeon Worgan lists mutton, pork, ducks,

kangaroo, fish, salads and pies, Portuguese and Spanish wines
and English porter. The extended royal family was toasted, as
well as all Pitt's Cabinet, 'who, it was observed, may be Pitted
against any that ever conducted the affairs of Great Britain'.
There did not seem any concern in Phillip's big Antipodean
marquee that these paragons of British statesmanship to which
the officers were drinking might forget to resupply New South
Wales, but the thought must have been there in some minds.

The day 'was a little damped by our perceiving that the
governor was in great pain', though 'he took every method to
conceal it'. He explained that he had intended to lay the first stone
and name the town Albion that day, but the lack of progress in
breaking the ground and the lack of skilled hands made naming
a premature act. But to honour the royal family he named the
Sydney area the County of Cumberland, the 'boundaries of which
is Broken Bay to the northward and Botany Bay to the southward
as far inland as a range of mountains seen from Port Jackson from
the westward'.

The soldiers were given a pint of porter each, on top of their
regular ration of grog, and men who had been surviving on the
rock named Pinchgut near the east side of the cove were pardoned and brought filthy, scrawny and haggard as shadows back
to the cove. About five in the evening an immense bonfire was lit.
Convicts had been gathering wood for two days and the eucalypt
trees in particular contributed by being great shedders of bark
and branches. Worgan thought the bonfire a noble sight, bigger
than the one traditionally set that day on Tower Hill in London.
A number of convicts formed ranks on the far side of the flames
and greeted Phillip with a verse of God Save the King.

But the Tawny Prince again took some of the honours that

night. The next morning everyone was astonished by the number of thefts that had occurred, in particular from the huts or tents of officers whose servants had been told to keep watch but had wandered away to nearby convict fires for companionable talk and drink. Passionate Captain Meredith of the marines, coming back from the bonfire, found a convict in mid-theft and struck him on the head with a club, disabling him and sending him to hospital. The convict caught so by Meredith, Sam Payton, was a type for which the British public had a lot of time – the gentleman convict, well-dressed and well-spoken. At his 1784 trial at the Old Bailey, Payton had been sixteen years of age. Earlier in the night of the King's birthday, before being stupefied by Captain Meredith's blow, he had stolen shirts, stockings and combs from Lieutenant Furzer's tent or hut, and had them with him in the swag he was carrying.

Payton spent his time awaiting trial under the care of Surgeon White at the hospital. 'I frequently admonished him to think of the perilous circumstances he then stood in.' White suspected he had accomplices and urged him to come up with their names rather than be hung and find oblivion in New South Wales at the age of twenty. With some credibility, Payton claimed that because of his head injury he could not remember robbing Lieutenant Furzer's place, let alone entering Captain Meredith's – though he would suddenly admit to both once sentenced.

As for the missing Corbett, during his nineteen days out of the settlement, he lived chiefly by what he could get by creeping down to the edges of the fledgling town by darkness. When food went missing from the houses of convicts and marines, Corbett was declared an outlaw, a further distinction for him.

On the afternoon of 22 June, a brief earth tremor ran through the settlement. It came, said young David Blackburn, master of the *Supply*, living ashore as so many of the ships' company did at that stage to build up their health, 'from the south-west like the wave of the sea, accompanied by a noise like a distant cannon. The trees shook their tops as if a gale of wind was blowing.' It was the decisive experience for the wandering Corbett, for he presented himself on the edge of the settlement again and was captured by the governor's perhaps most trusted servant, Henry Dodd, a free man who was already showing considerable skill as an agricultural supervisor of convicts.

The returnee Edward Corbett and gentlemanly Sam Payton appeared before the criminal court and were both condemned to death. They were to be hanged the next day at 11.30 am by the executioner convict, Freeman. Samuel Payton took the time to dictate a florid letter to his mother, wife of a well-respected stonemason in London. He no doubt had half an eye to the poignant impact such a letter would have on the London public, to whom, via inevitable publication, he may have been chiefly speaking. 'My dear mother! With what agony of soul do I dedicate the few last moments of my life to bid you an eternal adieu! My doom has been irrevocably fixed, and ere this hour tomorrow I shall have quitted this vale of wretchedness, to enter into an unknown and endless eternity. I will not distress your tender maternal feelings by any long comment on the cause of my present misfortune. Let it therefore suffice to say, that impelled by that strong propensity to evil, which neither the virtuous precepts nor example of the best of parents could eradicate, I have at length fallen an unhappy, though just, victim to my own follies.'

Both Payton and young Corbett 'died penaten', noted

Sergeant Scott, Payton in particular addressing the convicts 'in a pathetic, eloquent and well-directed speech'. Indeed, Reverend Johnson may well have reached his maximum efficacy at the gallows tree that day, 25 June, since both men prayed fervently, 'begging forgiveness of an offended God'. They expressed the hope too that those they had injured would not only forgive them, as they themselves already did all mankind, but would offer up their prayers to a merciful Redeemer. Then they were both turned off by Freeman, the steps taken from beneath first one and then the other, 'and in the agonising moments of the separation of the soul from the body', dangling and jerking, they 'seemed to embrace each other'. The execution of these two young men, said White, had a powerful impact on the convicts who watched. The big fig tree of Sydney Cove had become a regular Tyburn. The manner of death still appalled those Eora who happened to see it.

Thirteen

In mid-July the *Alexander*, *Friendship*, *Borrowdale* and *Prince of Wales* all sailed down the harbour and made ready for the journey home under the direction of Lieutenant Shortland, agent for the transports.

Phillip knew that by these vessels and those already departed there travelled many complaints drafted against him by Major Ross and Captain Campbell and directed to people of influence in Britain, especially to Lord Sydney and Evan Nepean. To Evan Nepean, Ross wrote, 'Take my word for it, there is not a man in this place but wishes to return home, and we have no less than cause, for I believe that never was a set of people so much upon the parish as this garrison, and what little we want, even to a single nail, we must not send to the Commissary for it but must apply to His Excellency, and when we do he always says there is but little come out [from England], and of course it is but little we get.' To Lord Ducie, Campbell complained, 'This man will be everything himself – Never that I have heard of communicates any part of his plan for establishing a colony or carrying on his work to anyone – much less, consult them.' What men like David Collins and Watkin Tench saw as Phillip's admirable composure and prudence, Campbell and Ross saw as selfish and pettifogging remoteness.

There must have been some genuine desperation and stress behind the officially framed pleadings in the dispatches Phillip sent off to Lord Sydney on different returning transports. He hoped, he had told the Secretary of State by the same ships which had carried the complaints of Ross and Campbell, that few convicts would be sent out that year or the next unless they 'should have at least two years provisions on board to land with them'. He suggested that putting provisions on one ship and convicts on another 'must be fatal if the ship carrying the provisions had been lost'.

All the provisions, Phillip told Nepean in a private letter, were now in two wooden buildings, which were thatched. Bloodworth had not yet made enough bricks to undertake the building of more substantial storehouses. 'I am sensible of the risk,' Phillip had confessed, 'but we have no remedy . . . if fifty farmers were sent out with their families, they would do more in one year in rendering this colony independent of the mother country, as to provisions, than a thousand convicts.' He confided to Nepean also that the masters of the ships had departed with whatever bonds and papers they had received on boarding their convicts in England. Surely this was a mistake not only on the part of the masters but on that of Phillip's office, of what might be called his secretariat, which consisted, after Mr Commissary Miller gave up his temporary post as the governor's secretary, of David Collins and other occasional auxiliaries like Harry Brewer.

The upshot was, as Phillip admitted to Nepean, that he had no record of the time for which convicts were sentenced, or the dates of their convictions. 'Some of them, by their own account, have little more than a year to remain,' he wrote, 'and, I'm told, will apply for permission to return to England, or to go to India, in such ships as may be willing to receive them.' But if they decided to remain on the basis of land being granted them, the government would need to support them for at least two years, and it was probable that one-half of them would need support even after that period. 'If, when the time for which they are sentenced expires, the most abandoned and useless were permitted to go to China, in any ship that may stop here, it would be a great advantage to the settlement.' But that was as close to daydream as Phillip could permit himself to come, for the most abandoned and useless were unlikely to get employment on a visiting vessel.

As the last transports vanished, the sense of isolation which would bedevil New South Wales became entrenched. In many cases it was doubtless expressed by those women ashore who had borne children and who saw their fathers, aloft in rigging, waving futilely (or with some cynical relief) as the transports receded down-harbour for the Heads. Captain Tench was sensitive to the nuances of feeling occasioned by the departure, the 'anxiety to communicate to our friends an account of our situation', which only the departing ships could relieve with the letters and reports they carried. Similarly, he wrote understatedly, 'It was impossible to behold without emotion the departure of the ships.' But the naval vessels *Supply* and *Sirius*, which were on station at Port Jackson, remained.

The convicts' experience of the world of authority, of the prisons and the hulks, made the idea they would be abandoned in their little huts on this abominably distant foreshore not unlikely to their minds. They did not know, and neither did Arthur Phillip, that one of the factors guaranteeing their future was that the criminal arts had not been diminished in Britain by their removal, that the gaols and hulks were newly, densely crowded. The government, which had thought of Phillip's fleet as perhaps the final answer to overcrowding, now knew it was but a partial relief. The inhabitants of New South Wales – or as the British press still referred to it, Botany Bay – did not know that their strange new domicile would figure more permanently in the plans of the Home Office.

On the three convict transports going home, but not by China – *Alexander*, *Friendship* and *Prince of Wales* – the crews suffered from the symptoms of scurvy and diarrhoea, especially of the kind called bloody flux. Surgeons like White had been assiduous in preaching their gospel of fruit and vegetables, but often the sailors, and even the convicts they had left behind in Sydney Cove, preferred their rough, salted food to any form of fruit, which after years of salt overload they found too acidic for their taste. And in any case, Sydney, unlike Rio, did not abound in obviously succulent native fruit. Scurvy sapped the strength of the crew of the *Alexander* and the *Friendship* to such an extent on their journey back to England that the *Friendship* had to be scuttled in the Straits of Macassar on 28 October, and her survivors transferred to the *Alexander*. It would be 28 May 1789 before the *Alexander* arrived off the Isle of Wight. The *Prince of Wales* had gone home by way of Cape Horn and reached Rio with its crew in great distress, but got home at Deptford a little earlier than *Alexander* on 30 April 1789.

These journeys undermined the assumption that scurvy could somehow be held at bay when it came to a long journey out to New South Wales, a sojourn in Sydney, and a return.

~

After the ships left, mutual small conflicts between black and white continued. On Thursday 21 August, two canoes landed

Eora people on the west side of the cove. Some of them distracted an officer with talk while others speared a goat. Grabbing the dead goat, the party decamped. They were pursued in a boat but the chase was given up. In Lieutenant Bradley's terms, 'It was too late, either to recover the goat or discover the thief.' There is no doubting Bradley's sincerity in defining the incident as the work of a *thief*.

As Bradley and the other gentlemen of New South Wales well knew, the Enclosure Acts in Britain had established a system in which the ordinary peasant's access to game on common ground, even to a rabbit for his pot, had vanished. The landlords of large estates were endowed with fishing and game rights which once were more commonly held. Many poachers would be sent to Botany Bay for entering enclosed land and taking, or trying to take, game or fish. Yet when birds and animals were shot in the woods about Sydney Cove, often to the great excitement of White and Tench, the enthusiastic naturalists, or fish taken from the harbour, it was done without any enquiry as to pre-existing rights, and the natives' stealing of a goat seemed as culpable an act to Bradley as the stealing of game under the Enclosure Acts.

Some commentators wish to attribute this failure of perception to malice, but it seems more a failure of cultural imagination. Many of the officers, including Phillip, were the sort of men who fancied themselves as well informed on the matter of savages as it was possible to be, and genuinely desired to behave with good will. Phillip recently had written to Nepean a letter (which had gone off with the returning transports) asking for government aid to supply clothing for the natives, which he believed they would accept gratefully. The failure to see any native claim on land and water and animals was a sad lapse of empathy which would blight the settlement's present and future, and produce victims on both sides of the divide, many more – in the end – on the side of the Eora.

~

The earth seemed to Phillip as resistant to kindly gestures as the natives. The first crop that year came from the mere ten to fifteen acres of wheat the convict supervisors had been able to persuade their fellows to plant in Phillip's government farm, and some further acres of corn. Much of the planting had failed to germinate and the crop promised to produce only enough for seed. Phillip calmly attributed the disaster to the seeds' having been overheated on the long journey from England and having been planted under a severe Australian summer sun.

Aware of coming famine after the crop's poor showing, Phillip approached his friend John Hunter and told him he had decided to send Hunter's cranky converted frigate, *Sirius*, to Cape Town 'in order to procure grain and at the same time what quantity of flour and provisions she can receive'. He wanted Hunter to leave behind his guns, powder, shot and other impedimenta to enable the *Sirius* to make as much speed and have as much deck space for supplies as possible.

At the time, Hunter was using an old convict on the task of caulking the ship. The fellow was making a bad job of it, but Hunter was unable to use his carpenter since that gentleman was ashore working non-stop for Phillip, building public and private structures. Captain Hunter was, however, a seaman since childhood, and showed all the alacrity and contempt of low grievance that was the mark of a good officer. The *Sirius* quickly prepared and set out on its emergency mission on 2 October. Because of the wind directions around the south of the Earth below 40 degrees, Hunter intended to sail east to Cape Town by way of Cape Horn, and then return to Sydney from the west. That is, he meant to sail around the world, on a track south of 40 degrees, a most gallant undertaking. He and Phillip must, at dead of night, when renal pain and discomfort woke the governor in his bed, and dreams of past *Sirius* near-misses woke Hunter in his, have wondered whether *Sirius* would survive such a circum-global shaking of its timbers.

The departure of *Sirius* left only the tiny *Supply* in Port Jackson, in the harbour which had recently teemed with ships. There must have been hope in the Eora clans that now the great ships had gone, the interlopers might wither. Many of them already showed harrowed faces to the blank bush of the hinterland or the dazzle of Port Jackson. Every year in New South Wales, Collins would later tell his father, a man aged two years. The disintegration of these intrusive white souls might sometimes have seemed almost certain to some native observers, as well as to Phillip and Ross.

But as the Antipodean spring came on, Phillip had plans to spread his hold on the earth, and prepared to send part of the garrison and a number of male and female convicts up the Parramatta River, to the extension of Port Jackson which he had explored the previous spring, to begin a new settlement at Rose Hill, or what would be called, in ordinary daily usage, Parramatta. He was pleased to appoint Major Ross the commandant of this inland settlement fifteen miles from Sydney Cove, and he seems also to have recognised that this major of marines would be competent when less irritated by the presence of a governor who did not treat him like a peer. Secretly, Phillip had decided that Rose Hill would be the place of his principal city, because it was surrounded by good farming land, and 'was beyond the reach of enemy naval bombardment', a reference to a grievance Ross had held against him during the previous months in Sydney and had complained to the Home Secretary about – that the marines had no point, or stronghold, where they could muster and resist civil unrest or enemy attack.

Ross and a garrison of twenty marines occupied the open ground by the banks of the Parramatta below Rose Hill, and Governor Phillip and the Surveyor General, Augustus Alt, accompanied by further marines and convicts, travelled to Rose Hill and marked out the town. Alt was a mature soldier with an expertise in surveying, more aged than Phillip, but like him a man raised in a German household. Phillip and Alt were able to converse in German as they worked at this pleasant task of city-making on the banks of the Parramatta.

Phillip was determined to end 'this state of petty warfare and endless uncertainty' between the races. He intended to kidnap one or more natives and retain them as hostages-cum-language teachers-cum-diplomats in Sydney Cove. He knew and seems to have accepted this would bring things to a head, either by inflaming the natives to vengeance, or preferably by creating a dialogue. Arthur Phillip explained the reasons for such an abduction to Lord Sydney: 'It was absolutely necessary that we should attain their language, or teach them ours, that the means of redress might be pointed out to them, if they are injured, and to reconcile them by showing the many advantages they would enjoy by mixing with us.'

On 30 December, Phillip sent two boats down the harbour under the command of Lieutenant Ball of the *Supply* and Lieutenant George Johnston of the marines with orders to seize some of the natives. At Manly Cove 'several Indians' were seen standing on the beach, 'who were enticed by courteous behaviour and a few presents to enter into conversation'. Two men who waded out to the boats were seized in the shallows, and the rest fled, but the yells of the two who had been taken quickly brought them back with many others, some of whom were armed with their long spears. One of the captured natives dragged the sailor who had hold of him into deeper water so the sailor had to let him go, and the native got away. The other captive, a slighter young native, was tumbled into one of the boats.

There was an immediate counter-attack on the boats – the natives 'threw spears, stones, firebrands, and whatever else presented itself, at the boats, nor did they retreat, agreeable to their former custom, until many muskets were fired over them'.

The male native they had fastened by ropes to the thwarts of the boat 'set up the most piercing and lamentable cries of distress'. He seemed to believe that he would be immediately murdered. His arrival at Sydney Cove was a sensation, women and children and off-duty marines milling about him. Most people in the Cove had not seen a native at close quarters for a year. Like everyone else, Tench rushed down from his hut to assess the hostage. He appeared to be about 30 years old, not tall but robustly made, 'and of a countenance which, under happier circumstances, I thought would display manliness and sensibility'. He was very agitated and the crowds who pressed round him did not help calm him. Every attempt was made to reassure him as he was escorted to the governor's brick house, now finished adequately enough for Arthur Phillip to live there. Someone touched the small bell which hung over the vice-regal door and the man started with horror. In a soft, musical voice, the native wondered at all he saw, not least at people hanging out the first-floor window, which he attributed to some men walking on others' shoulders. That lunchtime, calmer now, intensely observed by Arthur Phillip and fed by Mrs Deborah Brooks, wife of *Sirius*'s bosun, he dined at a side table at the governor's, 'and ate heartily of fish and ducks, which he first cooled'. He drank nothing but water, and on being shown that he should not wipe his hands on the chair he sat on, he used a towel 'with great cleanliness and decency'. It was observed that his front incisor tooth was missing, and it was later learned by the governor that it had been removed at initiation.

Phillip watched the Aborigine with less flippancy than the crowd who had accompanied him to the governor's house. As part of the potential peace-making between Phillip and the young man, his hair was close cut and combed and his beard shaved – though he did not submit to any of this until he saw the same work done on a sailor or convict. He seemed to be delighted with his shorn hair, full of vermin as it was, which he proceeded to eat, and only the 'disgusted abhorrence of the Europeans made him leave off'. He was now immersed in a tub of water and soap and Watkin Tench had the honour to perform part of the scrub.

Despite the young man's accommodating nature, he resisted telling people his name, and the governor therefore called him Manly, after the cove he came from. He seemed to belong to the Manly people named the Gayimai, but like all Eora speakers was known by other clans and shared various reciprocal hunting, fishing and ceremonial rights with them. To prevent his escape, a handcuff with a rope attached to it was fastened round his left wrist, and at first it seemed to delight him, since he called it *ben-gad-ee* (ornament). In the government house yard, he cooked his supper of fish himself that night, throwing it undressed onto the fire, then rubbing off the scales after cooking, peeling the outside with his teeth and eating it, and only later gutting it and laying the entrails on the fire to cook. An unnamed convict was selected to sleep in the same hut with him and to be his companion, or as Tench inevitably wrote, 'his keeper', wherever he went.

The next morning, as a cure for his depression, he was led across the stream and past the parade ground through the men's and women's camps to the observatory and introduced to Dawes, the young astronomer, who like Collins had a scholarly interest in the natives and would soon start putting together a dictionary of Eora now that contact had been reinitiated. It seemed that the purpose of this excursion was to amuse and instruct the native, not to parade him for mockery. But the camp housed men and women to whom all of life was a mock, and so there must have been hoots and catcalls.

The native could see across the water to the north side, where on a sandstone cliff-face a great rock-pecking depiction of a sperm whale had been made by people ritually and tribally connected to him. Spotting also the smoke of a fire lit by his fellows in the northern distance, 'he looked earnestly at it, and sighing deeply two or three times, uttered the word '*Gw-eè-un* [fire]'. Although depressed and despairing, he consumed eight fish for breakfast, each weighing about a pound. Then he turned his back to the fire and thought hard, but lying so close that at last the fabric of the shirt he had been given caught flame, and he had to be saved.

This young man of subtle and soulful features fascinated Phillip. On New Year's Day, Manly, as he was still called, dined heartily on fish and roast pork while sitting on a chest near a window, out of which, when he was finished eating, 'he would have thrown his plate, had he not been prevented'. A band was playing in the next room, and after the cloth was removed one of the company sang in a very soft and superior style. Stretching out on his chest, and putting his hat over his head, the native hostage fell asleep.

Phillip ordered now that he be taken back to Manly Cove for a visit, so that his people could see he had not been hurt. A longboat carrying armed marines conveyed him close to shore so that he could speak to natives on the beach, or those who edgily waded close. He chatted to his people with a good humour which even survived the return to Sydney. Some of his kinsmen obviously urged him to escape, but he pointed to an iron fetter on his leg. He told them he was kept at Warrane, Sydney Cove.

He was taken back to Manly again two days later, but no natives came near the beach this time, so that he and his keeper were let ashore to enable him to place a present of three birds, shot on the way down-harbour by members of the boat crew, into a bark basket left on the beach. He returned to the longboat without having heard a word of either acceptance or rejection. Either his clan considered him vitiated by his contact with the Europeans, or else they were frightened that he was placed on the shore as a bait to attract them, and that they would end up in his position.

Perhaps he realised he would never be an intimate of his people again, and he released his real name, or at least one of his names, to his captors. It was Arabanoo. The fleet's children, still impressed by his novelty, would flock around him, and he treated them with great sensitivity – 'if he was eating, [he] offered them the choicest morsels'. He does not seem to have had a volatile disposition and to have been wistful and gentle by nature.

Since everyone, including Phillip, was enchanted by him, his continued presence at government house almost became its own point. The fact was he did not learn English quickly, at least not to the point where he could make Phillip any wiser on the grievances of the natives.

And though he was an honoured courtier and ambassador during the day, every night Arabanoo was locked in with his convict. As he became aware that his rations would be regularly supplied, he ate less voraciously than he had on his first return from Manly, when he had eaten a supper of two kangaroo rats, 'each the size of a moderate rabbit, and in addition not less than three pounds of fish'.

These dietary details were recorded by young Watkin Tench, whose fascination with Arabanoo was based on his instinctive belief that the native was somehow Watkin on the far side of a dark mirror. If he could read the native, and the native read him, the humanity of both of them would be enlarged. Arabanoo's appetites and actions were therefore of crucial interest. Tench recorded, for example, a small excursion the native had on the *Supply* when it left for Norfolk Island in February 1789. Arabanoo and the governor and other gentlemen were aboard *Supply* simply for the journey down the harbour, but the native was in an agitated state as the vessel was lifted by the great swell of the Pacific through Port Jackson's heads. By now he had been freed from his shackle and was as attached in friendship to Phillip and Tench and others as they were to him, yet he seemed to fear they were taking him out of the known world, and every attempt to reassure him failed. Near North Head, he lunged overboard and struck out for Manly, attempting to dive, 'at which he was known to be very expert'. But his new clothes kept him up and he was unable to get more than his head underwater. Picked up, he struggled, and on board sat aside, melancholy and dispirited. His experience of having clothed himself in alien fabric that took away his power in the water served him as great proof of the inadvisability of his situation. But when the governor and his other friends descended into a boat to return to Sydney Cove and he heard them calling him to join them, 'his cheerfulness and alacrity of temper immediately returned and lasted during the remainder of the day. The dread of being carried away, on an element of whose boundary he could form no conception, joined to the uncertainty of our intention towards him, unquestionably caused him to act as he did', wrote Tench.

Still Arabanoo's presence brought no quick solution to the relations between the Aborigines and newcomers. On 6 March 1789, sixteen convicts, feeling vengeful towards the natives, left their work at the brick kilns set up by James Bloodworth to the south-west of the settlement and, without permission, marched south on the track which snaked along a forested ridge above bushy coastal headlands and beaches on one side and lagoons to the west, then down to the north side of Botany Bay. They had been troubled by occasional Eora visits to their camp, and had none of His Excellency's lenient feelings towards native murderers of convicts. They were also discontented with the sameness and nature of their short rations. They meant to attack the Botany Bay natives and relieve them of their fishing tackle and spears. So began the first vigilante expedition in New South Wales. 'A body of Indians, who had probably seen them set out, and had penetrated their intention from experience, suddenly fell upon them. Our heroes were immediately routed . . . in their flight one was killed, and seven were wounded, for the most part severely.' Those who ran back to Sydney gave the alarm, and a detachment of marines was ordered to march to the relief of the wounded, but the natives had disappeared and the detachment brought back the body of the man who was killed. At first the convicts claimed they had gone down to Botany Bay to pick sweet tea and had been assaulted without provocation by the natives, 'with whom they had no wish to quarrel'. Gradually, their story developed holes.

Seven of the survivors of this expedition appeared before the criminal court and were sentenced to receive each 150 lashes and wear an iron on the leg for a year, to prevent them from straggling beyond the limits prescribed to them. Tied up in front of the provisions store, they were punished before the assembled convicts. One of them was a man approaching 60 years, John Turner, who had once stolen 28 gallons of small beer from a landing in Kent.

For this flaying, the governor made a point that Arabanoo should accompany him down to the triangles in front of the stores, and the reason for the punishment was explained to the native, both 'the cause and the necessity of it; but he displayed on the occasion symptoms of disgust and terror only'.

At this time, for lack of any replenishment, and until *Sirius* returned from Cape Town, the ration had been reduced to 4 pounds of flour, 2½ pounds of pork and 1½ pounds of rice. The need for more than that in both quantity and variety was legible in the curio-hunting expedition the brick-kiln men had recently engaged in. Phillip had needed to reduce the working hours: now the working day lasted from sunrise to one o'clock. The same regulations operated for the people up the river at the newly surveyed settlement at Rose Hill. People could receive 10 pounds of fish as the equivalent of their 2½ pounds of pork, if fish were available, as it was intermittently.

As in so many other areas, Watkin Tench gives us a frank and telling example of how people lived then. 'The pork and rice were brought with us from England: the pork had been salted between three and four years, and every grain of rice was a moving body, from the inhabitants lodged in it. We soon left off boiling the pork, as it had become so old and dry that it shrank one-half in its dimensions when so dressed. Our usual method of cooking it was to cut off the daily morsel and toast it on a fork before the fire, catching the drops which fell on a slice of bread or in a saucer of rice.'

The shortage of pease, compacted pea porridge, deprived people of their chief source of vitamin B, and increased their vulnerability to infection, which showed up in a hollowed-out appearance and leg ulcers.

Arabanoo seemed exempt from these rations, and this surely became a cause for complaint on the part of some. But in case Arabanoo escaped back to his people, Phillip did not want the natives to know that the newcomers' hold on Sydney Cove was so tenuous, so threatened by hunger.

The Eora were threatened in a new way too. Sergeant Scott noted on 15 April 1789 that he went with a party to cut grass trees for thatching and, landing on a beach, found three natives lying under a rock, a man and two boys, but one of the latter dead from what looked like smallpox. Phillip took Arabanoo and a surgeon immediately by boat to the spot. It is interesting that the idea of smallpox amongst the natives aroused no great concern for their own safety amongst the whites. To a seaman like Arthur Phillip, scurvy, with its combination of wasting ailments, its lesions and its strange hellishness of depression, was of far more concern than would be a smallpox outbreak.

Though it could be lethal, smallpox was a disease most of the residents of Sydney Cove were used to. Many British people of all classes carried the pitted faces of survivors of the illness. The comeliest of Sydney's transported women were marked by having suffered smallpox earlier in their lives. By the standards of the eighteenth century it was eminently survivable, and on top of that, it seems that from early in the century, many Englishmen and women had already been inoculated against it. Indeed, that up-to-date surgeon, John White, had carried with him on Phillip's fleet a flask of 'variolous material', *variola* being the Latin name of smallpox, just in case he needed to inoculate the young against an outbreak in the penal colony. Phillip would soon check with White whether that tissue had somehow escaped its flask and thus spread itself to the natives.

Visiting the beach in Port Jackson where the sufferers had earlier been seen, Phillip and his boat party found an old man stretched before a few burning sticks. A boy of nine or ten years of age was pouring water on his head from a shell. The boy had the lesions on his skin too. Near them lay a female child, dead, and a little further away, her mother. 'The body of the woman showed that famine, super-added to disease, had occasioned her death: eruptions covered the poor boy from head to foot and the old man was so reduced that he was with difficulty got into the boat.' Arabanoo worked with his hands digging sand to prepare a grave for the dead girl – the officers did not point out to him the female corpse nearby. He 'then lined the cavity completely with grass and put the body into it, covering it also with grass, and then filled the hole'.

The man and boy were taken back to Surgeon White's hospital in Sydney Cove, where they were placed in a special quarantine hut.

Boat crews began to see dead natives everywhere, the bodies abandoned by streams and on beaches, or littering caves. The disease disqualified the victim from receiving from his fellow Eora the normal beneficent funeral rituals. The binding up of a body with various talismatic possessions in a sort of death canoe of paperbark, or the burial in shallow earth, or ceremonial cremation – all of which seemed to have been previously practised in the Sydney area – no longer occurred.

In Surgeon White's quarantine hut, the older native suffering from the disease looked into his son's cot, 'patted him gently on the bosom; and with dying eyes seemed to recommend him to our humanity and protection'. The boy's name, it appeared, was Nanbaree, for his father, shivering, called to him out of a swollen throat. When Nanbaree's father died, the boy is said to have surveyed the corpse without emotion and simply exclaimed: 'Bo-ee [dead]'. It was the gracious Arabanoo who placed the old man's body in its grave. Arabanoo was tentative about whether the body should be buried or burned, and Tench read this as his being solicitous about which ceremony would most gratify the governor. His hesitation might rather have come from the fact that he was not of the same blood as the dead man, and so was not entitled to carry out the full funeral rite. In any case, his behaviour that day, his tenderness and generosity towards the ill, persuaded Phillip to release him from his leg bracelet for good.

Nanbaree, the boy, slowly recovered. One day, offered fish, he responded suddenly with appetite and began cooking them at once on an open fire-pit. Despite the idea of quarantine, contagion was poorly understood, and so was the extent of the risk Arabanoo was running, and had earlier run on the beach, burying the dead child. Collins reported that many of the children of the fleet visited Nanbaree and another native child in hospital, and none of them caught smallpox. An American sailor from HMS *Supply*, however, not Nagle but another, was infected and soon after died. Two more Aborigines suffering from smallpox, a young man and a girl about fourteen, were also brought in by the governor's boat. The young man died after three days, the girl recovered. The names by which she would become commonly known were Abaroo and Boorong.

An estimated 2000 Eora were perishing of the smallpox virus in Port Jackson. But amongst the white community with their resistance to that infestation, hunger remained the issue: acute enough to undermine health and to corrupt and derange not only convicts, but some of the marines with the duty of guarding the food of Phillip's little penal commonwealth. By now the stores were held in two buildings of brick and stone designed and built behind government house under the supervision of that most promising convict, the bricklayer James Bloodworth, with the help of the former builder's clerk, Harry Brewer. Of Mr Commissary Miller, a shadowy and vulnerable figure who managed the supplies, Phillip would say that he fulfilled the task appointed him 'with the strictest honour and no profit'. Indeed Phillip doubted whether Miller made three shillings out of his faithful dispensation of rations in Sydney – an exceptional claim to respect in the eighteenth-century bureaucracy. Miller, in charge of rations in a society where everyone's body and mind were enslaved to dreams of food and liquor, and in which no form of currency existed, lived off the standard ration himself, despite the impact that had on his health. The stress of distributing food absolutely equally to convict and official alike, and facing the rancour of Major Ross, became an increasing weight on his mind.

One morning in March 1789, Mr Commissary Miller approached his storehouse and saw that the wards or shank of a key were still sitting in the padlock on the door. He had believed till that moment that all the keys were in his possession, and to a man of his disposition, the lock choked with an alien mechanism must have seemed a cosmic disorder. He was able to get the broken piece of key out of the lock, and opening the storehouse, he saw that a large cask had been opened and some provisions removed. He sent for the convict locksmith William Frazier. Earlier, Phillip had called Frazier to government house and showed him some locks for use on a public building and asked his opinion. Frazier asked for a crooked nail to be provided and opened them within seconds. Tench had a low but fascinated opinion of this Yorkshireman, Frazier, who had been transported with his wife, Eleanor Redchester. 'When too lazy to work at his trade, he had turned thief in fifty different shapes; was a traveller of stolen goods; a soldier, and a travelling conjurer. He once confessed to me that he had made a set of tools for a gang of coiners, every man of whom was hanged.'

The same thing was about to happen again, because Frazier told David Collins that he identified the wards, the business end of the key which had become stuck in the lock, as belonging to a key that had been brought to him by Private Joseph Hunt for alteration. Private Hunt had been in continuous trouble since the colony's beginning, but when the guards brought him before David Collins at the courthouse, he turned King's evidence, and he was able to name seven marines from various companies who were in the plot to loot the stores during their rotating sentry duties.

It turned out the key Hunt wanted altered in various ways came from a trunk belonging to the widow of Private Harmsworth, Alice. Private Harmsworth had died in the first few months of Sydney Cove's encampment; Alice had a daughter and son and had already buried another infant son in Sydney soil, as well as her husband, so that she could be described as a vulnerable woman, particularly in the presence of a powerful and dangerous figure like Hunt. Hunt had been sentenced to receive 700 lashes in the past month, was a brutal and brutalised soldier, and felt loyalty to little but his needs.

What had happened with the key was that a sentry-accomplice of Hunt's, doing duty at the door of the store, had inserted the key to enter the storehouse but had heard the night guard of marines approaching. He knew that the lock would be examined by the corporal of the night guard. In haste to remove the key from the lock, he broke it in two.

The plot involved men from each of the companies that made up the garrison. Some were established troublemakers, notably Privates Richard Dukes, James Baker, Richard Asky and Luke Haynes. The previous December all four of them had been lucky to beat a murder charge of having caused the death of Private Thomas Bullmore in a long-ranging brawl in the women's camp over a particular convict girl.

A court-martial now found them all guilty of plundering the

stores. Their execution, carried out on a scaffold erected between the two storehouses, not at the notorious convict hanging tree on the western side of the town, was an agony for the corps of marines. Private Easty, who found it sinister that the gallows had been erected before the sentence was passed upon them, was in the ranks of marines paraded to witness the hangings. By now his coat, like that of other marines, had faded and worn, and his shoes were falling apart. But the military rituals were still maintained, and he had his Brown Bess musket ready to present arms at the solemn moment. He noted that the marines to be executed told the assembled crowd that Hunt, who had escaped with his life, was the 'occasion of all their deaths as he was the first that began the said robbery, but that he received a free pardon. There was hardly a marine present but what shed tears, officers and men'. And yet in a strange way the corps accepted the inevitability of this public hanging. We are left to guess, however, how they accepted Hunt, who indeed received a free pardon and returned to duty in his company. One should not be surprised if they extended a grudging tolerance to him.

There had been less distinguished food plots. Mary Turner, a girl from Worcester, and Tamasin Allen – 'a lusty-ish woman with black hair' – who had earned her New South Wales hunger as an elegant thief by lifting a collection of diamonds and topazes from a client, had conspired earlier that year to steal six heads of cabbages out of a convict's garden. Allen and Turner were sentenced to 50 lashes each, '25 now and 25 on the next provision day – Saturday'. What did future lovers or husbands make of the junked backs of these women? In any case, David Collins's court went on grinding out the accustomed punishments to the hungry and the venal.

Turner had also been involved in the trial of the marines who had thieved from the stores, and had committed perjury in an attempt to save one of them, Private Baker, from the gallows. Captain Campbell and Major Ross had found her impudent and wanted her tried and condemned to death, but David Collins believed there was not enough evidence on which to hang her either as a perjurer or an accessory. Though Phillip called a meeting of marine officers to decide the matter, the officers refused to be drawn in, saying that the business involved 'in itself a point of law and a private disagreement'. It was Collins's business, and Collins had decided. Robbie Ross at Parramatta was outraged by the open recalcitrance of his officers. They had cooperated with Collins and Phillip by sitting on the criminal court against Ross's wishes, and now they were behaving like country lawyers to thwart him. Grievance and dislike ran deep in rancorous letters transmitted by rowboat up and down the Parramatta River in this immense yet strangely claustrophobic colony.

As the smallpox continued to rage among the Aborigines, Arabanoo became Phillip's liaison to the dying. Phillip was anxious that the Eora, who were in utter terror of the plague, would know the frightful disease was not *his* work, was not some weapon of malice. Arabanoo was taken round the different coves of the harbour to try to make contact with his fellows, but the beaches had been deserted. 'There were no footprints on them and excavations and hollows and caves in the sandstone rocks were clogged with the putrid bodies of dead natives. It seemed as if, flying from the contagion, they had left the dead to bury the dead.' For a time Arabanoo lifted up his hands and eyes 'in silent agony' and at last cried, 'All dead! All dead!', and hung his head in silence. Arabanoo had a word for the disease – *galgalla*, he called it, and so did other natives who survived it.

It was known that people from Macassar regularly visited far northern Australia to collect trepang, the sea cucumbers that were a high-priced delicacy and aphrodisiac throughout Asia. Could they have transmitted smallpox to the natives of the north? Then could it have travelled over time and through inter-tribal contact over a huge distance down to this south-east coast of New South Wales?

Phillip asked such a question in part because this epidemic genuinely puzzled him. The port authorities in both Rio de Janeiro and Cape Town had wanted to know of him on the way out if there were any signs of smallpox on board the fleet, and Phillip had been able to say no. Nor had there been any sign since. And White assured him that the disease did not arise from his flask of material, which was unbroken and secure on a shelf. Convicts did not covet it, and Aborigines themselves had not entered White's storehouse and taken the flask. So had there been a sufferer on the French ships, now gone? Yet Phillip had compared notes with La Pérouse on the very subject, and La Pérouse, having no reason to say otherwise, had declared there were no cases.

Had someone amongst the gentlemen, someone who hated the natives and saw them as an unnecessary complication, somehow managed to let the disease loose on them? There is no evidence of anyone's intention at this early stage to conduct biological warfare. As for the smallpox virus having survived the journey from England, experts believe it was unlikely to have survived in dried crusts or clothing for more than a year. So the question remains how it could have survived so long in the First Fleet to have reached out and struck the Eora fifteen or sixteen months after the arrival of the ships, two years after departing England.

American experience of epidemics amongst the native populations had already taught British surgeons that not all people around the globe had a similar level of immunity or resistance to all diseases, and the appalling size and density of the pustules on the bodies of the dead Eora people, as well as the lightning progress of the disease amongst living natives, was an issue of note to White and the others as well.

Two more serious diseases had certainly been transmitted to the Aboriginal women and men. After their journey on the transports, the spirochaetes of syphilis (*Treponema pallidum*) made an early landing in Sydney, and as a result of rape or willing congress afflicted the oldest society in the world. The abhorred chancres, nodular growths in the genital area, had already appeared in some Aboriginal women, along with the swelling of the lymph nodes which denoted primary-stage syphilis, and the disease had been transmitted to male natives. The pelvic inflammatory disease associated with *Neisseria gonorrhoea* had also by now made its first inroads. Like the smallpox virus, syphilis and gonorrhoea began their long and relatively fast journey north, south and west of the Sydney region, infecting, bewildering and killing people who had not yet seen a European. In a vacuum of immunity such as that offered by the long-protected bloodstreams of native people, European bacteria and viruses took much quicker possession of New South Wales than Phillip himself had the capacity to.

Arabanoo's nursing of the girl Abaroo and the boy Nanbaree

had been the cause of great admiration, and there was some concern that he himself would be attacked by the disease. Even when he grew ill, Tench and Phillip hoped that the symptoms came from a different cause. 'But at length the disease burst forth with irresistible fury.' Everything possible was done for him, given his centrality in both the affections and plans of Arthur Phillip. He allowed himself to be bled by the surgeons and took everything they had to offer. When he died on 18 May, hard-headed Collins declared the death was 'to the great regret of everyone who had witnessed how little of the savage was found in his manner, and how quickly he was substituting in its place a docile, affable, and truly amiable deportment'. The governor, 'who particularly regarded him', had him buried in the garden of the brick and stone government house, and attended the funeral to mourn and honour him. This would not be the first sign of Phillip's affection for the native people, and his feeling of closeness to Arabanoo must have aroused sneers, comment and rumour amongst some.

Fourteen

Not long before Arabanoo had been buried in Phillip's garden, *Sirius* relieved the hysteria over food by reappearing on the broad sweep of Port Jackson, or as it was commonly called, Sydney Harbour. Sent out the previous October to fetch supplies from the Cape of Good Hope, the vessel had survived a hard journey.

During the voyage the ship's company was afflicted with scurvy so badly that at one stage there were only thirteen sailors available to man the watch, along with the carpenter's crew. Maxwell, third lieutenant of the *Sirius*, displayed obvious insanity off Cape Horn, when he crowded on all sail before a gale. 'The captain,' Seaman Nagle remembered, 'got on deck in his shirt and began to take in sail as fast as possible, till she was under snug sail. He asked Mr Maxwell what he was doing.' Maxwell told the captain he would 'tip all nines' – sink the ship, that is – to see whether the vessel would re-emerge from the deep with the same set of damned rascals she was carrying. Hunter, 'finding he was delirious, ordered another officer in his watch'. Maxwell, forcibly carried below three times in one night, would remain permanently deranged.

Captain Hunter and the surgeon set to work in Cape Town to address the scurvy amongst the crew. Nagle said that the disease was so prevalent that when men bit into an apple, pear or peach, blood from their gums would run down their chins. The best cure, he thought, was fresh mutton and vegetables, 'and the captain allowed us to send for as much wine as we thought fit to make use of, the ship's company recovering daily, till we were well and hearty'.

While the *Sirius* was anchored at Robben Island off Cape Town, an incident occurred which showed the strange tension between discipline and the personal pride of veteran seamen, a tension wise commanders like Hunter could handle well. A midshipman presumed to beat the whole ship's company with his rattan cane, 'and being a stripling not more than fifteen years of age, I told him we would not be treated in such a manner by a boy. When we got on shore, five of us out of six left the boat, not intending to return any more. The other four never did return'.

This act of revolution showed that the men were aware Hunter needed them. How could he replace experienced men for a cruise whose only attraction was a return to a hungry penal nether-earth? Hunter had the wit to know it, and sent officers ashore looking for the lost men with the orders that their demeanour towards such veterans as Nagle was to be very amenable. He told his officers to stress to Nagle that his mess-mate Terence Burn missed him and hoped his friend would not abandon him for the journey back to Sydney. Accordingly, Nagle returned to the ship and approached Captain Hunter. Hunter remarked to his first mate, Bradley, in Nagle's hearing, 'No wonder, Mr Bradley, losing our men, when our young officer gives them such abuse against my orders!' He next confined the boy midshipman to his cabin for three weeks, and told Nagle to go to his hammock and get some rest.

They left Cape Town with twelve months supplies for the ship's company, and about four to six months of flour at full ration for the entire settlement, as well as various other stores, including six tons of barley, sundry private items and stores for officers in Sydney, and medical items ordered by Surgeon White. 'A most tremendous and mountainous sea' kept them laying to for 21 days. Surprisingly then, they had good weather until they got off the South Cape of Van Diemen's Land. In the darkness of a storm they found the luminescence of surf breaking higher than their mastheads on huge rocks ahead, and had to wear ship and stand to the westward. Even so, they found themselves with barely enough steerage room, 'embayed' as the term goes, with a heavy sea rolling in upon them and nothing but high cliffs under their lee and the gale to windward blowing them towards the rocks. The captain ordered close-reefed topsails and the mainsail to be set. Nagle heard Hunter cry out above the noise of sea and gale. 'He said she must carry it, or capsize, or carry away the masts, or go on the rocks . . . I don't suppose there was a living soul on board that expected to see daylight.'

This was not the result of any grievous fault of navigation by Hunter or Bradley. It was what happened amidst improperly charted perils with uncertain reliability of chronometers and in bad-luck weather. Hunter would later think it not improper to observe that to that point three days had elapsed without the weather allowing a sun reading, and three nights without a visible star. But suddenly the wind, to use Hunter's phrase, 'favoured us two points', and half-buried in the sea by the press of sail they had on, *Sirius* was able to round the rocky columns of the Tasman Peninsula and continue well eastwards before turning northerly towards Sydney. So the vessel survived one of the planet's most dangerous coasts. Had *Sirius* foundered then, not even Phillip might have been able to control the chaos which hunger would have brought to New South Wales.

On arrival through the heads of Port Jackson and then, to the great joy of all, at Sydney Cove, the *Sirius* looked beaten-about: she was missing the upper sections of her masts (the fore-topgallant masts), had split the upper part of her stem and lost the figurehead of the Duke of Berwick. Lieutenant Maxwell was brought ashore raving to the hospital, and would never recover his sanity. His family sent him a draft of 70 guineas from England, and in his fits he got hold of a hoe and buried the heavy coins singly all over the hospital garden, declaring he'd have a good crop of guineas the next year. If an appropriate ship ever arrived, he would be sent home on it.

Hunter, landing, went straight to report to a grateful Phillip, finding him in the company of 'a native man of this country, who was decently clothed, and seemed to be as much at his ease at the tea table as any person there'. But the smallpox was already at work in Arabanoo, and when Hunter remarked to His Excellency that the foreshores of Port Jackson seemed empty of natives, Phillip could tell him why.

How sincerely must Phillip have nonetheless wrung Hunter's hand. He had nonchalantly circumnavigated the southern globe so that the Earth's unredeemed might live another span of time. It had been a splendid and fraught journey in harsh waters, and he had been prompt about it. There were no newspaper columns or levees to greet Hunter, and yet he had made a remarkable journey without hope of great notice or publicity. What in the northern hemisphere would have gained him renown gained him here an invitation to the governor's dinner table, with the proviso that applied to all officers so honoured, that they bring with them their own bread roll.

Phillip could tell himself that his forthright decisions had saved the experiment in Sydney Cove, on Norfolk Island and in Parramatta. But he would as promptly have acknowledged Hunter's execution of policy.

Book Two

Fifteen

The departure of the First Fleet from Britain had been designed to create space in Newgate, in the hulks and the county gaols, once and for all. There had been no indication from any government document of 1786–87 that it was meant to be followed by further fleets and transports. But Phillip would have felt more secure about being resupplied from England if he knew about the speed with which all the vacated space created by his fleet had been filled. At the time Phillip was appointed, Botany Bay was perceived as a once-and-for-all alleviation of pressure on Britain's penal system. Now it might need to become a habitual one.

By August 1787, three months after Phillip's fleet had sailed, the Sheriff of London and Middlesex, Mr Bloxham, had written to Lord Sydney about the problem of overcrowding in Newgate gaol. Most of the 700 Newgate prisoners were living in crowded wards designed for two dozen people and crammed with twice as many. The sheriff worried about the coming winter, and the prospect of death from congestive disease and gaol fever (typhus) amongst his charges. Throughout Britain, gaolers wrote to complain that they had been promised that they would be able to move some of their prisoners down to the hulks once the convict fleet left in May 1787, and this promise had not been kept.

In October 1788, William Richards, the reputable London merchant contracted for the First Fleet, sent to the Treasury Department a detailed proposal for the transportation of further convicts. It was referred to the Home Office and the Navy Board. When Lord Sydney was asked about future plans, he told the Treasury he wanted to send at least 200 women from Newgate and the county gaols to New South Wales, but only when favourable reports of the new colony's progress arrived. Just in case the women could be transported, Richards was given a contract to 'take up' a suitable ship, and in November 1788 officials looked over a 401-ton ship named *Lady Juliana* at the Royal Navy's Deptford dockyard and found her to be fit to transport convicts, provided her hull was newly caulked and sheathed with copper. Richards was to be paid 9s 6d per ton for the hire of the ship for the outward voyage. While the *Lady Juliana* was in port he would be allocated ninepence per day for each adult convict on board, to provide them with fresh provisions, and while the ship was at sea, he was budgeted sixpence per day to supply the women with sea provisions. The charter party, or contract, also required the ship to make calls for fresh provisions at Teneriffe, Rio de Janeiro and the Cape of Good Hope, just as the First Fleet had been instructed to do.

Mr Richards appointed George Aitken her master. Aitken was conscientious in fitting the ship out. He was very willing also to cooperate with the naval agent put aboard her, Lieutenant Thomas Edgar. Edgar had been Captain James Cook's navigator on HMS *Discovery* on Cook's last voyage in 1776–79. A naval colleague would leave us the information that his nickname was Little Bassey because he was unable to pronounce *Blast ye!* in any other way. He was middle-aged and shocked at nothing, and determined to look after the women prisoners' physical and nutritional well-being. A younger man, the surgeon Dr Richard Alley, had a similar regard for the needs for the women. The concern of Edgar and Alley would express itself during the journey of the *Lady Juliana* in ways the respectable Richards could not have predicted.

By the end of 1788 a new outbreak of gaol distemper, a form of typhus, had been reported from Newgate. At the Old Bailey sessions just finished, all windows and doors had been kept open despite the bitter weather, to prevent the spread of the disease. But berths, or cradles, for the convict women aboard the *Lady Juliana* were not yet ready, and no loading would begin for some months. So the women were not immediately moved out of contagious Newgate, and the government, in any case, still hoped to hear from Botany Bay before they brought convict women aboard the ship. If the colony were judged to be in trouble, Captain Aitken might have to transport those aboard *Lady Juliana* to Nova Scotia, despite the hostility of the people of that province to the idea.

The New Year came and went, and it was not until March of 1789 that *Prince of Wales* arrived back in England with the first news of the colony. The Home Office must have been very anxious to get *Lady Juliana* loaded up, since Phillip's dispatches, though hopeful, and telling of a struggling yet healthily located place, were counterbalanced by the utterly negative voices of Ross and Campbell. Undersecretary Nepean put more reliance on Phillip than he did on Ross. There was enough basis to order that *Lady Juliana* could now conscientiously be filled up for her journey.

The *Lady Juliana* had been moved from Deptford to Galleon's Reach just off Greenwich, ten miles downriver from Newgate. One hundred and sixteen women from the prison were embarked during March and April 1789. There was a woman in the death cells of Newgate who would have loved to be with them. Catherine Heyland, in her mid thirties, had been sentenced to death on 2 April 1787, before Phillip's fleet left, for counterfeiting, and while male counterfeiting drew only the hanging sentence, female counterfeiting was subject to the same traditional punishment as witchcraft – burning at the stake. Police had raided a front garret in Lincoln's Inn Fields and seized scissors, files, crucibles, bellows, charcoal, a casting frame, scales, scouring paper, arsenic, *aqua fortis* (nitric acid) and blacking, and various other tools of counterfeiters. They arrested a male, William James, alias Levi, who tried to swallow some of his handiwork, and when arrested vomited black foam on the officer's sleeve.

There had been two women in the room, and down the bodice of one of them, Catherine Heyland, the officials found two bags of counterfeit sixpences. Throughout his own trial James/Levi, intervened frequently to say that Heyland had been innocent and he had merely used her as a hiding post. In court, a young Irish girl named Margaret Sullivan was found guilty of a separate act of counterfeiting, and she and Heyland were both condemned to death. James/Levi was to hang with Sullivan's accomplice in two days time, but Heyland and Sullivan were to be publicly immolated by fire. To enable her to complete an appeal for mercy, Heyland's execution was stayed. *The Times* the next day asked whether mankind must not laugh at long speeches against African slavery when 'we roast a fellow creature alive, for putting a penny-worth of quicksilver into a halfpenny-worth of brass?'.

Mr Bloxham, then Sheriff of the City of London, had a distaste for burning women, and believed Catherine Heyland did not deserve to burn anyhow. He had already been involved in the burning of a female in June the year before, and even though she was mercifully hung or garrotted while tied to the stake and before the flames devoured her, it had been a catastrophic and barbarous affair for everyone involved. Except, that is, for the spectators, who seemed to relish the high drama of burnings.

What can we make, in our own brutal-by-proxy world, of such public savagery? A Westerner who in this age saw eight friends and acquaintances twitch to death at a rope's end, as did the marine garrison of Sydney, or saw a young woman burned alive, as did any gentleman, woman or child who wanted to be a spectator in Newgate Street, would perforce be offered counselling. Not only did Boswell in the spring of 1785 watch nineteen criminals hanged outside Newgate without its spoiling his appetite, but later the same year he persuaded Sir Joshua Reynolds to attend the execution of five convicts at the same place. Perhaps it was the unquestioning certainty that such events were ordained for solemn instruction, for education and grievous sport, and the certainty that God acquiesced with British statute law, that made them less shocking to the mind of the eighteenth-century felon, soldier or citizen.

Margaret Sullivan seemed to face her unspeakable death in the spring of 1788 with great courage. She spent her last evening praying with a priest and rejected the offer of a treat of strawberries from Sheriff Bloxham's wife. On a Wednesday morning a crowd gathered in St Paul's churchyard and around the Old Bailey for the executions. As was normal at such times, neighbouring inns profited from the crush. William James/Levi and Jeremiah Grace, the accomplice of Sullivan, came through the covered walkway from the Debtors' Gate to the roar of 'Hats off' from mannerly gentlemen in the crowd. The chaplain of

Newgate preached for three-quarters of an hour. From her place in the condemned cells, Catherine Heyland heard the crowd, segments of the sermon and the drop of the trapdoor as Grace and James/Levi, to whom her relationship remains a mystery, plummeted into air. Fifteen minutes later Margaret Sullivan, dressed in a penitential white shroud, emerged with the priest. And it was all done as ordered. The morning *Chronicle* of 17 March 1788 records that Sullivan was 'burnt, being first strangled by the stool being taken from under her'. City worthies sat on a viewing platform nearby, the horrified Sheriff Bloxham amongst them.

Friends and strangers sent the doomed Catherine Heyland gifts, letters and messages of support as her month's grace passed and the stake was put in place again. Sheriff Bloxham went searching for the Secretary of State, Parliament having closed for the summer. Wherever Lord Sydney was, visiting some country house, Bloxham found him, was taken to his bedroom, and galloped back to London with a four-day stay of execution, arriving at Newgate two hours before the pyre was due to be set alight. The four days were designed to permit time for the King in Council to order a stay of execution during His Majesty's Pleasure. That pleasure was, as well as indefinite, unpredictable.

So Heyland saw the first lot of women leave Newgate for the *Lady Juliana*, and must have thought their destiny sweeter than hers. Another female counterfeiter, nineteen-year-old Christian Murphy, was meanwhile found guilty and publicly burned at the stake. We are not given any details of the anguish and resistance of victims, nor of the stench of the whole exercise, but if Catherine Heyland, who could hear the crowd and the procedure from the condemned cells, was not by now half-crazed, it must say something for her endurance and spirit.

When, to secure against escapes, *Lady Juliana* moved down-river further to Gravesend, Heyland seemed an unlikely candidate to join it. But out of nowhere, mercy descended on her. George III having recovered from his madness, bells were tolled, cannon were fired, and a restorative deity was praised by choirs in St Paul's. The normally five-day sessions at the Old Bailey in April finished in four days, and a spirit of forgiveness prevailed. The 23 female convicts then under death sentence were brought from their con-demned cell the following day to the Old Bailey. These women, all young, in various states of dress, were told by the recorder that His Majesty had granted pardon to them on condition that they undergo transportation for the terms of their natural lives.

Of the 23 women, only sixteen accepted the offer, a grateful Heyland amongst them. To the amazement of the court, seven refused transportation. Three of them were young accomplices in the same crime of assault and highway robbery. The victim, Solomon, was a glass-blower, who had been walking near Petticoat Lane when he was set upon by the three women who inveigled him away, and using 'very bad expressions', threw him on a bed, with one of them lying on top of him while another held his mouth. During his ordeal they stole 14 guineas and a further 10 shillings from his pockets. The oldest of these three girls, Sarah Cowden, now told the recorder, 'I will die by the laws of my own country before ever I will go abroad for my life. I am innocent and so is Sarah Storer.' Her two accomplices, Storer and Martha Cutler, made similar speeches, raising the issue that it had been on the glass-blower's word alone that the sum stolen had been fixed at 14 guineas and 10 shillings.

The astounded recorder warned that if they did not accept the King's reprieve now, it would be too late thereafter.

Nellie Kerwin, 29 years old, whom one of her shipmates would call 'a female of daring habits', had made a politer refusal of transportation in these words: 'I have two small children; I have no objection to confinement for life; I cannot live long.' She had kept a rakish boarding house for sailors at Gosport near Portsmouth, and was also a bum-boater – that is, she extended credit to seamen between their periods of remuneration as well as providing accommodation for them in port, and arranged berths for them for a commission. She had been found guilty of forging sailors' wills and representing herself as their relative – something like the crime of the Irishwoman Hannah Mullens in the First Fleet. When first sentenced to death, Nellie had to face a jury of matrons, immediately empanelled, who inspected her and reported to the judge that she was 'with quick child', and so would not face the scaffold until after her child was born and established in good health. But now she refused the King's mercy.

The recorder accused the women who refused the royal generosity of trying to delay things until after ships such as the *Lady Juliana* sailed. They were given twelve hours to think about it. If they refused this beneficence again, they would be sent down from the bar and, 'You will depend upon it that you will suffer death with the first culprits, at the next execution.' When that did not change their minds, he ordered them placed in solitary confinement and on a punishment diet until the June assizes.

As the seven hold-outs tested the patience of the Old Bailey and went into their solitary cells, Catherine Heyland, the reprieved forger, had by now escaped Newgate and gratefully boarded the *Lady Juliana* at Gravesend. Even for those already on the *Lady Juliana*, there had been fortunate reprieves. A maidservant named Anne Aborough was the only child of respectable parents willing to take her home and provide for her. 'Under these very favourable circumstances,' wrote Sydney, in response to a petition from them, 'I cannot but feel myself impelled to recommend her to His Majesty's royal mercy as the object of free pardon.' So she was rowed ashore and received back into Britain.

After a month of solitary confinement, the female recusants of Newgate were brought back to the dock of the Old Bailey. Two women immediately accepted the renewed offer of mercy, including Kerwin, as long as the court could give her some time to work out her affairs, 'but not to send me away in a day or two'. But Sarah Cowden was still arguing her innocence and that of her friend Sarah Storer. She would accept transportation if Storer's sentence was mitigated, she said. All the other women, including Storer herself, eventually accepted transportation and were marched from the court. Thus Cowden was left alone, and at last the recorder readmitted her to the ranks of the living. But we do not know if she came to New South Wales as intended, for her record fades out with her embarkation on the *Lady Juliana* in June 1789. Did she escape? And by what means? For there was no further mention of her in the relevant documents, nor can she be found in the records in New South Wales.

In journeying to New South Wales on the *Lady Juliana* and devoting a chapter of his journal to it, the ship's steward, John Nicol, a young Scot, gives us a rare view of the transactions between convict women and seamen. Nicol was a veteran sailor, 35 years old, who thought Captain Aitken 'an excellent humane man'. He had a positive nature himself, believing that aboard one found not 'a great many very bad characters' amongst the women. Most had committed petty crimes, he said. He came to earthy conclusions about why these women were being sent – there were a great proportion who had 'merely been disorderly, that is, streetwalkers, the colony at the time being in great want of women'.

Whilst the ship was in the Thames, he had seen a young Scottish girl die of a broken heart. 'She was young and beautiful, even in the convict dress, but pale as death, and her eyes red with weeping.' She sat alone in the same corner of the deck from morning to night, and did not make any friends. 'Even the time of meals roused her not.' When he offered her consolation as a fellow Caledonian, he found that it was useless: 'If I spoke of Scotland she would wring her hands and sob until I thought her heart would burst. I lent her a Bible and she kissed it and laid it on her lap and wept over it.'

It was Nicol's job to go ashore and buy supplies for the ship, but he also shopped for convict women who had money with them, particularly for a Mrs Elizabeth Barnsley, 'a noted sharper and shoplifter'. Barnsley was a high-class, superbly dressed thief, who had brought a splendid chest of clothes aboard with her and had asked Captain Aitken if she could wear them in lieu of convict dress. The captain refused, and told her she had to wear the convict uniform until the journey began. Nicol was a little shocked and awed by this potent woman. 'She herself told me her family for one hundred years back had been swindlers and highwaymen. She had a brother, a highwayman, who often came to see her as well dressed and genteel in his appearance as any gentleman.' Mrs Elizabeth Barnsley became *Lady Juliana*'s centre of authority and dispenser of favours amongst the women, who were all pleased to serve her and were rewarded with the groceries Steward Nicol bought for her ashore. In the meantime, to add to her other gifts of personality, she became the ship's midwife, one whom Surgeon Alley very much trusted and thus took advice from. He supported, for example, the women's requests for tea and sugar in lieu of part of their meat ration and also suggested that they be supplied with soap. He would eventually ask for 'a supply of child bed linen to be sent on board, for some of the women were pregnant . . .'

Mrs Barnsley had left behind in England a somewhat younger husband, Thomas, a musician by trade, now on the Thames hulk *Ceres*, but he is worth mentioning for his own brio and the fact that he would soon enough be dispatched to New South Wales too. He and an accomplice had stolen a 48-pound box of tea and an expensive trunk full of gentlemen's goods and clothing from the luggage rack of the Wiltshire, Bath and Bristol stagecoach while it was loading at Holborn Bridge. Elizabeth Barnsley, well settled in on *Lady Juliana*, hoped that she would be joined by him in Sydney.

Nicol had been working aboard *Lady Juliana* for three months when the great love of his life came aboard. Seventeen women from Lincoln Castle, riveted irons around their wrists, had come down to Greenwich, travelling 36 hours roped to the outside seats of a coach. Their condition after such a journey in English winter weather was pitiable: they were tattered, pale, muddied and chilblained. And the journey out to the *Lady Juliana*, then in Galleon's Reach, for girls who had never been on a large body of water before, must have completed the disorientation of the journey.

Nicol, as ship's steward and trained blacksmith, had the not entirely thankless task of striking the riveted county prison irons off the women's wrists on his anvil. In fact he could present a bill of 2s 6d to the keeper of the county gaol for each set of shackles he struck open. In a smithy shack on the windswept deck women bent low to have the task completed, and Nicol fell in love with one of them, despite her bedragglement, in the space of performing his task. 'I had fixed my fancy upon her from the moment I knocked the rivet out of her irons upon my anvil, and as firmly resolved to bring her back to England when her time was out, my lawful wife, as ever I did intend anything in my life.'

Sarah Whitelam, the object of this fervour, was a Lincolnshire country girl, thick-accented to Nicol's ear, and perhaps another victim of Enclosure. Nicol had a very broad streak of generosity in his demeanour, which this Lincolnshire girl saw in her extreme situation and latched onto. Not that she struck him as a gross opportunist like some of the London women. She was 'a girl of modest reserved tone, as kind and true a creature as ever lived. I courted her for a week and upwards, and would have married her on the spot had there been a clergyman on board'.

During their courtship Sarah told Nicol that she had borrowed a cloak from an acquaintance, and her friend had maliciously prosecuted her for stealing it, and she was transported for seven years for unjust cause. The sentence was the truth, and the fact that she had served nearly a year of it.

To allow the sort of courtship which Nicol describes, the *Lady Juliana* must have been a relatively relaxed ship, where for their own good the women were allowed on deck for exercise a considerable amount, and some were permitted access to the sailors' quarters to an extent not openly countenanced on most of the First Fleet. Not that Lieutenant Edgar and Captain Aitken were incompetent in managing the ship or maintaining discipline in its other forms. But they were Georgian pragmatists, not evangelical Christians. In a wooden ship of 400 or so tons, there was not a lot of room for private courting, but the poor of the time were used to cramped quarters, to cohabiting in one-room hutches, to copulating by stealth and with minimal privacy. So space for love was not the issue as Nicol chattered away to Sarah Whitelam. Sarah would be pregnant with Nicol's child by the time the ship left England. Thus, as in the First Fleet, the fallen young of Britain were busy at their associations, taking comfort from the random interest of sailors and generating an enlargement of the convict nation towards which they were headed.

Sarah's true crime, to whose record the love-stricken Nicol had no access, was that at Tealby in Lincolnshire, she had stolen an amount of material which included 6 yards of black chintz cotton, a Coventry tammy gown, a Norwich crepe gown, 7 yards of 'black calamomaco', a pink quilted petticoat, a red Duffin cloak, and a quantity more clothing. On the spur of whatever criminality or need, it seemed that she had cleaned out an entire small shop-load.

A number of friends and family of the women of the *Lady Juliana* made plots to rescue particular women before the transport left the Thames. The attempt at Gravesend on the night before sailing was the only successful one – four women of the convict party below decks went over the stern and into a boat. The escapee whose identity we know was 24-year-old Mary Talbot – one of an army of young shoplifters – who fled the ship with her baby, William. But she was later to be recaptured and would find herself in the end, without any of her children, wasting on a ship to New South Wales, the *Mary Ann*, and soon enough yielding up her bones to that soil.

In early June, *Lady Juliana* left the Thames to sail to Spithead off Portsmouth, where it was joined by 90 women from county gaols and five late arrivals from London who had been rushed down chained to the outside of wagons. The last load of women was brought on in Plymouth and it was July 1789 when the *Lady Juliana* sailed with a crowded prison deck.

Indeed, John Nicol says there were 245 women aboard *Lady Juliana* as she left Plymouth. The official records indicate about twenty fewer, but with pardons and vanishings they were not accurate either. To round out the personnel of this convict ship, Nicol tells us that 'We had on board a girl pretty well behaved, who was called by her acquaintance "a daughter of Pitt's",' that is, what gentlemen called 'a by-blow' of William Pitt, the prime minister of Great Britain. She much resembled him, said Nicol, but he did not name her.

'When we were fairly out to sea, every man on board took a wife from among the convicts, they nothing loath.' The same had happened surreptitiously on the First Fleet, but on *Lady Juliana* the practice seemed to be virtually official policy, and relieved the crowding on the convict deck.

As the *Lady Juliana* with Nicol and his pregnant Sarah Whitelam made its solitary way out of English waters, past Ushant and into the Bay of Biscay, it was in a sense a precursor, the first ship of an as yet not fully planned Second Fleet to get away. It carried on board a letter Home Office Undersecretary Evan Nepean had written to his friend Arthur Phillip in Sydney Cove informing him that 'in the course of the autumn I expect that about 1000 more convicts of both sexes will be embarked from the several gaols and dispatched to Port Jackson'.

Sixteen

As far away from Newgate as one could get, on Sydney Cove on 4 June, the King's birthday was celebrated again with a volley fired towards Port Jackson's brilliant sky. That day Phillip gave a dinner to all the officers, and in the evening convicts performed the George Farquhar play, *The Recruiting Officer*, a broad farce written by a hard-up Irish military officer and former actor more than 80 years earlier, a play with legs, however, which poor Lieutenant George Farquhar, sometime recruiting officer himself, did not live to reap financial reward from, dying at the age of 29 just as this play and his other masterpiece, *The Beaux' Strategem*, became a success. *The Recruiting Officer* was very English in a jolly, sentimental, affectionate way, and in telling its central love story, full of mistaken identities, maids posing as ladies, men dressing as women, and other devices, gave a picture of the dodges used by recruiting officers and sergeants to fill His Majesty's forces.

It is poignant to think that the convict cast took to this theatrical option. We do not know who their director was, but there must have been many enthusiastic rehearsals. Young convicts, spat out by Europe, unlikely to be seen by their former fellow citizens again, nonetheless felt bound to reproduce the

European rituals of the theatre, doing so even as others in Sydney Cove were honouring the Tawny Prince in theft and as the Eora struggled through their smallpox epidemic.

English exiles of all stamp would have laughed and cried that June night as the drama temporarily lifted them out of their remoteness, the peculiarity of their situation. Tench wrote a wonderful evocation of this first emergence of European theatre in the netherworld. 'The exhilarating effect of a splendid theatre is well known: and I'm not ashamed to confess that the proper distribution of three or four yards of stained paper, and a dozen farthing candles stuck round the mud walls of a convict hut, failed not to diffuse general complacency on the countenances of sixty persons, of various descriptions, who were assembled to applaud the presentation. Some of the actors acquitted themselves with great spirit, and received the praises of the audience; a prologue and an epilogue, written by one of the performers, was also spoken on the occasion.' Collins said that the performers 'professed no higher aim than "humbly to excite a smile; and their efforts to please were not unattended with applause."'

The fact that somebody brought the text of George Farquhar's *The Recruiting Officer* with them to New South Wales raises the question of which books, other than works of navigation and tides, people had chosen to travel with across the world. The Reverend Johnson's King James Bible and *Book of Common Prayer* are still on display in a small museum in Sydney. King used Jethro Tull's *An Essay on the Principles of Tillage and Vegetation* to plant a garden of wheat on Norfolk Island. Lieutenant Johnston brought on board the *Lady Penrhyn* a number of volumes of *The Spectator*, and they would have circulated around the gentlemen of the fleet for recreational reading. Fenelon's *The Adventures of Telemachus, The Son of Ulysses*, published in two volumes, also came with Lieutenant Johnston. Marshall Turenne's *Military Memoirs and Maxims* and the Reverend Alexander Crudin's *A Complete Concordance with the Holy Scriptures*, together with the *Gentlemen's Magazine* and the *Lady's Magazine*, accompanied officers and midshipmen. Other plays included Nicholas Rowe's *The Tragedy of Lady Jane Grey*, which Lieutenant Ralph Clark was reading at sea on Friday 7 December 1787, and was much affected by – 'she did love her husband but not half as much as I love my adorable Alicia'. Watkin Tench could quote Milton's *Paradise Lost* from memory, and could also recite Oliver Goldsmith's *Deserted Village*. He might have had copies with him. But as a well-rounded eighteenth-century gentleman he certainly owned Adam Ferguson's *An Essay on the History of Civil Society*, which endeavoured in a thorough-going Scot's way to 'set the ancient discipline of moral philosophy upon a modern scientific foundation'. Ferguson's advice was that indigenous people were embodiments of the primitive virtues, and thus should be respected.

It seemed that Watkin or one of his friends owned Oliver Goldsmith's *A Natural History of the Earth and Animated Nature*. When an emu was successfully hunted for the first time, Watkin Tench was able to look up Goldsmith's book and quote from his description of this giant flightless bird which Cook had first seen in Botany Bay in 1770. The construction of the feathers deserved notice, said Tench, finding something that Goldsmith did not refer to – they grew in pairs from a single shaft. Goldsmith had not mentioned either that the creatures could outrun greyhounds, for they had outrun Phillip's.

While Phillip had brought Cook's *A Voyage of the Pacific Ocean*, Collins, who knew he would be judge-advocate, had brought Blackstone's *Commentaries on the Laws of England* and Sir Matthew Hale's *Historia Placitorum Coronae* – texts found in every legal library across the vastening English-speaking world. Interestingly, John Lowes, the assistant surgeon on HMS *Sirius*, carried with him a number of the works of Emanuel Swedenborg. Alternative religions were of some interest to men who saw the Church of England as little more than a ceremonial and suasive arm of government, but who did not want to be fervent in the manner of the Reverend Johnson.

As for the magazines or books which entertained the women of the fleet, those who had their letters, we know very little. No *New Colony's Collection of Authorised Classics* accompanied the First Fleet, merely a random sampling of Western European literary and popular culture, with which the few literate men and women needed to be content.

By the time *Lady Juliana* had left England, Phillip was faced with the continuing problem of convicts saying their time was expired. Phillip's reply, that he regretted he had no records to verify these matters, was 'truly distressing' to many convicts. Several men told the governor that when the records *did* arrive, they would want to be paid for their labour as free men. One such man was mangled by his attempts to be heard. John Cullyhorn claimed to have been told by Major Ross that he could now do what he liked, his term having finished by July 1789. He came over the stream to make a direct appeal to the governor on 29 July 1789 for a full pardon on the grounds that his term was served. In the course of his conversation with Phillip, Cullyhorn asserted that Lieutenant-Governor Ross had told him that there were two years provisions available for any convict who finished their time, and he sought to claim them now. Ross denied having told the convict that, and demanded Cullyhorn be punished as a liar. At Ross's insistence, but with Phillip's consent, poor Cullyhorn was charged with calumny and sentenced to receive 600 lashes and to work in irons for the space of six months. That is, the court, its judgment influenced by a need to shut up the turbulent Ross, ordered what a later historian would rightly call 'a savage (and illegal) punishment for a free Englishman'. For documents arriving in Sydney later would prove Cullyhorn correct – his time had indeed expired.

Privately, Judge-Advocate Collins was not unsympathetic to such people, who were 'most peculiarly and unpleasantly situated'. But the reality was Phillip could afford to advance no person two years of rations. Despite the supplies *Sirius* had brought back from South Africa, by November 1789 the ration had to be reduced by two-thirds again. Amongst other factors, the storehouse supplies had proved to be very appetising to rats and to native marsupials – bush rats, potoroos, bilbies and possums. Nonetheless, said Collins, 'The governor, whose humanity was at all times conspicuous, directed that no alteration should be made in the ration to be issued to the women.'

Despite abiding hunger, by the end of the Antipodean winter of 1789 the camp of Sydney Cove had taken on the look of a permanent town. Two barracks were finished, two storehouses, and the large brick house the governor occupied. Many male and female convicts had brick huts. But the brick-makers were not always the servants of civilisation. Because of ongoing turbulent behaviour at night, and a conviction in the camp that the brickfield convicts who were camped a little way west of town came down to the men's and women's area to steal property, a Jewish Cockney convict named John Harris, a *Mercury* returnee, came to Captain Collins and asked him whether a night guard might be established, a patrol of reputable convicts.

This was an early example of the New South Wales conundrum, the overthrow of Phillip's initial intention that the positions of the free and the condemned should not become blurred. The convicts began to take on an official importance in the great open-air experiment of Sydney that they could not have achieved in Newgate or on the hulks. In a criminal kingdom, a clever and reputable man like Harris ended in a position akin to that of police chief, as, without a free police force to keep order, a night watch of eight convicts was indeed initiated. Collins wrote about this paradox. 'It was to have been wished that a watch established for the preservation of public and private property had been formed of free people, and that necessity had not compelled us . . . to appoint them from a body of men in whose eyes, it could not be denied, the property of individuals had never before been sacred. But there was not any choice.'

For the purpose of the night watch, the settlement was divided into four districts, and three men patrolled each. The watch, it seemed, was guarding the settlement not only from the nocturnal evil of convicts, but from other prowlers also. When one of the night watch stopped a marine in the convicts' compound, Ross viewed it as an insult, and Phillip was forced, wearily, to ensure it did not happen again. So efficient was John Harris's guard that Collins would record that by comparison with Sydney Cove, 'many streets in London were not so well guarded'.

Seventeen

Aging Viscount Sydney had now resigned from the Home Office. His replacement, and Nepean's new superior, was one of Pitt's young cousins and parliamentary colleagues, the 29-year-old William Grenville. Grenville, soon to be Lord Grenville, was an enemy of slavery and a campaigner for the emancipation of Catholics from the legal disadvantages which kept them out of civic life. A future prime minister, he was presently subject to the same political pressures as Sydney had been, and wrote to the Lords Commissioners of the Treasury in early July 1789 telling them, 'His Majesty has therefore been pleased to signify to me his Royal Commands that 1000 of the said convicts should forthwith be sent to New South Wales.' The dispatch of this further 1000 was exclusive of the women already on *Lady Juliana*.

The Navy Board immediately called for tenders from merchants to supply ships and stores. William Richards bid again, but the successful contractor was the slave-trading company Camden, Calvert and King, the largest slave transportation company in Britain. It is on the face of it a curious decision for an abolitionist to make. Perhaps Grenville wanted to wean Camden, Calvert and King off slaves and onto criminals. Grenville was energetic, too, and wished to do away with laxities in the Home Office. If, as a means of turning a new and more efficient page, he gave his ministerial consent to the Navy Board's choice of Camden, Calvert and King, he would come to regret it.

In August the contracts for a second fleet of ships were signed by the Navy Commissioners and the representative of Camden, Calvert and King. As had the charter parties for the First Fleet, they specified the rations for each mess of six male convicts for seven days, and similarly for each mess of six female convicts. The contractors were to be paid a sum of £17 7s 6d for each convict embarked, somewhat less than Richards had quoted. Five pounds would be paid to the contractors once the cabins and bulkheads had been fitted, and £10 when the stores had been loaded and the ships were ready to receive the convicts. The remainder was to be paid when a certificate was received in London from the commissary in New South Wales confirming that the stores had been delivered. There was no money held back pending the delivery in good condition in Sydney Cove of the convicts themselves.

The Australian legend that the British 'dumped' convicts in Australia was enhanced and very nearly justified by the horrors which would characterise this core section of the second flotilla – just as the *Lady Juliana* helped generate the concept that women's ships were 'floating brothels'.

The War Ministry had been thinking about New South Wales too, and decided that the marines who had travelled on the First Fleet would be gradually replaced, in part because of their internal dissension, the unwillingness of Ross to allow marine officers to serve as superintendents of convicts, the fact that half the officers were technically under house arrest over the quarrel about punishing Private Hunt, and because of the other conflicts Ross had with Phillip. During the summer of 1789, from England, Scotland and Ireland, 300 men were recruited for a new corps, and the first 100 privates and NCOs, along with two captains, three lieutenants, an ensign and a surgeon's mate would travel on the transports of the Second Fleet. The new unit, the 102nd Regiment of Foot, would be more commonly called the New South Wales Corps, but they were also referred to, whether ironically or otherwise, as the Botany Bay Rangers.

Three transports – *Neptune*, *Scarborough* and *Surprize* – were readied at Deptford for the journey. In the meantime another store ship had been sent from Spithead six weeks after the female convicts in the *Lady Juliana*. The ship in question was a naval frigate of 879 tons, the HMS *Guardian*, and it left Britain in September 1789 richly burdened with the supplies for which Phillip had asked, and with 25 'artificers', convicts with trades, for whom Phillip had also pleaded. In the crew was fourteen-year-old Thomas Pitt, a cousin of the prime minister. With all it carried, and with its small corps of talented convicts, the *Guardian* represented a secure future for the people of Sydney Cove.

Salvation could not indefinitely come from outside New South Wales. Some had to come from within the colony itself. And one of the iconic figures of redemption from within would be the young Cornish convict, James Ruse. He was the farmer who would maintain throughout his life that he was the first person from the fleet to step ashore on the east coast of New South Wales, when he carried Lieutenant Johnston from the *Supply* to the Botany Bay shore on his shoulders.

The clerks who had drawn up the lists for the First Fleet had not hesitated before including people who had already served the greater part of their sentence. And Ruse had been sentenced in 1782 for burglariously entering a house in Launceston to seven years transportation to Africa. He had spent five years on the depressing and brutal hulk *Dunkirk*, moored off Plymouth, before being loaded on the *Scarborough*. Without verification that Ruse's sentence had expired, Phillip nonetheless knew enough about him from his supervisory work at the government farm in Sydney Cove to decide to embark on an experiment with him, and turn him into New South Wales's first yeoman. Ruse had told Tench, who admired him: 'I was bred a husbandman, near Launcester [Launceston] in Cornwall,' and now Phillip gave him a conditional grant of 30 acres and convict help to clear it in the promising area known as the Crescent on the riverbank near Parramatta/Rose Hill. Phillip also authorised the issue to Ruse of necessary tools and seed for planting. Full title to the land was withheld until Ruse proved himself the first viable farmer.

Phillip, surrounded by men who regularly told him New South Wales could not serve as a place for settled agriculture, wanted to test whether it was possible for a skilled farmer to live off the land. Above all, he needed to rebut the nihilist voices such as that of Major Ross who hated New South Wales with an almost theological passion. 'I do not scruple to pronounce that in the whole world there is not a worst country that what we have seen of this. All that is contiguous to us is so very barren and forbidding that the main truth be said, here nature is reversed.' The perverse behaviour of the convicts confirmed Ross in a sense that he was stuck in an irremediably perverse land, a country of contrary, obdurate gods.

Indeed, it seemed to Ross that New South Wales bore the same motto as Lucifer the fallen angel – *Non Serviam*, I shall not serve. The terms 'will not serve' and 'will not answer' pepper the reflections of many diarists and correspondents, but Ross's above all. Ross, for example, criticised Phillip's choice of Sydney Cove for the settlement, declaring it would 'never answer'.

In the face of Ross's negativity, Ruse would symbolise the resourceful agriculturalist and be a living validation of the idea that the Australian earth was, after all, compliantly fruitful. Phillip's investment of government resources in him was wide-ranging and tipped the scales in Ruse's favour, starting him off with livestock and ultimately building him a brick house.

In legend Ruse is something equivalent to Johnny Appleseed, but not all his industry and energy could fully prevail over the recalcitrant, leached-down and grudging earth along the Parramatta River, and he would later move to the more remote floodplain areas along the Hawkesbury. At the time he got his land grant, there were others Phillip was willing to free and put to the task of sustaining New South Wales. But that was not to happen until he saw what befell this young Cornishman, and how he set about the task.

The other experiment which had been in abeyance was the Aboriginal diplomatic experiment which had ended with Arabanoo's death. Tench says that in making a further capture of natives, Phillip needed, amongst other things, to know 'whether or not the country possessed any resources, by which life might be prolonged'.

Reliable Lieutenant Bradley of the *Sirius* was sent out with two boats to capture natives, a task he found distasteful. Northwards, at Manly Cove, he found a number of natives on the beach, and in the prow of one of the cutters, a seaman held up fish, tempting two robust men, a mature fellow and a young man, into the shallows. 'They eagerly took the fish,' wrote Lieutenant Bradley. 'They were dancing together when the signal was given by me, and the two poor devils were seized and handed into the boat in an instant.' The two captured happened not to be local natives but two formidable visitors from the south side of Port Jackson. Both of them fought ferociously to get away from the melee of soldiers, sailors and convicts, but they were up against numbers, and soon shackles were on them. The other natives rushed from the bush and gathered on both headlands of the cove, shaking their spears and clubs.

Bradley wrote, 'The noise of the men, crying and screaming of the women and children, together with the situation of the two miserable wretches in our possession was really a most distressing scene.' The captives were howling out for help, but the boat pulled away. It was a bad day's business, Bradley thought, 'by far the most unpleasant service I was ever ordered to execute'. He illustrated his journal with a memorable picture of the capture.

At the governor's wharf at Sydney Cove, a crowd gathered to see the natives brought ashore, just as they had gathered to see Arabanoo. The boy Nanbaree, who had survived the smallpox and who now lived at the hospital where White had given him the name of Andrew Snape Hamond Douglas White, to honour White's former naval captain who had recommended him for the chief surgical job in the colony, shouted 'Colby' to the older of the two men and 'Bennelong' to the younger. He had often told Surgeon White about fabled Colby, who was his uncle. Both men still bristled with resistance.

Woolawarre Bennelong (this being just one of many alternative spellings of his name) was judged by Tench to be about 26 years old, of good stature and sturdy appearance, 'with a bold intrepid countenance, which bespoke defiance and revenge'. He was a man of lively, passionate, sociable, humorous character, and was well-advanced in ritual knowledge, ritual being the fuel and physics of his world, what kept it in place, what kept it so lovable and abundant. He did not quite have the *gravitas* and the power of eye to be a full-fledged *carrahdy*, a doctor of high degree, a curer and ritual punishment man. He did not seek solitude or penance. But he was well-liked around the harbour, even on its northern shores and beaches, and southwards too, around the shallow shores of Botany Bay, where people lived who were related to him by marriage, language and the great rituals of corroboree dance and other secret, communal ceremonies. Sometimes, it would be discovered, he fornicated with their women and bravely stood up under a rain of ritual punishment spears and took his scars and was proud of them. He had an ambiguous relationship with his least favourite relatives, the Cameraigal of the north shore, whose women he nonetheless also had a weakness for and in whose country he was at various times permitted to hunt, fish, socialise and join in corroboree – that is, take part in dances which preserved and sustained and continued the earth made by hero ancestors. Bennelong had a range of names in a society where people carried many names, and some of his others were Boinda, Bundabunda and Wogetrowey.

Colby was perhaps 30, more intractable, somewhat shorter but athletic-looking, and 'better fitted for purposes of activity', observed Tench. They had both survived the smallpox – 'indeed Collbee's face was very thickly imprinted with the marks of it'.

Hunter would claim Colby was 'a chief of the Cadigal', the Sydney Cove clan, and Midshipman Fowell called him 'the principal one of the two', and said that his full name was Gringerry Kibba Colby. *Kibba*, or *gibba*, was Eora for rock, and would enter the settlers' English before long – the children of the convicts and the free being commonly accused, in this settlement and beyond, of 'chucking gibbas' at each other. Colby *was* a rock, and behaved like one.

Both natives were taken up to the governor's residence. It was the first time Bennelong and Arthur Phillip saw each other eye to eye, a meeting as fateful and defining as that between Cortéz and Montezuma, or Pizarro and Atuahalpa. Bennelong and Phillip in particular were mutually enchanted and attracted, and both Bennelong and Colby could see through the deference other white people offered him that Phillip was the supreme elder – *Be-anna*, Father, as Arabanoo had called him.

Phillip knew that as with Arabanoo he would need to restrain the two natives to stop them running away. A convict was assigned to each of the men until they should become reconciled to their capture.

Banks had written in the journal of his voyage with Cook about the capture of Tupia, a Polynesian high priest. 'I do not know why I may not keep him as a curiosity, as well as some of my neighbours do lions and tigers at a larger expense than he will probably put me to.' Phillip's motives were perhaps equally as proprietary, but somewhat more elevated.

Nonetheless, the means used to detain the two men were in their way severe – they were tied at night to their keepers by both ankle chain and rope, and slept with them in a locked hut. At this treatment, Colby yielded no gesture of reconciliation. He planned escape. Genial Bennelong, 'though haughty', not only got on well with the Europeans but enjoyed the experience of doing so, and was his people's first enthusiastic anthropologist. Beneath his conviviality was a desire to work out how and what these people meant, and perhaps how to appease them and even make them go away.

After attempting to escape many times, Colby managed it on the night of 12 December 1789, while eating supper with Bennelong and their two minders. Colby was at the door, sitting just on the outside of the hut, and had some rations for his supper, 'which he pretended to be employed about . . . the end of his rope was in the hands of his keeper within; whilst those on the inside were thus amused, he drew the splice of his rope from the shackle and in a moment was over the paling of a yard and out of sight . . . he carried off his whole wardrobe'.

This was bad news for his minder. The convict who had been given charge of Colby received 100 lashes for 'excessive carelessness and want of attention'.

Bennelong had been trying to slip his shackle too, and now became much alarmed, expecting punishment or to be put to death, but after two or three days he became quite composed again. He boarded the *Sirius* without the smallest apprehension for his safety. 'He looked with attention at every part of the ship and expressed much astonishment particularly at the cables.' Bennelong was thus quickly revived by his interest in Phillip and the others. He was considered a family member, if a tethered one. Phillip took him with Nanbaree to the look-out post and signal station on the south head of the harbour, which had been established the December before. Bennelong still wore his leg shackle and despite it was able to put on a display of strength and accuracy by throwing a spear nearly 300 feet against a strong wind 'with great force and exactness'. On the way back the boat stopped near Rose Bay, a cove east of Sydney Cove, and from the boat, Bennelong called to a native woman ashore he was very fond of – a visiting Cameraigal named Barangaroo. Barangaroo and other women waded out and talked, and told Bennelong that Colby was fishing on the other side of the hill, but had been unable to remove the shackle from his leg.

A captive by night, Bennelong had the freedom of the governor's house by day. At Phillip's table, wrote Watkin Tench, Bennelong was quick to make clear to Phillip how many of his people had died of the smallpox epidemic the previous year – he claimed that one in two had perished, 50 per cent. Unlike Arabanoo, Tench observed, Bennelong became immediately fond of 'our viands' and would drink spirits without reluctance, which Colby and Arabanoo had not done. A deadly appetite was thus imbued in Bennelong. But for the moment, wine and spirits did not seem to have a more perceptible impact on him than they did on any one of the gentlemen who sat around him. He liked turtle, too, which he had never eaten before, but which the *Supply* had brought from Lord Howe Island. 'He acquired knowledge, both of our manners and language, faster than his predecessor had done.' He would sing and dance and caper, and talked about all the customs of his country in a mixture of rudimentary English and Eora on his side, and rudimentary Eora and English on Tench's and Phillip's. 'Love and war seemed his favourite pursuits,' wrote Tench, 'in both of which he had suffered severely. His head was disfigured by several scars; a spear had passed through his arm and another through his leg; half of one of his thumbs was carried away, and the mark of a wound appeared on the back of his hand.' But they served as a map of his adventures, and as well as telling the stories of his exploits, an exercise he loved greatly, he was also explaining a concept of blood justice, and preparing the European mind for the idea that they too might need graciously to receive similar wounds for their crimes. The plunders and even the occupation of earth by the Europeans violated the land. Bennelong hoped they could be taught that fact. It might have been one of the reasons he stayed so long in Sydney Cove, and risked his soul.

'But the wound on the back of your hand, Baneelon!' Tench asked him. 'How did you get that?' Bennelong laughed and told Tench it was received in carrying off a lady of the Cameraigal on the north shore of Sydney Harbour, across from Sydney Cove. 'I was dragging her away; she cried aloud, and stuck her teeth in me.'

'And what did you do then?'

'I knocked her down and beat her till she was insensible, and covered with blood.'

The story – Tench intending it to be more amusing than it seems to us – is credible despite the presence of that non-Eora word *insensible*. Bennelong frequently asked the governor to accompany him with the marines in order to punish and even obliterate the Cameraigal, with whom he had both passionate connection and passionate grievance. As for the governor, as well as sometimes calling him *Be-anna*, Bennelong exchanged his own honorific *Woolawarre* with him, calling him by that name, and thus being entitled to call himself *Governor*. The exchange of names was meant to do both parties great honour and convey closeness of soul. *Woolawarre* could have been a very significant name in other ways too, for it seems to derive from the Eora words for Milky Way and depart – Phillip being one who had departed the stars.

Phillip told the former Home Secretary, Lord Sydney, in a letter that he hoped Bennelong 'will soon be able to inform us of their customs and manners'. The Europeans certainly got to know of Bennelong's highest order of recreation: *boon-alliey* – kissing women.

As part of his British training, Bennelong was required to appear at the governor's table in trousers and a red kersey jacket, and Phillip was anxious to make him dependent on clothing. On Sundays the native wore a suit of buff yellow nankeen from China. He was not the least awkward in eating or in performing actions of bowing, drinking healths and returning thanks, all of which he did with a 'scrupulous exactitude'. He would raise his glass and drink a toast to 'the King', a term which Bennelong associated ever after with a glass of wine. Gentlemen tried an experiment on him by mixing brandy and water instead of wine and water, 'but he instantly finds the trick out, and on this occasion he is angry'.

He spoke much of the Cameraigal women, *Cameraigalleons*, as he called them. They were not so much enemy women, but certainly the women of rivals, and were alluring to Bennelong, especially the woman named Barangaroo, whom he said had him under a spell. This glamour of the foreign and the owned might have led to behaviour appalling in European eyes, but it was one of the mechanisms by which ancient societies avoided incest, by marrying out of their family group.

The Europeans had brought with them from the history of the

Americas and of European incursions into the Pacific a concept of tribes and chieftains, and attempting to categorise the New South Wales natives in those terms, found it a difficult task. There were no individual chieftains in Aboriginal society, though groups of elders, men and women, held much collective knowledge and power. There were perhaps two dozen or more clans that participated in the common language of the Sydney area. From the south head of Port Jackson to Sydney Cove, and southwards towards Botany Bay, the people were called Cadi and the tribe was the Cadigal, and Colby was an important man amongst that group. (The ending *gal* meant country.) On the south side of the harbour from Sydney Cove westwards, the tribe were the Wangal, of whom Bennelong was a member. On the opposite, northern, shore of the Parramatta River from the Wangal lived the tribe called the Wallumattagal. Then, on the broader reaches of northern Port Jackson were the Cameraigal, and at Manly the Gayimai, whom Colby and Bennelong had been visiting when captured. These neat divisions merely scratch the surface of the complexity of clans and families and geography. At particular times they all visited each other's territory, and were connected by favours, gestures, swapped names, marriage, ceremonies and ritual knowledge of how to sustain their shared earth and the known world given them by the adventures of their hero ancestors.

And then there were the inland people of the western basin of the Sydney region, the Burramattagal, who would give their name to Parramatta; and the people north of Botany Bay, the Bediagal; and to the south of Botany Bay, the Gweagal: all Eora-speaking, if with their own dialects, and all of them people known to each other. West of Parramatta lay a language group named the Dharug who had many contacts with and similiarities to the Eora, so that some experts count Dharug and Eora the same language. Later, for example, the Gweagal, Bediagal and Dharug would fight guerrilla war in each other's territory (now Sydney's southern and western suburbs), against the Europeans.

Apropos of clan borders, and the density of mystery or ritual sites, Phillip and King (the latter returned on leave from Norfolk Island), were accompanied by Bennelong to Parramatta, and walked to Prospect Hill through 'a pleasant tract of country', which, King remarked – as many an Englishman before and since have – 'appeared like a vast park'. King was impressed by the fact that in this four-mile walk they crossed eight Aboriginal districts. Phillip would record them in a language notebook.

In fact the authority system of the natives was like that of Freemasonry, but not even as pyramidal as that, for there was no overall grand master and there were many lodges with many masters. *Carradhys*, shamans, were other sources of power: healers and condemners, ritual punishment men, and binders and loosers of sins and curses.

By April 1790, the shackle was removed from Bennelong's ankle. Arthur Phillip demonstrated his trust, as he could never do with a convict, by letting Bennelong wear a short sword and belt, Bennelong being 'not a little pleased at this mark of confidence'. As well, in a time of great scarcity, Bennelong was still well supplied with rations. Phillip's stated motivation was the same as earlier, with Arabanoo: 'Had he [Bennelong] penetrated our state, perhaps he might have given his countrymen such a description of our diminished numbers, and diminished strength, as would have emboldened them to become more troublesome.' But Phillip was indulgent as well. Bennelong's allowance was received each week from the commissary stores by the governor's steward, the Frenchman Bernard de Maliez, 'but the ration of a week was insufficient to have kept him for a day'. The deficiency was made up with fish and Indian corn. For if he were hungry, Bennelong became furious or melancholy.

He was also in love and had a woman to pursue. On 3 May, he pretended illness, and awakening the steward, Maliez, who lay in the room with him, 'very artfully' begged to be taken downstairs, no doubt under apparent pressure of diarrhoea. Bennelong 'no sooner found himself in a back-yard, than he nimbly leaped over a slight paling, and bid us adieu'.

Along with his desire for Barangaroo, whom he probably knew Colby was trying to seduce, homesickness and hunger motivated Bennelong's escape. Collins was a little affronted that the governor's every indulgence had not delayed Bennelong's decamping. But Bennelong had agendas beyond Collins's imagining, including the necessity of performing ceremonials that were pending, and of reporting his experiences of the Europeans.

John Hunter, hearing of Bennelong's escape, made the joke of the season by saying Bennelong had taken 'French leave'. When boat crews, sent around to look for Bennelong, called his name in various coves and bays of Port Jackson, the native women laughed and mimicked them.

The British were meanwhile finding there was no comfort for them in the hinterland Bennelong was so anxious to embrace again. Lieutenant Dawes travelled west but was defeated by the great bush-entangled precipices of the Blue Mountains. And a former slave, Black Caesar, 'a notorious convict and native of

Madagascar' delivered himself up again to the officer at Rose Hill on the last day of the year. He had managed to stay free only since 22 December, when he escaped in a canoe from Garden Island. He had a musket with him and was able to drive Aborigines away from their camp fires and eat what they had been cooking. He had also robbed from gardens in Sydney and Rose Hill. When he lost the musket he found it impossible to subsist and was attacked by the natives and received various wounds. Though he would remain an enthusiastic escapee, he was incarnate proof of the uninhabitable nature of the hinterland.

Eighteen

With a sigh of relief but some concern for his charges, in March 1790 Phillip eventually consigned Ross from Parramatta to the command of Norfolk Island since Lieutenant King had been pleading a need to return to England, and Phillip thought of King as the most reliable man he could send home to report to influential Britons on the parlous state of things in New South Wales.

For the inhabitants of Sydney Cove, the ration at the time Ross was sent to Norfolk and King was summoned to go back to England and plead for the mouths of New South Wales provided daily about 1800 calories and 56 grams of protein, a minimum for survival. Tench, passing the provision store, saw a man who emerged with 'a wild haggard countenance having received his daily pittance to carry home. His faltering gait, and eager devouring eye, led me to watch him; and he had not proceeded ten steps before he fell. I ordered him to be carried to the hospital where, when he arrived, he was found dead . . . On opening the body, the cause of death was pronounced to be inanition'. Both soldiers and convicts found they were not able to fulfil tasks. The clothing store was near empty and some convicts lived in tatters and rags. In their camp the women were resourceful with needles and yarn Phillip had distributed, but many a guard detachment was mounted in which the majority of soldiers lacked shoes. Thefts of clothing increased and intense depression bred a thousand desperate pilferings.

In this emergency, Phillip 'from a motive that did him immortal honour', released to the general stores the three hundredweight of flour which was his personal store, 'wishing that if a convict complained, he might see that want was not unfelt even at government house'.

In March 1790, the *Sirius* and *Supply* both set sail for Norfolk Island with about 350 people. Phillip was unloading some of Sydney Cove's hungry onto Norfolk's richer soil. Amongst those travelling to Norfolk were John Hudson, the child chimney-sweep, and Lieutenant Clark. Major Robert Ross, as new commandant of the island, was also amongst the passengers. On the way down-harbour, the bulky *Sirius* got itself in an awkward situation near the rocks of the north head of Port Jackson, as it had earlier off southern Tasmania, and again clever seamanship just managed to avoid disaster and a huge accompanying death toll.

John Hunter and *Sirius* had not been to Norfolk before, and on arriving could not land at Sydney Bay on the south side of the island. At Cascade Bay on the north shore Hunter was able to land convicts and marines, 275 people in all. But his ship was blown out to sea by a gale before it could land any supplies for them. When the wind shifted Hunter tried again for Sydney Bay, and when the signal flags flying ashore indicated that the surf was calm enough to allow longboats to land, the unloading of stores began. After much had been landed, another wind shift caused the *Supply* to make sail and get away from a reef on the west side of the bay. Despite Hunter's best efforts, and a complicated series of manoeuvres with sails and helm, *Sirius* was blown stern-first howling and creaking onto the reef, where the surf began to batter her to pieces. Sailors began cutting away the masts and rigging and throwing them over the side in the hope that the loss of weight might refloat her: 'In less than ten minutes the masts were all over the side, the ship an entire wreck,' wrote Midshipman Newton Fowell. Provisions were brought up from the hold and stacked on the gun deck. If necessary, some of them could be floated ashore. Sailors were tied to ropes and hauled ashore through the surf.

Male convicts already landed volunteered to swim to the wreck as the sea subsided, and liberate the livestock. Having done so, they also raided the ship's cellar. Ross would issue a proclamation against those who 'in a most scandalous and infamous manner, robbed and plundered' items from the wreck. He declared martial law, fearing the pressure placed on resources not only by the newcomers but also by *Sirius*'s crew, who would be stuck on Norfolk Island for ten months.

Little *Supply* survived and left with King, also carrying to Sydney his convict mistress, Ann Innett, and their two small sons, Norfolk and Sydney, whom King intended to rear as his own, as a gentleman should.

With his declaration of martial law, Ross decided it was not possible to administer a necessary oath of obedience one by one to convicts and private soldiers. He said that if they would pass under the King's colours at the flagstaff, and between the colours of the detachment, it would equal a voluntary oath. He himself led the procession, the rest of the population following with 'chearfulness'.

In April 1790, a cheerful phenomenon indeed occurred which Hunter, stuck on the island in a small hut, considered an act of divine intervention. Thousands of birds of a species of ground-nesting petrels arrived on the hills of the island, and continued to land each night for four months. 'A little before sunset the air was thick with them as gnats are on a fine summer's evening in England,' noted Ralph Clark in wonder. They were of the mutton-bird species, and nested in particular on Mount Pitt, where they dug their ground nests like rabbit warrens. Settlers, free and bond, would climb the hill at night with lit pine-knots to search for the birds, who returned each evening to their burrows. Hunter, too, as *Sirius* began to break apart on the rocks, went on such excursions. The parties would arrive soon after dusk, light small fires to attract the attention of the birds, 'and they drop down out of the air as fast as the people can take them up and kill them'. Unfortunately for the species, the mutton-bird did not easily rise from flat ground and could not escape the slaughter. Their eggs in the burrows were also easily plundered. Throughout mid-1790, 170,000 birds were taken, and their feathers must have blown hither and thither on the island and coated the surrounding sea. 'They had a strong, fishy taste,' said Hunter. 'But our keen appetites relished them very well; the eggs were excellent.' As on the mainland, people also boiled and ate the head of the cabbage tree palm. The phenomenon of the birds coincided, however, with a plague of caterpillars and grubs that damaged the crops.

Ross seemed to feel freed from Phillip's influence and set up on Norfolk Island his own kind of commonwealth. He began to give allocations of land to groups of convicts, perhaps six people at a time, who were jointly responsible for growing what they needed on a particular, communally shared acreage. Thus the convicts would become their own motivators and regulators, and gang up on those who slacked off. As they produced their own food, the flour ration they got from the government would be successively reduced, it was initially proposed, but instead Ross decided to offer monetary and other prizes to those who put up for sale the most pork, fowls and corn. In his 'agrarian commonwealth', felons were exposed to the reforming impact of land of their own. One of the parties to this reform was John Coffin, who had been chained to two other recalcitrant convicts to work on the primitive roads of Sydney Cove, but who on Norfolk Island shared an allotment and a pig with a convict couple.

Captain Hunter, who observed the scheme at work, thought that in reality convicts were driven by it to steal from each other's gardens. Under the Ross system, the birth of every piglet was to be reported to the deputy commissary and the death of every sow was to be followed by an enquiry. If the cause of death was found to be an accident or a disease, the government would make up the loss, but if not, the convicts given the care of the pig as a group 'were to be considered responsible and were to be punished as criminals'.

Ross did not seem to be personally a great punisher or flogger, and on Norfolk, his ideals, unsuspected in Sydney and Parramatta, emerged. He offered his charges the allurements of a far more intense cooperativism than Phillip had in Sydney.

Nineteen

It was as well that Phillip, as he summoned King for his task as emissary, did not yet know what had happened to the store ship the British government had sent, the HMS *Guardian*. By 24 November 1789, the *Guardian* had been at Cape Town and its young captain, Lieutenant Riou, began the business of purchasing livestock for Sydney as fast as he could. He was an active and intelligent young man, and knew what joy and deliverance his cargo would bring to the population of New South Wales. He even carried a curate, the Reverend John Crowther, for the Reverend Johnson, although he wrote to his mother and sister, 'Protect me from such parsons. He has never hinted at giving us a sermon, and if he did, I have too great a respect for the credit of the clergy and more for the forms of our religion than to suffer him.' Riou also had aboard seven free superintendents of convict labour, recruited in London, and the young daughter of one of them.

The Dutch at Cape Town told Riou when he arrived that Captain John Hunter had been there earlier fetching supplies aboard the *Sirius*, issuing Admiralty bills of credit, and speaking of the harsh conditions of Sydney Cove, and that news increased Riou's determination to make all proper speed.

By 11 December, *Guardian* was ready to reach south-east to pick up the roaring forties which would take it to Van Diemen's Land and the turn northwards for Sydney. *Guardian* and its captain would be Botany Bay's saviours, a not unattractive idea to an intelligent and motivated young officer.

In this same December, the leisurely *Lady Juliana* was lying in Rio, and Mrs Barnsley was accompanied ashore by officers to do her shopping. The voyage thus far gave some indication of the entrepreneurial spirit of some of the women. In Teneriffe in the Canarys, Mrs Barnsley had treated her clique and followers to a cask of canary wine. At Santa Cruz, the capital of Teneriffe, the enterprising Sarah Sabola, alias Sarah Lyons, a young Jewish convict from the East End of London, having acquired lengths of black cloth, progressed with other convict women through the city barefoot and wan, bearing Catholic symbols such as crucifixes and rosaries, and attracted gifts of cash and goods from generous citizens.

Neither Lieutenant Edgar nor Captain Aitken seemed to have punished such enterprises. Nor did they cast judgment on the convict girls who accommodated Spanish gentlemen aboard, as had not been permitted in the First Fleet. The former London madam, Elizabeth Sully, who had run a lodging house at 45 Cable Street, East London, had been sentenced with three of her girls for robbing clients. (The watch of a client was found secreted in Sully's bed.) They and other former prostitutes welcomed visitors aboard, and after leaving St Jago in the Cape Verde islands, the *Lady Juliana* was accompanied for some distance by two Yankee slavers making for the Gambia. The two ships stuck close for the sake of 'the ladies', sailors being rowed over to the *Lady Juliana* from the slavers for evening recreation. Naturally, not all convict women were involved in the prostitution – for one thing, Sarah Whitelam, rural beloved of steward John Nicol, was by now heavily pregnant. But the former prostitutes who serviced the visitors from the whalers seemed to have been happy to build up their resources for the uncertainty of what was coming. One historian of the *Lady Juliana* believes that Nicol, Surgeon Alley, Captain Aitken and Lieutenant Edgar must have been in some way facilitators and profiteers of the flesh trade on the *Lady Juliana*, and it is hard to see how they could have been opposed to it. They certainly approached it all with a Georgian pragmatism unclouded by too much piety.

As some of the *Lady Juliana* women disported themselves in Rio, a city decked for an exuberant Christmas, the *Guardian* had left Cape Town and was at 42 degrees 15 minutes, a latitude generally too far north for icebergs. Nonetheless, the sailor of the masthead sighted ice. On Christmas Eve an extended ice pack stretched ahead. Riou brought the *Guardian* close in to one outcrop and two boats were hauled off to allow sailors to chop off lumps of ice to serve as water for the cattle. By the time the boats got back to the ship with their iceblocks, visibility had diminished. *Guardian* crept along, its captain looking for a safe passage, but a semi-submerged ice spur raked open the ship's keel. She tore free, but her rudder was left stuck in the ice. Water flooded into her hull.

Two days of frenzied endeavour began. Riou fothered his ship, that is, wrapped up the hull in a bandage of two layers of sail. After hours at the pump, some men found the liquor store and drank themselves stupid as a means of facing death. The day after Christmas, Riou gave those who chose, including the specialist artisan convicts, permission to give up the ship and take to the sea in the boats. Most of the seamen left, but the convict artificers stayed. It would turn out that theirs was the right choice. Only fifteen of those who took to the boats would survive.

Seven weeks later, covered in dirt and rags and with long beards, the group who stayed on *Guardian* sighted some whalers who led them back to the Cape of Good Hope. The *Lady Juliana*, fifty days from Rio, came into Cape Town to find the ruin of the *Guardian* low in the water and its masts and rigging in disarray. Most of the livestock Riou had bought on his first visit to Cape Town had been drowned or trampled in the ship's wreckage. Riou and Lieutenant Edgar of the *Lady Juliana* went ashore to search out an old friend also unexpectedly in Cape Town: Captain Bligh and the part of his crew of *Bounty* who had stuck with him following the mutiny led by Fletcher Christian. Bligh and his loyalists had sailed a cutter all the way from where the mutiny had occurred in the Pacific to Dutch Timor, and then had been conveyed to Batavia and Cape Town.

The *Lady Juliana* suffered its own emergency in port. 'While we lay at the Cape,' said Nicol, 'we had a narrow escape from destruction by fire. The carpenter allowed the pitch-pot to boil over upon the deck, and the flames rose in an amazing manner. The shrieks of the women were dreadful, and the confusion they made running about drove everyone stupid. I ran to my berth, seized a pair of blankets to keep it down till the others drowned it with water. Captain Aitken gave me a handsome present for my exertions.'

Riou had the sad duty of beaching the *Guardian* for careening, and ultimately of abandoning it. He had saved a flock of sheep and two Cape stallions, and these were trans-shipped to the *Lady Juliana* with wine, a small number of barrels of flour

and some Admiralty dispatches. Five agricultural work superintendents were also put on the *Lady Juliana*. One of them was
a former Hessian officer who had served George III in North
America, Philip Schaeffer, who came aboard with his ten-year-
old daughter.

All 25 of the convict artificers of *Guardian* would need
eventually to be delivered to Sydney Cove too. Riou had to find
quarters for them ashore, and intended to petition the authorities
to pardon them for their brave work in the saving of the
Guardian. It would indeed happen after they reached Sydney, but
not before Phillip first emancipated his brickmaker, Bloodworth.

Had the *Guardian* been able to continue to Sydney, it would
have arrived in March 1790 and saved Phillip from the further
reductions to the rations made in April 1790. By that time, weekly,
2½ pounds of flour, 2 pounds of pork and 2 of rice were the limit
for each British soul in New South Wales. Because of the energy
needed to fish and hunt, an extra measure of rations was set aside
for gamekeepers and fishermen. At the cooking fires in the men's
and women's camps, prisoners looked covetously at each other's
shares, and in the marines' huts wives asked their husbands how
they were expected to keep children healthy on a few flapjacks
a week, insect-infected rice and pork that shrunk to half its
weight as the brine cooked out. In late April it became apparent
that the pork in the storehouse would last only until 26 August at
the current low rate of consumption, and the beef similarly.

~

Back in the Thames, in a squally autumn and cold early winter
of 1789, following the departure of the *Lady Juliana* and
the *Guardian*, prisoners from Newgate were gradually

accommodated aboard the newly contracted vessels at Deptford – *Surprize*, *Scarborough* and *Neptune*. *Neptune* was the largest, 809 tons with a crew of 83. It was first commanded by Thomas Gilbert who had captained the *Charlotte* in the First Fleet and whose book, *Journal of a Voyage from Port Jackson, New South Wales to Canton in 1788 through an Unexplored Passage*, was about to be published in London to considerable interest. The *Scarborough*, which had already made the journey once, was half the size of the *Neptune*. The 400-ton *Surprize* was the smallest of the three and a very poor sailer. It was captained by Donald Trail, a former master to Bligh, who had recently commanded one of Camden, Calvert and King's slave ships.

On 15 October 1789 the ships were ordered to move out of the Deptford docks on the south bank of the Thames and embark soldiers and convicts in the river. One hundred soldiers of the New South Wales Corps were on board, at least in theory, from early November. They were accommodated in the gun rooms, forecastles and steerage areas of the ships, around the convict decks. The rumour was that some of these fellows were less than prime soldiery, and it was said by the press that some were ruffians recruited from the Savoy military prison. Many of this new regiment, particularly some of the young officers, tolerated the inconvenience of being sent so far abroad because they hoped for power, influence and riches from New South Wales.

Almost all the convicts taken aboard in the river had been confined for some years, having traded the death sentence for a period of transportation to New South Wales, generally for life. Some came directly from Newgate, but the *Neptune* prisoners came as well from the *Justitia* and *Censor* in the Thames. They were a sullen and angry cargo, but cowed and already weakening.

The ships would sail around the south-east coast to collect prisoners from the *Lion* and *Fortune* hulks in Portsmouth, as well as from the notorious *Dunkirk* hulk at Plymouth. The *Dunkirk* topped up the prison deck population of the transports by sending 290 convicts on board. Among those who came onto the huge *Neptune* at that time was a lusty young man in his mid-twenties, Robert Towers, who had stolen silver tankards and pint-pots from an inn in north Lancashire and then tried to sell them to a silversmith in Preston. His health had gone down a little on the damp lower decks of *Dunkirk*, but on the crowded prison deck of *Neptune*, where he wore slaver shackles around his ankles and wrists and got insufficient exercise, he began to feel really poorly. The *Neptune*, at anchor and at sea, would ultimately finish him, though it would take seven months until they brought his corpse up to deck and committed him to a distant ocean.

In late November when the *Neptune* was lying in Plymouth, the Secretary of State found that there was room for 40 more women – at 18 inches of bed width per person. The *Surprize* had earlier embarked 98 convicts from the hulks at Gravesend and then took on 130 male convicts from the *Ceres* hulk in Portsmouth and a few from the *Fortune*. Thus there was a heavy admixture of West Country and East End accents on the prison decks. By raw mid-December all three ships were anchored on the Motherbank off Portsmouth, making final preparations.

There had been a rough criterion this time for selecting those who went aboard – the idea was to remove the convicts who had been in the hulks the longest time. But, as with the First Fleet, that meant there were prisoners being transported who had already served years of their sentences. In committing them to deep space, the desire to clear out the gaols and hulks seemed to be the primary motive, but it must have occurred to more than one or two clerks and officials that it would also ensure that those prisoners sentenced to seven- or fourteen-year terms were unlikely to return from New South Wales. Thus they must have added names to the lists with the eugenic purpose of locating bad blood permanently in the south-west Pacific, without asking too closely what the implications might be for society in New South Wales. New South Wales was to be the great oubliette, in which convicts could be deposited and forgotten by British society at large.

Exemplifying this attitude was the Duke of Richmond, who was in charge of fortifications in Portsmouth Harbour, where 280 convicts worked on harbour defences. He asked that these men not be transported, even though their stonemasonry skills and relative reliability would have made them welcome citizens in New South Wales.

On *Neptune*, even between Plymouth and Portsmouth, where the men were racked by catarrh and congestive disorders, a number of the convicts had already died, but there was general and unquestioned agreement that it was a consequence of the physical condition in which they had arrived from the hulks and prisons. There were other signs of indifference to convict welfare, however, early on. Either Trail or Shapcote, the naval agent, ordered many of the convicts' chests thrown overboard with their possessions in them. Women who had thought to dress better and more warmly while at sea were now reduced to the basic convict dress – striped jacket and petticoat, navy shoes, inadequate blankets.

By early December 1789, while the healthy women of *Lady Juliana* were in Rio, Undersecretary Evan Nepean had become anxious about reports of the conditions on board the Second Fleet, and told the naval agent that he was to 'examine minutely into the manner of confining the convicts, as it has been represented that they are ironed in such a manner as must ultimately tend to their destruction'. Secretary of State Grenville sent Governor Phillip an ominous dispatch urging him to disembark the prisoners as early as possible when they arrived, 'as from the length of the passage from hence and the nature of their food, there is every reason to expect that many of them will be reduced to so debilitated a state that immediate relief will be found expedient'. It is a letter which reflects some culpability on the Home Secretary.

Male convicts were suddenly told that they could bring their wives on the voyage, if they chose, but only three women and three children turned up in Portsmouth by 21 December. Three or four other free women embarked in the following days, interesting volunteers, lovers of various convicts willing to take the step, on the eve of Christmas, into the void.

Amongst them was Harriet Hodgetts, wife of a 24-year-old blacksmith-cum-burglar from Staffordshire, Thomas Hodgetts. She had followed her husband down from Staffordshire to London, where she lived with their three small children in acute squalor in Whitechapel. It seems that the churchwardens and overseers of the parish of St Mary's Whitechapel took an interest in her case and were anxious to get Harriet aboard, since she had no other prospects at all.

That made her fit for New South Wales. Her revenge was to live till 1850 and to give birth to nine colonial children.

Twenty

There were two young men aboard the *Neptune* who would find a large place in New South Wales history.

One of these men of some future significance had a new rank and was a touch bumptious about it. He was John Macarthur, a little over twenty years of age, and a lieutenant in the 102nd Regiment, the newly created New South Wales Corps. His father was a Scots draper who lived at the back of his business in Plymouth. He had been able to obtain, that is, buy, an ensign's commission for John for a regiment intended to be sent to fight the American colonists. When that war ended, it left young men at a loose end and John Macarthur did some farming, considered the law, returned to full pay in 1788 as an ensign, but then in June 1789, when the formation of the New South Wales Corps was announced, saw the chance of promotion and became a lieutenant.

He had married the previous year a robust-spirited and handsome girl named Elizabeth Veal, a Cornish woman who considered her ambitious and volatile husband 'too proud and haughty for our humble fortune'. It was Macarthur and his fellow officers, not the convicts, who introduced turbulence into Captain Tom Gilbert's *Neptune*.

Captain Nicholas Nepean of the New South Wales Corps, brother of Evan Nepean, the Undersecretary at the Home Office, and Lieutenant John Macarthur were demanding young men. Macarthur and his young wife were billeted in a cramped space next to the women's convict deck and could hear their shouts and curses. These were not women of Elizabeth's gentility, and yet when Captain Nepean spoke to Gilbert about it in Macarthur's presence, Gilbert 'flew into one of his passions', saying that he did not understand people making mountains out of molehills, and threatening to write to the War Office to have Macarthur thrown off his ship. Macarthur called him an insolent fellow, but was pushed aside.

When the ship anchored in Plymouth in November 1789, Macarthur went up to the quarterdeck and upbraided the captain for his 'ungentleman-like conduct', and called him a 'great scoundrel'. Gilbert responded by saying 'he had settled many a greater man' than Macarthur. So the two agreed to meet at four o'clock in the afternoon for a pistol duel at the Fountain Tavern on Plymouth Dock. Accompanied by an Irish surgeon as second, Macarthur faced Gilbert on the stones of the Old Gun Wharf. The two duellists fired at each other. Macarthur's ball sizzled through Gilbert's greatcoat. Then Gilbert's missed altogether. Their seconds came running in and stopped the confrontation, and both men decided that their honour had been satisfied.

But enmity continued. The army officers, Captain Nepean on the *Neptune*, and Captain Hill on the *Surprize*, insisted that they have command of the convicts. Captain Gilbert would not surrender the convict deck keys to them. Anthony Calvert, of the contractors Camden, Calvert and King, was drawn into the argument and so, most potently, was Evan Nepean, Undersecretary of State. Evan Nepean declared, 'I trust that both sides, when out of the smell of land, will find it in their interests to live quietly together.'

In any case, a decision was reached between the Navy Board, the Home Office and the contractors to remove Thomas Gilbert as master of *Neptune*. Macarthur and Nepean and the New South Wales Corps would eventually bring down bigger fish than Gilbert, but they were pleased with themselves for their first triumph.

The other fascinating passenger of *Neptune* was a young Irishman, D'Arcy Wentworth, aged about 27, a highwayman-cum-surgeon, a voluntary passenger in one sense, a virtual convict in others. He was tall and good-looking and spoke English with an Ulster brogue. He had acquired notoriety in Britain throughout the 1780s as 'a gentleman of the road', whom the public and even magistrates distinguished from 'the lower and more depraved part of the fraternity of thieves'.

D'Arcy Wentworth was the son of an Ulster innkeeper, a relative of the noble Fitzwilliam clan of Portadown. He served as an officer in the Ulster volunteers, a militia unit, during the North American emergency. But the militia was not sent to America, and the end of the emergency left D'Arcy careerless. He suffered from a not uncommon problem of Irish younger sons of the Protestant tradition: he had a strong sense of being a member of the Ascendency in Ireland, and an appetite for the wealth and station that should attend such a status, but in dismal Portadown he was not well-connected enough to achieve it. Earl Fitzwilliam had no interest in supporting the youngest son of a distant kinsman, so D'Arcy was left both with a sense of his own worth, confirmed in him by his seven doting older sisters, and no wealth to affirm it.

Before serving in the militia, he had completed an apprenticeship with an Irish surgeon and in 1785 he left for London,
where the Court of Examiners of the Company of Surgeons
certified him an assistant surgeon. Now he set himself to 'walk
the hospitals', but the impoverished Irish medical student in
London's great world did not have the temperament to live
quietly and carefully. In criminal society at the Dog and Duck
Tavern in St George's Field south of the river, he could pass as a
real toff, live fairly cheaply, encounter raffish society, and attract
women with his tall frame and his vigorous Irish banter. His best
respectable patron was James Villiers, Member of Parliament,
second son of the Earl of Clarendon, and an old friend. During
1787 Villiers tried without success to get him a commission in
a regiment. By November that year, however, Wentworth had
been arrested. He had held up a man on Hounslow Heath. The
victim described the perpetrator as a large, lusty man who wore
a black silk mask and a drab-coloured great coat. The next day
Wentworth's mistress, Mary Wilkinson, sold a silver watch to a
pawnbroker in Soho. Four days later still, a gentleman, his wife
and a female friend were held up on Hounslow Heath by a
solitary highwayman on a chestnut horse with a white blaze.
Two Bow Street runners intercepted Wentworth as he returned
to the city and brought him before a magistrate. During his
examination by the magistrate Wentworth declared with
apparent sincerity that if Miss Wilkinson were 'brought into
trouble upon his account, he would destroy himself'. Wentworth
stood trial in the Old Bailey in December 1787. Though he
inveighed against the press for swinging the jury against him,
his victims seemed reluctant to identify him. By now he was
to some a glamorous figure, but one wonders what coercion

was used by his Dog and Duck associates to prevent a definite identification.

Behind Greenwich and south-east of the Dog and Duck lay the plateau called Blackheath, with Shooters' Hill rising from it. In January 1788, Wentworth was the so-called masked gentleman highwayman who rode out of the roadside heath and held up two travellers. In the same month on Shooters' Hill, three highwaymen held up Alderman William Curtis (who owned ships in the First Fleet) and two other gentlemen. These two hold-ups netted goods valued at over £50. One of D'Arcy's accomplices, William Manning, was captured in Lewisham, and an address in his pocketbook led Bow Street runners to Wentworth's London lodgings, where they arrested him again.

Before the magistrates and later in Newgate, Wentworth pleaded his family's good name and said that he had become degraded by the evil influence of the clientele of the Dog and Duck. Not only did he have to face a number of charges of highway robbery, but the trial was moved to Maidstone, Kent, where the Lent assizes met, in the hope of finding a jury who would convict without fear or favour.

That was the month the eleven ships of the First Fleet had gathered on the Motherbank, preparatory for departure. One commentator said he saw Wentworth on board the *Charlotte*, and that he had the job of ship's surgeon, but if it was so, the authorities did not in the end allow Wentworth's friends to intervene in this way and get him out of the country to save his noble relatives' embarrassment.

Acquitted in Maidstone, because of uncertainty of identification, Wentworth met Earl Fitzwilliam, his young kinsman, in London for a solemn talk. But by the end of November 1788, D'Arcy had been arrested again for holding up a post-chaise carrying two barristers of Lincoln's Inn across Finchley Common north of Hampstead Heath. Two masked highwaymen carried out the exploit. Stripping the gentlemen of the bar of their valuables, one of the highwaymen whispered, 'Good morrow'. One of the lawyers said to his companion, 'If I was not sure that D'Arcy Wentworth was out of the kingdom, I should be sure it was him.' It must have been believed by these worthy gentlemen that D'Arcy *had* been got out of the country to New South Wales by influential supporters.

The following year, 1789, someone identified as Wentworth asked a surgeon to come and operate on a friend of his, 'Jack Day', suffering from a pistol wound. Wentworth's associate had to be taken to hospital, was grilled by Bow Street officers, and the result was Wentworth's own arrest and interrogation in November.

This time his trial at the Old Bailey was such a *cause célèbre* that it was attended by members of the royal family, including the Duke and Duchess of Cumberland. On 9 December, when the *Surprize*, *Neptune* and *Scarborough* were assembled on the Motherbank, Wentworth appeared before a lenient judge and his lawyer victims did not prosecute, having known him socially. The jury came back with a verdict of not guilty, and the prosecuting parties were pleased to announce that Mr Wentworth 'has taken a passage to go in the fleet to Botany Bay; and has obtained an appointment in it, as assistant surgeon, and desires to be discharged immediately'. Lord Fitzwilliam had agreed to fit his kinsman out and pay his fare to New South Wales on the *Neptune*.

In fact, D'Arcy Wentworth had no official position aboard the ship. The quality of Great Britain often got rid of their wild relatives by *de facto*, above-decks transportation, and Wentworth would be an early well-documented instance of what would become a habitual recourse for embarrassed British families. Now he was alone in a little hutch aboard, bouncing on the swell of the Motherbank, amongst pungent odours and people he did not know, and at 27 was still without a post.

After Captain Gilbert was removed from *Neptune*, Captain Trail, the 44-year-old Orkney Island Scot and one-time master to Captain Bligh, took over command. He had sailed on *Camden*, *Calvert* and Kings *Recovery* as master, along the African coast 'recruiting' slaves. Now he came over with his wife from the *Surprize* to take over the fleet's biggest ship, *Neptune*, and it would prove a dismal day for *Neptune*'s convicts.

The *Neptune* alone now held over 500 – 428 male and 78 female – of the 1000 convicts to be shipped. Most of them were housed on the orlop deck, the third deck down, 75 feet by 35, with standing room below the beams of the ceiling only 5 feet 7 inches. The convicts slept in four rows of sleeping trays, one row on either side of the ship and two down the middle. Lanterns burned on the convict deck till eight o'clock at night, and each ship had to carry the latest ventilating equipment in the hope that air would reach the convict deck even in the tropics. In port, and for much of the journey, each convict was chained by the wrist or by the ankles, in many cases on *Neptune* two and two together, and indefinitely so. Trail must have known the impact this would have on individual cleanliness and health.

As usual, each group of six men or women chose their mess steward, and the food these mess orderlies collected morning and evening was cooked in communal coppers above deck. In bad weather the food had to be cooked below deck in the oven and coppers that were used first for the rations of the crew and soldiers, with the result that many of the convicts went without cooked food during wild weather.

The sanitary arrangements were very primitive – on the orlop deck large tubs were provided to 'ease nature'. These would be knocked over by accident or carelessness or rough seas. Some of the smells reached the Macarthurs in their little cabin by the women's prison area on a higher deck. Mrs Macarthur found the malodour hard to bear: 'together with the stench arising from the breath of such a number of persons confined in so small a spot, the smell of their provisions and other unwholesome things, made it almost unbearable'. But Elizabeth Veal *did* bear it for the sake of her dreams. In British colonial history she would be a more kindly, more loyal and more enduring Becky Sharp, to the extent that she broke that mean mould and became her own woman, clear-eyed even amongst the miasmas of *Neptune*. Her as yet callow husband would be harder to admire so unconditionally.

The 78 female convicts of *Neptune* were housed in a section of the upper deck and were not chained. They were allowed the range of the poop and quarterdeck during considerable parts of the day while at sea. It was an age when women were considered to have different dietary needs from men, and so they received smaller portions of meat and a larger proportion of bread. But they also got a ration of tea and brown sugar, as the *Lady Juliana* women had. The agent and captain of the *Lady Juliana* had allowed seamen considerable sexual freedom with the women, and in that spirit, a few days after the Second Fleet left England, the crew of the *Neptune* sent a petition to the captain regarding a promise they believed he had made in port to let them have access to the female convicts. Trail denied having made any promise to allow them sea-wives, and he punished men who had any unauthorised contact with the women. But still sailors got to women, and vice versa – in some cases through a break in the bulkhead between the carpenters' shop and the women's prison.

As for D'Arcy Wentworth, he seems to have fallen quite passionately in love, passion being his forte, with a pretty Irish convict of seventeen years named Catherine Crowley. She had been sentenced in Staffordshire for one of the usual offences, stealing clothing – although in her case it was a considerable amount of clothing. Catherine was sent down from Stafford gaol to London on the outside of a coach with three other girls, and boarded the *Neptune*. Wentworth had at first taken this young woman on as his servant, and she would have welcomed the relative freedom inherent in that situation. With Captain Donald Trail's at least tacit consent, D'Arcy made her his mistress soon after he joined the ship.

Without reflecting on Crowley's individual and demonstrably loyal motives, Wentworth, despite his status as the Second Fleet's only paying passenger, was a gentleman with accompanying entitlements – and a vigorous lover. In reality, D'Arcy may have been a more lonely figure aboard *Neptune* than Crowley was. And he remained so, not interfering, not being invited to interfere as a physician in what befell Catherine Crowley's convict brethren.

So, in close quarters on *Neptune* could be found two furiously ambitious young men: one a reclusive, prickly officer, John Macarthur, with his wife, Elizabeth, pregnant; and the other the founding social outcast of penal New South Wales, D'Arcy Wentworth, with his lover, Catherine Crowley, pregnant. Catherine would have been as surprised as the politer Macarthurs to find out that the child she carried on *Neptune* would one day become Australia's first great constitutional statesman. But all that future was mired in shipboard squalor, stench and dimness, and they sailed towards a place whose future was un-guaranteed in any case.

Twenty-one

The three ships now gathered in Portsmouth were joined by a store ship named the *Justinian*, loading with flour, pork, beef, pease, oatmeal, spirits, oil and sugar. There were also 162 bales of clothing and a quantity of coverlets, blankets and cloth, and a portable military hospital, prefabricated for assembly in New South Wales. Four hundred gallons of vinegar were shipped for use as disinfectant and mouthwash. The three transports also carried supplies.

The wind kept the new convict fleet shuttling between Portsmouth Harbour and the Isle of Wight, but on 7 January, a Sunday morning in the new year of 1790, a westerly allowed them to tack their way down the Channel. The store ship *Justinian* left Falmouth the same day as the other three ships left the Motherbank.

Twenty-two-year-old Elizabeth Macarthur kept herself absorbed by writing a stylish journal of the voyage. In the Bay of Biscay the sea 'ran mountains high', she wrote. Down the coast of west Africa, wind sails operated over the deck to keep the lower areas of the ship refreshed, but the terrible heat, particularly in the men's prison deck, could not be dealt with very well. Here was Georgian Hades, the convict deck of an eighteenth-century ship, the pumps on deck having no air to distribute, and men and women locked up with their complex screams and groans and surrenders.

After sailing, the soldiers complained to Lieutenant Macarthur that they were receiving short rations, that they were victims of purloining, that is, short weighting. Nepean did not seem to want to attend to the matter. Similarly, the passage the Macarthurs had formerly had to the upper deck was nailed down, and they could get to the deck only via the women's prison. Nepean told a protesting Macarthur that 'the master of the ship had a right to do as he pleased'. Increasingly, Elizabeth Macarthur stuck to her cabin. 'Assailed with noisome stenches', she used oil of attar but that did not dispel the reek. The Macarthurs' rations were also cut by Captain Trail, without resistance by the incapable Lieutenant Shapcote or by Nicholas Nepean. Nepean dined in Captain Trail's cabin and the two had become cronies, but the Macarthurs 'seldom benefited by their society'.

On *Scarborough* was a neurotic and vulnerable apprentice-goldsmith convict, Samuel Burt, who had already engaged in what seemed a self-destructive bid for the gallows. He had forged a bank draft in his employer's name and had been saved from death by the kindness of witnesses and jury, since he was thought to have committed the forgery as a result of being rejected in love. The girl he desired visited him in Newgate after all, but caught gaol fever through the bars from a louse-bite and died of it. In the Atlantic, he became afraid there was a plot to take over *Scarborough*, his ship. As a result of his information, the captain and officers tried seventeen men, found most of them guilty, and confined five of the ring-leaders for a final determination by

Phillip. This could not have done much for fellow feeling aboard the *Scarborough*.

Captain William Hill, a cultivated and sympathetic young member of the New South Wales Corps, who would soon make friends of the more intellectual of the officers already in New South Wales, particularly Tench and Dawes, was sailing on *Surprize*, where he did himself great honour by being a critic of the contractors from the start. 'The irons used upon these unhappy wretches were barbarous; the contractors had been in the Guinea trade, and had put on board the same shackles used by them in that trade, which are made with a short bolt, instead of chains that drop between the legs and fasten with a bandage around the waist, like those at the different gaols; these bolts were not more than three-quarters of a foot in length, so they [the convicts] could not extend either leg from the other more than an inch or two at most; thus fettered, it was impossible for them to move, but at the risk of both their legs being broken.' Forced inactivity on this scale, Hill feared, was an invitation to scurvy, 'equal to, if not more than salt provisions'. Even when disease struck, there were no extra comforts offered. 'The slave trade is merciful, compared with what I have seen in this fleet; in that it is the interest of the [slaver] master to preserve the health and lives of their captives, they having a joint benefit, with the owners. In this [fleet], the more they can withhold from the unhappy wretches, the more provisions they have to dispose of in a foreign market; and the earlier in the voyage they die, the longer they [the masters] can draw the deceased's allowance for themselves . . . it therefore highly concerns government to lodge in future a controlling power in each ship over these low-life barbarous masters, to keep them honest, instead of giving it to one man [a single agent], who can only see what is going forward on his ship.'

At Cape Town on 19 February, after an argument with Nepean, Macarthur and his wife, child and servant transferred to the *Scarborough* in protest, where they shared a small cabin with Lieutenant Edward Abbott. Elizabeth liked the ship's master of *Scarborough*, John Marshall, more than Trail. Marshall had a wife and three children in England 'of whom he speaks in the tenderest terms'. Her husband was incapacitated for five weeks by fever, during which time, Elizabeth Macarthur complained, the other New South Wales Corps officers did not make 'the slightest offer of assistance'. He was beginning to walk again as *Scarborough* neared Port Jackson.

The three main transports of the Second Fleet having reached Cape Town, the convict artificers who had behaved so well during the wreck of the *Guardian* and who had been stranded, were taken on board the *Neptune* along with some of the *Guardian*'s saved supplies. By now, *Neptune* had lost 55 men and a woman from scurvy, though the Lancashire silverware thief Robert Towers was hanging on. Young Lieutenant Riou of *Guardian* could foresee an accelerating calamity. He bluntly wrote to Evan Nepean, 'If ever the navy make another contract like that of the last three ships, they ought to be shot, and as for their agent Mr Shapcote, he behaved here just as foolishly as a man could well do.'

All four surgeons employed aboard the fleet had already written to Shapcote about the potential seriousness of the ships' unhealthy milieu. They urged him to get fresh supplies of beef and vegetables aboard. Surgeon Grey of the *Neptune* wrote that 'without they have fresh provisions and greens every day, numbers of them will fall a sacrifice to that dreadful disease'. Yet at the Cape, Trail made sure his prisoners were securely ironed, which did not contribute to their rehabilitation through whatever fresh fruit and vegetables were acquired ashore.

Surgeon Harris, the military surgeon to the 100 soldiers of the fleet, was concerned about *their* condition also. William Waters, surgeon of *Surprize*, reported 30 convicts suffering from scurvy. In the *Scarborough* ten soldiers were affected, five of them 'very bad'.

But Shapcote was strangely unconcerned, and may himself have been suffering from the famous lethargy of scurvy or from some other incapacity. He died suddenly in mid-May, after dining with Captain Trail and his wife. Between 3 and 4 am a female convict 'who had constantly attended Mr Shapcote' came to the quarterdeck with news of his death.

The fleet entered now the zone of storms. On *Surprize*, the New South Wales Corps soldier Captain Hill felt pity for 'unhappy wretches, the convicts', who often 'were considerably above their waists in water, and the men of my company, whose berths were not so far forward, were nearly up to the middles'.

The cold, damp, hunger and continued shackling were killing Robert Towers, and he was aware that if he died, as men were dying every day down here, his mess-mates would not tell anyone but would go on drawing his rations as long as they could, till putrefaction made his condition clear.

In the dispirited colony of New South Wales, June had opened rainy and hungry, but on the evening of 3 June, there was a cry throughout Sydney Cove of 'The flag's up!' It was the flag on the look-out station on the harbour's south head, and was visible from Sydney Cove itself. Tench left a passionate account of what this meant to him and others. 'I was sitting in my hut, musing on our fate, when a confused clamour in the street drew my attention. I opened my door and saw several women with children in their arms running to and fro with distracted looks, congratulating each other, kissing their infants with the most passionate and extravagant marks of fondness.' Tench raced to the hill on which government house stood and trained his pocket telescope on the look-out station. 'My next-door neighbour, a brother-officer, was with me; but we could not speak; we wrung each other by the hand, with eyes and hearts overflowing.'

Watkin begged to join the governor in his boat which was going down-harbour to meet the ship, and it was while they were proceeding that a large vessel with English colours worked in between the heads. But a full-blown wind, of the kind Sydney folk quickly came to name southerly busters, seemed to be blowing her onto the rocks at the base of the cliffs of North Head. 'The tumultuous state of our minds represented her in danger; and we were in agony.' She survived, however, and the governor sent out a boat to hail her, and when he knew who she was, the *Lady Juliana* with a cargo of women in good health, he crossed from the vice-regal boat to a fishing boat to return as fast as he could to Sydney, to prepare for the reception ashore of this new population. Meanwhile the seamen and officers in the governor's cutter 'pushed through wind and rain . . . At last we read the word "London" on her stern. "Pull away, my lads! She is from old England; a few strokes more and we shall be aboard! Hurrah for a belly-full and news from our friends!" – Such were our exhortations to the boat's crew.'

Tench was still overwhelmed as they boarded, so that he saw the women on board not so much as the fallen but as 'two hundred and twenty-five of our own countrywomen, whom crime or misfortune had condemned to exile'. Letters were brought up from below, and those addressed to the officers who had boarded were 'torn open in trembling agitation'.

The *Lady Juliana* was moored in Spring Cove on the Manly side of Port Jackson for some days, as the women prepared for landing. Then it came down-harbour and the women finally got ashore on 11 June 1790. They were better dressed than most of barefoot New South Wales, having been permitted to replenish wardrobes in Rio and Cape Town, and they made their way as paragons of health through mud to the huts of the women's camp on the west side of the town. Sarah Whitelam left John Nicol, her sea-husband, aboard, and the captain intended a brisk turn-around for the *Lady Juliana*, so that Nicol knew a sad parting was imminent.

But the presence of the *Lady Juliana*, and the bad news of the *Guardian*, were at least signs that the settlement had not been forgotten by Whitehall. Above all, so was the appearance of the store ship *Justinian*, a few weeks later. 'Our rapture,' wrote Watkin, 'was doubled on finding she was laden entirely with provisions for our use. Full allowance, and general congratulation, immediately took place.' The *Justinian* had taken only five months to make its trans-planetary journey. The profound gratitude and almost personal affection which would have gone Lieutenant Riou's way had the *Guardian* not been lost was now directed at *Justinian*'s young captain, Benjamin Maitland, for his ship carried the bulk of the stores Phillip needed, including nearly 500,000 pounds of flour and 50,000 pounds of beef and pork, as well as sugar, oil, oatmeal, pease, spirits and vinegar. Here was the end of famine, and the return to full and varied rations! And from what the *Justinian* told them, the settlement knew to look out for three more convict ships.

The first of the new ships, the *Surprize*, under jury masts from damage in a Southern Ocean storm, was seen from the look-out on South Head on 25 June. By the next day it was anchored in Sydney Cove, with its convicts, and one captain, one lieutenant, one surgeon's mate and 26 other ranks of the New South Wales Corps. The officers from Sydney Cove who boarded it might have expected the degree of health found in the *Lady Juliana*. In fact the peculiar disorders of the Camden, Calvert and King ships could be smelled for a hundred yards off. Phillip and King found the ill health of the New South Wales Corps soldiers was in stark contrast to the women of *Lady Juliana*, and the contrast with the convicts of *Surprize* was even more marked. Many of the *Surprize* prisoners were moribund. Upwards of 100 were now on the sick list on board, and 42 had been buried at sea during the journey. The portable hospital which had arrived by the *Justinian*, measuring 84 by 20½ feet, was assembled to take some of the spillage from White's timber-and-shingle hospital building, for the other transports were believed to be close, 'and we were led to expect them in as unhealthy a state as that which had just arrived'.

The other two transports were spotted by the look-outs on South Head two days later. On *Neptune*, Lieutenant John Macarthur's fever caught at the Cape had spread throughout the ship. In the mad southern seas men and women had perished amongst the jolting, incessant swell, and beneath the scream of canvas and wind. Aboard *Neptune* in particular, according to later witnesses, a black market had broken out for lack of proper supplies. It might cost 1s 6d for an additional pint of water, a pair of new shoes for a quart of tea or three biscuits, a new shirt for four biscuits, two pairs of trousers for six. Crew members would later sign a statement swearing that they sold food and drink to convicts on board at these elevated prices.

The *Neptune* and the *Scarborough* now entered Port Jackson. A visit by White and others showed them that the health of the people aboard *Neptune* was much worse even than that of the convicts on *Surprize*, and Collins was appalled by their condition. Indeed, Phillip and all the garrison officers looked judgmentally at masters like Captain Trail of *Neptune* but got back the unembarrassed stare of self-justified men. With all Phillip's power, he lacked the capacity to try them before his Admiralty court, so he was reduced to condemning them in dispatches.

Extra tents had to be pitched on the west side of the cove by the hospital to take in the 200 sick of *Neptune*, seriously ill with scurvy, dysentery or infectious fever. Several people died in the boats as they were being rowed ashore, or on the wharf as they were lifted out of the boats: 'both the living and the dead exhibiting more horrid spectacles than had ever been witnessed in this country'.

Much of it was attributed, said Collins, to severe confinement, such as had not occurred on the First Fleet: confinement in irons, that is, on the convict deck, without fresh air, without being permitted to exercise on deck. In many cases, convicts had been ironed together for the duration of the voyage. Collins thought Captain Marshall of the *Scarborough* had done a reasonably good job. Sixty-eight men had been lost on his ship, however. 'On board the other ships, the masters who had the entire direction of the prisoners never suffered them to be at large on deck, and but few at a time were permitted there. This consequently gave birth to many diseases.'

The sick told an astonished Collins and others that sometimes, on board, when one of their comrades died in irons, the other men in the chain sequence had concealed the death for the purpose of sharing out their allowance of provisions amongst the living. 'Until chance, and the offensiveness of a corpse, directed the surgeon . . . to the spot where it lay.' Such indeed had been the fate of Robert Towers.

The misery of the people of these three ships did not lead Collins, however, to wish that the mutiny on *Scarborough* had succeeded, for he applauded the convict who had too much principle to enter into the plot.

Visiting the wharf and the hospital tents, Captain Watkin Tench was also outraged by what he saw. 'The sum paid, per head, to the contractor, £17, was certainly competent to afford fair profit to the merchants who contracted. But there is reason to believe that some of them who were employed to act for him violated every principle of justice, and rioted on the spoils of misery, for want of a controlling power to check their enormities.' Tench did not, however, see the problem as a systemic one: 'No doubt can be entertained that a humane and liberal government will interpose its authority to prevent the repetition of such flagitious conduct.' Captain Collins summed up the problem in a paragraph: 'Government engaged to pay £17 7s 6d per head for every convict they embarked. This sum being as well for their provisions as for their transportation, no interest for their preservation was created in the owners, and the dead were more profitable . . . than the living.'

No sooner were the convicts unloaded than the masters of the transports, including Trail, opened tent stores on shore and offered goods for sale which 'though at the most extortionate prices, were eagerly bought up'. Since cash was lacking, though some – including Mrs Barnsley – had brought quantities of it with them, the goods were in part sold to those amongst the population who had money orders and bills of credit, and even to the commissary for bills drawn on the Admiralty.

Phillip's final figures were that 158 prisoners died on board the *Neptune*. Others said 171, 36 aboard the *Surprize*, and 73 aboard the *Scarborough*. Nearly 500 convicts in all were landed sick. Given the weakened state of the arrivals, at first officers could see no benefit to society from the newcomers until they might recover and join the labour force, whose rations and work hours had at least returned to normal for the present.

The Reverend Johnson, who had avoided the hulks after his first visit to them in the Thames, and who seemed to avoid visits to the convict decks on the way to Botany Bay, had become inured to the proximity of convicts and to the universal squalor of Sydney Cove and entered the below-decks of the first of the three scandalous ships to arrive, the *Surprize*. He was galvanised by what he saw. 'A great number of them lying, some half, others nearly quite naked, without either bed nor bedding, unable to turn or help themselves. I spoke to them as I passed along, but the smell was so offensive that I could scarcely bear it . . . Some creeped upon their hands and knees, and some were carried upon the backs of others.' Johnson did not quite manage to carry his Christian compassion to the other holds – the captain of the least fatal ship, *Scarborough*, urged him not to descend into the death hole of its convict prison.

Attentive at the hospital, however, Johnson found many of the ill unable to move and 'covered over almost with their own nastiness, their heads, bodies, clothes, blankets all full of filth and lice. Scurvy was not the only nor the worst disease that prevailed among them.' The convicts had not lost sufficient craftiness to beg clothing from Johnson and then sell it almost at once for food, but when it came to food, those who were stronger stole from the weak, as was the case with the blankets as well.

Parties of convicts were sent out collecting the acid berry, also known as the native currant to combat the widespread scurvy. Since White found the quantity available was not sufficient to treat everyone, he also made use of a plant growing on the seashore greatly resembling sage, and a kind of 'wild spinage' (samphire) as well as 'a small shrub which we distinguished by the name of the vegetable tree'.

By early August, the Reverend Johnson wrote that he had buried 84 of the convicts, one child and one soldier, nearly all of them from the Second Fleet. People would afterwards remember the dingoes howling and fighting over the bodies in a sandy pit over the hills above the Tank Stream. By 6 August, Phillip reported an improvement in convict health, with the sick list down to 220, but deaths continued.

Captain Hill, landed from *Surprize*, suffered the normal shock of arrival but was pleased in some respects with his landfall. 'It is now our winter quarters, and had I superior abilities to any man that ever wrote, it would be possible for me to convey to your mind a just idea of this beautiful heavenly clime; suffer your imagination to enter the regions of fiction; and let fancy in her loveliest moment paint an Elysium; it will fall far short of this delightful weather. It is well we have something to keep up our spirits, everything else is unpromising. And did the gloomy months prevail here as in England, it is more than probable that the next reinforcement on arrival would find a desolated colony.'

But he was not happy with the amenities of his life. 'Here I am, living in a miserable thatched hut, without kitchen, without a garden, with an acrimonious blood by my having been nearly six months at sea, and tho' little better than a leper, obliged to live on a scanty pittance of salt provision, without a vegetable, except when a good-natured neighbour robs his own stomach in compassion to me.' Fresh meat cost 18d a pound, fish was not abundant (for it was winter), and 'should one be offered for sale, 'tis by far too dear for an officer's pocket'.

All the healthy male convicts from the Second Fleet were sent to the farming settlement at Parramatta. Captain Hill began surveying and laying out an enlargement of that township, 'in which the principal street will be occupied by the convicts; the huts are building at the distance of 100 feet from each other, and each hut is to contain ten convicts . . . and having good gardens which they cultivate, and frequently having it in their power to exchange vegetables for little necessaries, which the stores do not furnish, makes them begin to feel the benefits they may draw from their industry'. He found that people who had lived in huts with their own gardens for some time rarely abused the confidence that was placed in them, and if they did it was to plunder some other convict's garden.

Women convicts were put to work making clothes out of the slops, the raw cloth brought out on sundry ships. The population had by now quadrupled, and so when on 1 August the *Surprize* left for China, Phillip leased it to drop off 157 female and 37 male convicts at Norfolk Island on the way.

D'Arcy Wentworth had been working on a voluntary arrangement with Surgeon White, but was now sent to Norfolk Island with his convict paramour, Catherine Crowley, with the provisional post of assistant surgeon, based on the help he had given in the grounds of the Sydney hospital. There is no record of how he felt, the angry pride at being on probation and therefore not receiving wages. His sense of exile and of being neither bond nor free threw him more and more into the company of pregnant Catherine, and it seemed to have been adequate for him.

When the *Justinian* turned up at Norfolk on 7 August, the ration on the island was down to 2 pounds of flour and 1 pint of tea per person weekly, and only fish and cabbage tree palms and mutton birds and their eggs had saved the population. The *Surprize* joined her late that afternoon, with D'Arcy Wentworth and his eighteen-year-old convict woman aboard, but the Wentworths did not have a high priority for landing, so when the ship had to back off again and go to Cascade Bay on the north side of the island to shelter from a gale, Catherine Crowley gave premature shipboard birth to a son who was to be named William Charles Wentworth. D'Arcy Wentworth helped his son from his mother's womb, cut the cord and washed him, noticed an in-turned eye, but wrapped, warmed and caressed the baby. It took some weeks of tenderness and care to ensure his survival.

Wentworth landed into a turbulent scene, every human's negative passion enhanced by hunger and isolation and the limits of a small island set in consistently dangerous seas. He saw that the officers of the *Sirius* snubbed Major Ross and would not pay him the normal respects. Appointed quartermaster-general, Ralph Clark was now seen as Ross's favourite, even though Clark's opinion of the man had not previously been high. Clark's new posting gave him a tin-pot power, but it was also power of life and death over those who served time on Norfolk. D'Arcy Wentworth, fortunate to be free of all that, found five other surgeons and assistant surgeons on the island, and liked most of them: the fellow Irishmen Thomas Jamison and Dennis Considen, then Surgeon Altree, and the former convict John Irving. Irving, sentenced in Lincoln, had served as assistant surgeon on his own ship in the First Fleet, *Lady Penrhyn*, and after the arrival of the portable hospital in the Second Fleet had done such conspicuous work there that Phillip granted him an absolute pardon and appointed him to assist Considen. Back in Sydney, he had a grant of 30 acres awaiting him.

Dennis Considen befriended Wentworth at once and began to instruct him in the use of native plants for treating disease, an area of practice in which he had been a leader in Sydney. Indeed, in a letter to Sir Joseph Banks he had written, 'If there is any merit in applying these and other simples to the benefit of the poor wretches here, I certainly claim it.' As well as promoting the use of native sarsaparilla and spinach, red gum from angophora trees, yellow from grass trees, and oil from the peppermint eucalyptus tree, he found that the native myrtle would serve as a mild and safe astringent in cases of dysentery.

Wentworth was appointed surgeon to the little inland hamlet of Charlotte's Field, soon to be known as Queensborough, in the interior of the island, to which at first he walked each day. Wentworth had to treat, above all, diarrhoea and dysentery. He also had to attend lashings. Clark seemed to think flogging increasingly appropriate. For some time, Wentworth was a mediator between the lash and convicts. There had been the case of John Howard, former highway robber, already lashed early in 1790 for stealing potatoes and selling his clothes in return for food and drink. Later in the year, he would be ordered to receive 500 strokes for selling the slops issued to him by the public store and for telling a lie about it to Major Ross. Wentworth humanely called off the punishment when he had received 80 strokes – though Howard was still, in theory, to receive the remainder when he had recovered. Wentworth also attended when a man of almost 70 was given 100 lashes for stealing wheat and neglecting his work; and a young convict boy received 13 strokes on the buttocks for robbing his master.

Ralph Clark gave later Australian feminist historians every opportunity of accusing him of rancour against the women convicts. He said of First Fleeter Rachel Early that she was 'the most abandoned woman that I ever knew or heard of', but that seemed to be a definition Clark applied to whichever woman he had last been required to punish. He was embarked on an affair with Mary Brenham, a First Fleet woman of about nineteen years of age with a son who had been born to one of the *Lady Penrhyn* sailors. She would soon be carrying Clark's child. He seemed to take the relationship seriously – ultimately he would call the girl-child born of Brenham *Alicia*, to honour his wife, irrespective of whether she would ever find out or not.

As claustrophobic as the cheek-by-jowl society of Sydney and Parramatta were, the even narrower tensions of Norfolk Island sometimes made men like Clark sound nearly unhinged. He wrote, for instance, of a fellow officer, Lieutenant Creswell: 'I am a damned thorn in his side as he thinks I will get some thing by my volunteering this business of building a town out at Charlotte's Field [Queensborough]. I don't care how much he grins but by God, he must not attempt to bite for if he does this world will be too small for both of us to live in.'

The marine garrison showed they suffered obsessions of their own, to match those of the convicts and gentlemen, by refusing to take their provisions, alleging that the convicts were better off through getting preferential treatment and extra greens. Their hunger was no doubt sincere, but Clark was convinced that what they wanted was to test whether they or Major Ross were to be the masters here. He believed that the air of revolution, let loose in France, had reached even this remotest post.

Captain Johnston and his officers called the roll of the two companies, parading without arms in front of the barracks preparatory to implementing orders from Ross to march them disarmed to the store with their supply bags. Would they resist this order, even run inside to their bunks for their weapons? The authority of the Crown felt tenuous here, and yet, haunted by the possibility of severe punishment, the ranks broke and left their muskets in place and marched to the store to take their rations. 'This day has been near one of the most critical days in my life,' Clark sighed. 'Never was club law near taking place in any part of the world than it was in this – I wish that we were fairly away from this island, for I am afraid if we stay much longer we will not get away without a great deal of bloodshed, for our men here are the most mutinous set I ever was amongst and are ripe for rising against any authority.'

On Monday 2 May 1791, Clark 'went out to Queensborough to take Richardson with me (which is the man that flogs the people), and give them as many lashes as I think they deserved'. The flogger in question was James Richardson, a young man sentenced at eighteen for highway robbery and sent out on the

First Fleet. Richardson was very muscular and had been the public flogger for some months. The previous May, he had been required to lash five members of a boat crew who had concealed part of their catch, but had found himself subjected to 50 'for neglect of duty for not flogging the above five men as he ought to have done'. That is, he had not lashed them with sufficient vigour.

At Queensborough, Clark found that Katherine White and Mary Higgins had stolen corn out of the public fields. A woman in her early twenties, Katherine White had once lifted £65 in bank notes from an office in Woolwich, but the jury had soft-heartedly valued them at only 39 shillings to save her from the gallows. 'When I ordered Katherine White and Mary Higgins 50 each, White could only bear 15 when she fainted away. The doctor [Wentworth] wished I would order her to be taken down which I did.'

Clark then records that Mary Tute received 22 of her 25 lashes 'when she fainted away when I ordered her to be cast loose – I hope this will be a warning to the ladies out at Queensborough'. The pattern continued. Later in Ross's reign, Clark ordered another young woman to receive 50 lashes for abusing Mr Wentworth, but she received only 16, 'as Mr Wentworth begged that she might be forgiven the other 34'. Clark considered the girl in question – one Sarah Lyons – a 'D/B', his code for 'damned bitch'. Wentworth's tender-heartedness would not save Sarah Lyons from further floggings.

As much as these punishments were countenanced in the eighteenth century, and indeed administered to members of the armed forces with equal mercilessness, there is a growing coarseness of sensibility in Clark's journal which is an index of the effects of flogging on the entire society. What was occasional in the Royal Navy was close to daily on Norfolk Island, and obviously Wentworth did not like it. Clark's voice is the voice of a small-minded and savage authoritarianism, and there must have been days when Wentworth thought highway robbery was honest work beside this.

Back on the mainland, something promising was happening. James Ruse, the governor's agricultural Adam, was fulfilling his symbolic significance on his farm in the Rose Hill area. He was a young man who was no stranger to rage at what had befallen him, and liked to soften the edges of his life as a probationary felon–yeoman with gambling, talk and drink. Phillip was willing to live with those realities and took them as read. What he wanted were signs of agricultural hardihood and industry, and Ruse gave him that.

Ruse's 1790 harvest would produce a token 17½ bushels of wheat from 1½ acres, but by February 1791, Ruse would draw his last ration from the government store, an event of great psychological potency for Phillip, Ruse and all the critics. By then Ruse had met and married a convict woman from the *Lady Juliana* named Elizabeth Perry. Elizabeth at 21 had stolen items of clothing, including a bombazine gown and shoes, from her employer, a milk vendor's wife, to whom Perry had represented herself as 'a country girl just come to town'. She had been sick for the week before absconding with the goods. She claimed innocence, and argued that the clothes she was arrested in were her own, and given the shaky nature of the criminal justice system, she might indeed have been right.

The Ruse–Perry marriage rounded out the idyll. Phillip's land grant to Ruse was confirmed when in April 1791 the young convict would receive title to his land, the first grant issued in New South Wales. His place near the Parramatta River would become known appropriately as Experiment Farm. Elizabeth Ruse often heard her husband complain of the unsuitability of his ground at Parramatta, and he comforted himself for the smallish returns for his excessive labour and agricultural cleverness by drinking and gambling with other Parramatta convicts, notably with Christopher Magee, who had spent part of his adolescence in America and seems to have had republican and deist ideas, and thus was a good companion for irreverent conversations.

Twenty-two

His goods profitably sold in Sydney, scandalous Captain Trail, treating the governor's contempt with easy indifference, and blaming the death of his prisoners on the late Lieutenant Shapcote, prepared to return to England.

In late July 1790, the *Lady Juliana* was also due to sail for China and home via Norfolk Island, and ship's steward Nicol faced being immediately separated from Sarah Whitelam, his convict woman, and the child they shared. It had been a busy time for John Nicol: 'I saw but little of the colony, as my time was fully occupied in my duties as steward, and any moments I could spare I gave them to Sarah. The days flew on eagles' wings, for we dreaded the hour of separation which at length arrived.' Marines and soldiers were sent around Sydney Cove to bring the lovestruck crew of the *Lady Juliana* from the township on board. 'I offered to lose my wages, but we were short of hands . . . the captain could not spare a man and requested the aid of the governor. I thus was forced to leave Sarah, but we exchanged faith. She promised to remain true, and I promised to return when her time expired and bring her to England.' He wanted to stow her away, but at times of sailing the convicts were strictly guarded by the marines, and repeated searches were made of departing ships.

Amidst his grief at separation, Nicol had time to observe impressionistically the high fertility of New South Wales's convict women and attribute it to the sweet tea herb, *Smilax glyciphylla*. 'There was an old female convict, her hair quite grey with age, her face shrivelled, who was suckling a child she had borne in the colony . . . Her fecundity was ascribed to the sweet tea.'

As *Lady Juliana* made ready to leave, a leviathan came to Port Jackson, a huge sperm whale which entered and became embayed within the harbour. It had ever been so, one or two such creatures entering through the heads, sometimes with their calves, on their yearly migration from Antarctica to Hawaii. Some boat crews from the various transports went trying to hunt it, and threw harpoons its way without success. Then on a July morning it rose from the harbour deeps to smash a punt occupied by three marines and a midshipman from the look-out station on South Head. 'In vain they thro' out their hats, the bags of our provisions, and the fish they had caught, in hopes to satisfy him or turn his attention. Twice the whale rose out of the deep buffeting the punt with its back.' Only one marine survived, swimming ashore to Rose Bay.

By late August, however, the whale, still trapped in the harbour, ran itself aground at Manly. The beaching of a whale was a significant event for all Eora people, who gathered together on the beach from various clan areas to participate in the great meat and blubber feast. They used the sharpened shell on their *woomeras*, spear-throwers, to cut the whale flesh.

In the middle of the Eora whale-meat feast at Manly, an expeditionary party from Sydney Cove landed there. It included Surgeon John White; Captain Nicholas Nepean; the governor's shooter, John McEntire; and White's young native companion,

Nanbaree. They planned to head north overland for Broken Bay to hunt. The feasters, cooking blubber and flesh at their fires, scattered at the first sight of the party, but Nanbaree got up in the boat and reassured them. Bennelong and Colby stepped down the beach to meet the group. Other natives followed. The Europeans thought Bennelong was much changed, was 'so greatly emaciated, and so far disfigured by a long beard'. Colby proudly showed them that he had got rid of the iron shackle from his leg. Bennelong asked whether the visitors could provide a hatchet, which would be very helpful in speeding up the butchering of the dead whale, but Surgeon White said there were no hatchets. He gave him a shirt, and when Bennelong seemed awkward in putting it on, Surgeon White directed McEntire, the Irish huntsman, to help him. But Bennelong forbade McEntire to come near, 'eyeing him ferociously and with every mark of horror and resentment'. To the Aboriginals, McEntire was one of Phillip's chief avatars of malice.

Nonetheless, Bennelong kept enquiring after Phillip, and expressing a desire to see the governor, with whom, after all, he had exchanged names. At Bennelong's request, White fetched him from someone's kit a pair of clippers, and Bennelong began to trim himself. Looking at the women who would not come any closer, White asked Bennelong which was his old favourite, Barangaroo, 'of whom you used to speak so often?'

'Oh,' said he, as later set down in elevated English by Tench, 'she has become the wife of Colby! But I've got *Bul-la Mur-ee Dinnin* (two large women) to compensate for her loss.' White observed Bennelong bore two new wounds, one in the arm from a spear and the other a large scar over his left eye.

As the boat that was carrying the expeditioners was leaving to land them in another inlet, the natives crowded up with lumps of blubber for the governor, but by the standards of the Europeans, the meat was already putrescent. Bennelong insisted just the same on putting in a specially large piece as a gift to Phillip. The gift was not ironic – far from it. It was intended to get Phillip there, to Manly, to the great festival of the whale.

The party from Sydney Cove landed for their tramp to Broken Bay and told their coxswain, on the return to Sydney Cove with the lump of putrid whale meat, to let the governor know Bennelong was looking for him. Back in Sydney, His Excellency was engaged in discussing with Bloodworth and Harry Brewer the building of a pillar on South Head to serve as a direction-finder for ships at sea. The governor could be impetuous in rearranging his affairs to accommodate the natives, but then their relationship to him was high on his agenda. Now he gathered together all the weaponry immediately available – four muskets and a pistol – and set out in his boat to meet Bennelong. He was accompanied by Captain Collins and Lieutenant Waterhouse of the navy.

Waterhouse was a personable young man, newly promoted to the rank of lieutenant to replace the insane Mr Maxwell. He had become infatuated with Elizabeth Barnes, who had come off the *Lady Juliana* three months before, a slightly older woman than he, and possibly, as a former prostitute, more worldly. He may have been nervous making this excursion to Manly with the governor, given that many thought the governor somewhat reckless and over-trusting in his willingness to approach the natives. But Waterhouse would have been consoled at least to be with solid Captain Collins.

On landing, Phillip found the natives 'still busily employed around the whale'. He advanced alone, with just one unarmed seaman for support, and called for Bennelong, who was mysteriously slow in approaching. Collins and Waterhouse also landed, and given that Bennelong had a special liking for Collins, the native now came forward. So did Colby. Bennelong seemed delighted to see his old acquaintances 'and asked after every person he'd known in Sydney, among others the French cook and servant from whom he'd escaped, whom he'd constantly made the butt of his ridicule, by mimicking his voice, gait, and other peculiarities, all of which he again went through with his wanted exactness and drollery'. He asked particularly after a lady of the colony, surely Mrs Deborah Brooks, Phillip's housekeeper, from whom he had once ventured to snatch a kiss. When he was told she was well, he kissed the fresh-faced Lieutenant Waterhouse whom he obviously thought had a complexion like that of the lady, and laughed uproariously. But when the governor pointed to Bennelong's new wounds, the native became more sombre. He had received them down in the southern bay, Botany Bay, he announced, and he solemnly pointed out their contours to Phillip.

The governor promised to come back in two days with hatchets and tomahawks. He had brought a bottle of wine with him – the servant was carrying it, and on Phillip's order uncorked it and poured a glass, at which Bennelong uttered the toast, 'The King!' and drank off the wine. During this conference, 'the Indians filing off to right and left, so as in some measure to surround them', Phillip remained calm. Bennelong, wearing by now two jackets, one brought by Phillip and the other by Collins, introduced the governor to a number of the people on the beach, including a 'stout, corpulent native', Willemering. On the ground was a very fine barbed spear 'of uncommon size'. The governor asked if he could have it. But Bennelong picked it up and took it away and dropped it near a place where Willemering stood rather separate from the rest. Bennelong brought back another gift for the governor instead, a throwing stick.

Willemering was a wise man, a *carradhy*, amongst other things a ritual punishment man invited in from another place, in fact the Broken Bay area. He struck the watching Europeans as a frightened man, and he may have been, but he was probably more a tense and intent man, coiled for his task.

For it was time for the governor, who had had the grace to present himself, to be punished for all of it – the fish and game stolen, the presumption of the Britons in camping permanently without permission, the stolen weaponry and nets, the stove-in canoes, the random shooting of natives, the curse of smallpox, the mysterious genital infections of women and then of their men. Phillip was about to pay for all the damage which had befallen the Eora people. There was no malice on anyone's part in this punishment, which explained why Willemering showed all the nervousness and then unexpected decisiveness of a bride-groom. But the scales needed to be adjusted by august blood, and the most august of all was Phillip's. To Bennelong, Colby, and to the visiting punishment man from Broken Bay, Willemering, Phillip needed to pay for his unruly children.

Thinking Willemering was nervous, Phillip gamely advanced towards him, as if begging the spear. Captain Collins and Lieutenant Waterhouse followed close by. Phillip removed his own single weapon, a dirk in his belt, and threw it on the ground. Willemering reacted by lifting the spear upright from the grass with his toes and fitting it in one movement into his throwing stick, and 'in an instant darted it at the governor'. In the last moment before the spear was thrown, Phillip thought it was more dangerous to retreat than to advance and cried out to the man, 'Werre, Werre!'

Given the force with which the spear was projected, Phillip would later describe the shock of the wound to Tench as similar to a violent blow. The barb went into the governor's right shoulder, just above the collar bone, and ran downwards through his body, coming out his back. Willemering looked at his handiwork long enough to ensure the spear had penetrated, and then he dashed into the woods, with miles to travel to his home ground in the Pittwater–Broken Bay region.

There was instant confusion on both sides. Bennelong and Colby both disappeared, and the party of Europeans retreated as fast as they could, but Phillip's escape was hindered by the fact that he carried in his body, pointing skyward when he was upright, a lance twelve feet long, the butt of it frequently striking the ground as he reeled and further lacerating the wound. 'For God's sake, haul out the spear,' Phillip begged Waterhouse, who knew it was potentially fatal to try to draw out the barb and instead tried to break off the spear shaft. Waterhouse, wrongly expecting a massacre, one eye on the advancing natives, struggled to break the thing off close to the wound and at last managed to do so. Another thrown spear from an enthusiastic native struck Waterhouse in the hand as he worked on the shaft. Now spears were flying thickly, as happened at such exchanges of blood, as the ordinary folk, the laity if you like, joined in the ritual event.

Phillip was lifted with the point of the spear protruding from his back into his boat and brought across the harbour, bleeding a considerable amount on the way. 'The boat had five miles to row before it reached the settlement,' wrote Collins. Indeed it had longer, for the distance was seven miles. 'But the people exerting themselves to the utmost, the governor was landed and in his house in something less than two hours.' It was feared in the boat that 'the sub-clavian artery' might have been punctured. Since Surgeon White was away from Sydney, his Scots assistant, William Balmain, a quarrelsome man in his mid-twenties, took on the task of extracting the spearhead from Phillip. There, at government house, on a cot, his blue coat sodden with blood, lay the settlement's pole of stability and awesome reasonableness, without whom all was lost. As Balmain prepared his instruments, what sedation or anaesthesia, if any, was administered we do not know, but the young surgeon earned the joy of Phillip's disciples by declaring the wound non-mortal and by safely extracting the barbed point of the spear. 'The governor remains in great agonies, but it is thought he will recover, though at the same time His Excellency is highly scorbutic.' The wound would heal slowly, but it *would* heal.

This result would not have surprised the blubber-feasting natives of Manly Cove. They knew it was not intended to be a fatal wound: they knew the barb was meant to be extractable, they knew Willemering was an expert at placement, they knew there were no infectious, magic-laden, glued-in fragments of bone and stone designed to stay in the wound and cause ultimate death. But to the Europeans, Phillip's recovery was a matter of rejoicing, at least for those who knew how much the settlement depended upon him. Phillip, no doubt given laudanum for the pain, had time to order that no natives were to be fired on, unless they first were 'the aggressors, by throwing spears'. White's hunting party was fetched back by marines with the news of

Governor Phillip's wounding. The boat crew sent to retrieve them told the party that Colby and Bennelong had been talking to them and had 'pretended highly to disapprove the conduct of the man who had thrown the spear, vowing to execute vengeance upon him'. Was this a token offered to the wounded Phillip? Were the two natives striking attitudes just to please him?

David Collins was sure that the only reason the spear was thrown was fear on the part of the native Willemering that he was about to be seized and taken away. Indeed, Collins thought the spearing would not have happened if only a musket had been taken ashore with Phillip. 'The governor has always placed too great a confidence in these people . . . he had now, however, been taught a lesson which it might be presumed he would never forget.'

In general, no one blamed Bennelong directly for Willemering's gesture. It was accepted that Willemering acted out of personal panic, though the people from Sydney Cove found Bennelong's behaviour typically mystifying. But if the accounts of witnesses, including Lieutenant Waterhouse, are looked at, one sees that Bennelong very clearly showed his new scars, which his adventures and sins had merited, to Phillip as a sign and a reassurance, and that in refusing to give Phillip the spear he asked for, and taking it away and putting it within reach of Willemering's foot, he had shown it possessed another ordained purpose. The forming-up of warriors in a half-circle creates an impression of a conclave of witnesses to a ritual penalty.

And with considerable perception, in the end Phillip thought that it was a cultural manifestation, that though Bennelong probably was glad his friend and name-exchanger, the governor, had survived, there was no doubt that the natives 'throw their spears, and take a life in their quarrels, which are very frequent, as readily as the lower class of people in England stripped to box'.

The ritual spearing of Phillip seemed to be a new direction in Eora policy, though to put it in those terms is callous to the reality of the bewilderment of the Eora soul. There had been hope for a time that the visitors would vanish, but the ships had multiplied in number, coming by way of lesions in the cosmos though the gates of the great harbour. Some ships had departed, but now a number had taken their place, and the ghosts multiplied both by new shiploads and by human generation. Though on the day of the spearing one convict amongst the victims of the Second Fleet, a man of 24 named Samuel Allen, former buckle-maker, former gentleman's gentleman, former drummer to an Irish brigade in the French army and now a declared silverware thief, was brought from the morgue at the hospital and buried in Sydney's earth, this decrease by death did nothing in numbers to produce a visible crisis in the camp of the whites, or provide a sign that they would be finally borne away and return the coast to its normal state.

Phillip's wound took six weeks to get better, and throughout that time, hoping to use Abaroo and Nanbaree as intermediaries, Phillip still had his men out looking for Bennelong, hoping there would be reconciliation. Several officers went to visit the Eora on the Manly side. Surgeon White and the new commissary, John Palmer, former purser of *Sirius*, veteran of the American wars who had replaced the exhausted Andrew Miller, were the ones who at last found Bennelong, for whom a momentous change had come about. He had been joined by his beloved Barangaroo, a spirited woman who had left or been divorced by Colby. Barangaroo already knew that she needed to watch Bennelong very closely, and did so. She did not seem as noticeably pleased as he to know that the governor was well. Bennelong claimed, through the interpretation of the two children, Abaroo and Nanbaree, to have beaten Willemering as a punishment. It might have been the truth, another adjustment of universal order.

The party asked Bennelong to help them arrange a husband for Abaroo, someone who could go to and from the settlement without causing trouble. At once, Bennelong suggested Yemmerrawanne, a slender and handsome youth about sixteen years old. He called the lad out of the people milling nearby. For smiling Yemmerrawanne, this would prove a fatal nomination in the end, but he came forward on being invited, went immediately up to Abaroo and offered 'many brandishments which proved that he had assumed the *toga virilis*. But Abaroo disclaimed his advances, repeating the name of another person, who we knew was her favourite'. On a return visit later in the day though, Yemmerrawanne pressed his suit 'with such warmth and solicitation, as to cause an evident alteration in the sentiments of the lady'.

There was a contest between Abaroo and the older woman Barangaroo, Barangaroo trying to talk Abaroo into rejoining her people, and Abaroo, as a means of validating her choice to live amongst the Europeans, offering Barangaroo a petticoat to wear, which Barangaroo put on but was then mocked out of, or became ashamed of. 'This was the prudery of the wilderness, which her husband joined us to ridicule, and we soon laughed her out of it. The petticoat was dropped with hesitation, and Barangaroo stood "armed cap-a-pee in nakedness".'

Now that the wounding of Arthur Phillip had established the principles of responsibility, Bennelong complained to Tench that his countrymen had lately been plundered of fizgigs, spears, the gift of a sword and many other articles by some of the convicts and others, and said he would hand back a dirk the governor had dropped during the attack by Willemering. The next day, after a search of the settlement, a party of officers, sailors and soldiers went down-harbour again with the collected stolen property. Bennelong was not there – he had gone fishing with Barangaroo. Yemmerrawanne came forward and grabbed the sword, which had been an earlier gift to Bennelong, and fought a mock battle with a yellow gum tree, engaging in all the 'gestures and vociferations which they use in battle'. He now laid aside the sword and joined the party, 'with a countenance which carried in it every mark of youth and good nature'.

Tench saw an old man come forward and claim one of the fizgigs, 'singling it from the bundle and taking only his own, and this honesty, within the circle of their society, seemed to characterise them all'. Chancing upon Bennelong, they found he was grateful for the return of the materials, though they still possessed some unclaimed items, one of which was a net of fishing lines, which Barangaroo now took possession of and flung defiantly around her neck. Bennelong did not return the governor's dirk, however, and pretended not to know much about it. Perhaps it was kept for some chant to be sung into it, something to bring wisdom to Phillip, to end the calamity. Watching him imbibe wine they had brought, the officers pressed him to name a day when he would come to Sydney. Bennelong said that the governor must first come and see him, 'which we promised should be done'.

When the governor was well, he travelled by boat down-harbour to visit Bennelong, opening his wound-inhibited arms.

His apparent willingness to forgive created not always approving comment. But Bennelong was not ready to visit Sydney Cove yet. It was arranged that the natives would light a fire on the north shore of the harbour as a signal for the Europeans to visit them further.

Again Phillip accepted these terms. Certainly Bennelong was the sort of wilful man who delighted in setting tests, but even so he might have still been trying in a way to educate Phillip, who asked to be notified as soon as look-outs saw the signal fire. When it was seen, Phillip and some others set off immediately in their cutters. 'We found assembled Baneelon [Bennelong], Barangaroo, and another young woman, and six men, all of whom received us with welcome. They had equipment with them – spears, fish gigs and lines, which they were willing to barter.' Bennelong and his party thus attempted to create the principle on which they would make friends with the settlement. Implements and items in general should be bartered, not plundered. 'I had brought with me an old blunted spear, which wanted repair,' wrote Tench. A native took it, carried it to the fire, tore a piece of bone with his teeth from a fizgig and attached it to the spear to be repaired with yellow eucalyptus gum, which had been 'rendered flexible by heat'. The meeting was probably considered a success by both parties, but there were major lessons on both sides which remained unlearned.

Another day, when Surgeon White, Watkin Tench, the Reverend Johnson, the native girl Abaroo or Boorong, and a young, educated convict, John Stockdale, ran into Bennelong and Barangaroo on the north side of Port Jackson, they tried to persuade him and three other natives to visit Phillip in Sydney Cove. Barangaroo, more suspicious than the impetuous, vulnerable Bennelong, did not want her husband to go to Sydney with Tench and White. She snatched up one of Bennelong's fishing spears and broke it against rocks in protest at her lover's gullibility.

In the end, the Reverend Johnson, Abaroo and Stockdale remained with Barangaroo as hostages against a safe return of Bennelong and the other men. The boats and the native canoe tied up on the east side of Sydney Cove at the governor's wharf, and then everyone set off for Phillip's residence. There was a reunion at which Bennelong told Phillip that Willemering was at Broken Bay. Bennelong was delighted to see the governor's orderly sergeant, whom he kissed, and a woman who attended in the kitchen, probably Mrs Deborah Brooks. But again he snubbed the gamekeeper McEntire. He showed his friends around government house, explaining what various implements were for. Since the Aboriginals could not pronounce the letter 's', Bennelong amused Tench by pointing to a candle-snuffer and saying, 'Nuffer for candle.' He demonstrated its use, employing his forefinger in the role of the candle. 'Finding that even this sagacious interpretation failed, he threw down the snuffers in a rage, and reproaching their [the other Aboriginals'] stupidity, walked away.' He was more tender-voiced with the children of the settlement who came to see him. At last, he departed and was rowed back to Barangaroo, whom they found sitting by a fire with the Reverend Johnson, making fishhooks.

'From this time our intercourse with the natives,' wrote Tench, 'though partially interrupted, was never broken off. We gradually continued, henceforth, to gain knowledge of their customs and policy; the only knowledge that can lead to a just estimate of national character.' But that Bennelong might have been involved in a study of *him* was something not even generous and perceptive Watkin mentioned.

One day in October that year, a sergeant and three soldiers were out beating the bush for an escaped convict when they met up with Bennelong and Colby and a party of other natives. Bennelong asked the sergeant to come with him south and kill a particular man, a man who was 'well-known for having lost an eye', a Botany Bay warrior named Pemulwuy. The soldiers joked with him, but he was serious. Near the shores of Botany Bay Bennelong had fought a ritual battle with the father of a desirable girl, and although he claimed to have won the contest, his passions ran high against Pemulwuy, the girl's kinsman, who must have taken some part that annoyed Bennelong. But as ever with Bennelong, the woman was forthright and not submissive. She was named Karubarabulu, a Bediagal kinswoman of Pemulwuy, and Bennelong had desired to take her as a second wife.

Bennelong had a temperament which participated passionately in all these inter-clan squabbles, but the difference between himself and Pemulwuy ran deeper than mere scars. Pemulwuy stayed remote from the Europeans. He would never investigate the whites or try to work them out. He wished to exorcise them and restore the normal world. While Bennelong was conciliatory, Pemulwuy was a hard-liner. Both would suffer unutterably for the positions they took.

Aside from tribal conflicts, it seemed that a sort of compact now existed between the Eora, in the person of Bennelong, and Phillip's invading culture. Bennelong seemed well aware of his status as chief peacemaker, the one with whom above all Phillip wanted reconciliation, and he was not above asking for material rewards for fulfilling that role. He requested a tin shield – he rightly thought it might save him many a wound – and a brick house in Sydney Cove. The mutual gifts of hatchets and spears, and the intermittent arrival and departure of Eora people in Sydney sealed the deal. Bennelong read the gifts he received from Phillip and others as personal, but also more than that – as acknowledgements of Eora rights in this country and in these waters. The officers failed to see them as equivalent exchanges, and remained half-amused by Bennelong's demands for hatchets. They thought they were giving appeasing gifts to troublesome Aborigines, rather than sealing an informal but important treaty.

A visible sign of the compact was in the making. A brick house was built for Bennelong, as requested, on the eastern point of Sydney Cove, Tubowgulle. Bennelong had chosen the place himself, according to Tench. 'Rather to please him, a brick house of twelve feet square was built for his use, and for that of his countrymen as might choose to reside in it, on a point of land fixed upon by himself.' He had got his shield too – it had been double-cased with tin and represented an exponential leap for Eora weaponry. Of Bennelong's new stature with both whites and Eora, Tench observed, 'He had lately become a man of so much dignity and consequence, that it was not always easy to obtain his company.' The point chosen by him for his residence had significance – given its position at the head of the cove (where the Sydney Opera House now stands), it could be seen as a symbol of Eora title to the place. It was almost certainly seen that way by Bennelong, and all Barangaroo's warnings went for nothing.

Twenty-three

By mid-1790, Collins would write that native women would barter sex with convicts for a loaf of bread, a blanket or a shirt. 'Several girls who were protected in the settlement had not any objection to passing the night on board of ships.' They would try to conceal the gifts given them by sailors, thus, said Collins, learning shame. Europeans seemed both attracted and repelled by the indigenous women – there were complaints about the odour of their flesh, anointed with fish oils to drive off insects. Yet even Arthur Phillip was not immune from their allure. One of the native women, noted Phillip, had 'pleasing features . . . had she been in a European settlement, no one would have doubted her being a Mulatto Jewess'.

The natives shared with the British lower classes a full-blown willingness to beat their wives, although spirited women like Barangaroo hit back, giving Bennelong a severe gash on the forehead to go with his ritual wounds. Outside his hut at Tubowgulle, Bennelong would severely beat Barangaroo for breaking a fishing spear and a *woomera*, or throwing stick, and she needed to be taken to White's hospital across the stream for sutures. It certainly seemed that Bennelong was in a volatile condition – the Europeans were left to wonder whether all

Aboriginal husbands felt it was right to damage their wives, or whether it was a temperamental flaw in Bennelong himself.

Phillip observed a tender moment between Bennelong and Barangaroo when she complained of a pain in the belly. 'I went to the fire and sat down with her husband who, notwithstanding his beating her occasionally, seemed to express great sorrow on seeing her ill, and after blowing on his hand, he warmed it, and then applied it to the part affected, beginning at the same time a song, which was probably calculated for the occasion.' A bystander offered him a piece of flannel he could use to make his hand warm. '. . . he continued his song, always keeping his mouth very close to the part affected, and frequently stopping to blow on it, making a noise after blowing in imitation of the barking of a dog'. In the end they sent for the surgeon who treated her with tincture of rhubarb, which worked to give her relief.

But the standing of Bennelong, at least in Captain Tench's view, suffered further damage from his behaviour towards his second, new and younger wife, Karubarabulu, the young woman from the north side of Botany Bay who, despite the earlier battles over her, had now come to live at Tubowgulle. One day in November, Bennelong came to the governor's residence and presented himself to Phillip – he seemed to be able to get an interview any time he liked. Holding a hatchet, and trying out the sharpness of it, he told Phillip that he intended to put Karubarabulu to death immediately. Bennelong obviously believed Karubarabulu had committed adultery, and that this gave him the right to bludgeon her to death, and his visit to government house beforehand was a warning to Phillip not to interfere in laws that were none of his business. But Phillip was alarmed enough to take his secretary, Captain Collins, and Sergeant Scott, the orderly, with him to observe proceedings. On the road from government house down to Tubowgulle, Bennelong continued to speak wildly and incoherently and 'manifested such extravagant marks of fury and revenge' that his hatchet was taken away from him, and a walking stick was given to him instead. After all, English males were themselves relatively comfortable with the idea of hitting errant women with walking sticks.

Karubarabulu was seated at the communal fire outside the hut with the other natives. Bennelong, snatching a sword from one of the soldiers, ran at her and gave her two severe wounds on the head, and one on the shoulder.

The Europeans rushed in and grabbed him, but the other natives remained quiet witnesses, a sign that they considered Bennelong entitled to his vengeance. Phillip and the officers noticed that the more they restrained Bennelong, the more the other male Aborigines present began to arm themselves, as if to support Bennelong's right to what he was doing.

Fortunately the *Supply* was in the intimate cove – on Phillip's orders, it was immediately hailed and a boat with armed sailors was sent ashore, and Karubarabulu was hustled away on this across the cove to the hospital. A young native came up and begged to be taken into the boat also. He claimed to be her lawful husband, which she declared he was, and pleaded that he might be allowed to accompany her so that he also would be away from Bennelong's rage. 'She is now my property,' Tench has Bennelong saying, like a character in an eighteenth-century drama. 'I have ravished her by force from her tribe: and I will part with her to no person whatever, until my vengeance shall be glutted.' He told the governor and others that he would follow her to the hospital and kill her. Phillip told him that if he did, he would be shot at once, but he treated this threat 'with disdain'.

A number of natives visited the girl in hospital and 'they all appeared very desirous that she might return to the house, though they must have known that she would be killed; and, what is not to be accounted for, the girl herself seemed desirous of going'. After an absence of two days, Bennelong came back to Phillip's house and told him he would not beat the girl any further. He himself had a new husbandly shoulder wound from an argument with Barangaroo. His wife and he should go to Surgeon White's hospital and have their wounds dressed, Phillip suggested. But Bennelong would not go because he believed Surgeon White would shoot him, and he refused to stay in the settlement in his house because he had come to believe White, outraged by the damage he had done to Karubarabulu, would assassinate him by night.

The argument was sorted out, however, and soon he was over in the hospital to have a plaster applied to his shoulder. Once this was done he visited Karubarabulu, and to Barangaroo's outrage took Karubarabulu by the hand and spoke softly to her.

Thus Bennelong's *ménage à trois* remained turbulent. It is remarkable the way Phillip, across the barrier of racial incomprehension, entertained and tolerated it. Karubarabulu was at last taken to the governor's house so that she could be safe. From the government house yard, Barangaroo stood hurling curses up at the girl's window, even grabbing some of Bennelong's spears to launch at the offender, and had to be disarmed of them by the marine guards at the gate. But in the evening, when Bennelong was leaving to go back to his hut, the girl Karubarabulu, on whom the governor had lavished such care, demanded that she go too, for a messenger had come saying that Barangaroo would not beat her anymore and was now 'very good'. Phillip reluctantly let her go and looked down from his hill towards Tubowgulle, the headland where Bennelong's hut lay, outside which fires burned and from which cries and conversation and arguments could again be heard. All violent domestic quarrels have their aspects of dark comedy and excess, and to what extent this brawl was characteristic of native society is hard to fathom.

Bennelong continued to confuse the officers with his signals. On the one hand he said a relative had been killed by the Cameraigal, but then he was seen on the north shore picking wild fruit with members of that group. And then on 21 November, Bennelong and Barangaroo as a couple pleaded with Phillip to give them protection in his house. The governor did so. In fact, if a native family were under some cloud with their own or other people, they often came to camp in the garden of government house. In this case, Bennelong told Phillip the Cameraigal had killed one of his 'brothers', a friend or relation, and had burned his body. When Phillip said he would send soldiers to punish them, Bennelong was all in favour of such action. The expedition, however, never took place.

The behaviour of the governor's chief huntsman, John McEntire, had not been changed by Phillip's wounding, and so the long list of infringements of which he was guilty in Eora eyes, and in which he continued, had not been absolved. On one occasion, when he was hunting, the natives had set one of the indigenous dogs, a dingo, on him, and he had shot it.

Phillip would later observe an initiation ceremony during

which native elders crawled on their hands and knees with a stick stuck through a waistband and lying across their backs like the tail of a native dog. When McEntire turned and shot the dingo dead, he was assuming the role of an initiated man, and another crime was added to the mortal list.

Preparations were made amongst the Eora for his punishment. For Phillip was amazed to observe that Bennelong entertained at his hut for some nights the man named Pemulwuy whom he had previously told Phillip and others was his enemy.

Men like Pemulwuy became *carradhys*, or as one scholar puts it, 'Aboriginal men of high degree', by being selected in childhood for their piercing, flecked eyes and precocious air of authority. Throughout eastern Australia there are many initiations, processes and tests for the making of a *carradhy*. The candidate was often thrown on a fire while in a state of trance, or hurled into a sacred waterhole. Prayers were recited by the initiate and the elders to the most important cult heroes and sky beings, Gulambre or Daramulan, as the candidate was brought out of the water or fire. The elders woke the candidate from his trance by laying their hands on his shoulders, and he was given quartz crystals to swallow and an individual totem to help him cure people. In all this, as in Western rites of preparation for the priesthood, fasting and endurance and time spent alone before the candidate went through initiations were considered important.

A *carradhy* always played a leading part in the rituals of the Dreamtime, for which he was painted with arm blood or red ochre sanctified by the chants that accompanied its application to the skin. All the crises of Aboriginal life were dealt with by magic, by rituals, by spells and by the sacramental paraphernalia owned by the *carradhys*. The *carradhys* also interpreted dreams, which were taken very seriously by Aboriginals.

The powers exercised by *carradhys* were sometimes symbolised externally by the handling of bones or of crystals of quartz or other rare stones. It was believed *carradhys* were capable of eroding a human being while he slept by extracting fat from within his body without making a mark. But it was McEntire's lifeblood Pemulwuy would apply himself to.

On 9 December, a sergeant of marines took three convict huntsmen, including McEntire, down to the north arm of Botany Bay to shoot game. They settled down in a hide of boughs to sleep and wait for the kangaroos to emerge at dusk. At about one o'clock in the afternoon the party was awoken by a noise outside the hide, and saw five natives creeping towards them. The sergeant was alarmed but McEntire said, 'Don't be afraid, I know them.'

Indeed he did. He knew Pemulwuy from earlier expeditions. The sergeant and the other convicts noticed that 'he had been lately among us' as 'was evidenced from his being newly shaved'. Pemulwuy had a deformed foot which enabled him to make confusing tracks, and the particular characteristics of the eyes, including a strange fleck in his left eye, which went with his office. As McEntire advanced to greet him, Pemulwuy retreated a little, jumped on a fallen log and with great sudden energy hurled his spear into McEntire's side. McEntire declared, 'I am a dead man.'

One of the party broke off the shaft of the spear and the other two took up their guns and futilely chased the natives. Then they carried McEntire back to Sydney Cove and got him to the hospital early the next morning. The governor was away at

Parramatta at the time, but was shocked by the news on his return. One of Phillip's characteristics was sometimes to invest affection and unremitting loyalty in people of flawed character who were effective in a limited range of skills: Harry Brewer, for example, and McEntire. Phillip detailed a sentry to wake the ever loyal Captain Watkin Tench. As Tench walked up the hill in the still, pre-dawn cool of a summer's night, he may have had a sense that for the first time in his Sydney experience, Mars was calling and battle was close.

He met a Phillip who was grimly and uncharacteristically enraged. He instructed Watkin to lead a punitive party of armed marines. Excited by the accounts of the two convicts and sergeant who had been with McEntire, the governor at first envisaged that Tench's party would track down a group of natives, put two of them instantly to death and bring in ten hostages for execution in town. None of these were to be women or children, and though all weapons that were encountered were to be destroyed, no other property was to be touched. After prisoners had been taken, all communication, even with those natives 'with whom we were in habits of intercourse, was to be avoided'.

Tench was horrified to hear that his party was required to cut off and bring in the heads of the two slain – hatchets and bags would be supplied for the purpose. But teased and annoyed by the ambiguity of native manners, Phillip argued that no signal 'of amity or invitation' should be made to the natives, and if made by any native was to be ignored.

In explaining his tough policy, Phillip told Tench that since the British had arrived seventeen people had been killed or wounded by the natives, and he looked upon the Bediagal clan, who lived on the north side of Botany Bay, as the principal aggressors.

Phillip was convinced the natives did not fear death individually, but what they particularly dreaded was to lose numbers relative to the other native groups. He had delayed using violent measures because of his belief that 'in every former instance of hostility, they had acted either from having received injury, or from misapprehension. "The latter of these causes," added he, "I attribute my own wound; but in this business of McEntire, I am fully persuaded that they were unprovoked, and the barbarity of their conduct admits of no extenuation".' He complained that Bennelong and Colby had promised to bring in Pemulwuy, but they had failed to do so and were now engaged on other tasks. Bennelong, 'instead of directing his steps to Botany Bay, crossed the harbour in his canoe, in order to draw the fore-teeth of some of the young men'.

Indeed, for the sometimes hated Cameraigal, Bennelong was now acting the part of distinguished visitor for an initiation ceremony. As for Colby, he had gone off in his canoe and was 'loitering about the look-out house' on South Head. 'I am resolved to execute the prisoners who may be brought in,' said Phillip, 'in the most public and exemplary manner, in the presence of as many of their countrymen as can be collected, after having explained the cause of such punishment, and my fixed determination to repeat it, whenever any future breach of good conduct on their side shall render it necessary.'

The governor at this point asked Watkin for his opinion, and the young officer suggested the capture of six might do just as well, and out of this number, a group should be set aside for retaliation if any further outrage occur, and only a portion executed immediately. The governor decided that should Watkin find it possible to take six prisoners, 'I will hang two, and send the rest to Norfolk Island for a certain period, which will cause their countrymen to believe that we have dispatched them secretly.'

McEntire was not dead, indeed he seemed to be recovering at the hospital, but Phillip believed the lesson still had to be taught. The expedition was to set out at 4 am on the humid morning of 14 December. Tactful Tench included the New South Wales Corps's urbane Captain Hill in the group. He had also chosen Lieutenants Pouldon of the marines and Dawes, the astronomer.

Lieutenant Dawes was conscience-stricken about the objectives of the expedition and spoke with his friend the Reverend Johnson about its morality. Even though in Chesapeake Bay he had been wounded by the French in alliance with the revolutionary Americans, Dawes saw himself above all as a student of people, a surveyor of surfaces and skies, not as a combat soldier. He had spent a great deal of time putting together his dictionary of the Eora, who liked him greatly. Above all, he admired Patyegarang, an Aboriginal girl of about fifteen named for *Pattagorang*, the large grey kangaroo, who was one of his sources for his language collection. She became his familiar and stayed in his hut as his chief language teacher, servant and perhaps lover. Rightly or wrongly, in a society in which the life expectancy was less than forty years, an affair with a fifteen-year-old would not be considered too grossly improper, and the language of Patyegarang recorded by Dawes might indicate that he was either a very affectionate mentor or something more. *Nangagolang*, time for rest, Patyegarang said when the tap-to, military lights-out, was beaten from the barracks square near the head of the cove. And *Matigarabangun naigaba*, we shall sleep separate. *Nyimang candle Mr D*. Put out the candle, Mr Dawes.

It was Patyegarang who interpreted the motives of her people to Dawes. A white man had been wounded some days before in one of the areas down-harbour to Warrane, Sydney Cove, and Dawes asked her why. *Gulara*, said Patyegarang. Angry. *Minyin gulara Eora?* asked Dawes. Why are the black men angry? *Inyan ngalwi*. Because the white men settled here. And then, further, said Patyegarang, *Gunin*, the guns.

These exchanges must have played a large part in Dawes's refusal to hunt the natives. On the day the expedition was ordered, he wrote a letter to his superior officer, Captain James Campbell, in which he refused to take part in the expedition. Dawes was an officer who had corresponded with William Wilberforce, renowned leader of the campaign against slavery, and the objectives of this mission were abhorrent to him. Campbell could not persuade Dawes to change his mind and the two of them brought the letter to Phillip, who 'took pains to point out the consequences of his being put under arrest'. Phillip told Dawes he was guilty of 'unofficerlike behaviour' and threatened him with a court-martial. But Dawes simply refused to submit to one.

Though he ultimately agreed to go, he would later publicly declare he was 'sorry he had been persuaded to comply with the order'. And though this would further outrage Phillip's feelings, Dawes refused to retract his statement.

Three sergeants and 40 privates made up the rank and file of this expeditionary force, and some of the low soldiery carried the hatchets and bags for the collection of two heads. The force tramped south on a familiar track between bushy slopes and paperbark lagoons, sighting the Pacific to their left through the contours of the land. They reached the peninsula at the northern arm of Botany Bay at nine o'clock in the morning. They searched in various directions without seeing a single native, so that at four o'clock they halted for their evening camp. At daylight they marched fruitlessly in an easterly direction, then southwards, and then northwards, often beset by insects in marshy country. Back near the north head of Botany Bay they saw 'five Indians' on the beach, whom Tench attempted to surround, but the five vanished. 'A contest between heavy-armed Europeans,' said one commentator, 'and naked unencumbered Indians, was too unequal to last long.'

Phillip took comfort from the fact that some local natives at the hospital already knew the name of the killer, Pemulwuy, and were upset to see McEntire in this condition. Phillip read their sympathy as unconditional, whereas they might have felt awed to find themselves in the presence of a walking dead man.

After Tench's military expedition set out, the governor had tried to stop Colby going to Botany Bay, offering him a blanket, a hatchet, a jacket to distract him. On top of that, he was diverted by food – the officers tried to *eat* him down. 'It was hoped that he would feed so voraciously, as to render him incapable of executing his intention.' He was given a huge meal of 'a light horseman' (a New South Wales fish) and 5 pounds of beef and bread. But then 'he set out on his journey with such lightness and gaiety, as plainly showed him to be a stranger to the horrors of indigestion'.

He told the gentlemen he had to go south not to thwart any military expedition but to see a kinswoman, Doringa, who was about to give birth. But his chief purpose was probably to warn people, especially Pemulwuy and his own *damelian* – his namesake – the Botany Bay native who shared the name Colby.

Meanwhile, the British military force under Tench moved towards 'a little village (if five huts deserved the name)', but no one was there. In the native *gunyas* or huts, they found nothing except fishing spears, fizgigs, which they left untouched. Tench used bags certainly enough, but chiefly to bring home samples of the thin, sandy soil of lagoon-studded Botany Bay. Some canoes were seen and possibly fired on, because we know that Botany Bay Colby was wounded.

Returning to their baggage, which they had left under the care of a small guard of soldiers, the party saw a native fishing in shallow water about 300 yards from land. Tench seems to have been relieved that it was not practicable at that distance to shoot him or seize him, so decided to ignore him. But the native himself did not ignore the party. He turned and started calling various of them by name, and 'in spite of our formidable array, drew nearer with unbounded confidence'. It was Colby from Sydney. Tench was under orders to ignore old native friends, but how could he shoot Colby down? Single handedly, Colby psychologically dis armed the group 'with his wanted familiarity and unconcern'. In theory, his head should have gone into one of their bags. Instead, he recounted how the day before he had been at the hospital for the amputation of a woman's leg by Surgeon White, and he re-enacted for them the agony and cries of the woman. In fact, he was having exactly the blunting effect on the expedition he probably wanted to have. The longer he talked and used his dramatic tricks, the harder it became for them to consider killing him.

Overnight he vanished. The next day the British party resumed their dispirited march and camped at three in the after-noon by a freshwater swamp: 'after a day of severe fatigue, to pass a nice night of restless inquietude, when weariness is denied repose by swarms of mosquitoes and sandflies'. Fortunately for Tench and the other soldiers, the mosquitoes of New South Wales carried neither malaria nor yellow fever. But the next day, 'after wading breast-high through two arms of the sea, as broad as the Thames at Westminster', they were glad to find themselves at Sydney between one and two o'clock in the afternoon. Private Easty, who had served in the expeditionary ranks, called the return to Sydney 'a most tedious march as ever men went in the time'.

Phillip at once ordered a second expedition – his orders for the first had not been a matter of passion but the establishment of principle, and he did not seem to have blamed Tench for failure, since, wrote Watkin, 'the "painful pre-eminence" again devolved on me'. This time the party pretended they were setting off for Broken Bay to punish Willemering. Since the moon was full, they would move by night, to avoid the heat of the day. Crossing the broad estuaries of Cook's River and the swamps behind the beaches of Botany Bay, the soldiers carried their firelocks above their heads and their cartouche boxes were tied fast to the top of their hats. Pushing towards the village they had visited the first time, they met a creek which when they tried to cross sucked them down waist-deep into its mud.

There is a perhaps unconscious comedy in Tench's description. 'At length, a sergeant of grenadiers stuck fast, and declared himself incapable of moving either forward or backwards; and just after, Ensign Prentice and I felt ourselves in a similar predicament close together. "I find it impossible to move; I am sinking", resounded on every side.' At length the soldiers not yet embarked on the creek cut boughs of trees and threw them to the men that were stuck, but it took half an hour to drag some out. The rope intended to go round the wrists of captured natives had to be used to drag the sergeant of grenadiers free.

With their mud-smirched uniforms, the military pressed round the head of the creek and on to the village. Tench, dividing his party into three so that they could attack from all sides, sent the troops rushing amongst the huts to find them absolutely empty. And now, unless the marines set out for camp at once, the river estuaries they had crossed since the point where they left their supplies and bags would be cut off till night. The struggle back exhausted many soldiers, their physical condition undermined by dietary deficiencies.

Again, with caked mud on his uniform and wrists, Tench had an opportunity to reflect. This country extolled by Cook was covered with high, coarse rushes, 'growing in a rotten spongy bog, into which we were plunged knee-deep at every step'. They made another attack on the village in the following small hours, with the same results, and so marched back to Sydney, relieved at their own failure.

Meanwhile, the wounded Irish gamekeeper was still well enough to walk around the hospital. Though many had spoken to McEntire about the appropriateness of openly confessing any injuries he had done the natives, just in case he needed soon to face God, 'he steadily denied . . . having ever fired at them but once, and then only in defence of his own life, which he thought in danger'. And yet those Eora who watched from the fringes of bush or were permitted in the town despite the edict against it knew that he was a walking dead man. He died quite suddenly on 20 January. The surgeons did an autopsy and found pieces of stone and shells inside the left lobe of the lung. Along with the magic which had been sung into them, they had contributed to the lung's collapse.

After missing all the drama of the two expeditions, Bennelong had by now returned to Sydney with Barangaroo from Cameraigal country across the harbour. He had been asked to officiate at certain ceremonies there – knocking out the front teeth of initiates and raising various scars on the skin of the young men. Phillip saw that Barangaroo's body was exceptionally painted to mark the ritual importance of herself and her husband, red ochre colouring her cheeks, nose, upper lip and small of her back, while dots of white clay spotted the skin under her eyes. Bennelong and Barangaroo proudly wore crowns of rushes and reed bands around their arms. Barangaroo was after all a Cameraigal woman, and had returned to her people with her distinguished husband to be made a fuss of. Bennelong showed Phillip a throwing stick which had been specially designed to remove the teeth of the initiates. Two friends of Governor Phillip were amongst their number: the youth named Yemmerrawanne and another youth who had lived at Governor Phillip's house, probably Ballooderry (whose name meant leather-jacket, a type of fish). Each had had a snake-like black streak painted on his chest, and his front tooth knocked out. In fact, Yemmerrawanne had lost a piece of his jawbone along with his incisor.

The removal of a tooth, the upper incisor, was a rite which ancient skulls recovered throughout Australia would prove to be millennia-old. In Collins's journal, the preparations for the knocking out of a tooth are both illustrated and graphically described. The elders danced until one of them fell suddenly to the ground, seemingly in a state of agony. The other elders continued dancing, singing loudly while one or more beat the fallen one on the back until a bone was produced from his mouth and he was free of his pain. This bone chisel would be used on one of the initiates, who thus believed it to have come from the elder's body. Then one by one the other senior men threw themselves on the ground in this manner, and in each case a bone to be used the following day to remove an initiate's tooth was produced.

For the ceremony, the young initiate, surrounded by spear- and shield-carrying elders, was seated on a kneeling relative's shoulders and the tooth was extracted by a man holding a chisel of bone in his left hand and a striking stone in his right. Collins acquired the name for this tooth-excising ceremony – *erah-ba-diang*, jaw-hurting. Amongst all the names initiated men carried, some too secret to be uttered to the Europeans, there was added after this ceremony the title *kebarrah*, a man whose teeth had been knocked out by a rock. The associated words, *gibber* or *kibber*, meaning a stone, had already been picked up by the English speakers of New South Wales. Another word which would long survive in Australian English was *corroboree*, which came from the Eora *carabbara* or *carribere*, the ritual involving singing and dancing.

'Full of seeming confusion, yet regular and systematic,' Watkin Tench wrote of corroboree, 'their wild gesticulations, and frantic distortions of body, are calculated rather to terrify, than delight, a spectator. These dances consist of short parts, or acts, accompanied with frequent vociferations, and a kind of hissing or whizzing noise; they commonly end with a loud rapid shout, and after a short respite, are renewed'. Bodies were decorated with white for the dance, and there were waving lines from head to foot, crossbars, spirals or zebra-type stripes. The eyes were often surrounded by large white circles. There were occasional dances of romance as well – Nanbaree and Abaroo performed one for Phillip and the officers.

Corroboree was an exultant experience and Bennelong

returned to Sydney full of the exhilaration of the recent Cameraigal ceremonies. He cheerily told Governor Phillip that he had met Willemering there. In Bennelong's mind this was no more remarkable than it would be to a European to mention that they had met a given judge socially. But to Phillip it seemed another instance of unreliability in Bennelong.

When Bennelong said goodbye and moved down the slope with Barangaroo and some of his clansmen to his hut at Tubowgulle, his younger wife, Karubarabulu, again left the shelter of government house, stripping off her European gown, keeping only her nightcap because her head had been shaven, to take residence at Bennelong's house.

An incident was about to occur which came close to convincing Bennelong to sever his association with Phillip, his name-swapper. Though there were no more Botany Bay military expeditions, after Christmas a raid was made by some natives who dug and stole potatoes – the natives called them *tarra*, teeth – near Lieutenant Dawes's hut. One of the Eora threw his fishing spear at a convict trying to scare the marauders away and wounded him. Led by Phillip, a small party went chasing the potato thieves, and two of them were found sitting with women by a fire. One threw a club, which the marines thought a spear, and three muskets opened fire. Both men fled, and the two women were brought in, slept the night at government house, and left well fed the following morning.

One of the two natives fired at was wounded. A surgical party led by White and accompanied by some Sydney Cove natives went looking for him and found him lying dead next to a fire.

Bark had been placed around his neck, a screen of grass and ferns covered his face, and a tree branch stripped of bark formed an arch over his body. He was covered in green boughs except for one leg. The musket ball had gone through his shoulder and cut the sub-clavian artery. He had bled to death. None of the Eora who went with the surgeon to look for him would go near him, for fear that the *mawm* spirit in him, the spirit of shock or mortal envy, would overtake them.

Bennelong was angry that death had been the punishment for the minor crime of stealing potatoes. At government house he was plied with food, but refused to touch anything. Besides, the fruits of the earth were communally owned by his people, and here were the interlopers making a sop or a bribe out of them.

Later, Bennelong appeared at the head of a group of several warriors in a cove where one of the fishing boats was working, and took the fish while threatening the unarmed convicts and soldiers that if they resisted he would spear them. When he next saw Phillip, the governor asked an armed guard into the room during a session in which Bennelong passionately argued the case for taking the fish. Bennelong saw as justice what Phillip saw as robbery. When confronted with two of the whites who had seen him in the boats, Bennelong launched into a rambling, insolent protest, 'burst into fury, and demanded who had killed Bangai [the dead Aborigine]'. Then Bennelong walked out on Phillip, and as he passed the wheelwright shop in the yard, he picked up an iron hatchet and disappeared with it.

Amongst the population of Sydney Cove was an anonymous painter who produced a striking watercolour portrait of Bennelong wearing white paint while angry and mourning the news of Bangai. Both Phillip and Bennelong had now become exceptionally enraged over their dead. Phillip gave further orders that no boat should leave Sydney Cove unless it carried arms, and forbade the natives to go to the western point of the cove, where the crime of potato-stealing had occurred. This prevented them from visiting their respected friend, Lieutenant Dawes.

But even this breakdown of their relationship did not prevent the amiable Bennelong from stopping fishing boats to ask them how Phillip was, and to find out if the governor still intended to shoot him.

Captain Collins had a clear grasp of the policy of 'sanguinary punishments' by the natives, for 'we had not yet been able to reconcile the natives to the deprivation of those parts of this harbour which we occupied. While they entertained the idea of our having dispossessed them of their residences, they must always consider us as enemies; and upon this principle, they made a point of attacking the white people whenever opportunity and safety concurred.'

On a personal level, Phillip refused Bennelong entry to government house and placed him on the same level as the other natives.

Twenty-four

When Lieutenant Ball of the *Supply* had been in Batavia in 1790, gathering supplies and sending Lieutenant King on his way to Whitehall on a Dutch ship, he had chartered a snow, a small, square-rigged ship which carried an additional sprit-sail mast aft of the mainmast, to bring further supplies to Sydney. Sailing in *Supply*'s wake, the snow *Waaksamheyd* (*Wakefulness*) of about 300 tons, under the Dutch master Detmer Smith, lost sixteen of her Malay crew along the way from fevers that had been incubating in them as they left Batavia. A young British midshipman who travelled on the snow as Ball's representative was in a shockingly skeletal and fever-ridden condition when landed from *Waaksamheyd* in Sydney in December 1790. No one was surprised, given Batavia's repute as an unhealthy place. The snow also brought the news that the sick crew members Lieutenant Ball had left at that port as too ill to safely sail back to Sydney Cove had all died except one. As Tench eloquently wrote, 'Death, to a man who has resided in Batavia, is too familiar an object to excite either terror or regret.'

The snow brought with it a cargo of rice and some beef, pork, flour and sugar as well. By an arrangement not uncommon in food distribution to this day, the British were willing to lose

5 pounds in 100 of the rice, but after that deduction was made there was a nearly 43,000-pound deficiency in the rice Detmer Smith landed. Smith had rice and flour aboard which he claimed was his own, and then proceeded to sell to the commissary in return for money or butter.

At some stage Phillip would decide that despite Detmer Smith's chicanery, this would be a good ship to contract for taking the officers and ship's company of the *Sirius* back to England for the *pro forma* court-martial which always followed the loss of a British naval vessel. Stranded Captain Hunter, fetched back with his crew by the *Supply* from Norfolk Island in the new year of 1791, did not think the Dutch snow was suitable, 'for, anxious as I was to reach England as soon as possible, I should with much patience rather awaited the arrival of an English ship, than to have embarked under the direction, or at the disposal, of the foreigner'. Phillip, too, found dealing with Detmer Smith very hard, believing him impertinent, perverse and crass. 'The frantic, extravagant behaviour of the master of her, for a long time frustrated the conclusion of a contract. He was so totally lost to a sense of reason and propriety, as to ask for £11 per ton, monthly, for her use . . .'

To pressure Phillip, Smith made as if to sail with *Waaksamheyd*, but merely dropped down-harbour to bushy Camp Cove and waited. At last a contract was achieved, and Hunter and the crew of *Sirius* boarded the Dutch vessel. Not all the crew would travel – perhaps Bosun Brooks and Mrs Deborah Brooks, who had earlier enchanted Captain Phillip, remained in Sydney, though there is no evidence either way. But it was above all upon the officers that the duty lay of presenting themselves to the Admiralty and facing court-martial for the loss of *Sirius*.

Phillip wrote to the Home Secretary by way of the Dutch snow with a new request to match an earlier one he had sent, expressing a desire to return to England on account of 'private affairs'. To the 'matters of serious concern' he had already mentioned was added the statement that he found his health so much impaired that he was obliged 'on that account' to request permission to leave the colony.

The private affairs were to do with his estranged wife, Margaret, particularly as to what his future might be in the light of any legacy she left him, or bills she expected him to meet after her death. When he left for New South Wales in 1787, he was aware she had been ill and unlikely to live many years, and he saw both benefits and horrific legal responsibilities potentially arising out of her death, if in her will she made him responsible for all the liabilities attached to the estate he had run for her at Lyndhurst. He wondered whether his future was to be one spent on half-pay, in cheese-paring gentility, or in affluence.

But in the request he gave Grenville, Secretary of State, was the added information that for the past two years, 'I have never been a week free from a pain in my side, which undermines and wears me out, and though this colony is not exactly in the state in which I would have wished to have left it, another year may do much, and it is at present so fully established, that I think there cannot any longer be any doubt that it will, if settlers are sent out, answer in every respect the end proposed by government in making the settlement.'

That word *answer* had arisen again. By the same ship, Collins had told his father that 'this colony, under the present system of supplying it, will never answer'. It was as if the place was being asked a question, and gave only a subtle response, which Phillip alone could hear.

The recurrent bouts of pain he sincerely complained of were due to calcium deposits in his urinary tract, a condition which was then one of the seaman's occupational hazards, because of the use of salt to preserve food. Earlier he described it as 'a violent pain in my left kidney'.

Just as the *Waaksamheyd* had been about to depart, four officers, of whom the most senior was Captain Tench, who had been placed under arrest by Major Ross for bringing down an alternative sentence on Private Hunt in the colony's early days, sought to draw to Phillip's attention the fact that it was three years since the day they were placed under arrest, and that the Act of Parliament regulating the marines stipulated that no one should stand trial if on shore more than three years since the commission of the alleged offence. They still felt very heated about their arrest and about Ross's insistence that they revoke their sentence, and were 'indignant at the novelty and disgrace of the situation unexampled in British military annals'. As it was possible that a promotion in the corps in which they served might have taken place since the date of the last dispatches from Britain, 'there is but too much reason to dread that we may have been passed over as prisoners who had forfeited the common claim of service. Dear as promotion is to a soldier, we deem it but a secondary consideration when put in competition with the honour and preservation of our characters in the military profession'.

They asked Phillip to release them from their technical confinement, which he did, and transmit a copy of his letter doing so to the Lords Commissioners of the Admiralty. They also begged Phillip to make it clear to their Lordships that 'we have not by misconduct forfeited our pretensions to their favour'.

Phillip also sent off by *Waaksamheyd* a letter to Sir Joseph Banks which rings strangely to later ears. '. . . I am sorry that I cannot send you a head. After the ravages made by the small-pox, numbers were seen in every part, but the natives burned the bodies.'

Surgeon White, too, appealed to Grenville to allow him to go home to England because of 'the failure of [an] agent, who had in his hands my whole patrimony'. Naval men employed agents to mind their affairs, chase up back pay and bounty money. But with White the issue must have been resolved, since he stayed on in New South Wales for years yet.

Hunter was well reconciled to the *Waaksamheyd* by the time the Dutch ship departed. On the journey home, he undertook a policy of calling meetings of his officers and Detmer Smith – for example, to discuss their water situation, the water casks having been built from 'old worm-eaten staves, which had been lying exposed to the sun for more than a year'. They were to try to land on Norfolk Island on the way if they could, and were unable to because of weather, but on that short leg 'we had lost by leakage full three weeks water'. Hunter and Smith veered north-ward, running into adverse winds again off New Caledonia, and hoped to reach Timor by a new route by sailing around the north of New Guinea, in order to avoid the fever port of Batavia on Java. It became necessary for them to go to Java however, since contrary winds delayed them so long.

It would take Hunter and the other surviving sailors till the following year to reach Portsmouth. Their voyage was marked by Hunter's wisdom and inventiveness. He proved the exact location of the reef-girt Solomon Islands, and discovered a passage between Bougainville and Buka, a passage which would in a much later war in the twentieth century become a graveyard for Australian, American and Japanese sailors. Twenty-two of Hunter's sailors had fever when they left Batavia, and three would die by Cape Town, where at Hunter's insistence the *Waaksamheyd* would wait sixteen weeks, until mid-January 1792, to allow recuperation.

In April that year, the snow reached Portsmouth. Hunter faced his court-martial and was exonerated.

~

In New South Wales in April 1791, with the *Waaksamheyd* seen off, another exploration of the hinterland was planned. The expedition's aim was to cross the Hawkesbury River near Richmond Hill and then push on to those same western mountains whose deep canyons and cliffs had earlier turned Dawes back. Phillip had named them the Carmarthens, but everyone called them the Blue Mountains.

Apart from Phillip, Watkin Tench was one of the expeditionary group that also intended to find out whether the Hawkesbury River to the north-west and the Nepean River to the west were one and the same watercourse. Dawes, Collins, White, Colby, the youth Ballooderry, two marine sergeants, eight soldiers and three convicts who were assessed to be good shots made up the party. Dawes steered north-west by compass, an instrument to which Colby and Ballooderry gave the title *naamora*, to see the way.

The country immediately west of Rose Hill did not much scare Colby, who said that most of the people from there, the

Bidjigals, had died of the *galgalla*, smallpox. Further west still was the Hawkesbury River clan called the Booroo Berongal, and encountering one of their encampments, Colby and Ballooderry felt at risk and wanted to burn down the few shelters. They said these inland people were not trustworthy, and native huts, easily rendered of bark and brush, were reproducible compared to hunting weapons or other laboured-over implements, the stealing of which would have constituted a serious insult.

When they reached the bushy banks of the Hawkesbury River, the problems the Europeans had walking through the entangled undergrowth and their frequent falls caused amusement to Colby and his young friend. If the person who fell 'shaken nigh to death' got angry with them, 'they retorted in a moment, by calling him every opprobrious name which their language affords'. Their favourite term of insult was *Gonin patta*, an eater of human excrement.

Again, Phillip was defeated by the country and was unable to scale the Blue Mountains. Meeting some Broken Bay, Hawkesbury River Aboriginals, Tench noticed that 'they spoke different dialects of the same language'. One of those they met, Yarramundi, was a great *carradhy* and, on request, treated Colby for an old wound below the left breast caused by a short, two-pronged spear. Colby began the consultation by asking for some water, and Tench gave him a cupful which he presented 'with great seriousness' to Yarramundi. Yarramundi took the cup and filled his mouth with the fluid, but instead of swallowing it, threw his head into Colby's chest, 'spit the water upon him; and immediately after began to suck strongly at his breast, just below the nipple. The action was repeated with great seriousness and after a time, Yarramundi pretended to take something into his mouth which he had drawn out of Colby's chest. With this he retired a few paces, put his hand to his lips, and threw into the river a stone, which I had observed him to pick up slyly, and secrete'. Returning to the fireside, Colby assured everyone that he had 'received signal benefit from this operation'. He gave Yarramundi for his services some of his supper and a knitted woollen nightcap.

Everyone was impressed by the tree-climbing capacity of the Hawkesbury River natives, and a young man gave his coastal brothers Colby and Ballooderry and the gentlemen an exhibition in climbing the smooth and slippery trunks of eucalpyts, looking for possums.

Phillip was excited to tell Sir Joseph Banks later in the year about the journey and to note the difference of the Hawkesbury language from that of the coastal people – indeed, he went so far as to see them as two separate languages. Collins, on the other hand, like Tench, noticed that 'our companions conversed with the river natives without apparent difficulty, each understanding or comprehending the other'. By now Colby and Ballooderry had grown uneasy amongst the inland strangers and were keen to return to known parts. They kept up a chant of 'Where's Rose Hill; where?' On the return journey, the explorers shot ducks which Ballooderry refused to swim for.

It was typical of those early explorations that bush or water or steep terraces of sandstone would defeat the part-time explorers of Sydney and Parramatta. In fact the most astounding of the journeys of this era of heroic journeying was one plotted and undertaken by the convict couple William and Mary Bryant in the hope of becoming the first to rise from their pit and appear again on the shores of the known world.

In February 1789, Will Bryant had been sentenced to be flogged for trading in fish on his own behalf. After the flogging of 100 lashes, he had been kept on in the fishing service because, as Captain Collins said, 'Notwithstanding his villainy, he was too useful a person to part with and send to a brick cart.' Bryant burned inwardly however. Like her husband, Mary also resented his punishment, and hated being cast out of her privileged position on the east side of the cove and made to live with her infant daughter, Charlotte, in the squalor of the convict camp in the Rocks (as the west side would become known).

There, in the general camp, not only did she need to listen to the mockery of fellow prisoners and references to her fallen status, but she and her family were exposed to the full hardship of the Sydney Cove diet. Into such deprivation was Mary's second child, Emmanuel, born, and baptised by the Reverend Richard Johnson on 4 April 1790. The dilemma of people like William and Mary Bryant was reflected more urbanely in a slightly overstated but valid letter Surgeon White wrote in April 1790 to a dealer in hams, tongues and salt salmon in the Strand, London. 'Much cannot now be done, limited in food and reduced as people are, who have not had one ounce of fresh animal food since first in the country; a country and place so forbidden and so hateful as only to merit execration and curses; for it has been a source of expense to the Mother Country, and of evil and misfortune to us, without there ever being the smallest likelihood of its repaying or recompensing either. From what we have already seen we may conclude there is not a single article in the whole country that in the nature of things could prove of the smallest use or advantage to the Mother Country or the commercial world. In the name of Heaven, what has the Ministry been about? Surely they have quite forgotten or neglected us? . . . This is so much out of the world and tract of commerce that it could never answer.'

The Bryants were by no means the only ones who desired escape in those months. In Rose Hill in September 1790, newly arrived John Terwood (or Tarwood) proposed an escape to Tahiti to five others. Terwood was a former sailor and a highway robber and stock thief in the London area. Collins thought him 'a daring, desperate character, and the principal in the scheme'. Terwood's accomplice in a theft of bullocks from marshlands at Poplar, on the edge of the city of London, and three others as well, were willing to go along with him. John Terwood must have heard of the joys and plenty Tahiti offered from being acquainted with accounts of Cook's time there, and above all would have been impressed by the rich sensual experiences of Cook's crew.

One night, the group led by Terwood came down the Parramatta River from Rose Hill and into the harbour, and then stole 'a wretched weak boat' from the look-out station at South Head, and got away. They were not heard from again for years, and were presumed to have died at sea. Five years later, four of them would be found at Port Stephens some way up the New South Wales coast, very scrawny, praising the kindness of the natives but anxious for return to their own kind. The fifth and oldest man of the group, Sutton, had by then died.

Bryant knew that in his turn, he would go much better equipped than Terwood and company, and that his boat wouldn't be 'a wretched weak' one.

When towards the year's end, the *Waaksamheyd* arrived in the wake of the *Supply*, Captain Smith and William Bryant made repeated contact with each other. If the English thought little of Smith, Smith was willing to return the favour and at some stage, in secrecy, sold Will Bryant a compass, a quadrant and a chart covering the route to Batavia via the eastern coast of New South Wales and Torres Strait. Then, towards the end of February 1791, Bryant called a meeting with five other convicts in his hut proposing the stealing of the boat in which he was employed. A passer-by overhead the discussion, and it was reported to the governor, who ordered that a watch be kept on Bryant. It was the next day, however, that an accident – the near overturning and swamping of the fishing boat – put the likelihood of an escape out of everyone's mind but Bryant's.

It was an event whose main point at the time seemed to be that it helped heal the relationship between Phillip and Bennelong. Bennelong's sister, Karangarang, was fishing in the government cutter with William Bryant, his crew members and two native children when it was hit by an unexpected and typically violent Port Jackson southerly storm. The boat was over-burdened with a fish catch, and was swamped with water. Karangarang took the two children on her shoulders in a moment and swam ashore with them. Several natives ashore, including Bennelong, seeing that the boat was being driven onto rocks, gave every possible assistance, 'without which, in all probability, one of the crew would have been drowned . . . in these friendly offices Bennelong was very assiduous: this behaviour gave Governor Phillip an opportunity of receiving him in a more kindly manner than he had done since his bad behaviour'.

Everyone thought that the accident to the boat had put an end to Bryant's plans, since it had demonstrated the unsuitability of the cutter for what he had in mind. But he had been enthused, as the officers had been, by the news that had come to Sydney by *Supply* and *Waaksamheyd* of the mutiny on *Bounty*, and of Captain Bligh's journey in an open launch from the mid-Pacific site of the mutiny to Timor. What Bligh could do, Bryant believed he could reproduce. And because of the recent overturn of the boat, it had been refitted at government expense with new sails, mast and oars.

An additional motive for him was that though he knew his term of transportation had expired – he had been sentenced in 1784 – he must have doubted that the papers proving his time had been served would ever turn up. In 1790, Phillip had written to Nepean, asking for further information about how to deal with the people whose time had expired. 'We have now near thirty under the circumstances, and their number will increase as well as their discontents.' In *his* discontent, Bryant had by now acquired two muskets and various supplies. His and Mary's accumulated secret cache for their proposed escape included 100 pounds of flour, 100 pounds of rice, 14 pounds of pork, about 8 gallons of water, a new net, two tents, carpenter's tools and fishing gear. Mary Bryant had also collected a little pharmaceutical kit, included amongst it the triple-veined leaves of the native sarsaparilla. (Some of her *Smilax* leaves would end up, as souvenirs of her escape, all over the world.)

Since seven other convicts accompanied them, one can only think that they contributed to this serious accumulation of stores as well. Not all of them had seamanship, but Samuel Bird and the former seaman, William Morton, both did. Four of Bryant's escapees had come in the Second Fleet. William Allen, a man in his mid-forties who had stolen 49 linen half-handkerchiefs from a shop in Norwich, had had a trusted role as servant to the rather demanding Captain James Campbell of the marines. Nathaniel Lilly had broken into a house in Sudbury with two other men, both of his accomplices having been sentenced to death, in part on his testimony. Samuel Broome was a middle-aged Second Fleeter who also went by the name of John Butcher, and James Cox, a colonial cabinet-maker, had been one of those who had skipped ship as a result of the mutiny on the *Mercury* in 1782. The wood of New South Wales did not suit his craft. He had a life sentence, and was ready to flee. Before he left, Cox left a letter to his lover, Sarah Young, in the hut where he pursued his cabinet-making. The letter called on her 'to give over the pursuits of the vices' which, he told her, prevailed in the settlement. He left her whatever property of his remained, and explained that it was the hopelessness of his situation, 'being transported for life, without the prospect of any mitigation, or hope of ever quitting the country', which drove him to take part in Bryant's plans.

Between nine and midnight on the evening of the day the *Waaksamheyd* departed Sydney, the Bryant party, some of whom were rostered on for fishing that night, stole the government boat and crept down-harbour past the light at the look-out station where Sergeant Scott and his men were obliviously posted. They met with gratitude and exhilaration the pulse of the Pacific racing in through the Heads. The laughter, the curses, the cries of triumph which must have characterised that sturdy cutter as the Bryants and their friends went to meet the moonless night of the Pacific would in coming weeks be imagined and sucked on by those without the skill or endurance to match these escapees. This boatload should have been self-doomed, but it worked with an exemplary degree of cooperation. It was not so just that night, but in days to come as well. Mary had delivered her swaddled children, lying in the stern, from bondage.

The day after the escape, Bryant's hut was searched and 'cavities under the boards were found'. The authorities knew he had talked about escape, but the search showed that his plans were well thought-out and more capable than the authorities had expected. Most of the escapees 'were connected with women' and Collins declared, 'if these women knew anything, they were too faithful to those they lived with to reveal it'.

The governor would enforce an edict that hereafter only smaller boats be built – in fact, he had already decided on that before the escape, and now he reiterated it with force.

Though great intensity of feeling went into this escape, it was not lightly embarked on. Private Easty declared sympathetically, 'It's a very desperate attempt to go in an open boat for a run of about sixteen or seventeen hundred leagues and in particular for a woman and two small children, the oldest not above three years of age, but the thought of liberty from such a place as this is enough to induce any convict to try all schemes to obtain it as they are the same as slaves all the time they are in this country.' Like Easty, Captain Tench expressed something close to sympathy and good wishes 'to this little band of adventurers'. There was little doubt, said Tench, 'that a scheme so admirably planned, would be adequately executed'.

The Bryants were escaping a colony in which, despite what the *Supply* and the Dutch snow had brought in from Batavia, the ration was reduced again shortly after their departure, this time to 3 pounds of rice, 3 pounds of flour and 3 pounds of pork per week. Hunger would again have the effect of driving people to raid gardens, and to make small thefts. Mary Morgan, transported for stealing linen yarn from a bleaching yard in Shropshire, stole a black tin dish, the property of Mrs Elizabeth Macarthur. Mary Whiting was charged with drunkenness and with 'falsely aspersing' the character of Zachariah Clark, the deputy commissary, over his distribution of food. A woman in her forties recently married to a male convict, Whiting was found guilty and sentenced 'to receive 100 lashes, at four different times – each time to be at a serving of provisions, and then to declare with what injustice and falsehood she accused Mr Clark of robbing the store'. Food was the subject of deranged behaviour – but the Bryants had escaped all that desperation.

In another sense the absent Bryant had a lasting effect on the scrawny, misbegotten society of New South Wales. It was reported to Phillip that he had frequently been heard expressing what was a common sentiment on the subject amongst convicts – that he did not consider his marriage in this country as binding. It was a marriage for the sake of the alternative world in which fortune had placed him, but he asserted to other convicts that it would not bind him should he return to reality, the established and accustomed earth. Phillip, hearing of Bryant's attitudes after his escape, saw how dangerous this concept was to his community, to all the business of inheritance and ordered life of which monogamy was the keystone. Men who were proven to serve their time and had the means, if former sailors, to sign on with visiting ships and return to the outside world might share that belief and leave behind destitute wives and children who would become a burden on the settlement. Phillip issued an order that no time-served convict could leave behind in the colony any wife or children who could not support themselves.

'This order was designed as a check on the erroneous opinion which was formed of the efficacy of Mr Johnson's nuptial benediction.' Here was another instance of Arthur Phillip declaring that New South Wales was not virtual reality, it was *their* world, and the contracts made here bound people to the same pieties as contracts made anywhere. Thus, he intended to centre their lives in the colony. In so doing, he was making the first families of a non-Aboriginal Australia.

David Collins thought, with some injustice towards Mary, that Will took her along only as a means of preventing her from betraying his great scheme. Certainly, she saw her connection with Bryant as the chief hope for her children, but in all other aspects of her life that we know of, she was no mere token of fallen womanhood, but a vigorous and equal participant. Like many a male, Bryant might have had fantasies of flight, but he was not likely to get away without Mary as fellow-spirit and conspirator. Indeed Captain Tench would later declare that he admired both of them, and he obviously saw Mary as something more than the convict's token, south-west Pacific wife. The journey they were about to make, to this day one of the two longest open-boat excursions in maritime history, could not have been made without a united, refined and mature sense of purpose.

Twenty-five

The following year, the by now famous or notorious William Bligh, restored to normal naval command after the mutiny on the *Bounty*, and promoted to post-captain, called again at the Dutch port of Koepang in Timor and heard the tale of the Bryant party's voyage from the Dutch officials who were still talking about it. The Dutch governor at Koepang gave Bligh a journal entitled *Remarks on a Voyage from Sydney Cove, New South Wales, to Timor*, which was said to be Bryant's true account. All we retain of it is what an enthused and remarkably sympathetic Bligh extracted for inclusion in his own journal. He did not have time to copy more than a quarter of the account, and one of his officers was able to get more of the account of Bryant and the others down. The other source for the Bryant journey is an extraordinary document written by at least one of the escapees and entitled *Memorandoms*, later published in London in 1792.

Early in the journey, we learn by reading Bligh and the *Memorandoms*, only two days sail north of Sydney, the Bryant party put in through the surf to a creek where so much coal lay 'we thought it was not unlikely to find a mine . . . we picked with an axe as good coals as any in England – took some to the fire, and they burned exceedingly well'. It is interesting that there is a certain patriotic pride in that 'as any in England'. Bryant saw himself as a Briton, fulfilling a destiny – freedom – and the remark implied that he, Mary and the others saw England as their destination, not some lotus-eating island in the Pacific.

It was hard and skilled work beaching the boat and getting it out again through the waves. But despite the perils, regular landings and rest periods were essential for the health of all the parties to the adventure.

There was a night when rain drenched them, and a typical coastal storm in which the seas ran 'mountains high' – that recurrent nautical description – while two of the crew bailed feverishly. What nursery rhymes and songs did Mary sing to soothe the children at such a time? Resting ashore when a landing was possible, they kept a fire burning and a system of watches for the natives, many of whom along the coast of New South Wales and the reef-girt shores of what is now Queensland were friendly, though some were hostile. With all the aplomb of such gentlemen as Tench or Phillip, Bryant claimed that shooting above the natives' heads always dispersed them. As they travelled north, temperatures increased. And although the draught of their cutter was not deep, the Irish convict Martin needed all his navigational skills amongst the reefs, islands and inlets of the Barrier Reef coastline. At one point the party was driven out of sight of land for 'near three weeks' and by the time they reached a beach again were 'much distressed for water and food'.

Nevertheless, from what we know, at this stage there was a remarkable air of unity and intent amongst a group normally considered incapable of such cohesion.

As they passed Cape York into Torres Strait, between New Guinea and Australia, they encountered several small islands occupied by natives. The Torres Strait Islanders were of Melanesian background, but had interbred with coastal Aboriginals. These natives' canoes were more sophisticated than those found in Sydney Cove – 'The sails seemed to be made of matting.' The escapees 'fired a musket over them, and immediately they began firing their bows and arrows at us'.

The party crossed the Gulf of Carpentaria, that great indentation on the northern Australian coast, in four and a half days. Then Martin navigated them across the treacherous Timor Sea where they met the southern shore of Timor and reached the Dutch port of Koepang on 5 June 1791. Their prodigious open-boat journey had only been eclipsed by the earlier journey of Bligh, after he had been cast off the *Bounty* two years before. They had covered 3254 nautical miles and it had taken them, rests ashore included, ten weeks.

As they had agreed, they explained themselves to the Dutch Governor of Timor, Mynheer Timotheus Wanjon, as survivors from the wreck of a whaler named *Neptune* in Torres Strait, and claimed 'that the captain and the rest of the crew probably will follow in another boat'. This was a credible enough scenario. 'The governor,' Martin wrote, 'behaved extremely well to us, filled our bellies and clothed double with every[thing] that was wore on the island.'

Koepang proved a delightful place, favoured for recuperation by those who had suffered fevers in Batavia. Its landscape of hills and headlands was spectacular, but it was not free of curses – an ugly skin disease marred some of its inhabitants. But there was no question that after the journey they had made, it represented deliverance to the Bryant party, and Charlotte and Emmanuel, the children, were revived by it. Adding a further dimension to the stylishness of their escape, Bryant and his party drew bills on the British government and so were supplied with everything they needed by the administration.

～

By the time of the escape of the Bryants, there was a great deal of conjecture in Sydney Cove about the fate of the *Gorgon*, a 44-gun frigate converted into a store ship, which Phillip knew was on the way to Sydney. In fact *Gorgon* had been delayed in port and had only just left England that March of 1791. She sailed alone, as the other ship that sailed independently as part of Camden, Calvert and King's new deal with the government had already set out. The *Mary Ann*, 298 tons, commanded by her part-owner, Mark Munro, had left England a month earlier with 150 female prisoners. So the ruptured heavens of the English criminal punishment system shed more and more ghosts towards New South Wales.

Already a larger third flotilla, the Third Fleet, had been authorised by Whitehall. The contract was made in November 1790, and nine ships would sail on 27 March 1791. For the overall contract, Camden, Calvert and King were to be paid up to £44,658 13s 9d, but they had plans beyond that – six of the Third Fleet transports were also chartered to trade in Bombay cotton on the company's account after they had discharged their duty of convict transportation. The other ships of the group would go whaling off New South Wales and in the Southern Ocean. Camden, Calvert and King's own ships carried about £30,000 in coin, to lay the foundations of monetary exchange in New South Wales.

The government and its bureaucracies such as the Navy

Board, having made an outrageously inappropriate contract, seemed content that the disaster of the Second Fleet should go unreported in London. But via the Second Fleet ships returning, a letter from a literate unnamed female convict from the *Lady Juliana* would make its eloquent way into the *London Chronicle* of 4 August 1791, and arrest the attention of the British public. The woman reflected on seeing the victims of Camden, Calvert and King and their officers brought ashore. 'Oh, if you had but seen the shocking sight of the poor creatures that came out of the three ships, it would make your heart bleed. They were almost dead, very few could stand, and they were obliged to fling them as you would goods, and hoist them out of the ships, they were so feeble; and they died ten or twelve a day when they first landed . . . The governor was very angry and scolded the captains a good deal, and I heard, intended to write to London about it, for I heard him say it was murdering them . . . What a difference between us and them.' The writer expressed gratitude to the good agent of the *Lady Juliana* – Lieutenant Edgar. For the *Lady Juliana* had landed 223 women and twelve children in good health after only three women and one child died on the voyage.

Those Britons outraged by the murderous policies of Camden, Calvert and King, and particularly of Captain Donald Trail of the *Neptune*, included an activist London attorney, Thomas Evans, who brought *Neptune* seamen before magistrates to swear statements against Trail and his first mate, William Ellerington. Evans did not mind whether the death for which they paid the price would be that of a convict or a seaman, but it was ultimately for the murder of a seaman that Trail and Ellerington were tried at the Old Bailey Admiralty sessions in 1792, long after the Third Fleet had already been sent.

Evans became another victim of the Sydney experiment. Neither the Navy Board nor the Home Office welcomed the attention the trial attracted. But in the end the charges failed, the judge mysteriously discounting the evidence and directing the jury to bring in a not-guilty verdict. The attorney-general, encouraged perhaps by Evans's over-exuberance in prosecution, refused to allow a second trial, and it was Evans who suffered, being eventually disbarred.

The same attorney-general produced a report for the King in July 1792 in which he nonetheless partly agreed with Evans and attributed the 'unusual mortality' in the Second Fleet to the 'tonnage of the ship being less than was capable of containing for so long so large a number of persons without hazard of their lives'. If this was so, if the tonnage of the *Neptune* had been fraudulently exaggerated as a way of overcharging government, then no one paid for it, the Navy Board simply wanting the whole embarrassment to vanish. Trail, a mass murderer, would return with impunity to the Royal Navy and serve as a master to Lord Nelson. 'I considered him one of the very best masters I had ever met with, and from what I have seen since I have no reason to alter that opinion,' wrote Nelson in the coming decade. As for Camden, Calvert and King, after putting together the third convict flotilla, the company was thereafter never used again.

The chief scandal of this Third Fleet would prove to be the alleged short rations for the Irish convicts on the *Queen*. On 26 February 1791, the *Freeman's Journal* of Dublin reported, 'The gaoler of Limerick set off for Cork with a number of prisoners, where a large transport is waiting to carry all the convicts in the kingdom to Botany Bay.' It was not all the convicts in Ireland who fitted aboard the *Queen*, but 133 men and 22 women, plus four children. A receipt for these prisoners, dated 11 April 1791, was signed by the naval agent and given to the Mayor and Sheriff of the City of Cork, Sir Henry Brownhose, a United Irishman nationalist who would himself one day be sent to New South Wales for administering a traitorous oath. The *Queen*'s indent list, however, would be left behind and, echoing earlier oversights, would not reach Sydney until eight years after these convicts had arrived. A future governor of New South Wales, John Hunter of the *Sirius*, would complain of the manner of transportation from Ireland as 'so extremely careless and irregular'.

For many Irish convicts of *Queen*, their time would expire and they would not be in a position to prove it. Amongst the vessel's passengers was James Blake, a twelve-year-old Dubliner who had stolen a pair of silver buckles, and who would die four months after arriving in Sydney, never recovering from the rigours of his voyage to New South Wales.

The nine ships of the Third Fleet proper sailed from England in two divisions just before the *Queen* left Cork: the *Atlantic*, the *Salamander* and the *William and Anne*, with Lieutenant Richard Bowen as naval agent, left Plymouth on 27 March, less than two weeks before the store ship *Gorgon*, and the same day the *Albemarle*, the *Active*, the *Admiral Barrington*, the *Britannia* and the *Matilda* left Portsmouth under agent Lieutenant Robert Parry Young. *Queen*, though belonging to the Portsmouth division, embarked her convicts at Cork and had her own naval agent, Lieutenant Samuel Blow. The Irish newspapers noticed that women seemed more keen to go than the men. *Queen* sailed at the beginning of April with orders to rendezvous with the rest of the division at St Jago in the Cape Verde Islands.

So a great number of ships were on the interminable seas making for Sydney Cove. The *Mary Ann* was well ahead with her 150 English female convicts, nine of whom would die at sea. She did not call in anywhere but the Cape Verdes for fresh supplies, and that ensured a brisk passage. The converted frigate, HMS *Gorgon*, the store ship which also carried 29 male convicts selected for their trades, would lose only one male. The Third Fleet proper followed, and some of them would overtake the *Gorgon*.

Separated at sea, the *Atlantic*, *Salamander* and the aged *William and Anne* all met up at Rio, and then made the journey to Port Jackson without stopping at the Cape. The *Atlantic* had eighteen deaths but these were blamed on the condition in which men had been loaded from the *Dunkirk* hulk at Plymouth. At least a dozen of the men Surgeon James Thompson had been required to take on board were so weak that they had been unable to climb the ship's side and needed to be lifted up in a chair. Surgeon Thompson had wanted to exchange them for men physically able to face the passage, but a hindrance to this were the harbour works proceeding in Plymouth for which the fittest men from *Dunkirk* were needed still. Six of the newly boarded died before sailing. But Surgeon Thompson took many pragmatic steps on diet and exercise time spent on deck to prevent scurvy developing. So that while only nine men had to go from the *Atlantic* to the hospital in Sydney Cove, the old 370-ton *William and Anne* would land a great number of convicts who were very ill on arrival. Its master, Captain Bunker, was ultimately fined for assaulting and beating some of the Irish members of the

New South Wales Corps during the passage, so the conditions for the prisoners must have been harsh indeed.

The ships from the Portsmouth group, *Matilda*, *Britannia*, *Admiral Barrington* and *Albemarle*, were blown apart by a gale, and the *Albemarle* was on its own in the North Atlantic when the convicts attempted an uprising. The rising on *Albemarle* began with an assault on the quarterdeck, where an officer of the watch shot the leader of the mutiny, Siney, just as he was about to cut down the helmsman. The mutineers retreated to the convict deck, where they were rounded up. The wounded leader, Siney, and his confederate, Lyons, were hanged at the fore-yardarm, and several others were subjected to floggings. But the convicts would hand Lieutenant Bowen a document in which they argued that the mutiny had been encouraged by two seamen who also had a dream of America. These two sailors had equipped the prisoners with knives, which mutineers had converted into files so that they could escape their bonds. The two seamen believed to be responsible were landed in Madeira in irons, and that was that.

The men who took the job of agent aboard these ships were sometimes older men, cat's paws for the captains. The agent on *Queen*, Lieutenant Blow, would later be reprimanded by the Navy Board for his lack of interest in the convicts' welfare. The second mate, who would later claim he was working on behalf of the captain, Richard Owen, ordered that the leaden weights used to determine rations be scraped by one of the Irish convicts, who was rewarded with adequate provisions. The 4-pound weight had 6 ounces scratched out of its base, the 2-pound weight almost 3 ounces. The convicts were also cheated of food by the use of a 4-pound weight in place of a 5-pound weight, and a 3-pound for a 4-pound.

The Irish convict mess orderlies turning up at the cooking shack on deck found that the cook frequently complained of not being able to work out how to divide the reduced amounts of meat between all the messes. The prisoners appealed to Lieutenant Blow, and he told them to elect one of their own to stand beside the second mate during the weighing. The prisoners also complained to Ensign Cummings of the New South Wales Corps, who in turn asked Lieutenant Blow to intervene, but Blow replied, 'My dear fellow, what can I do?'

Magistrates in New South Wales to whom the convicts complained after landing would eventually find that the rations stipulated in the contract with Camden, Calvert and King had not been supplied, that frauds had been committed, and that those who should have seen that the full ration was served had failed to exercise their authority. The magistrates passed the matter on to Phillip, who believed that he lacked the jurisdiction to have the captain prosecuted. He wrote in his dispatch to the Secretary of State, 'I doubt if I have the power of inflicting a punishment adequate to the crime.'

We know little about this first Irish ship precisely because it would be so long before their sentencing papers caught up with them. If they were like later shiploads, the crimes of the women were at least in part motivated by want when the potatoes gave out in the spring, and shoplifting and theft became an option for those who needed cash or goods to trade for oatmeal. A certain number of the males, about two dozen, were members of an Irish peasant secret society, the Defenders, who had arisen as local groups to protect Catholics against the raids of a similar Protestant organisation named the Peep-of-Day Boys. Many Protestant land-lords disapproved of the radical, house-burning tendencies of the

Peep-of-Day Boys, especially in the Armagh area, where raids upon and murders of Catholics and burning of cabins and farmhouses occurred throughout the mid-1780s. Some Protestant landlords advised their Catholic tenants to arm themselves, even though it was illegal for a Catholic to own or carry a gun. Public sentiment both sides of the sectarian chasm at first had some sympathy for the men who called themselves Defenders. Feelings deepened, however, when the Defenders moved to the offensive against suspected Peep-of-Dayers, and when they refused to buy any good or trade with any business which had Peep-of-Day connections or sympathies.

Secret societies would account for a sizeable minority of Irish convicts to reach New South Wales over the following decades. Even to recruit another peasant to take the oath of membership of the Defenders incurred a seven-year sentence, and men were convicted for fourteen years for posting a threatening notice against a landlord, agent, or tithe proctor. In their own heads, many of their crimes had political colour, so that the first Irish political prisoner ever sent to Australia was arguably some largely unknown figure, or a series of figures, on the muster list of the *Queen*.

These people who owned so little were bolstered by enduring myths of the kind which grow amongst the defeated. Christ was their fellow-sufferer and was close to them, and would in the end exalt them, confounding their enemies and destroying the British apparatus of landlord and magistrate. Peasant legends arose which depicted the Irish armed with nothing but cornstalks turning back the armies of England. Such desperately-held hopes came to New South Wales with the two dozen or so Defenders and their more numerous sympathisers aboard *Queen*.

But it was not all a matter of Defenders and legend. When, in Dublin, the prisoners had been moved from the new gaol to the ship, 'Rositer, the woman who had been condemned to die for robbing one of the rooms at the Linen Hall, called out to the soldiers, "Clear the way", 'til she mounted into the landau.' That air of defiance, arising out of a hope of a great God-given reversal of Irish fortunes, characterised many of the convicts of the *Queen*, and combined with their use of Irish language, brought a new level of complexity to the New South Wales equation.

The forerunner of this Third Fleet, the little *Mary Ann* with her female convicts aboard, appeared off Sydney on the morning of 9 July 1791. She had made the quickest passage yet – four months and sixteen days. But the captain, Mark Munro, not only had no private letters aboard, 'but had not brought a single newspaper'. The officers on the *Mary Ann* could tell Tench – to his relief, since it meant his chances of ultimate promotion were not too severely inhibited by being under Ross's open arrest – that there was 'No war; the fleet's dismantled'.

'When I asked whether a new Parliament had been called, they stared at me in stupid wonder.'

'Have the rebelliousness French settled on their form of government?' Tench wanted to know further.

'As for that matter I can't say; I never heard; but d—n them, they were ready enough to join the Spaniards against us,' came the reply.

The disembarking women were all very healthy and spoke highly of the treatment they had received from Munro. Phillip was pleased by the *Mary Ann* also in that only three, all of whom were already suffering from disorders when they were loaded aboard in England, had died on the passage. Tench, too, thought that Captain Munro should be praised. 'The advocates of humanity are not yet become too numerous: but those who practise its divine precepts, however humble and unnoticed be their station, ought not to sink into obscurity, unrecorded and unpraised, with the vile monsters who deride misery, and fatten on calamity.' The *Mary Ann*, which carried sufficient stores to enable the rice ration to be increased at once by 2 pounds, also brought the happy news that the store ship *Gorgon* was definitely on the way.

Mary Ann additionally carried instructions for the governor that were of unforeseen importance to an as yet unenvisaged southland nation named Australia. They confirmed the policy he had already been following since May 1791. From that time, too late for the escaped Bryant, allotments of ground were parcelled out by the governor even to selected well-behaved transportees, as well as to time-expired ones who voluntarily offered to become settlers in the country. If they continued to cultivate their land for five years, the conditional grant would become permanent in title. Many of the grants were in the hilly area to the south-west of the source of the Parramatta River.

It was now also confirmed British policy that though those convicts who had served their period of transportation were not to be compelled to remain in the colony if they could somehow get home, 'no temptation' should be offered to induce them to quit it. The desire to prevent the felons returning to Britain and their former practices was one of the principles which under-pinned the New South Wales experiment. It was not simply a matter of being free that enabled a man or woman to transport themselves out of the country. They had to be able to deal with the needs of all encumbrances – dependants and families – and pay off all debts of a public nature. So the mere prison camp had already become a society which made its own demands of civil piety.

And so the founding element of New South Wales, and of the embryo nation it would make, was the practical inability of most time-served convicts to leave. The more the population of convicts built up, the more limited the means became of working a passage back home. Thus, for most of the convicts, in no sense was New South Wales the chosen land. Though some *did* choose it, for many it was the country where people got stuck, and having served time became, willy-nilly, citizens of New South Wales. Watkin Tench would eventually visit such people and noted their attitudes to their new homeland. 'Some I found tranquil and determined to persevere, provided encouragement should be given: others were in a state of despondency and predicted that they would starve, unless a period of eighteen months, during which they were to be fed and clothed, should be extended to three years.'

Amongst the infant children of convicts who could now be found playing around the camps, a new identity would emerge, one to which Europe and Britain were a rumour – though such a new race did not figure in the Home Secretary's nor the Admiralty's intention. A later governor, William Bligh, would call the children born in New South Wales 'National Children', but it was an administrative, not a visionary term. Now, with varying degrees of reluctance and acceptance, further time-served convicts moved out that July of 1791 to their land grants around

Parramatta. Some former convicts did not need to take on the labour of such grants – Henry Kable, for example, who at this time had work as a supervisor and constable, and in whom an entrepreneurial spirit was being awoken by early contact with the highly entrepreneurial officers of the New South Wales Corps.

The ships which arrived after *Mary Ann* did not maintain her high standards of care for prisoners. The 450-ton *Matilda* made a record passage of 127 days and yet Phillip was not as pleased to see her. She had buried two dozen convicts in the sea, he lamented, and she needed extensive repairs from the hard driving her captain, Weatherhead, had given her. An ensign and twenty privates from the New South Wales Corps landed from *Matilda*, and many of the *Matilda* convicts were transferred to the *Mary Ann* which took them straight to Norfolk Island.

The convicts who were landed sick would have been interested to see Bennelong at the hospital, being treated for what he called *Tyibul*, a form of scabies, which had struck the natives that winter. The surgeons were trying to heal him with applications of sulphur. Bennelong resembled, said Phillip, 'a perfect Lazarus'. Though 'he was easily persuaded to go to the hospital and rub himself, yet it was not possible to make him stay there till he was cured'. The presence of fretful souls of the dead made the hospital a perilous place to Bennelong. Collins guessed the scabies might be a dietary matter, based on the seasonal unavailability of fish, and perhaps it was a dietary matter in another sense: that Bennelong was taking in food with which the Eora had been for millennia unfamiliar – potatoes, pumpkins, melon, bread, coffee, salt beef and pork from Bengal.

The *Atlantic* came in on 20 August with its male convicts very weak, and soon 40 of them were lying at the hospital. The *Salamander*, which anchored the day after, also delivered its 154 male convicts in an emaciated state, and complaining loudly that they had not had proper attention paid to them. The government had again sent Phillip a parlous gift. 'Although the convicts landed from these ships were not so sickly as those brought out last year, the greatest part of them are so emaciated, so worn away by long confinement, or want of food, or from both these causes that it will be long before they recover their strength, and which many of them never will recover.' The master of *Salamander* was ordered to proceed to Norfolk Island with convicts, stores and provisions. Phillip sent the majority of the convicts he retained on the mainland to Parramatta, employing them to open up new ground at a short distance from the settlement.

The slow *Admiral Barrington* and her crew and convicts had suffered a hard time in the Southern Ocean and even off the New South Wales coast, where she was dragged out to sea by a ferocious southerly gale. She was 206 days on the ocean from Plymouth and had suffered 36 deaths when she reached Sydney on 16 October 1791.

Mrs Parker, the wife of Captain John Parker of the *Gorgon*, took the trouble when the store ship arrived in Sydney to visit the convicts of the Third Fleet then in hospital. She was shocked to find herself 'surrounded by mere skeletons of men – in every bed, and on every side, lay the dying and the dead. Horrid spectacle! It makes me shudder when I reflect that it will not be the last exhibition of this kind of human misery that will take place in this country, whilst the present method of transporting these miserable wretches is pursued'.

Yet in these grim vessels two convicts arrived in New South Wales who would become notable entrepreneurs. Simeon Lord was a thief of linen who, once landed, acted as servant to a captain in the New South Wales Corps. It is not certain which of the vessels of the Third Fleet he arrived on. He would later become one of the former convict front men who would retail goods purchased by the officers of the corps. Another entrepreneur in the making, a young felon named James Underwood, came on the *Admiral Barrington* and would go into the shipping business. But their glory days, along with those of most of the Rum Corps officers and of Henry Kable, were some time off yet.

An army chaplain, the second minister of religion in New South Wales (the Reverend Crowther having turned back when *Guardian* sank), arrived also on the Third Fleet. It was not necessarily the relief Johnson had been yearning for, though the Reverend James Bain seemed a practical young man, who brought with him a promise from the Archbishop of Canterbury to support any schoolteacher Bain could find to start a school for the young of New South Wales. Johnson reflected on Bain that 'as yet he seems to be greatly caressed by our great ones, and I fancy, is not suspected of being a Methodist', the suspicion under which Johnson laboured. Johnson's tone was more ironic than bitter, and despite all he seemed to like New South Wales life. He and his wife had recently moved 'out of our little cabbage tree cottage, and are now in a house as comfortable and convenient as I can wish – my garden too is in a flourishing state'. In Parramatta, when on duty there, he was able to find a room to stay on Saturday and Sunday evenings, 'which gives me an opportunity of visiting the convicts in their huts, and I declare to you that I've found more pleasure at times in doing this, than in preaching etc'.

Phillip chartered two of the convict ships, *Britannia* and *Atlantic*, to go to India for supplies for the settlement. Five of the transports were to go whaling off the Australian coast. The remaining four merchantmen went to India where the East India Company had given them sanction to load with cotton. It was all shaking down into a pattern. After the delivery of convicts, it was a matter of cotton and tea, and now whaling.

Twenty-six

The store ship *Gorgon* had arrived in the midst of all the questionable ships of the Third Fleet. 'I will not say that we contemplated its approach with mingled sensations,' wrote Tench, by now a veteran of such arrivals. 'We hailed it with rapture and exultation.' *Gorgon* contained six months full provisions for about 900 people, with stores for His Majesty's armed tender the *Supply* and for the marine detachment as well. Lieutenant King, having returned to England to be married, arrived back on the *Gorgon* with the new rank of commander, accompanied by his wife, Anna Josepha Coombe, a generous-spirited woman who would look to the welfare of his children by the convict Ann Innett as well as to that of the child she herself was carrying. Obviously King had been frank about them before marrying Anna Josepha at St Martin-in-the-Fields between successful conferences with Sir Joseph Banks, Grenville and Nepean. He had returned with assurances about ongoing support for New South Wales, and these he passed on to Arthur Phillip. These verbal guarantees must have been crucial in convincing Phillip that the settlement was now, for all its hungry times and desperate internal pressures, assured, and fixed in the map of the Britannic world.

Indeed, an extraordinary validating device had arrived on the *Gorgon* and been delivered to Phillip's office at government house. It was the Great Seal of New South Wales. On the obverse, the King's arms with the royal titles in the margin; on the reverse, an image of convicts landing at Botany Bay, greeted by the goddess Industry. Surrounded by her symbols, a bale of merchandise, a beehive, a pick-axe and a shovel, she releases them from their fetters and points to oxen ploughing, and to a town rising on the summit of a hill with a fort for its protection. In the bay, the masts of a ship are to be seen. In the margin lie the words *Sigillum. Nov. Camb. Aust.* [Seal of New South Wales]; and for a motto, *Sic Fortis Etruria Crevit*, 'In this way Tuscany grew strong' – a reference to Tuscany having once received the criminals of other places.

King would go back to administering Norfolk Island, and took his young son, Norfolk, and the infant, Sydney (and perhaps even their mother), with him to raise them alongside the son borne by Anna Josepha, Phillip. He would ultimately have the three of them educated in England. Having made the dangerous island landfall in November 1791 and relieved Major Ross of his post, King received a group of convicts who brought a petition which claimed that they had been 'forced into independent habits' they could not sustain, and that they would never meet the major's harvest targets. Though this petition was signed by less than half of the people in allotments, King would order the pigs returned to government ownership, and abandoned the socialist project, applying Phillip's style of governance from then on.

In his review of the island administration, he would find the superintendent of convicts at Queensborough, the little inland settlement, unsatisfactory, and would appoint the Irish surgeon D'Arcy Wentworth in his place. Wentworth, said Phillip, 'had behaved with the greatest attention and propriety as assistant-surgeon, which duty he still continued to discharge'. The Irish tearaway had become a minor imperial official.

But enduring exile in his little house at Queensborough, Wentworth still felt uncertain about his situation. He had earlier written to Governor Phillip to seek a clarification of when his posts might become official. The governor replied through David Collins, saying that both Hunter and Jamison had praised him, and that he would finalise his future residence and employment as soon as he received directions from England. The frustration for Wentworth was that both his positions were described as *acting*, and carried no salary except as a prospect. He privately despaired of ever being a man of substance, and thought that the people at home on whom he had relied to advance his interests had either been lazy about arguing on his behalf once they got him away on *Neptune*, or had been rebuffed by the government.

At least at Queensborough, Wentworth was some miles away from the centre of turbulence down at Kingston, the main settlement on the coast. His home was idyllically located. Ten acres of wheat and 30 of Indian corn grew there, and all those who occupied the place were concerned that it should ripen and come to harvest without ground grubs or caterpillars inflicting damage on it. The convict women of Queensborough were cutting reeds for thatching roofs; the men were widening the road between the inland and the coast. There must sometimes have been a not unpleasant atmosphere of combined endeavour, but if so, there were many discontents and much malice close to the Arcadian surface. Queensborough had its own gaol and stocks to accommodate the imperfections of its inhabitants, and Clark, so quick to detect fault in the convicts, was stationed now at nearby Phillipsburgh.

In narrow Norfolk, where Wentworth continued to cohabit with Catherine Crowley, there were rumours that he was already married in England, and doubts must have been muttered about her child's paternity, given that D'Arcy did not come aboard the *Surprize* until December 1789. Nonetheless, D'Arcy remained devoted to the boy, and his generous spirit extended to his relationships with others on the island. Authority had not made him a martinet, and he was well liked by gentlemen and convicts both because of his democratic manner. Without being a philosopher, he had imbibed some of the spirit of democracy driving the American and French revolutions and the coming trans-sectarian rebellion of United Irishmen, many of them of his class and higher, which would break out in Ireland in 1798. He had also had many lessons in the fragility of life, and of the thin filament that lay between respectable and criminal society. Norfolk Island was his purgatory, and during it, as super-intendent at Queensborough, he developed a gift for supervising agricultural work and for breeding livestock.

From the modest brig *Active*, which arrived in Sydney Cove on 26 September 1791, came Sydney's first genuine celebrity criminal, an Irishman named George Barrington. D'Arcy Wentworth had been a considerable gentleman of the road, but Barrington was a brand name of crime, like Jesse James, Ned Kelly, Dick Turpin or Al Capone. His origins were, as people said then, mysterious. He was sent to Dublin Grammar School at the instigation of people in authority, and a rumour was spread that he was of royal descent. At Dublin Grammar he stabbed another school boy in a fight, was flogged, and in response stole money and a watch and ran away. He joined a band of strolling players, and was taught by an expert actor–pickpocket, who took him to London as his young protégé. In 1773, his senior partner was transported to America.

As his own operator, George Barrington achieved the status of prince of pickpockets, living splendidly despite having to spend a year in the hulks. The victims of his confidence tricks and lifting skills included the Russian Prince Orlow, from whose pocket he extracted at Covent Garden Theatre a snuff-box inlaid with diamonds and said to be worth £30,000. Various peers of the realm were caught out by Barrington, and some of 'the brightest luminaries in the globe of London'. Tried at the Old Bailey in September 1790 for stealing a gold watch and chain at the Enfield racecourse, he was sentenced to transportation for the light term of seven years. The press reported that he had attempted to escape from Newgate in his wife's clothes, and that he had commiserated with other rogues in the general wards about the fact that they were all to be sent to a country where the natives had no pockets to pick.

After his transportation, his name still remained in use in British true-crime pamphlets and chapbooks. Having been the generic gentleman pickpocket, he now became the generic redeemed thief, and the idea of New South Wales as a place of redemption for deficient Britons gained great currency. In 1793 a small but popular tract named *An Impartial and Circumstantial Narrative of the Present State of Botany Bay*, and in 1802, *The History of New South Wales*, would be published under his name, but may or may not have come from his hand. In the second, more credible book, he is quoted as saying that the appearance of the convicts at the time his ship arrived was truly deplorable, 'the generality of them being emaciated by disease, foul air, etc., and those who laboured under no bodily disorder, from the scantiness of their allowance, were in a bitter plight'.

Phillip, meeting Barrington, found him sober-minded, as if transportation had had an impact on his legendary flamboyance. He was sent to work at Toongabbie, west of Sydney, where he began his convict life in a hut shared with lower-class criminals. They no doubt found sharing their table with him a great privilege and novelty, and pressed him for stories of his glittering, bold career. Though Barrington no doubt satisfied these demands, his seriousness, probably arising in part from depression, lasted, and on the basis of his changed demeanour and his 'irreproachable conduct', he was quickly appointed a superintendent of convicts and ultimately to the night watch. Barrington had found in Parramatta a life not utterly lacking in pleasure: 'having had several young native dogs given to me, from time to time, I take great delight in kangaroo hunting, it is not only an agreeable exercise, but produces a dish for the table, nearly as good as mutton and in the present dearth of livestock is not an unacceptable present'.

By the Third Fleet, Governor Phillip received from Secretary of State Grenville an answer to his earlier petition for leave. Grenville said he was much concerned that the situation of Phillip's private affairs would not be such as to intrude on his services in New South Wales which 'are so extremely important to the public. I cannot, therefore, refrain from expressing my earnest hope . . . that you may be able, without material inconvenience, to continue in your government for a short time longer'.

But it *was* intended that the bulk of the marine garrison, now relieved by the purpose-recruited New South Wales Corps, return to England on the *Gorgon*. In deciding what to do, Lieutenant Collins was caught between his dislike of Captain Nepean of the New South Wales Corps and his detestation of the departing Major Ross. Had Collins given up his task as judge-advocate and governor's secretary, for which he received only half-pay, and returned to a full-paid but purely military function, he would have been reduced to serving in New South Wales as junior to Nepean, and would have found that distasteful. 'I have no prospect of getting on in the army, and I very much dislike the generality of the officers who compose the Corps.' But though he mentions his wife Maria's letters, and worries about her welfare, there is no hint of longing to be back with her via *Gorgon* in his remarks, even accounting for the reserve that was natural to him. Indeed, he was in an association with Ann Yeates, alias Nancy, the young milliner from *Lady Penrhyn,* who had borne him two sons.

As for returning on the *Gorgon*, Major Ross took his passage in that ship, 'and with him I would not sail were wealth and honours to attend me when I landed'.

In reality, however, he could not reconcile it to his mind to leave Governor Phillip, 'with whom I have now lived so long, that I am blended in every concern of his'. Even so, the work he had to do for Phillip 'is increased to more than double what it was at first, and my salary has decreased one-half of what it was at first'. But for the moment, stay he did, even though he felt he was spending the prime of his life at the furthest part of the world, 'without credit, without, or with but very little, profit, secluded from my family, my connections, from the world, under constant apprehensions of being starved, and constantly living on a reduced ration of provisions'.

Collins was disgruntled that though the masters of the Third Fleet ships admitted they could have brought out a further thousand tons of provisions, instead they had loaded up with copper, iron, steel and cordage for sale at Bombay 'on account of their owners'. Dependent for his survival on this strange balance of beneficence and greed in shipping merchants, he decided ultimately that he would seek permission to go home and take 'the first opportunity that offers of escaping from a country that is nothing better than a place of banishment for the outcasts of society'.

Meanwhile, in distant Koepang, in Dutch Timor, some of Bryant's party of escapees had taken jobs. 'We remained very happy at our work for two months,' said Martin, 'till Wm Bryant had words with his wife, went and informed against himself, wife and children and all of us . . . we was immediately taken prisoners and was put in the castle.'

Tench, who would later investigate the case, wrote: 'The Dutch received them with kindness, and treated them with hospitality; but their behaviour giving rise to suspicions, they were watched; and one of them at last, in a moment of intoxication, betrayed the secret. They were immediately secured, and committed to prison.'

Their imprisonment does not seem to have been severe and they were allowed out of the castle two at a time for whole days, and this continued until the arrival of another group of British, the worst group possible for Will and Mary Bryant. Captain Edward Edwards of HMS *Pandora* had been sent to Tahiti to round up the men who had mutinied on the *Bounty*. Fletcher Christian and a small group of others, knowing that such vengeance would be dispatched, had sailed away on the seized *Bounty* across the Pacific towards South America to remote Pitcairn Island, where they could continue to enjoy a form of freedom. The majority remained on the far more kindly islands of Tahiti. There Captain Edwards, 'a cold, hard man devoid of sympathy and imagination', arrived on *Pandora* on 23 March 1791, about the same time the Bryant party was escaping Sydney. He found fourteen mutineers and detained them on board the *Pandora* in a structure 11 feet long and 18 feet wide that he had built on the outer quarterdeck. This imprisonment shed would become known in infamy as '*Pandora's* box'. The only entry was by way of an iron hatch on top, and inside the box the mutineers were attached by leg irons to heavy ring bolts. *Pandora* headed across the Pacific towards the northern tip of the Australian east coast and through Torres Strait, intending to return its prisoners to England by way of Batavia and Cape Town. Instead she ran aground on an outcrop of the Great Barrier Reef. A few of the prisoners from *Pandora's* box were released immediately to work at the pumps, but the rest were left chained inside. As the ship sank, three more were let out, but the hatch was again slammed down, closed and barred. The bosun's mate delayed taking to the sea himself to unbar the manhole to let the rest out, some of whom were picked up by the ship's boats.

On a little island where the survivors gathered and boats were prepared for the row to Timor, the mutineers were not allowed the use of tents, and they were put to the oars mercilessly by Edwards. They got more sympathy from the surgeon, Hamilton, who would also extend many clemencies to Mary Bryant, her children and her colleagues when the whole group reached Timor in September.

If, as Martin said, it was Bryant who gave the group away while drunk, they were all to pay a massive price for it now that Edwards had appeared. In the castle at Koepang, without the help of the Dutch colonial police, Edwards interrogated the prisoners one by one. 'We told him we was convicts and had made our escape from Botany Bay,' wrote Martin. 'He told us we was his prisoners.' They were no longer allowed any freedom of movement. Edwards had already shown a tendency to care not so much for bringing his captives back to England for punishment as accounting for them. His behaviour during the wreck of the *Pandora*, even taking into account his many distractions, was not that of a man who wanted at all cost to save the lives of the *Bounty* mutineers and bring them to trial.

By early October 1791, Edwards had chartered a Dutch vessel, the *Rembang*, to take himself and his crew, his *Bounty* prisoners and his 'Botany Bay ten', to Batavia. He put the Bryants and their party below decks clamped in bilboes, 'irons attached to a long sliding iron bar to confine the prisoner, fastened at one end to the floor by a lock'.

On the way to Batavia, off the island of Flores, the *Rembang* ran into a cyclone. 'In a few minutes,' wrote the surgeon of the lost *Pandora*, 'every sail of the ship was shivered to pieces; the pumps all choked and useless, the leaks gaining fast upon us.' The *Rembang* was being driven towards a lee shore seven miles away, but the cyclone passed before she was smashed against it.

THE COMMONWEALTH OF THIEVES • 379

There was no evidence, one way or another, about whether Will and Mary, the two children and the others would have had the bilboes removed for escape during the crisis. Based on Edwards's record, one doubts they would have been unlocked by him.

Batavia, near the northern end of Java, was the chief port of the Dutch East India Company in the Indonesian islands. A magnificent Dutch town square opened up from the harbour, just as in Cape Town. Here, where the jungle still pressed close, could be found the same enterprising Calvinist mind as existed in any other Dutch principality, and the Dutch themselves were said to thrive on the swampy exhalations of the place. But for everyone else it seemed to be, to quote Surgeon Hamilton a 'painted sepulchre, this Golgotha of Europe which buries the whole settlement every five years'.

The Botany Bay ten were put aboard a Dutch East India Company ship lying in the roads of Batavia. Smothering heat hung over them and an unhealthy damp filled their prison deck like mist. There are no accounts, either from the party itself or from observers, of bitter recriminations amongst the group, even though survival seemed unlikely. Mary knew, however, that if she could get her two children back to England alive, they would have the privilege of breathing softer air. For many others of the party, death seemed an intimate certainty.

Twenty-seven

Speaking their own language, and bound together in many cases by secret oaths and compacts, the Irish who had come into Port Jackson on *Queen* on 26 September 1791 presented particular problems. A later Irish genius would call Ireland *John Bull's Other Island*, and the officers in New South Wales would have nodded as ruefully as any Anglo-Irish magistrate on Irish soil at the Gaelic wrong-headedness of Irish convicts' refusal to behave like Englishmen, and to speak English. Irish was still the first language of over 80 per cent of Irish hearths, and now it was heard, to the discomfort of the officers and officials, in the fringes of the bushland of New South Wales. What were they plotting, what was behind their frequent, secret laughter?

One thing about them was the ready – some would say gullible – comfort they took in millennial fantasies. After all, a new century was nearing, and at its dawn the justice of Christ might reverse the order of the world, putting the first last, and the last first. In Sydney and Parramatta, there developed amongst them like a fever 'the chimerical idea' of finding China from New South Wales, the idea that it was beyond the mountains to the north-west of Sydney Cove. In terms of the Enlightenment it was a preposterous idea. In terms of their extreme poverty and of religious belief and Irish psychology it made perfect sense. Somewhere on earth there *must* exist a veil the Irish could penetrate, beyond which they would have their old powers and remembered spaciousness restored to them. A faith in Christ's promise of the meek inheriting the earth, and of the humble actively seeking redemption, was not laughable to the Irish-speaking convicts of the *Queen*. Their ignorance of strict geography was something chosen for them by their masters – the schooling of Irish Catholics was contrary to the penal laws of Britain – and so they made up a geography of hope from fragments of information, namely that New South Wales was part of the same unknown zone as China. They drew their compasses on a piece of paper, with the arrow fixed on north, a practice which would be laughed at by their betters. Yet the Defenders and other secret societies were influenced by Freemasonry, to which the Irish nationalist Protestants such as Robert Emmet, Napper Tandy and Wolfe Tone belonged, and in Freemasonry, and other secret societies too, there was an inherent importance and a power in the representation of the compass. The north was potent, even if invoked merely on paper, and the Irish convicts, eating bitter rations by the camp fires of Sydney and Parramatta, had caught the belief that not too many days walk northwards from the Parramatta River and Port Jackson, a habitable kingdom lay awaiting them.

One sight of the dense bush around Parramatta and Sydney was enough to make many delay their Chinese pilgrimage. The strangeness of the natives, matched by the strangeness of the forests, the tangles of ungodly acacias and melaleucas, the spiteful sharpness of narrow-leaved shrubs determined to survive fire and drought, and the feeling of godlessness and lack of familiar presences in the place had been for three years sufficient to stop most convicts walking away, and promised to be effective well into the future. Yet on 1 November – All Saints' Day – twenty male Irish convicts and one pregnant female in Parramatta took a week's provisions, tomahawks and knives, and set out into the bush to find China. Collins and others suspected that this was a cover story, and that their real purpose was to steal boats and get on board the transports after they had left Sydney waters. But he almost certainly mis-stated their ambitions.

A few days later, sailors in a boat belonging to the *Albemarle* met the pregnant Irish woman down-harbour. She had been separated from her group for three days. The woman's husband was also later found and gave the same 'absurd account of their design' to the officials back in Sydney. Thus the proposition of Irish stupidity made its entry onto the Australian stage.

Other men were captured to the north near Broken Bay, and despite their suffering, attempted escape again a few days afterwards. Thirteen of those who first absconded 'were brought in, in a state of deplorable wretchedness, naked, and nearly worn out with hunger'. They had tried to live by sucking flowering shrubs for their honey and by eating wild purple berries.

Phillip ordered the convicts at Parramatta to be assembled, and told them that he would send out parties looking for them with orders to fire on sight, and if they were recaptured he would land them on a part of the harbour whence they could not depart, or chain them together with only bread and water during the rest of their term of transportation. The declaration did not staunch the magnitude of their hopes.

Typically, Watkin Tench visited the Irish convicts who had made the dash for China – it was he who called them 'the Chinese

Travellers'. Four of them lay in hospital, variously wounded by the natives. Watkin's enquiries were not contemptuous, but grew from genuine human impulses of investigation. He asked them if they really supposed it possible to reach China, and they informed him that they had been told that at a considerable distance to the north lay a large river, 'which separated this country from the back part of China'. When they crossed this Jordan, they would find themselves among a copper-coloured people who would treat them generously. On the third day of their wanderings towards this hoped-for place, one of their party died of fatigue, and another was butchered by the natives as they fled the scene. They had reached Broken Bay and the Hawkesbury River, where the wide entrance and estuary stopped them from going further.

Though a great proportion of the Irish were of farming backgrounds or had agricultural experience, and though this was a hopeful aspect, Hunter would later describe them as 'dissatisfied with their situation here', and 'extremely insolent, refractory, and turbulent'. For the Irish combined their dream of China with a keen sense of their small quota of rights. The convicts of *Queen* at Parramatta were the first to stage an organised public protest, outside government house in Parramatta in the humidity of December 1791, demanding that the issue of rations be changed back from weekly to daily. There was a certain justice in this. A weak or sickly person might be deprived of a week's rations by a bully in one swoop, but if the ration was doled out daily, the weak could appeal to the strong to prevent any large-scale ration-snatching.

There was a pregnant Irish girl named Catherine Devereaux aboard *Queen* who did not seek China but stuck close to camp for the sake of her unborn child, who would be christened James, taking the name of his father – the *Queen*'s cook, Kelly. James Kelly would reach young manhood under the tutelage of two entrepreneurial former convicts, Henry Kable and James Underwood, and in Van Diemen's Land would become a whaling, sealing and shipping tycoon of some renown before dying in 1859. But all that was in a future version of Australia, the mercantile one.

Despite a few nods towards mercantilism in the founding of Sydney, such as murderous Captain Trail setting up his general store with impunity in a tent at Sydney Cove, it was not a trading post, and Phillip did not want it yet to be one. But he was interested in how the three Third Fleet transports which had gone off to try the whale fishery on the coasts of New South Wales and Van Diemen's Land fared. The *Britannia* returned with seven sperm whales in November, having hunted in company with *William and Anne*, which had caught only one whale on its own account. Thirteen barrels of oil were procured from the whales killed by *Britannia*, 'and in the opinion of Mr Melville [*Britannia*'s captain], the oil, with its containing a greater proportion of that valuable part of the fish called by the whalers the head matter, was worth £10 more per ton than that of the fish of any other part of the world he had been in'.

Though the master of the *Mary Ann* had been as far south as 45 degrees without seeing a single whale, the *Matilda* stayed off Jervis Bay, south of Sydney, and saw a great many whales, but was unable to chase them because of the weather. The initial performance of the South Seas whale fishery seemed mediocre.

William Richards Jr, who had dispatched the First Fleet, had commercial dreams for the far-off colony he had never seen, and remained in touch with New South Wales through his Botany Bay agent, Zachariah Clark, who was now the commissary of stores in New South Wales. Still a visionary eccentric, Richards hoped to take over the convict-handling business, and combine it with other forms of trade between the south-west Pacific and Britain. The whole idea was irksome to Campbell, the contractor for the Thames hulks. But if Francis Baring, chairman of the East India Company, would describe Sydney as 'the serpent we are nursing at Botany Bay', William Richards was prepared to be both father and midwife to that serpent. He was willing to receive a land grant and to live permanently in New South Wales as Sydney's shipping magnate. Outraged by stories of the Second Fleet, the devoutly Christian Richards had moved towards the twin beacons of utility: a settled, regular, low-yield market in the conscientious transportation of convicts, and on the other side, high-yield trading with India and China and what he may have been convinced would be an increasing traffic of whalers. His ideas, an accurate depiction of the future of New South Wales though they were, were not well-received. Indeed, in a year or two he would become bankrupt due to other contracts gone bad, and some of his children would be left to consider New South Wales as an option for free settlement. But far more than anyone else in the penal equation, Richards had desired New South Wales. Not many did. Even Tench would write, 'If only a receptacle for convicts be intended, this place stands unequalled . . . when viewed in a commercial light, I fear its insignificance will not appear very striking.'

In December 1791, as the *Gorgon* lay in Sydney Cove ready to return the marines to Britain, offers were made to the non-commissioned officers and privates to stay in the country as settlers or to enter into the New South Wales Corps. Such offers could only have derived from a British government with a sense of population pressure. Three corporals, a drummer and 59 privates accepted grants of land on Norfolk Island or at Parramatta, as Rose Hill was by now officially named. The rest wanted to return – indeed, of those who stayed, Tench thought the behaviour of the majority of them could be ascribed to 'infatuated affection to female convicts, whose characters and habits of life, I am sorry to say, promise from a connection neither honour nor tranquillity'. As for tranquillity, only the parties to the relationships could say anything, but it is a matter of record that many of the remaining soldiers and their women were founders of enduring Antipodean stock.

Before packing to leave on *Gorgon*, in the summer of 1791–92, Tench made a reconnaissance around Prospect Hill and the ponds along the Parramatta River. Looking at the settlements with the eyes of a man about to depart forever, Tench gave a report of mixed skill and ineptitude on the part of convict and other farmers, and of New South Wales as something less than a bountiful garden. Its tough and plentiful flora might seem to promise a form of Eden, but here in the Sydney basin it all grew from an ancient, leached and worn-down earth that demanded great skill and determination from those who would profit from it.

For its natural fertility, Tench admired the Parramatta farm of the former sailor and highway robber, John Ramsay. Ramsay had settled there with his wife, Mary Leary, from the Second Fleet. Like Ruse's wife, Elizabeth Perry, Mary Leary might have been unjustly transported, and was a woman with an unresolved and burning grievance against her mistress, the wife of a London attorney. She claimed that the woman not only docked her pay but sold used garments to her for exorbitant prices. When the lawyer saw some of his wife's clothing on Leary, his wife swore under oath that she had never 'sold her any one thing in my life'. On the farm in New South Wales, Leary probably enlisted her husband's belief in her innocence. No doubt, at their rough-hewn table, she reiterated the extremely credible tale to Captain Tench. Tench thought Ramsay 'deserves a good spot, for he is a civil, sober, industrious man. Besides his corn land, he has a well-laid-out little garden, in which I found him and his wife busily at work. He praised her industry to me; and said he did not doubt of succeeding'.

By contrast Tench found Joseph Bishop, former fisherman and convict, had planted a little maize 'in so slovenly a style, as to promise a very poor crop'. To survive here as a farmer, thought Tench, a man 'must exert more than ordinary activity. The attorney's clerk, Matthew Everingham, I also thought out of his province, and likely to return, like Bishop, when victualling from the stores ceased, to drag a timber or brick cart for his maintenance . . . I dare believe he finds cultivating his own land not half so heavy a task, as he formerly found that of stringing together volumes of tautology to encumber, or convey away that of his neighbour'.

It would turn out that Everingham, son of an earl, whose crime was to have acquired legal textbooks under false pretences, and his wife, Elizabeth Rymes, Spitalfields bed-linen thief from the Second Fleet, would succeed, however touch-and-go it might have seemed in that early summer of 1791, and would give birth and habitation to nine small 'cornstalks' or Currency children, as native-born New South Welshmen came to be called.

Later in his last New South Wales summer, Tench would visit Phillip Schaeffer's farm on the Parramatta River. Schaeffer had served as a lieutenant in the Hesse-Hanau Regiment in the American War, and he and Tench had the bond of having been fellows in arms.

Herr Schaeffer had proved ineffective as a superintendent of convict farm work, but Phillip liked him as a fellow German-speaker, and had given him a land grant and five convicts to work for him. Although his maize was 'mean' and his wheat 'thin and poor', he had 900 vines planted – the only other vines in the country being in the garden of Phillip's second government house in Parramatta. He told Tench that his father had owned a small estate on the banks of the Rhine, and that he himself had loved from an early age working in the vineyard. Tench found that Schaeffer spoke very realistically about his prospects. Sometimes he nearly despaired and had often weighed up whether to relinquish the farm. But he always remembered that hardly any hardship could not be overcome by vigour and perseverance.

Directly across the river from Schaeffer's 140 acres lay the more modest but 'very eligible' farm of Christopher Magee, a neighbour of the initial farmer, James Ruse. Magee – alias Charles Williams – had been a farm labourer in England for eight years and had worked in America, and although sentenced in 1784 at the Old Bailey, had soon after his landing been made a convict overseer on the government farm. Though he entertained some revolutionary ideas, he was described by David Collins as having 'extraordinary propriety of conduct'. His wife, a former hawker and – if some of the evidence at her trial can be believed – prostitute, worked with him on the farm. 'I asked by what means he had been able to accomplish so much? He answered,

"By industry and by hiring all the convicts I could get to work in their leisure hours."' His greatest problem was that he needed to bear all the water he used half a mile from the river, for having sunk a well he found the water from it brackish.

Magee's idyll on the Parramatta River was fragile, for after Tench had left the colony, Magee's young wife, Eleanor McCabe, drowned in the river, and Collins would record that Magee subsequently gave himself over 'to idleness and dissipation'.

Tench's reconnaissance before departure showed that the Parramatta River area did not speak overly well for the fertility of eastern Australia. It was in Australian terms a short river which did not descend from any great elevation. North and south along the coast lay mighty and often turbulent rivers which created fertile floodplains, but these went unvisited for now, and the merely middling fertility of the land around Sydney and Parramatta made success fragile.

Before leaving Parramatta for the last time, Watkin went to visit Barrington. The tall Irishman approached six feet, was slender, and his gait and manner bespoke 'liveliness and activity. Of that elegance and fashion, with which my imagination had decked him . . . I could distinguish no trace. Great allowance should, however, be made for depression and unavoidable deficiency of dress'. Tench admired his strong cast of character, his penetrating eye, his prominent forehead. 'His whole demeanour is humble, not servile . . . Since his arrival here, his conduct has been irreproachable . . . his knowledge of men, particularly that part of them into whose morals, manners and behaviour, he is ordered especially to inspect, eminently fitting him for the office.' And here Tench went on to a refined reflection. 'I cannot quit him without bearing my testimony that his talents promise to be directed, in future, to make reparation to society for the offences he has heretofore committed against it.' This was a mirror of what Barrington had promised at his trial, that his colonial reformation would be held up as an example of an internationally famous criminal being reduced to good order by the convict transportation system.

Sydney, where Tench had spent the bulk of his time in New South Wales, was by the turn of 1791–92, as Tench said goodbye, the lesser village to Parramatta. In Sydney lived 1259 persons, with 1625 in Parramatta and its farming areas, and 1172 at Norfolk Island. He concluded there were just in excess of 4000 European people perilously surviving the Sydney experiment. He would leave the colony with fond remembrance, but no desire to return.

The always composed Phillip did not record his feelings in losing both such friends as Watkin and such enemies as Major Ross and Captain Campbell. But Robbie Ross was delighted to march the marines aboard the *Gorgon* on 13 December. His now pre-adolescent son, Lieutenant John Ross, was in their ranks. Ross had only the week before found reason to fight a duel with Captain Hill of the New South Wales Corps, from which though both fired two shots, both came away unhurt. Back home, Ross would be made a recruiting officer and then get plenty of action about His Majesty's warships during the long war with Revolutionary and Napoleonic France, and would be last heard of serving in the East Indies aboard the *Sceptre* about 1808.

Gorgon dropped down the harbour three days after the marines marched aboard, and vanished back to the known world the next day. Sergeant Scott and his family were returning to England on *Gorgon*, but a company of marines remained behind waiting for the arrival of the remainder of the New South Wales Corps.

The *Gorgon* on departure carried not only returning soldiers, but was to an extent an Australian ark: 'our barque was now crowded with kangaroos, opossums, and every curiosity which that country produced', including plants and birds and the other antediluvian mysteries of New South Wales.

By the time the *Gorgon* left Sydney, the twenty-month-old voyager, Emmanuel Bryant, had died in the Dutch East India Company prison ship moored off Batavia, where Mary Bryant and her two infants were kept prisoner. Will had already been moved ashore into the Dutch East India Company's hospital, where he too died, no doubt raving about the British excise men and their vileness. Captain Edwards, avenger of Bligh, was in the meantime in good lodgings in the elegant Dutch quarter of Batavia, organising passages for himself, his prisoners and the *Pandora's* company on three Dutch ships to go home by way of the Cape.

When the arrangements were concluded, Mary and her daughter, Charlotte, were put aboard the *Horssen* with two of the Bryant group. The others went aboard a ship called the *Hoornwey*. As they traversed Sunda Strait, James Cox either fell or jumped overboard from the *Horssen*. He had been Will Bryant's closest conspirator outside Mary. John Simms and William Martin, two members of the party, were sickening and would die before the Cape. It did not appear that Captain Edwards, on his way home for the *pro forma* court-martial for the loss of *Pandora*, considered the death rate of the Bryant party abnormal, or that it was untoward that they should pay so heavily for their skilled escape.

Twenty-eight

Through his gifts of iron hatchets to a number of selected Aboriginals, including Bennelong, Phillip might have unwittingly created a new elite – the *Mogogal*, the hatchet men. But even ownership of a hatchet did not give Bennelong psychological dominance over his wife Barangaroo Daringah, something of a woman-warrior. She carried two scars from spear wounds received in the give-and-take of inter-clan relations. The spear that caused one of them had passed right through her thigh. She was forceful and good-looking. 'She is very straight and exceedingly well-made,' wrote Phillip. 'Her features are good, and she goes entirely naked, yet there is such an air of innocence about her that clothing scarcely appears necessary.' The septum of her nose had also been pierced – an uncommon feature with Port Jackson women.

Tench had described Yuringa, Colby's wife, as 'meek and feminine', but Barangaroo by contrast as 'fierce and unsubmissive'. She seemed slightly older than Bennelong and had two children of a former husband, both of whom were dead, possibly from the smallpox. Now she was about to give birth again and Phillip noticed that she, like other Aboriginal mothers, planned to wrap up her new baby in the soft bark of the tea-tree.

Before the birth, Barangaroo had visions of being delivered of her baby in Phillip's house, and had already asked him about it. Phillip thought it a mere touching request. But it would give her child a claim on government house as his place of birth, and seemed to carry with it, apart from genuine affection and reverence, a new strategy – if the ghosts could not be made to disappear, the Eora should try to outclaim and out-title them. Barangaroo thus avoided the hospital, where Phillip wanted to send her, for the obvious reason that it was full of *mawm*, the bad spirits of the dead. In the event, the birth seemed to occur suddenly, and did not in fact take place at government house. The child was a girl named Dilboong.

Soon after, at the end of 1791, Barangaroo died. The cause of death was unknown, but might have been post-childbirth complications or perhaps marital contest, the latter seeming for once the least likely of factors. Bennelong and Barangaroo were always fighting, but Tench said, like a good Georgian man, that 'she was a scold, and a vixen, and nobody pitied her . . . the women often artfully studied to irritate and inflame the passions of the men, although sensible that the consequence will alight on themselves'. As Barangaroo lay dying, the desperate Bennelong summoned the great *carradhy*, Willemering, the wounder of Phillip. When he did not arrive in time to save her, Bennelong would seek him out and spear him in the thigh. Indeed, in Barangaroo's honour, or more accurately to adjust the world to her death, many spears were thrown by Bennelong and her Cameraigal relatives, for death was always the result of some sorcery. The idea that punishment for death was owed to some malign influence, and that spirits needed to be avenged before they could go to the sky, lay solemnly upon a passionate husband like Bennelong.

In intense grieving, he asked Phillip, Surgeon White and

Lieutenant David Collins to witness his wife's cremation. He cleared the ground where the funeral pyre was to be built by digging out the earth to about five inches below the surface. Then a mound of sticks, bushes and branches was made about three feet high. Barangaroo's body, wrapped in an old English blanket, was laid on top of this with her head facing north. Bennelong stacked logs on the body and the fire was lit. The English spectators left before the body was totally consumed.

After the ceremony, Bennelong seemed cheerful and talked about finding a nurse amongst the white women for his daughter, who still needed breast-feeding. Dilboong, the child, was suckled by a convict woman, Midshipman Southwell noting that some of the Eora women 'gladly forego the dear pleasure of nurturing their own brats, and leave them in perfect security to the care of several of the convict women, who are suitably rewarded by the governor'.

The day after the funeral, Bennelong invited the gentlemen for the scraping up of Barangaroo's ashes and powdery bones with a spear.

With Watkin Tench gone, David Collins and Lieutenant Dawes and Phillip himself remained as the chief observers of the natives. Collins retained an exhaustive interest in native society and recorded what he saw in detail and without any deliberate cultural malice. He was also perceptive when it came to shifts in the relationship between the Europeans and the Aboriginals. Since the period of peace-making in late 1791, when stolen goods were returned to the natives, there had been no 'interruption by acts of hostility', he wrote. 'Several of their young people continue to reside among us, and the different houses in the town were frequently visited by their relations.'

But Collins and others were aware that aside from British–Eora conflict, the old ritual battles of the Eora continued. There had been a confrontation between the Sydney and Botany Bay natives in April 1791 over the uttering of the name of a dead man. The natives knew that the uttered name could summon havoc from the spiritual realm onto the physical earth. After a death, the deceased became 'a nameless one', said Collins. Mourners often warned Collins and other officers not to use the names of the dead.

A corroboree dance-rite was held at night that summer at 'the head of the stream' on a rise to the south-east of government house. During it a Gweagal man from southern Botany Bay, who had earlier been involved in beating a Cadigal, was suddenly attacked. Colby thrust his spear at the man and another native struck two heavy blows to his back with his club. Wounded and bleeding, the unarmed man rose to his feet and let himself be upbraided by Colby and his ally. Bennelong came up and wiped the blood from his wounds with grass. That evening David Collins saw the Gweagal man with a ligature fastened very tightly round his head, for it 'certainly required something to alleviate the pain he must have endured'. According to the practice of the country, said Collins, the victim did not wash the blood off.

An incident occurred in May 1792 which gave the whites a further bewildered insight into the rigidity of native law. A woman named Noorooing came into town to tell the whites of the ritual killing of a south Botany Bay native, Yellaway, who had abducted her. She was clearly not an unwilling abductee, since she threw ashes on herself in sadness and refused all food, and other Aboriginals explained that she was *go-lahng*, in a state of ritual mourning and fasting. Soon after, Noorooing, travelling in the bush near Sydney Cove, met and attacked a little girl related to the murderer of Yellaway. She beat the little girl so cruelly that the child was brought into town almost dead, with six or seven deep gashes in her throat and one ear cut to the bone. She died a few days later.

The English were not sympathetic to Noorooing, but other Aboriginals explained to them 'that she had done no more than what custom obliged her to . . . The little victim of her revenge was, from her quiet, tractable manners, much beloved in the town; and what is a singular trait of the inhumanity of this proceeding, she had every day since Yellaway's death requested that Noorooing should be fed at the officer's hut, where she herself resided.' The native who had committed the murder for which his little kinswoman suffered escaped apparently unpunished. In some way that the Europeans could not understand, the blood debt had been fully settled by the girl's death.

Colby's wife, Yuringa, like Barangaroo, would die soon after childbirth. In recent times, Yuringa had visited Mrs Macarthur in the Macarthur hut made from cabbage tree posts framed with wattle and daub, and sturdy Mrs Macarthur had observed the mantle made of soft bark in which the child was wrapped. At Yuringa's burial, the British onlookers were horrified to see Colby place the baby with its dead mother in a shallow grave. Colby looked down on his wife and his child and threw a large, murderous stone on the corpse and the living infant, and the grave was instantly filled in. 'The whole business was so momentary, that our people had not time or presence of mind sufficient to prevent it; and on speaking about it to Colby, he, so far from thinking it inhuman, justified the extraordinary act by assuring us that as no woman could be found to nurse the child it would die a much worse death than that to which he had put it . . .'

Meanwhile, because of settlement at Parramatta, and the area known as Toongabbie to the north-west of Parramatta, many of the Burramattagal were pushed west. Here the warrior Pemulwuy of the Bediagal from the north shore of Botany Bay began to cooperate with the Bidjigal. If Bennelong had come to some accommodation with the accumulating waves of Europeans or ghosts, Pemulwuy had not. Near Prospect Hill west of Parramatta in May, seven native men and two women stole clothing and corn, and a convict worker on the farm fired at a man preparing to throw his spear. The party fled, abandoning nets containing corn, blankets and spears. The natives took a fast revenge. A convict employed on well-digging on a farm near Prospect Hill walked to Parramatta to collect his clothing ration. On the way back he was attacked, his head was cut in several places and his teeth were smashed out. His dead body gaped with wounds from spears.

So here was the contrast. Bennelong was victualled from the store – he took the rations as recompense for damage done his people. Pemulwuy, who was involved in the murder of the convict, would not deign to receive that sort of requital. He would not take Phillip's appeasing flour, or any other gift. Gift-giving was continuous amongst natives, and the basis of prestige and human cohesion amongst groups and relatives. Those who did not participate were named *damunalung*, a word which was translated into English by Lieutenant Dawes as 'churl'. But Pemulwuy would not enter into gift-swapping with the newcomers.

It would have confirmed his worst suspicions had he known Arthur Phillip still had an ambition to send an Aboriginal skull to the great Sir Joseph Banks. The whites had raked through burial mounds to find remaining bones which might be of scientific interest, and at one, Captain John Hunter discovered a jawbone. But Phillip managed to acquire a skull at last – we do not know whose it was – and sent it to Banks, who in turn sent it on to Professor Johann Friedrich Blumenbach of the University of Göttingen. The male skull had its front tooth missing, as Banks had warned Blumenbach would be the case, 'according to the custom of these savages'. Blumenbach was a pioneer in the branch of science known as physical anthropology. Caucasians, according to Blumenbach, who coined that term from an Aryan skull he had retrieved from the Caucasus Mountains, were the founding form of the human group, while other races had degenerated from this primary type because of climatic variations. The skull he received from Banks would go to support his theory, though Blumenbach himself, who would live until 1840, was repelled by the political use to which his dissertations were put. The perversion of his ideas would reach its apogee in Nazi ideology, when Blumenbach's collection at Göttingen 'became a core of racist, pan-Germanic theory, which was officially sanctioned by the National Socialist Party when it came into power'.

Twenty-nine

The age of convict fleets had ended, but transportation by regularly dispatched individual ships had begun, the government retreating shamefaced from its dalliance with Camden, Calvert and King. It was as an individual transport that a large ship named the *Pitt*, of 775 tons, had sailed on 17 July 1791 carrying nearly 400 male and female prisoners. The owner of the *Pitt*, George Mackenzie Macaulay, was an alderman of the city of London and one of the Scots merchants of Blackheath who had such a powerful connection to shipping sent to early New South Wales. Macaulay was what the East India Company called a 'husband', that is, a contractor who regularly chartered his ships to the company and was reputable. Yet he was also canny to a fault.

The *Pitt* had originally embarked nearly 450 prisoners, but a complaint about overcrowding was made to the Commissioners of the Navy, and as a result of an inspection it was decided she could not accommodate more than 410 on the two-level benches which made up her sleeping quarters. The inspecting officers remarked in their report that 'if a sickness should happen, a sick [person] and a person in health must touch each other'.

On the gun deck, below the quarterdeck, three separate coops in front of the main cabin were set apart for the women's quarters. The 58 women convicts would therefore have better ventilated spaces, though were equally as cramped as the men – in fact, an extra shack needed to be built on the gun deck to take their overflow.

Smallpox struck the prison deck soon after the *Pitt*'s departure from Yarmouth Roads, and even before the Cape Verde Islands there were fifteen deaths amongst the convicts. In the doldrums off Africa, the prisoners developed ulcers on their bodies from lack of vitamin B and showed symptoms of scurvy. A fever struck, killing 27 people – soldiers, sailors and their families – in a fortnight. The crew was left so short-handed that some of the convicts with maritime experience had to be recruited up from the prison deck to help sail the vessel.

Aboard this vessel travelled Major Francis Grose, on his way to assume command of the New South Wales Corps. He would be the new lieutenant-governor, and came from a rather more privileged background than Phillip. His father was a renowned antiquary, and his grandfather a jeweller who had counted George II among his clients. He had a much more genial nature than Ross – if anything he would become over time too accommodating to the desires of the officers of his corps for land and wealth. Grose, like the majority of officers, had campaigned during the American Revolution, fighting in the summer of 1778 at Monmouth Courthouse in New Jersey, a battle site at which the heat may well have killed as many men as were shot, though he was amongst the latter. After nearly six years on half-pay, he was delighted to be appointed lieutenant-governor of New South Wales and commandant of the New South Wales Corps which, as a professional recruiter, he had helped to raise.

Grose reported from Rio on 22 October 1791 that the sick, including soldiers' and convicts' children, were landed on an island – perhaps the island the Portuguese had appointed for the use of Phillip's First Fleet four years earlier. The serving of fresh provisions there helped restore the health of many, though five convicts tried to swim for the mainland and were believed drowned in the attempt.

When at last *Pitt* arrived at Port Jackson in February 1792, a further twenty male and nine female prisoners had died, and 120 of the men were landed sick. Surgeon White's hospital was again required to deal with a huge medical emergency. So though Macaulay's ship did not create quite the massacre of the Second Fleet, it was still a ship of disgrace. The ship's officers, including the master, Edward Manning, set up a store ashore to sell goods they had brought out at their own expense. 'The high price at which everything was sold, the avidity with which all descriptions of people grasped at what was purchased was extraordinary, and could only be accounted for by the distance of our situation from the Mother Country, the uncertainty of receiving supplies thence, and the length of time which we had heretofore the mortification to find elapse without our receiving any.'

The *Pitt* brought for the commissary store mainly salt beef, enough to extend the provisions of the settlement for 40 days, and the ship was subsequently employed in taking a proportion of the supplies to Norfolk Island.

Having landed and inspected his garrison, Major Grose was enthused by what he saw in Phillip's Sydney Cove and Parramatta. 'I find there is neither the scarcity that was represented to me, nor the barren sands I was taught to imagine I should see; the whole place is a garden, on which fruit and vegetables of every description grow in the greatest luxuriance . . . within five miles of my habitation there is food in abundance for many thousand head of cattle . . . Could we once be supplied with cattle, I do not believe we should have occasion to trouble Old England again. I live in as good a house as I desire; and the farm of my predecessor, which has been given to me, produces a sufficiency of everything for my family. The climate, though very hot, is not unwholesome, we have plenty of fish, and there is good shooting.' There was at last, in Grose's picture, the promise of a settled colony and a habitable place.

Even though Grose saw Sydney Cove in such positive light, it was indeed a hot season, and those male convicts of *Pitt* who had been passed as healthy on landing were put to work cultivating and clearing public ground beyond Parramatta. They found it hard under that hammering February sun, in New South Wales's most humid month. Many of them began to join their prison-deck mates in hospital. The offer of full and more justly distributed rations could not save some. The record of burials, chiefly of newcomers, during that late summer is sobering. On 16 February, four convicts were buried, and six the next day, and a further six on 20 February. Five were buried the next day, a further two the day after, on 23 February a further six, on 25 February another four – and these just at Parramatta. And so through the first week of March the burials continued. On 8 March there were five male deaths, and on the next day two more and that of a child, Margaret Tambleton. The regular multiple burials of men continued throughout the month. By May 1792, of 122 male convicts who came out in the *Queen*, only 50 were still alive.

Yet the vigour of the settlement had affirmed itself for Phillip when in late February he issued 52 further land grants to former convicts, chiefly in the Parramatta–Prospect Hill area – and all without reference to the interested Eora parties. He would write, however, to the third Secretary of State he would deal with, Sir Henry Dundas, a former Edinburgh lawyer, older than Grenville and a veteran of government, in not entirely positive terms: 'What I feared from the kind of settlers I have been obliged to accept has happened in several instances.' The convict settlers in some cases grew tired 'of a life so different to that from which they have been brought up' and abandoned their grants or sold their livestock to purchase from stores like that set up by the master of *Pitt* 'articles from which they do not reap any real benefit'. Even so, of dozens of settlers around Parramatta, only half a dozen had actually lost or given up their land in this way, and a number of ex-convict farmers had convicts working for them and being supported by them. Nonetheless, Phillip knew that 22 time-expired men and nine women intended to go home on the *Pitt*. 'Thus will the best people always be carried away, for those who cannot be received on board the ships as seamen or carpenters pay for their passage.'

Henry Dundas, the newest Home Secretary, had been born in Scotland in 1742, and was a close friend of Sir Joseph Banks, both belonging to the Dilettante Club, of which Horace Walpole, parliamentarian and poet, said that the supposed qualification for membership was to have travelled in Italy, but the real one was to be a drunk. Dundas, a not always approving friend of that other great Edinburgh man, the writer James Boswell, remained crucial to delivering the Scottish vote to Pitt, and had been rewarded with the Home Office.

In the Sydney area and along the Parramatta River, the burials of convicts continued through winter and into spring, but the man who conducted them was thinking of the children of convicts and their education as well. By the *Pitt*, Richard Johnson told a friend in England, came 'a man convict' who for some years had been accustomed to the profession of teaching. The man was now schoolmaster at Norfolk Island, but on the mainland there were no classes at all, and Johnson thought it was a great chance gone begging not only for mainland children of convicts but for convicts themselves who could have been instructed to read.

By this time, in early 1792, Johnson's house was crowded with native children, while Mrs Johnson was 'far gone with child', and domestic life was under pressure. One could not with entire justice depict Johnson as the dull, unimaginative evangelist who neglected the natives. He was still engaged with a struggle against Phillip's indifference to religion as anything more than a form of social regulation. The foundations of a church had been laid at Parramatta the previous spring, but before it was finished it was converted into a gaol, and then into a granary. Phillip had at one stage put aside 400 acres for church use as a glebe, but did not give Johnson any help to cultivate it. 'What, sir,' Johnson asked one of his London friends, 'are 400 or 4000 acres full of large green trees unless some convicts be allowed to cultivate it?'

He was still holding services at a boathouse along the foreshores of Sydney Cove and in the open, and in any shelters indoors or out he could find in Parramatta or Toongabbie. 'The last time I preached at Sydney was in the open air,' he admitted with reasonable pride but some resentment. He was troubled by migraine, and often dreaded the coming of Sunday and the glaring Sabbath sun.

On the day he wrote his plaint he had to bury another six convicts, most of them men, but one of them a woman, Eleanor

Lowry, another newcomer via *Pitt*. Death in such numbers must itself have been a form of stress on a soul whose resources were limited.

Johnson's daughter in Christ, brave Mary Bryant, was at this time still being taken home to England on the lower deck of a Dutch ship. When the three Dutch vessels Captain Edwards had hired in Batavia reached Table Bay off Cape Town in March 1792, they found that the HMS *Gorgon* with Major Ross and other marines aboard, including Watkin Tench, was already moored in the roads. Edwards decided to send aboard her the ten remaining *Bounty* mutineers 'and the convict deserters from Port Jackson'. Mary, her four year-old daughter, Charlotte, and William Allen were the first to be transferred, and then Martin, Butcher/Broome and Nathaniel Lilly. Here there were some familiar faces, men of the marines, and Watkin Tench in particular took time to interview the party, in barely disguised admiration of their successful escape as far as Koepang. 'We was well known by all the marine officers which was all glad that we had not perished at sea,' James Martin wrote. 'I confess that I had never looked at these people, without pity and astonishment,' declared Watkin. 'They had miscarried in a heroic struggle for liberty; after having combated every hardship, and conquered every difficulty . . . and I could not but reflect with admiration at the strange combination of circumstances which had again brought us together, to baffle human foresight, and confound human speculation.'

The *Gorgon* left Table Bay for England in early April. At first there were many days of fine weather, and as Clark said, 'a charming trade wind'. The island of St Helena came into sight: 'nothing but a barren rock, worse than any part of New South Wales'. None of the children aboard were well, even after spending time in a shore camp in Cape Town being nursed and fed for the continuation of their long voyage. Corporal Samuel Bacon and his wife, Jane, had already lost one child on the first evening out from Cape Town – 'it was ill on shore'. A little over two weeks later, the other of the twins of Corporal Bacon died. Clark wrote: 'Several more of the young children will, I am afraid, die. This hot weather is playing the devil with the children – down here it is as hot as hell – I wish to God we had got 20 degrees the other side of the line.'

Edward Divan, son of Sergeant Divan, quartermaster in Captain Campbell's company, born aboard the *Charlotte* on the way out, saw both his younger brothers, Dennis and Mark, committed to the sea from the broiling deck of *Gorgon*. Then Sergeant Andrew Gilbourn's child perished. 'I am very sorry for poor little John – he was a fine child,' wrote Clark. William Mapp, the child of Private James Mapp and the late Susan Creswell, a convict, died a few days later, just as Clark was committing to his journal his hope that if 'this little good breeze continues . . . we will be out of the southering part of the world, into that my love lives in. I hope that we shall be in the same side of the world that my Betsy is in before twelve o'clock at night.'

In early May another child, the youngest of Private John Turner and his wife, Susannah, was sent to the deep. Mary Bryant heard the weeping and keening of women from the crowded troop quarters, not much preferable to the ones she occupied, where the atmosphere must have been funereal. These lost children had all gone into the making of the great Sydney experiment, and were victims of a most peculiar imperial enterprise. Bentham's panopticon prison might have saved their lives.

With so many barely consoled women howling close by, their children worn out by the distance between Sydney and London, Mary must have known that Charlotte, who had been through more than any other child aboard, was unlikely to survive. But even though genial Captain Parker allowed Mary and Charlotte regularly on deck, even though Mrs Parker would have talked to her and may have given her comfort, she understood that Charlotte was under the axe of the same dietary exhaustion and fevers as the other children.

'Last night,' wrote Clark on May's first Sabbath, 'the child belonging to Mary Broad, the convict woman who went away in the fishing boat from Port Jackson last year died about four o'clock, [we] committed the body to the deep, latitude 5 degrees 25 minutes North.' The ship was surrounded by sharks which had learned that a regular supply of flesh trailed from this vessel, the child of a marine having died only two days before Charlotte.

The *Gorgon* arrived at Portsmouth on 18 June 1792. Transport was arranged at once to take Mary and the other escapees to London, where, towards the end of the month, they appeared before Magistrate Nicholas Bond, and were identified all too willingly by that grand stickler Captain Edwards. The magistrate sent them to Newgate but 'declared he never experienced so disagreeable a task as being obliged to commit them to prison, and assured them that, as far as lay in his power, he would assist them'.

As grim as the wards of Newgate were, the escapees all declared that they would sooner suffer death than return to Botany Bay, according to a contemporary broadsheet. The *London*

Chronicle said they found the prison 'a paradise, compared with the dreadful sufferings they endured on their voyage'.

James Boswell, famed companion of Dr Samuel Johnson, generous by nature and with a taste for handsome and robust girls of the lower orders, appealed repeatedly to his friend Dundas and to the Undersecretary Evan Nepean for a pardon for Mary and the others. He collected 17 guineas as a subscription for Mary to purchase comforts in prison, and enquired into the nature of her family in the West Country by consulting the Reverend William Johnson Temple, his 'old and most intimate friend' in Devon. The Reverend Temple reported that Mary's relatives were 'eminent for sheep stealing'.

When Mary and the others appeared at the Old Bailey on 7 July 1792, the prosecutor did not seek the statutory death penalty for their return from transportation. 'Government would not treat them with harshness, but at the same time, would not do a kind thing to them, as they might give encouragement to others to escape.'

Boswell decided to visit Mary in Newgate and take up the cause for her pardon. He had twenty years of practice at the Scottish bar behind him when he began the process of writing Samuel Johnson's life, and he was an ardent counsel, in the old days often defending accused against the then Crown Prosecutor of Scotland, Henry Dundas, these days of course Secretary of State for that realm of thieves in New South Wales.

Boswell had always been fascinated and horrified by capital punishment. Typical had been his concern for a client, John Reed, a sheep thief whom he had defended in 1774 in Edinburgh. He realised after Reed was found guilty that the man had lied to him and wanted a withdrawal of the lies for the sake of the sheep thief's eternal soul. So he entered into a fantastic scheme to have the man revived immediately after his hanging, in the hope that revivifying him would save his life and soul. 'He may curse you for bringing him back,' an advisor told Boswell. In any case, Boswell gave up at last on Reed, but seventeen years later his raising of money for the girl from Botany Bay was characteristic of this great Scotsman's spacious sympathies.

The final judgment of the Old Bailey court had been that the Botany Bay escapees were 'to remain on their former sentences until they should be discharged by due course of law'.

That was not good enough, Boswell thought, and asked Dundas for an appointment, but failed to get one. So on 16 August 1792, he wrote to Dundas again. 'The only solution you can give me for this unpleasant disappointment is to favour me with two lines directed Penrhyn, Cornwall [where Boswell had gone to see the Reverend Temple], assuring me that nothing harsh shall be done to the unfortunate adventurers from New South Wales, for whom I interest myself, and whose very extraordinary case surely will not found a precedent.' Dundas replied, promising 'to duly consider' Boswell's petition.

On 2 May 1793, the Home Secretary advised the Sheriff of Middlesex that Mary Bryant had received an unconditional pardon. Released from Newgate, she remained in London, seemingly at Boswell's expense, until the following October. Amongst Boswell's papers is a record headed 'Mary's Money', which lists amounts paid for her lodgings and for a bonnet, a gown, shoes and a prayer book. Reverend William Temple wrote to Boswell to tell him that subscribers to a fund to help settle her back in Cornwall were put off by the allegation that her family were still engaged in stealing livestock. Nevertheless, a sister of Mary's, Mrs Puckey of

Fowey, wrote to Boswell telling him that Mary would be kindly received if she were to return to her home town.

In June 1793, Boswell, still talking to Nepean and Dundas about the 'unfortunate men', Mary's companions, was mugged and left unconscious in the street on his way home after a night's drinking. But by August, he was well enough to visit the four men in Newgate to assure them that he was doing all in his power for them, and on 2 November, they were at last released. One of the four had already followed a stratagem of his own to seek freedom. In January 1793, John Butcher, alias Samuel Broome, had written from Newgate to Sir Henry Dundas offering to return to Botany Bay on the terms that 'having been brought up in the thorough knowledge of all kinds of land' he was 'capable of bringing indifferent lands to perfection'. His offer was not accepted, but when he was released through Boswell's generous offices, he enlisted in the New South Wales Corps anyhow and returned there, and received a land grant 'in the district of Petersham Hill', west of Sydney. Having spent so much effort getting away, he had now gone to lengths to return. He was an early instance of an ordinary man seeing New South Wales as quite habitable under conditions of freedom.

Mary Bryant, meanwhile, left London for Fowey on 13 October, on the *Anne and Elizabeth*. The evening before, Boswell took a hackney coach to her room in Little Titchfield Street and collected her and her box. His son James was with him, and was to wait in a nearby house till his father returned from Beale's Wharf, Southwark, where Mary was to embark. 'I sat with her almost two hours,' wrote Boswell, 'first in the kitchen and then in the bar of the public house at the wharf, and had a bowl of punch, the landlord and the captain of the vessel having taken a glass with us at last. Mary was uneasy about going, and becoming a figure who would be pointed out in the limited society of Fowey.' She was frightened her relations would mistreat her.

Boswell consoled Mary by assuring her he would send her a sum of £10 yearly as long as she behaved well. The annuity would be paid half on the first of May, and half on the first of November. Though she could not write very well, they rehearsed a particular form in which she would inscribe the letters 'MB', and affix them to any letter purporting to be from her, as a sign of its authenticity. The last known receipt from Mary, acknowledging the payment of £5, would be dated 1 November 1794.

The poet William Parsons assumed that there had been an amorous connection between Boswell and Mary, and that Mary was sad to leave him.

'Though every night,' Mary is depicted as saying, 'the Strand's soft virgins prove/On bulks and thresholds thy Herculean love,' she nonetheless remains Boswell's *inamorata*, and asks him:

> *Was it for this I braved the ocean's roar,*
> *And plied those thousands leagues the lab'ring oar?*

Mary is further depicted as being sure that,

> *Thou, relenting, shall consent at last,*
> *To feel more perfect joy than all the past;*
> *Great in our lives, and in our deaths as great*
> *Embracing and embraced, we'll meet our fate.*

And then, facing the rope together (since wits said Boswell deserved it):

First let our weight the trembling scaffold bear,
Till we consummate the last bliss in air.

Nearly 150 years later, in 1937, amongst Boswell's possessions was found an envelope with the words in his handwriting: 'Leaves from Botany Bay used as tea'. It was the same *Smilax glyciphylla* which Mary Bryant had taken on the cutter with her and which comforted the scurvy-ridden and debased citizens of New South Wales.

Thirty

Old Harry Brewer, lucky to have any post at all and still working as provost-marshal and building supervisor without official confirmation from the home government, was conscientiously searching *Pitt* before it left to return to England and found a recently arrived convict woman stowed away, with the connivance of one of the mates, Mr Tate. Tate was brought ashore and tried for the offence and acquitted, so that whether it was to escape New South Wales or for the love of that sailor that the girl was secreted on *Pitt*, we do not know.

Why would she and others not want to flee? For the funerals continued, and the stores were still proving inadequate to sustain healthy lives. 'The convicts dying very fast, merely through want of nourishment,' wrote a newly arrived refugee from bankruptcy, Surgeon Richard Atkins. 'The Indian corn served out is of little use in point of nourishment, they have no mills to grind it and many are so weak they cannot pound it. At present there is not more than eight weeks ration of flour at 3 pound per man at the store. Oh! Shame, shame!'

By now, desperately hungry men and women crept into the maize fields and stole the cobs from the centre of the crops, and being caught, were too weak to face punishment. The ration of salt meat remained as before, but *Gorgon*'s flour was giving out, and the ration was reduced to 1½ pounds, though 3 pounds of unmilled maize would be given instead to each adult, and to every child ten years of age. In the absence of proper grinding facilities, maize would become a byword for useless food, as it also would more than 50 years later, during the Irish famine. To make enough meal for each person's survival, 'hand mills and querns were set to work to grind it coarse for every person both at Sydney and at Parramatta; and at this latter place, wooden mortars, with a lever and a pestle, were also used to break the corn, and these pounded it much finer than it could be ground by the hand mills; but it was effected with great labour'.

By May 1792, the flour *Gorgon* had brought, initially believed to be adequate for six months, was giving out, and could last the settlement only another 24 days at 1½ pounds per week, and the salt meat provisions would be depleted within three months. 'Had not such numbers died, both in the passage and since the landing of those who survived the voyage, we should not at this moment have had anything to receive from the public stores; thus strangely did we derive the benefits from the miseries of our fellow creatures!'

It was 'afflicting', said Collins, to observe the emaciation of those who remained. A fishery was set up at the South Head look-out station exclusively for the use of the sick. The bulk of game was directed towards the hospitals. The huntsmen were given a reward of 2 pounds of flour and the head, one forequarter and 'the pluck' of any animal they brought in. Collins expressed the nature of the scurvy beginning to prevail in graphic terms – a very want of sufficient strength in the constitution to digest nourishment.

Phillip now found himself issuing maize from the store to supplement shortfalls in other items. Yet the threat of capital and other punishments for food theft could hardly have entirely prevented the strong stealing from the more vulnerable when the chance presented, particularly since the weak, from the time of the Second Fleet onwards, had become so numerous. Camden, Calvert and King had a great deal they and their captains would never be called to answer for.

Richard Atkins, newly arrived surgeon and deputy judge-advocate of New South Wales, was characteristic of the personnel from which many colonial governors had to fill their bureaucracies. He was the fifth son of a baronet, and such men would frequently find themselves employed, for want of something better, in some post along one of the further tendrils of empire. Fleeing insolvency by resigning a commission as adjutant of the Isle of Man Corps, and sailing for Sydney in the *Pitt*, he would retain in the colony a reputation as a toper, a libertine and an unreliable borrower of money. Yet he got by on the strength of his family repute, for he had renowned brothers, one in public life, one an eminent soldier who would end his career as a lieutenant-general, and the other an admiral in the making, to lend him some colouration of talent. Despite his drinking, Phillip made him magistrate at Parramatta and then appointed him registrar of the Vice-Admiralty Court, even though it soon became apparent that he could not be trusted to pay his bills, raising again the old conundrum about who was the more corrupted, the gaoler or the gaoled. John Macarthur would ultimately describe Atkins as 'a public cheater living in the most boundless dissipation'.

Yet there is something extremely amiable in the way he writes. When he went to breakfast at the governor's house the first time,

Atkins came amply supplied with contrary opinions of Phillip by a number of gentlemen in the colony. But he decided, 'His situation is by no means a desirable one in point of duty, for except the civil and military departments he has nothing but a set of rascals to deal with who require a watchful eye . . . The overseers for themselves are convicts and are not to be depended on. At Parramatta some of them are rigid to a degree, which proceeds from a fear of being thought too indulgent, and probably from what will almost universally operate upon weak minds, a thirst for power and dominion over the rest of our fellow creatures. The lash is in their hands at present, they ought to use it with lenity, lest they themselves should fall under it. Their power here hangs by a thread.'

For what it was worth, Atkins remained loyal to Phillip, impressed by the energy with which he visited his farmers, himself accompanying the governor on a tour of the ten or so settlers at the Ponds along the Parramatta River. Atkins found them very comfortably lodged, with plenty of vegetables and Indian corn, and able to keep two or three pigs and a few acres under wheat. 'In short, they are in every particular much better situated than they could possibly be in England. Indeed too much praise can't be given to the governor for (I may say) the paternal care and encouragement he gives to all and each of them who deserve it.'

Atkins found that hunger was the general convict plea against accusations of theft, 'but unfortunately in this country it cannot be admitted, for was it, no private property could be secure. Indeed, to act as a magistrate here with efficacy, you must in a great degree lay aside that philanthropy and goodwill towards men that adorns human nature'.

He noted that, just as earlier in the colony's history ships had been passionately waited for, now people were desperately hoping for the early arrival of the *Atlantic* and the *Britannia*, convict ships of the Third Fleet, which Phillip had sent on to Bengal for provisions.

By now the law of diminishing returns had hit New South Wales. 'Few, however, in comparison with the measure of our necessities,' wrote Collins, 'were the numbers daily brought into the field for the purpose of cultivation; and of those who could handle the hoe or the spade by far the greater part carried hunger in their countenances; independence of Great Britain was merely "a sanguine hope or visionary speculation".'

Indeed, even the First Fleeters' resistance to disease had been depleted by years of poor and reduced rations. Augustus Alt, the settlement's surveyor, a former Hessian soldier, was in too bad a condition to attend to surveying farms. A young man named David Burton, whose appointment as superintendent of convicts Sir Joseph Banks had recommended and who had come out on the *Gorgon*, took up the task, and Phillip came to like him. Since Phillip was concerned that New South Wales had acquired a bad reputation internationally, he asked Burton to prepare a report on the agricultural potential of the Sydney basin, and Burton spent the summer of 1791–2 attending to this task. Phillip sent the result to Dundas with the note that Burton 'may be supposed to be a much better judge of the good or bad qualities of the ground than any of those persons who have hitherto given their opinions'. Burton had already remitted 60 tubs of plants and sundry boxes of seeds and specimens to Sir Joseph Banks, his patron, via the *Gorgon* and the *Pitt*, and had many tubs ready to send on the *Atlantic*, whenever it should return to Sydney from Bengal.

But sadly the useful Burton was taken away from his grateful governor. He had been out with some soldiers of the New South Wales Corps to kill ducks on the Nepean River. He carried his gun awkwardly, said Collins, and the first time it went off, it 'lodged its contents in the ground within a few inches of the feet of the person who immediately preceded him'. Then, on the river, resting the butt of his piece on the ground, he put his hand over the barrel to pull himself upright. The gun discharged, and the shot entered his wrist and forced its way up between the two bones of his shattered right arm to the elbow. It took till five o'clock the next day before his companions got him back to Parramatta, and by then an inflammation had set up in the wound. In the opinion of the surgeons, amputation would have hastened his death, so he was allowed to die in what could be called peace. Phillip approached young Burton as he lay the evening before his death, and found him very collected. 'If I die, Sir Joseph Banks knows my family, and my intentions towards them – I have brothers, and a father and mother – I wish everything to be sent to Sir Joseph Banks, for my father and mother.' In him, Phillip told Banks, 'I lost one whom I cannot replace and whom I could ill spare.'

At last, on 20 June, 'to the inexpressible joy of all ranks of people in the settlements', the *Atlantic* store ship arrived, 'with a cargo of rice, soujee and dholl from Calcutta'. She also brought two bulls and a cow with her, and twenty sheep and twenty goats, which Collins thought a very diminutive species. By way of the *Atlantic* news of the wreck of the *Pandora* and the recapture of William and Mary Bryant and their party reached Sydney Cove, as if to prove to its inhabitants that even an escape was no guarantee of freedom.

But the deliverance from hunger *Atlantic* seemed to offer was illusory. It had brought only grain and dholl – a species of split pea – and so the ration of salt meat had now to be reduced. Phillip had promised both soldiers and convicts that back rations 'being the same as are allowed His Majesty's troops serving in the West-India Islands, excepting only the allowance of spirits', would be made up to everyone once adequate provisions arrived. Atkins said that in lieu of 2 pounds of pork per week, the stores now gave out 1 pound of Indian corn and 1 pound of dholl. All parties were united in a democracy of want. 'The convicts dissatisfied with their ration, not thinking it adequate to what they had before; 'tis hard.'

Some were cheered at the mid-winter wheat crop in the Parramatta area, but there was need for more rain if the next harvest were to succeed. Though the yearly rainfall in the Sydney basin was approximately 48 inches, it was subject to what we now know as the El Niño southern oscillation, which, from the frequent references to drought made in Sydney from 1790 onwards, seems to have had an impact on the first European settlers. The Eora were used to this phenomenon: it was one of the factors which inhibited their transition to what the Europeans, at least in theory, would have desired them to be – farmers. When it rained in Sydney, as it did in the first days of the settlement and to the discomfort of such people as Lieutenant Ralph Clark, it rained torrentially and with massive energy, with the pyrotechnics of electricity thrown in. When it refused to rain, as in the winter of 1792, one pleasant blue-skied day succeeded another.

To free women for direct or indirect service to the production of crops, the governor suggested to Evan Nepean that ready-made clothing for the settlement should be purchased in Calcutta. The women of New South Wales had been employed until now

making clothes out of slops. But there was full enough employment for all the women as hut-keepers, mothers of small children
and at labour in the fields without the further task of manufacturing clothing, and in any case there were 'many little abuses
in the cutting out and making up of clothing' that could not be
wiped out without superintendents. Phillip suggested that frocks,
trousers, shirts, shifts, gowns and petticoats be made in India for
the colony, but with a specific thread of a different colour being
inserted into the convict provision, so that what was intended
for the prisoners could not readily be sold to the soldiers or free
settlers.

What sales there were, legal and illegal, still occurred by barter
or by bills of various kinds – cheques or written orders which
were re-endorsed by one payee to a further one. Sometimes there
was a list of crossed-out payees' names on the back of a bill, with
only the last legal recipient's name uncrossed. People did not
always trust this sort of document as bills could be forged. Yet the
specie of various kinds and nations brought to New South Wales
by the Second Fleet did not cover all the necessary transactions
even of a modestly commercial place, and so bills had to do. Then
when the commissary, John Palmer, sent a subordinate aboard
Atlantic with a money order for £5 to purchase articles, the purser
devalued it to a mere £1 4s. Thus were all bills discounted, and all
New South Wales prices hugely inflated.

Government intervention was clearly essential and Harry
Brewer was sent to the master of *Atlantic* with a writ to enquire
into the massive, usurious discounting of bills. But the problem
remained.

In mid-July, as rain came and the last of the stores were being cleared from the *Atlantic*, another signal was made from the South Head look-out station, and the *Britannia* store ship, returning from India, came down the harbour and anchored in the cove. There had been rumours conveyed by Aborigines along the coastline that more than one ship had been seen south of Port Jackson, and again the feverish state of mind associated with anticipation and hope was set in motion among the Europeans. In the event, *Britannia* sailed alone, but aboard was twelve months clothing for the convicts, four months of flour and eight months beef and pork, so that 'every description of persons in the settlement' could be put back on full issue. Suddenly, Sydney Cove was redolent with the baking of flapjacks and the frying of salt beef. *Britannia* also brought news that Captain Donald Trail of the *Neptune* was being prosecuted, and people were cheered by that and thought that justice and reform were possible.

The restored rations gave Collins hope for the day when journal-keepers like himself would not need to 'fill his page with comparisons between what we might have been and what we were; to lament the non-arrival of supplies . . . to paint the miseries and wretchedness which ensued; but might adopt a language to which he might truly be said to have been hitherto a stranger, and paint the glowing prospects of a golden harvest, the triumph of a well-filled store, and the increasing and consequent prosperity of the settlements'.

But, as usual, the prospects weren't as bright as they first appeared. Not all the supplies Commissary Palmer received were of high quality. Phillip himself visited the storehouses and opened and peeped into a series of casks. He was reduced to shaking his head, and told Palmer that only those provisions considered 'merchantable' should be paid for. Many of the casks of beef were deficient in weight, and the meat lean, coarse and bony and 'worse than they have ever been issued in His Majesty's service'. Such a claim meant the product was near inedible. 'A deception of this nature would be more severely felt in this country . . . every ounce lost here was of importance.' Collins was reduced to considering this cargo from India as an experiment 'to which it was true we were driven by necessity; and it had become the universal and earnest wish that no cause might ever again induce us to try it'.

It does not seem to have been a dodge to save rations when that month Phillip granted Elizabeth Perry, the possibly innocent wife of James Ruse, founding farmer, an absolute remission of her term of imprisonment. She was already supported by the industry of her husband, who also supplied his two convict labourers independently of the public store. This and the Ruses' continuing good conduct were the reasons assigned in the document which gave her back the rights and privileges of a free woman.

But the governor felt the need to refine the regulations for that increasing minority of convicts whose sentences of transportation had expired. Having finished their time, 'many of them seemed to have forgotten that they were still amenable to the regulations of the colony, and appeared to have shaken off, with the yoke of bondage, all restraints and dependence whatsoever'. For example, Benjamin Ingram, a man who had been sentenced for stealing a one-shilling handkerchief in 1784 and whose sentence had now expired, was tried for breaking into the cottage of a female convict and packing up her belongings for removal. He was found guilty, sentenced to death, and was permitted to ascend the ladder under the infamous fig tree before he was informed that he had been pardoned on condition of transportation to Norfolk Island for the rest of his life. Norfolk Island had been at the beginning a sanctuary for the less corrupted, but had grown to be, at least in part, a catchment for those who offended notably on the mainland. While waiting to go to the island, Ingram told Collins and other officials he was 'frequently distressed for food'. This 'depraved man' would eventually be returned to the mainland and would commit suicide while in prison charged with yet another burglary.

The food supplies from *Atlantic* and *Britannia*, deficient as they were, could not prevent some remarkable acts of food theft. In September all hands were busy bringing in the Indian corn, and even though the seed crop was steeped in tubs of urine to keep it from being pilfered, 'some of the convicts cannot refrain from stealing and eating it'. In a letter to Dundas on 2 October, Phillip wrote of the persistent need for so many articles of food and industry amongst a population which had not eaten amply for four years. They needed iron cooking pots nearly as much as they needed provisions, he said, and all the cross-cut saws, axes and various tools of husbandry were in short supply or disrepair. Further hunger was inevitable. He went through the sort of weary figures he had been remitting to London since the start: 'There remains at present in this colony, of rice and flour and bread, sufficient for 96 days at 2 pounds of flour and 5 pounds of rice per man for seven days, salt [meat] provisions sufficient for 70 days on a full ration, and of pease and dholl, sufficient for 156 days at 3 pounds per week for each man.' But the last year's crop of maize, he said, injecting a soupçon of hope, was nearly 5000 bushels, despite the drought. 'Six hundred and ninety-five bushels reserved for seed and other purposes, and not less than

1500 bushels were stolen from the grounds, notwithstanding every possible precaution.'

Salt meat provisions for New South Wales, he counselled, should only be acquired from Europe – since those from other sources, such as India, were appalling.

Phillip himself remained a victim of the rations and an earth which was only gradually being persuaded to submit to European expectations. The newly arrived son of one of his merchant friends, wrote of the governor at this stage that his health 'now is very bad. He fatigues himself so much he fairly knocks himself up and won't rest till he is not able to walk'.

For in October 1792, Phillip was still awaiting explicit approval from England for his return home. He was anxious to be relieved, and there had never been any idea that he, the uncondemned, would choose to remain indefinitely in this temperate, beguiling but harsh garden. He was enlivened when on 7 October, the largest ship to enter Port Jackson up to that hour, the 914-ton *Royal Admiral*, arrived with a large cargo of convicts. The ship also brought one of the last detachments of the New South Wales Corps, an agricultural expert, a master miller and a master carpenter, along with its 289 male and 47 female convicts. The ship, owed by a London 'husband' who frequently contracted his ships to the East India Company, Thomas Larkins, was the antithesis of some of the appallingly run transports of the past few years. The *Royal Admiral* had embarked considerably fewer convicts than the overcrowded *Pitt*, whose men had died in such numbers throughout the New South Wales autumn. The naval agent for *Royal Admiral* was the former surgeon of the notorious but healthy *Lady Juliana*, Richard Alley, and the master and the ship's surgeon collaborated well with him in matters of convict health. There had been a conspiracy of some type on board, but it had been aborted and mildly punished, with one prisoner receiving three dozen lashes and seven others two dozen each. The *Royal Admiral* had made a very fast passage of 130 days from Torbay, even though she had spent 21 of those days in Simon's Bay at the Cape. Then, south of Africa, with the roaring forties in her sails, she had made over 3000 miles in just sixteen days.

'She brought in with her a fever, which had much abated by the extreme attention paid by Captain Bond and his officers to cleanliness,' Collins recorded. The officers had also supplied the prisoners 'with comforts and necessities beyond what were allowed for their use during the voyage'. The master and officers were speculators nonetheless – they had freighted out over £4000 worth of their own goods to sell ashore.

These days, the governor judged it necessary to send most newly arrived convicts straight up the river to Parramatta where work was to be done, since Sydney possessed 'all the evils and allurements of a seaport of some standing'. Phillip felt there would be difficulties in removing prisoners from Sydney once they settled in there. Even within a penal universe, under conditions of hunger, Sydney was already taking on what it would never lose – the allure of a city of pleasures and vices.

One convict, who for his special gifts was allowed to stay in Sydney, was the Scots artist Thomas Watling. He had been amongst the over 400 convicts who sailed in the *Pitt*, but had escaped in Cape Town. He had been arrested by the Dutch after the *Pitt*'s departure, put in gaol and then taken aboard *Royal Admiral*. Well-educated, and having worked for a time in Glasgow as a coach and chaise painter, he would become the most important artist of early New South Wales. He had been banished to the settlement in the first place through the temptations posed by his talent. In Dumfries in November 1788 he had been charged with making forged guinea notes on the Bank of Scotland. Rather than risk conviction and execution, he pleaded guilt, asked to be transported and was sentenced to fourteen years.

Upon landing, almost at once he was snatched up by Surgeon White, who as a naturalist made great use of Watling's artistic skills, especially for drawing rare animals. Watling would find White an exacting master, and would sometimes feel overworked.

Another arrival on *Royal Admiral*, this one significant only in retrospect, was Mary Haydock, thirteen when put aboard the transport, and now assigned as nursemaid to the family of Major Grose. She had been convicted of stealing a horse, but her crime seems to have been the Georgian equivalent of joy-riding. She had already been courted on *Royal Admiral* by a young agent of the East India Company, an Irishman, Thomas Reibey, who was making his way to India via Port Jackson. He would ultimately return and marry her, and the Reibeys would become wealthy, beginning their mercantile career as civilian associates of the emergent trading force of the New South Wales Corps.

For the newly arrived officers of the Corps were quick to sense the advantages of the place and dealt with their state of want by themselves chartering the *Britannia* to travel to Cape Town and Rio for supplies, including boots for the soldiers. Phillip was not easy about it, since it was an interruption to the duty the *Britannia* had in relation to collecting her cargo under East India Company charter. The officers also expected land grants, but Phillip feared that in giving them any, he would 'increase the number of those who do not labour for the public, and lessen those who are to furnish the colony with the necessaries of life'.

Collectivist New South Wales was under pressure from these new men, men similar to the ambitious Lieutenant John Macarthur, who was already dreaming of being an importer as a means of becoming a landowner. Phillip, by contrast, feared too much enterprise would make the penal community of New South Wales hard to control, and that barter would develop in spirits, for which the convicts were crazy. The shops set up in Parramatta and Sydney for the sale of private goods out of the *Royal Admiral* were permitted to sell porter, but they were found to be selling spirits as well, with deplorable results. 'Several of the settlers, breaking out from the restraints to which they had been subject, conducted themselves with the greatest impropriety, beating their wives, destroying their stock, trampling on and injuring their crops in the ground, and destroying each other's property.' In New South Wales, all the rage of exile and want was unleashed by liquor, but the officers of the New South Wales Corps could sniff not a social crisis, but an opportunity.

Almost as a passing distraction, the little *Kitty* arrived, the last ship of that year, carrying ten male and 30 female convicts and various supplies. On the *Kitty* too came 870 ounces of silver in dollars to pay the wages of superintendents. Fifteen Quaker families who had made a proposal to be settled in New South Wales were also to have made their passage on *Kitty* and other ships, but the plan to leaven the convict mass of New South Wales fell through, perhaps because it demanded that 500 acres be allotted to each of the Quaker settlers.

Sir Joseph Banks would later say that 'Governor Phillip . . . was so ill when he left Sydney as to feel little hope of recovery'. In dreaming of his return to England, Phillip must sometimes have imagined death coming from his exhaustion and chronic ailments, but at other, more energetic times, might have mused on the chance of military service arising from conflict with republican France. Being in such a remote place as New South Wales at such a crucial time as this could be itself a torment. Yet he hoped he had done enough not simply to satisfy his masters, but to validate his own honour as an officer, to recognise the demands of his culture, and to put its mark on the shore of New South Wales. Indeed, he would leave certain traditions indelibly implanted behind him – an insistence on the supremacy of law, an enlightened authoritarianism rather than republican rights, and a sense of community which the cynics would not have thought possible. Authority and equality were the two trees which Phillip planted in Sydney Cove, and perhaps too the tree of grudging cooperative endeavour, into which the convicts were forced by circumstance. He had never invoked happiness, but he had invoked cohesion and its benefits, and that tree too would grow to become a sense of commonwealth, from which, however, Bennelong and the clans he loved and hated would be excluded.

So now, despite merely ambiguous permission from Dundas, Phillip had decided. Regardless of the rationing problems, whose end he saw in sight if the government and private farms were successful, he would sail home on the *Atlantic*, due to leave Sydney in December 1792. For by the time Phillip packed his papers and assembled his samples, he had imposed on this version of the previously unknown earth the European template. There were 3470 acres under grant to various time-expired criminals and others. Some 417 acres were in private cultivation, but the timber had been cleared from 100 more, and 1012 acres were in cultivation on public land at Sydney Cove and Farm Cove, Parramatta and Toongabbie. There was a good crop of corn and a summer harvest of wheat for cutting.

'A striking proof of what some settlers had themselves declared,' said David Collins, 'on its being hinted to them that they had not always been so diligent when labouring for the whole, "We are now working for ourselves."'

As well as livestock on farms under cultivation, the stock belonging to the public was kept at Parramatta and consisted of three bulls, two bull calves, fifteen cows, three calves, five stallions, six mares, 105 sheep and 43 hogs. The governor gave each of the married convict settlers, and each settler from the marines and from the *Sirius*, one ewe for breeding purposes. Though it would later be argued that Australia's ancient, leached, thin soil was not well-suited to hard-hoofed European animals, such questions did not exist for Phillip. Livestock stood for a European imperative more profound than theology. The new place should be graced by such identifiable, Biblical and fruitful beasts.

Still, there was 'not a place dedicated to divine worship amidst all the work,' but convicts now lived in brick huts because of the good clays of the Sydney basin. Gradually, but relentlessly, the strange southland was adapted to European needs and ways.

There were a number of reasons the Sydney experiment seemed now, and despite all, in a promising condition. One was that the home government was still confronted with an epidemic of crime, and a growth of unrest and rebellious sentiment amongst Methodist radicals and Scottish and Irish seditionists. Thus New South Wales needed to be remembered and supplied. But Phillip's own stubborn certainties had a lot to do with the experiment's success-cum-survival as well. His insistence on equity in rationing must have been a new experience for many convicts used to the corrupt systems of supply in prison and hulk. His decision to elevate convicts to civic positions as super-intendents, overseers and settlers imbued in them a new sense of opportunity and potential influence. Only in New South Wales did land come to the convict who completed his time, and with it the sense of social order which accompanied ownership. Phillip had created a system of punishment and reward which, as repugnant as some of its elements might be to modern sensi-bilities, reliably delivered for the convict and soldier–settler.

In his last days in Sydney, soldiers, convicts and servants carried Phillip's baggage down from his two-storey government house past its garden and the edge of public farmland to the government wharf on the east side of Sydney Cove. When Phillip himself came down on 11 December, dressed for departure, full of unrecorded impulses and thoughts, unsure of his future but fairly sure of the survival of New South Wales's curious society, the red-coated New South Wales Corps under Major Grose presented arms. They dipped their colours and did him honour. Grose, whom Phillip got on with, would take over the management of New South Wales until the next governor arrived. (It would be turn out to be John Hunter, former captain of *Sirius*, Phillip's Scots friend.)

Phillip must have hoped that, leaving a place so little understood by the world at large that it would always seem to others to be out of the known universe, he would have a chance to advance towards greater responsibility and higher glory. But in fact it was with the children of his convict, free and military settlers, whom he was pleased to wave off, that his name would achieve its immortality. Though greater formal honours awaited him, his chief remembrance would be in this cove, in this harbour, and in the continent beyond. And even so, his abiding presence in the imagination would be more akin to that of a great totem than that of breathing flesh. He would not glisten for the children of this and other generations, he would not glow with the amiability or deeds of a Washington, a Jefferson, a Lafayette. He did not seek or achieve civic affection. He would forever be a colourless secular saint, the apostle of the deities Cook and Banks. He would be lodged not in our imaginations, but rather in our calculations of the meaning of the continent and its society forever. Yet his spirit, pragmatic and thorough, is still visible in Australia.

Thus the New South Wales Corps, which would acquire a questionable reputation, earned or not, saluted Phillip as he passed in his clouds of gravity.

One of the most intense fears of the natives was, and would remain, that figures like Phillip would attract men and women out of their accustomed circuits and spirit them away from this world which for the Eora was the centre of things, the sole habitable universe. And it was happening with Bennelong and Yemmerra-wanne, 'two men who were much attached to his person; and who withstood at the moment of their departure the united distress of their wives, and the dismal lamentations of their friends, to accompany him to England'. They knew no map for where they were going, only that it was *outer*, at an unspeakable distance, and that it was a region of incomprehensible darkness.

Bennelong's researches into and interest in Phillip would lead him profoundly away, and the risk that he could belong to neither world was one he bore relatively lightly on this high summer day as he sniffed the aroma of the eucalypts, tinged with smoke from western bushfires, and went aboard the *Atlantic*. It is likely that many of his people thought he was under an enchantment and thus vitiated forever. Some might have thought also that Abaroo's ultimate rejection of Yemmerrawanne as a suitor could have added to that handsome youth's readiness to travel with his kinsman Bennelong.

Early the next morning the *Atlantic* dropped down-harbour in semi-darkness, past the now familiar sandstone headlands and dun bush, and took Phillip away from New South Wales, forever. The desert interior of the continent conjured a summer south-westerly to send him out of Eora land, past the Cameraigal headlands of the north shore towards a last sight of the beach at Manly where he had taken the chief wound of his incumbency. As he left it, the state of the colony seemed far better than at any time since the settlement was made.

At Christmas, 'Phillip gave every mess a joint of fresh pork and some pumpkin and half a pint of spirits to each man to celebrate the redeemer's natal day.' In January, off Cape Horn, 'there were a great many islands of ice', and many squalls, but rapid progress. They made Rio in February in time for Easty to express disapproval of the 'grand and magnificent' Romish behaviour of candles, and statues of heads of patriarchs, and the Virgins at crossroads which people appealed to, 'instead of looking to Jesus Christ as a complete Saviour of the world'.

They celebrated the crossing of the Equator with the normal ceremonies, Bennelong and Yemmerrawanne being alarmed to see Neptune appear over the side of the ship. Within days, 'David Thompson fell overboard and drowned, Private Jackson died of a violent purging': two men who had survived strange waters to die in more accustomed ones. Finally, Bennelong and Yemmerrawanne stepped ashore with Phillip at Falmouth towards the end of May 1793, to catch the London stagecoach. It was their turn to enter a mystery.

Epilogue

Some of Phillip's convicts, a minority, would return to Britain, a few by escape, some on their own resources, a small number as crew members. Elizabeth Barnsley, for example, *Lady Juliana*'s Queen of Sheba, would first be reunited with her husband when he arrived as a result of his stealing that trunk off the Wiltshire, Bath and Bristol coach loading at Holborn. For a time the couple found themselves on Norfolk Island, and Thomas, once his time was up, travelled back to Sydney to raise money by gambling, musical performance or trading for the cause of taking his family back to England. It seems he succeeded, since soon after Elizabeth and their two children joined Thomas in Parramatta in 1794, the flamboyant pair disappeared from the New South Wales record, returned to Britain.

Characteristic of many others, however, were Bloodworth the brick-maker and Sarah Bellamy. In 1790, Sarah, the country girl, became James Bloodworth's common-law wife, marriage being impossible because it was well known he was married in England. Bloodworth was the architect in the construction of the two-storey, six-room building which became the governor's house, and a range of other public buildings. In December 1790 Phillip pardoned four selected convicts, of whom James

Bloodworth was one. But return to England was not possible until his full term expired. The next year he was appointed building superintendent of New South Wales with an excellent salary of £50 per year, and Phillip praised the 'pain he had taken to teach the art of brick-making and brick-laying, and his conduct was exemplary'. With some help from Harry Brewer, he built a soldiers' barracks, a clock tower, and houses for the surveyor general and judge-advocate.

Sarah Bellamy lost a second son in infancy, but then six more children were born to her and Bloodworth. Of Sarah's eight children, four survived to adulthood. In 1794 Major Grose would grant 50 acres to James and 20 acres to Sarah. They later added 200 acres to their property. Interestingly, Bloodworth stood as an Englishman by the King who had transported him, and served as a sergeant in the Sydney Loyal Association, a militia brought into being by the arrival of Scottish Republicans and United Irish prisoners from the 1798 uprising in Ireland. He died at the age of 45 in 1804, virtually insolvent, though with many people owing him money. In 1805, his wife, Sarah, rented a room in her house to a lodger on condition he would teach her children to read and write. In the Female Register compiled by the censorious Reverend Samuel Marsden, it is said of her cohabitation with Bloodworth that 'no relationship could have been more respectable, devoted or tenacious than theirs'. And in the census of 1828 she was one of only nineteen women still surviving from the great voyage of 1787. Sarah died in Lane Cove, Port Jackson, on 4 February 1843, aged 73.

The Australian Adam, James Ruse, sold his land at Parramatta in 1793, and toyed with using £40 he thus acquired to return to England. He decided instead to settle on the Hawkesbury, but by

1801 was in hardship, having mortgaged his property because the region had not yielded as well as everyone had hoped. Indeed poverty, caused by the distance from Sydney and Parramatta, the uncertain market for produce and frequent flooding, was the normal condition of smallholders of that area at the time. He tried to supplement his poor returns by running a gambling school at his farm, but the authorities clamped down on that. Using his friendship with Henry Kable, he apprenticed his sturdy colonial son, also named James, to the company of Kable and Underwood. In 1809, Ruse moved to the south-west of Sydney, a region around newly settled Bankstown, and then to the Windsor district, where he farmed into the 1820s. By 1828 he was working as well as an overseer at a large farm at Minto. In his advanced years, he joined the Catholic Church, and died a year later in 1837. Even though he had never been a wealthy farmer, his gravestone at Campbelltown would show he was aware of his primary place in the Sydney experiment.

> Sacred to the memory of james Ruse who departed this
> life sep 5 in the year of Houre Lord 1837. 'Natef of
> Cornwall and arrived in this coleney by the Forst Fleet,
> aged 77.
> My mother reread me tenderly
> With me she took much paines
> And when I arrived in this coelney I sowd the forst
> grains
> And now with my heavenly father I hope for ever to
> remain.

Hannah Mullens, Irish will-forger, having married Charles Peat, one of the founders of the convict night watch, was by 1802 the owner of a grant of 30 acres and the mother of four children. She would live into the second decade of the nineteenth century. Nellie Kerwin, the woman who ran a house of accommodation and had also forged a sailor's will, quickly married once she arrived in Sydney, but her new husband, Henry Palmer, a thief of fine glass, sent to Norfolk Island, was killed by a falling tree four months later. Kerwin was considered a reliable woman and travelled, perhaps as a servant, on *Supply* with the crew of wrecked *Sirius* back to Sydney, living in Parramatta for a time before returning to Norfolk Island. She may have continued her career as a bum-boater, a broker and moneylender for sailors in Sydney and Norfolk Island, even while serving her sentence. Now, with the resources to travel to England, she would have been the rare case of a convict woman returning home to the children she had left behind at transportation. At last she embarked for England via India in October 1793, on a ship named the *Sugar Cane*.

Olivia Gascoigne, one of the well-behaved convicts whom Phillip sent to Norfolk Island in 1788, married Nathaniel Lucas, a freed convict, or as people began to call such expirees, an emancipist. During a storm on Norfolk Island they suffered 'the unspeakable misfortune' of losing their twin daughters when a Norfolk pine tree fell on their house. In 1805 they left the island and returned to Sydney, where Lucas worked as a builder. When Olivia died in October 1820, she left eleven children and her sons were carrying on Nathaniel's business. Lucas himself, after building many government structures, had taken his own life in 1818.

There had been a number of military–convict alliances among the early settlers. Originally sentenced for stealing from a man who had refused to sleep with her, Sara Burdo, one of *Lady Penrhyn*'s midwives, married Private Isaac Archer in 1794, and they later settled at Field of Mars, an area along the Parramatta River put aside for marine land grants. By 1802 they had six children. Sara farmed with her husband and continued to act as a colonial midwife, and by 1828 was living in comfort in Clarence Street, Sydney. She would die in July 1834. Her history is only one of many which raises the tormented question of whether the female convicts of the early fleets were 'loose women' or matriarchs. In some cases it would seem that they were both at various stages of their lives. The new penal settlement and its cruelties could destroy some unwillingly landed there, yet, with its peculiar flexibilities, could also allow women of enterprise to find an honourable place for themselves in the new society.

The dismissal of colonial women as 'wanton' or as 'vile baggages' seems to have derived from the British press, and from clergymen who considered all common-law marriages to involve 'a concubine'. Compared to British society, New South Wales countenanced or at least tolerated many marriages which trans-cended class barriers, such as that between Esther Abrahams and the wealthy military officer George Johnston.

Catherine Heyland, who had escaped burning at the stake for forgery, established herself as an energetic woman on Norfolk Island and was given land in her own name. She lived with John Foley, a First Fleet marine turned farmer, and prospered so adequately that by June 1805, the couple could employ an educated convict, John Grant, to work for them and teach their two boys. The relationship was a strong one, and the family nursed Grant back to health once when he was flogged, and again after he had been exiled for sixteen weeks on a small island off Norfolk. In 1807, the Foleys moved to Van Diemen's Land. Catherine Heyland, once marked for a gruesome death, died peacefully on 18 October 1824, aged 79 years.

The convict lock-wizard Frazier and his wife, Eleanor Redchester, had two sons in New South Wales before Frazier died at Concord on the Parramatta River from the effects of hard drinking in June 1791. Eleanor formed a partnership with William Morgan, a former soldier, and they had six children. But they quarrelled over land and the ownership of certain pigs. She would outlive him and prosper, dying on her land at Concord in November 1840.

The children Captain David Collins had by the convict woman Ann, or Nancy, Yeates were Marianne Letitia, born in November 1790, and three years later, George Reynolds. When the last marine detachment left in the *Atlantic*, Collins remained as judge-advocate. He left the colony for the first time in the *Britannia* in 1796. In December 1794 he had been granted 100 acres of land on the south side of Sydney Harbour, and it is believed that he assigned the grant to Ann Yeates. Collins applied to resume active duty in the marines but since there was discrimination against officers who served lengthy periods in staff appointments, he would have lost eight years seniority. He chose ultimately to remain on the inactive list, although he was promoted brevet lieutenant-colonel in January 1798. After the publication of his *History of the Settlement of New South Wales*, he was chosen as head of a new penal settlement in the Port Phillip or Melbourne area, and was transferred to Van Diemen's Land in 1803.

He died insolvent and suddenly in 1810, leaving his widow, Maria, in England, in straightened circumstances. He had by then formed an association with a sixteen-year-old Norfolk Island-born woman, Margaret Eddington, the daughter of a convict. Eddington bore him two children.

His former mistress, Ann Yeates, and her children had returned to England in the *Britannia*, but re-emigrated to the colony in the *Albion* in 1799. She married the convict John Grant, who was to work for Catherine Heyland, in November 1800. George Reynolds Yeates entered the navy in 1807 under the name of Collins and rose to the rank of lieutenant.

The case of Private William Dempsey, one of the marines who in October 1791 decided to remain in New South Wales as a settler, is interesting in the light of comments that those who remained were chiefly influenced by attachments to unsatisfactory women convicts. Dempsey had been the victim of an attack by marine Private Joseph Hunt in 1788, in the famous court-martial that split the officer corps. At Norfolk Island, farming sixteen acres at Cascade Stream, Phillipsburg, he was by 1794 selling grain to the public stores, and the same year married a young *Lady Juliana* convict, Jane Tyler. She had been seventeen when sentenced to death at the Old Bailey in April 1787 for stealing money from her master, a Gray's Inn Lane victualler, and was one of the seven women who caused a sensation by refusing the King's offer of pardon on condition of transportation for life. 'I will never accept of it to go abroad,' she had declared.

In 1807 Jane and Dempsey moved to Van Diemen's Land, which offered more spacious possibilities for land ownership. Though childless, they adopted an Aboriginal girl, Mary Dempsey. William Dempsey would die in 1837, and his wife in 1840.

Mary Haydock, Major Grose's teenage nursemaid, married Thomas Reibey, the former East India Company official, in 1794. The Reibeys became involved in farming on the Hawkesbury River and in the cargo business, coming to specialise in transporting coal from the nascent colonial mines, as well as cedar, furs and skins. By 1809 the Reibeys' ships were trading to the Pacific islands, China and India. Thomas Reibey's death in 1811 left canny Mary in sole control of the business and of their seven children. She acquired ships in her own name and enlarged her warehousing and shipping enterprises. In 1820 she was able to travel back to Lancashire on her own ship, the *Admiral Cockburn*, visiting the scene of her childhood mistake with her daughters Celia and Eliza. She did not retire from business until nearly 1830, and lived off her extensive property holdings in what was by then the city of Sydney, a city many of whose more elegant commercial sites she had herself built. She would die in her house at Newtown in 1855.

James Larra, a convict who reached New South Wales with the Second Fleet on the hungry *Scarborough*, was a Cockney Jew who began the most famed colonial restaurant serving beef, lamb and seafood, and located at Parramatta. Larra would live until 1839 and was buried in the Jewish section of Devonshire Street Cemetery, Sydney.

The famous Irish pickpocket, George Barrington, was conditionally pardoned in 1792, the condition being that he never return to Britain. In 1796, Governor John Hunter made his pardon absolute and appointed him chief constable at Parramatta. He acquired two 30-acre land grants at Parramatta and bought 50 acres on the Hawkesbury. In 1800, an 'infirmity' overcame him. People associated it with his heavy drinking and his guilt over misuse of government property, but it proved to be lunacy. He died at Christmastide, 1804. It turned out that hardly any of the countless works written in his name and published in Britain came from his pen. Nor did he ever receive any form of payment for them.

When governor of New South Wales, Captain John Hunter wrote, 'Some of the very dregs of those who have been sent here [as] convicts are now in possession of their horses and chaise, servants, and other symbols of wealth.' Entrepreneurial convicts increasingly served and worked with the ever more powerful officer corps: 'Not wishing to soil their gentility by too blatant a descent into the marketplace, they [the officers] permitted the retail trade to fall into the hands of ambitious and able (if uneducated) men with no gentility to lose. By doing so they made affluent those who would oust them from their position of privilege.'

One such ambitious and able man was Henry Kable. In 1796, Kable become head constable and gaoler of Sydney Cove, and in 1797 was granted a license to operate an inn in the Rocks area of Sydney. He was also one of a syndicate of twelve which the governor authorised to build a boat for coastal trading. He was dismissed as head constable in 1802 for trying illegally to import pigs from a visiting ship, for he was by then a trader, and he also invested after 1800 in the sealing industry and became a partner with another former convict, James Underwood, in a boat-building business. Later, these two would form a business association with the most successful of all convict merchants, Simeon Lord, the Manchester cloth-thief who had arrived in Sydney in 1791. Their complicated tradings in whaling, sealing, sandalwood and wholesale and retail commerce would break down by 1809, and create a welter of litigation which would continue until 1819.

But for Kable, as for Mary Reibey, his land holdings were his ultimate security. He had been granted two farms at Petersham Hill on the Parramatta River and ultimately owned four farms around Sydney, five along the Hawkesbury and 300 acres west of Sydney in the area known as the Cow Pastures, as well as a house and storehouses in Sydney. In 1811 Kable's house in lower George Street, Sydney, would be advertised for lease in these terms: 'Convenient and extensive premises . . . comprising a commodious dwelling house, with detached kitchen and out-offices, good stable, large granaries, roomy and substantial storehouses, a front retail warehouse, good cellarage and every other convenience suited to a commercial house, the whole in complete repair, and unrivalled in point of situation.'

During their governorships of New South Wales, Philip Gidley King and John Hunter thought that this husky, red headed man, who as an adolescent had escaped the Norwich gibbet, had a dubious reputation, and Kable was certainly hostile to Governor Bligh, whom the New South Wales Corps, by then known ironically as the Rum Corps, would overthrow in 1808.

Henry Kable had used a cross to represent his name on his wedding certificate. His sons were highly literate, and though Henry Kable junior would severely injure his right arm during the launch of one of his father's ships in May 1803, it would not blunt his cleverness. In 1822, he was able to address a petition to the governor, Sir Thomas Brisbane, seeking 'a grant of land, and the requisite indulgences as allowed to settlers of respectability'. The request was refused, though young Kable asserted that, 'His aged father being some years unfortunately embarrassed in his circumstances, in consequences of unavoidable mercantile losses at sea.'

Later in life, Kable and his wife, Susannah, moved to the area named Windsor on the Nepean River, where Kable ran a store and a brewery. His business interests and his land holdings declined somewhat, but they lived comfortably enough and reared ten children. Henry had transferred most of his wealth to his son, Henry junior, the baby of Norwich gaol, to make it safe against claims from Simeon Lord, and the young man went on to become a knowledgeable and successful businessman. Another of Henry and Susannah's sons, James, was murdered by Malay pirates in the Straits of Malacca, piloting one of his father's boats back from China. A third son, John, became a famous boxer in the 1820s. Susannah Kable died in November 1825, but Henry lived on another twenty-one years and died in March 1846. His army of descendants are prominent in Australian society.

Nanbaree, the Eora boy who survived the smallpox epidemic, served as a seaman on HMS *Reliance*, and in 1803 was for a time with Lieutenant Matthew Flinders, circumnavigator of Australia, on the *Investigator*. He died aged about 40 in July 1821 at Kissing Point, at the home of the convict innkeeper James Squires, and was buried in the same grave as Bennelong.

Pemulwuy, the executioner of the huntsman McEntire, went on opposing white settlement with his son Tedbury, and in 1795 they were blamed for leading raids on farms north of Parramatta. In March 1797, a punitive party of New South Wales Corps troops and freed convicts pursued about a hundred natives to the outskirts of Parramatta, but found themselves in turn 'followed by a large body of natives, headed by Pemulwuy, a riotous and troublesome savage'. A number of the soldiers and settlers, turning back, tried to seize Pemulwuy, 'who, in a great rage, threatened to spear the first man who dared to approach him, and actually did throw a spear at one of the soldiers'.

The soldiers opened fire. 'Pemulwuy, who had received seven buckshot in his head and different parts of his body, was taken ill to the hospital.' He escaped and was seen in his home country near Botany Bay, an iron still fixed to his leg. Collins reported that an Aboriginal mythology had grown up around Pemulwuy. 'Both he and they entertained an opinion that, from his having been frequently wounded, he could not be killed by our firearms. Through this fancied security, he was said to be the head of every party that attacked the maize grounds.' Pemulwuy was still at large in November 1801, when Governor King outlawed him, it being believed that he had aligned himself with two escaped convicts, William Knight and Thomas Thrush, in murderous raids upon homesteads. When he was at last hunted down and shot, Governor King sent his head to Sir Joseph Banks for passing on to his German colleague, Professor Blumenbach. Tedbury fought on and though wounded, seems to have been alive as late as 1810.

Bennelong and Yemmerrawanne had an ambiguous experience in Britain. The *Atlantic* reached the Thames on 22 May 1793 and the *London Packet* of 29 May was quick to express an opinion, perhaps common among returning officers and marines, which would condemn Aborigines to a lowly status in law and cultivated British perception. 'That instinct which teaches to propagate and preserve the species, they possess in common with the beasts of the field, and seem exactly on a par with them in respect to any further knowledge of, or attachment to kindred. This circumstance has given rise to the well founded conjecture that these people form a lower order of the human race.' Two days after arrival, Bennelong and Yemmerrawanne were presented at court by Phillip, though there are no records in the correspondence of George III on what impact the two natives had upon him during a brief levee. The cold of England dispirited Bennelong, who was unjustly described by some press as 'the Cannibal King', and gave Yemmerrawanne congestive illness. The extent to which Phillip involved himself in their English experience is not known. The two of them were seen, dressed as English gentlemen, gazing into a shop window in St James's Street. They yearned for New South Wales. Yemmerrawanne would die of pneumonia in Essex in early 1794 and suffer the fate of being buried not in ancestral ground, but in a cemetery at Eltham. Hunter got Bennelong aboard the ship *Reliance* in August 1794, but it did not sail until early 1795, and Hunter confessed his concerns for Bennelong's health and broken spirit. Surgeon George Bass, in whose honour the as yet uncharted strait between Van Diemen's Land and the mainland would be named, helped treat Bennelong for his chest illness.

When he landed in Sydney in September 1795, Bennelong made a splash and settled down again at his house at Tubowgulle. But his young wife, Karubarabulu, who had taken up with another man in his absence, disdained him. He found himself fully accepted neither by the new administration in Sydney Cove nor by his own people, and in two years had become 'so fond of drinking that he lost no opportunity of being intoxicated'. He suffered further serious ritual wounds, perhaps as a result of the violence liquor evoked from him. As late as 1805 he was engaged in combat with Colby over Karabarabulu. By the time he died at Kissing Point on the Parramatta River in 1813, the *Sydney Gazette*, New South Wales's first newspaper, wrote, 'Of this veteran champion of the native tribe little favourable can be said. His voyage to and benevolent treatment in Britain produced no change whatever in his manners and inclinations, which were naturally barbarous and ferocious.' But his name lives on in modern Australia, not least because the Sydney Opera House stands on Tubowgulle, Bennelong Point.

That good friend of Bennelong's, Watkin Tench, the genial diarist, would be engaged in the long war against France, spending six months as a prisoner of war, then typically publishing a book, *Letters from France*, about the experience. Exchanged with a French officer, he served the rest of the war in the Channel fleet, rising to the rank of major-general by the time Napoleon fell. On half-pay for three years, he returned to the active list as commander of the Plymouth Division, retiring as a lieutenant-general in 1821. He and his wife had no children but adopted those of Mrs Tench's sister. His *Narrative of the Expedition to Botany Day* and *A Complete Account of the Settlement at Port Jackson* were published in 1789 and 1793. One can imagine him during his times ashore as the sort of charming, good-natured, cultivated fellow who would bring the light and warmth of his character to Jane Austen-esque drawing rooms.

Captain Philip Gidley King would be governor of New South Wales from 1800, and thus faced the great problem of the monopolist traffickers in liquor, generally members of the New South Wales or Rum Corps. D'Arcy Wentworth, back from Norfolk Island, had entered that market also. King has been described as being 'rather over-excited at the time of the Irish conspiracy in 1804,' and indeed, having received many transported United Irishmen from the rebellion in Ireland of 1798, he treated them with a provocative brutality over a number of years and suppressed their uprising in 1804 with a ferocity of hangings and floggings which will always stand to his shame. Not that he did not pay with his own health, for he returned to England in 1808 very ill, and died soon thereafter. His sons by Ann Innett and his wife and all but one of his four daughters lived to adulthood and many married into colonial families, including the Macarthur family.

Ann Innett herself would marry the emancipist farmer, Richard Robertson, supposed horse-thief, and be granted 30 acres of the Northern Boundary farms in 1794. In 1804, as governor, King would grant her an absolute pardon. She later ran a butchery with her husband, continuing to manage it after he left for England, sailing off herself for the near-forgotten homeland in March 1820.

If the Reverend Johnson had hoped for a more piety-respecting administration under Major Grose, he was disappointed. 'I can't pass over this business,' wrote Grose, 'without observing that Mr Johnson is one of the people called Methodists, [and] is a very troublesome, discontented character.' In 1793 Johnson received 100 acres at Kissing Point on the Parramatta River in return for relinquishing his claim to a glebe, that is, a church-farm. Though he made a reputation as an orchardist, he did not return to England as a wealthy colonist when he left New South Wales in late 1800. A monument was ultimately erected to him in St Mary Aldermary, London, stating that he was a former rector there and had died in 1827 aged 74 years. Mary Johnson lived until 1831.

John and Elizabeth Macarthur, who had travelled in squalid, loud and smelly cubbyholes to reach New South Wales, would begin to be rewarded for their troubles with grants of land and favours from Major Grose. Macarthur would build a fortune not only out of land and trade but through his development of world-beating Australian fleeces from his merino flocks at the Cow

Pastures south-west of Sydney. Litigious and rebellious, he would involve himself in the overthrow of Governor Bligh and would perforce leave the colony for some years to avoid the legal consequences of that rebellion, trusting his affairs to his capable wife. Macarthur would live until 1835 and be survived by Elizabeth, and by sons prominent in early New South Wales politics.

Ralph Clark, having returned to England with considerable joy even though placed on half-pay, was soon back on active service against the French. His beloved Betsy Alicia died in 1794 giving birth to a stillborn child. In the same year his son, a midshipman, was serving with Ralph on a British warship in the West Indies and perished below of yellow fever the same day Ralph Clark himself was shot dead on deck by a French sniper. His only remaining family were the convict, Mary Brenham, and her daughter, Alicia, christened in Sydney on 16 December 1791.

Major George Johnston, paramour of the Cockney Esther Abrahams, ruthlessly suppressed the uprising of United Irishmen in New South Wales in 1804, and survived the opprobrium of having overthrown Bligh, though he had to face a court-martial in England and be deprived of his rank. In 1814, he regularised his marriage to Esther. He enjoyed great success as a farmer and grazier in New South Wales, and he and his wife are buried together in a family vault designed by the convict architect, Francis Greenway.

After his bitter exile on Norfolk Island, D'Arcy Wentworth returned to Sydney in 1796 and would ultimately rise to become principal surgeon of the Civil Medical Department in 1809. He was appointed a justice of the peace and would sit on the Governor's Court. A commissioner of the first turnpike road to Parramatta, he was also treasurer of the police fund, which received three-quarters of colonial revenue. Governor Bligh had him arrested in 1808 for misusing the labour of sick convicts for his private advantage. Wentworth was understandably sympathetic to the rebels, such as Macarthur and Johnston, who overthrew Bligh that year.

He involved himself in victualling and clothing patients in colonial hospitals, and in 1810, in conjunction with two other businessmen, he contracted to build Sydney Hospital for Governor Macquarie in return for a monopoly on the rum trade. Wentworth claimed to have lost money due to the expense of building this 200-person hospital, but his trade in rum and other interests would make him perhaps the richest man in the colony. In 1816 he would help establish the Bank of New South Wales, of which he was the original director and the second largest shareholder. Wentworth's brushes with the Old Bailey, and his alliance with the convict woman, Catherine Crowley, tended to somewhat isolate him in his fine house on the road to Parramatta, yet when he emerged for social events he was much beloved by fashionable Sydney. Dying at his estate, Homebush, in 1827, he was described in the *Sydney Monitor* as 'A lover of freedom; a consistent steady friend of the people; a kind and liberal master; a just and humane magistrate; a steady friend and an honest man.' His son with the turned-in eye would ride his father's horses to victory in the races at Hyde Park – a barracks square near the source of the Tank Stream – and would be, with two other settlers, the first of the Britons to cross the Blue Mountains and see the illimitable inner plain. As a colonial statesman, William Charles Wentworth saw Australia not as a potential American-style republic, as some of his contemporaries did, but 'a new Britannia in another world'. A Tory to the extent many New South Wales democrats would mock, he was a leader in achieving constitutional government in New South Wales.

As for New South Wales itself, in his 1814 *Voyage to Terra Australis*, the navigator Lieutenant Matthew Flinders, dying of consumption, wrote, 'Had I permitted myself any innovation upon the original term Terra Australis, it would have been to convert it into Australia.' This latter name crept into use. The children of convicts and settlers found it easier to say they were Australians rather than New South Welshmen. William Charles Wentworth, son of Irish highwayman–surgeon D'Arcy Wentworth and of convict woman Catherine Crowley, advocated the use of the name *Australia* in his *Statistical Account* of the colony, and another early settlement child, Phillip Parker King of the Royal Navy, son of Philip Gidley King, used the term in his maps which the Admiralty published the same year, 1826.

A confusing range of opinions would be uttered in Britain and in New South Wales about the children of Australia, the issue of the first free or convict settlers. It was assumed by many that they would be criminal spawn. It was believed that they would be abandoned by their 'unnatural parents' or raised amidst scenes of criminal activity and daily debauchery. In fact the colonial experience and later research shows that they emerged 'as a remarkably honest, sober, industrious and law-abiding group of men and women'. By comparison with British society, the family life of early New South Wales children would be stable and sturdy. In New South Wales the child labour, hunger and vicious treatment which characterised the factories of Great Britain were missing, and although convict families sometimes lacked funds, they sought to apprentice their children to stay their hands from the youthful follies that had seen their parents transported in the first place. 'The family links among these skilled workers,' writes one expert, 'were strengthened by the marriage of sons and daughters of men who had been convicted together in Britain, or had arrived on the same ships, had served in the Royal Marines or New South Wales Corps, or who had worked at similar or allied trades in Sydney or Parramatta.' Former convicts (including Ruse) actively sought apprenticeships for their sons, often with government concerns in the Sydney dockyards and lumber yards. Here their teachers were generally convict and ex-convict trades-men who knew their parents. Firms such as Kable and Under-wood, and Simeon Lord's enterprises, also trained colonial youths in a range of crafts. 'Apprenticeship in the colony, therefore, had none of the connotations of exploited child labour.'

The native-born New South Welsh folk of that first generation, also known as Currency children or cornstalks, would be the first Europeans to escape the limits of the Sydney basin, the Cumber-land Plain, and begin to occupy land north and south of Sydney and west of the Blue Mountains. All the inter-racial incompre-hensions and savageries would be played out again, as Australian wealth abounded, and the law, the King James Bible, the songs and plaints of Britain and Ireland reached corners of deepest wilderness beyond the wildest imaginings of their creators.

As for opponents of the Sydney experiment, Jeremy Bentham was to prove tenacious. Throughout the 1790s, he sought information on how much per head 'the Botany Bay scheme' was costing. He had some success lobbying for the adoption of his panopticon prison plan, and would continue to collect information about the ineffectuality of penal colonies. Throughout his career he decried transportation as a poor punishment because it was so uncertain, since no one knew beforehand how much or how little pain was going to be inflicted by the experience on the offender. Death might in practice be occasioned by scurvy or drowning, while for another convict, transportation might be a favour. When criminals had been sent to America, Bentham argued, they entered an established society with its civic and moral virtues. In New South Wales, they *were* the society. There were not enough people to supervise them, or to impose order and discipline from above. Pointing to Collins's journal, Bentham argued that it did not give evidence of the reformation of humans by transportation to New South Wales.

Bentham was given enough ammunition to persuade Prime Minister Pitt to inspect a model of the panopticon, and Cabinet authorised him to proceed with the work. But the project met savage opposition from citizens and business interests in every neighbourhood in which Bentham proposed to build it. New South Wales won for the time being. It was too distant to infringe on the amenity of any British district except its own.

Bentham himself was eventually told by the Home Office that New South Wales was successful enough to relieve the kingdom of any need for his panopticon, and this caused him in 1802 to publish an impassioned tract, *Panopticon versus New South Wales*. For the next 30 years, a number of parliamentarians would attack transportation using Bentham's arguments. Bentham also found a disciple in the charming evangelical activist, William Wilberforce, who would oppose transportation on philosophic grounds – for one thing, its kinship with slavery.

It did have such a kinship, and native Australian patriots and liberals would be the ones who, in the end, put an end to it. But only a few of the felons of our story would live to see that day.

Arthur Phillip found when he returned to England that he had nearly had an opportunity to achieve a *tour de force* while out of the world, in New South Wales. In 1789, the Viceroy of Mexico, asserting Spain's right to trade along the west coast of America, sent ships and a garrison to Nootka Sound, near Vancouver Island on the present western Canadian–US border, to scare away American and British whalers and sealers wishing to collect sea-otter furs there. A plan was developed at the Admiralty in 1790 to send the *Gorgon*, the ship then about to carry troops and supplies to New South Wales, and another war vessel to Port Jackson, where Phillip would supply and command a joint naval–military party to cross the Pacific to the north-west coast of the Americas. But in the end, a report that the Spanish force was stronger than originally suspected led to the mobilisation of the entire fleet, and a Spanish backdown. Phillip remained in Sydney Cove, ignorant of the near-glory which had passed him by.

Phillip's estranged wife, Margaret, had died by the time he returned to Britain, but in her will she had released him from all obligations he had acquired during their relationship, so that he did not need to repay debts on the New Forest estate. As he defended and explained his administration to officials in White-hall, spoke to Lord Hawkesbury at the Board of Trade and to Sir Joseph Banks, he became by July 'convinced by those I have consulted that the complaint I labour under may in time require assistance which cannot be found in a distant part of the world'. So he asked the Secretary of State and the King for permission to resign his governorship permanently. By October, his resignation had been accepted and he was back on half-pay. But early the next year, he received a spacious pension of £500 per year in honour of his New South Wales service. Phillip now had adequate resources to take a residence in Bath, consult specialists, and begin to take the Bath waters.

His health improved and he offered himself to the service again. He began to visit and then married Isabella Whitehead, the 45-year-old daughter of a wealthy northern cotton- and linen-weaving merchant. Though Phillip had shown a tendency to 'marry up', his relationship with Isabella was a happy one, possibly not blurred by excessive passion or sexual appetite. Passion seemed reserved still for possible government appointments, and for glory as an administrator or a warrior. He was still bedevilled by a sense that he lacked connections, important friends who felt that he *must* be advanced.

Under Major Grose, he learned to his distaste, liquor had been used as a vehicle of exchange by powerful interests in the New South Wales Corps at Sydney and Parramatta, and the ewes and goats, crops and even land of some of his emancipated convict farmers were sold in return for spirits. In 1796 he complained to Banks that news from New South Wales was that individuals, including officers of the corps, were making fortunes at the expense of the Crown.

In 1799 Philip Gidley King was appointed to take over governorship of the colony, and Phillip advised his friend that he should expel those officers and officials 'who had been the principle means of ruining the colony'. Serving officers should not be granted land, and the Irish convicts should be separated from the rest, lest they infect the whole at this time of rebellion in Ireland.

Phillip continued to suffer galling reminders that he was just another competent captain. In February 1796, he went down by coach along the rutted, icy highways from London to Portsmouth to take command of the *Atlas*, but found that by a bureaucratic mix-up the command had been given to someone else. The following month, however, he *was* appointed captain of the *Alexander* and later in the year of the *Swiftshore*, a 74-gun battleship. In 1797, a number of naval mutinies broke out, one at Spithead, one at the Nore, the work of men – English, Welsh, Scots and United Irishmen alike – engorged by American and French revolutionary ideas. As Admiral Collingwood complained, the problem was the work of sailors who discussed constitutional issues and belonged to 'corresponding societies', organisations which passed on revolutionary material to each other.

Phillip dealt with any mutinous infection aboard the *Swiftshore* as he had dealt with New South Wales – with decision, adaptability, the weight of law and dispassion – and Lord St Vincent of the Admiralty declared the *Swiftshore* 'in the most excellent order and fit for any service'. The *Swiftshore* helped Nelson blockade Cadiz, but then Phillip was sent north to guard against an imminent Spanish–French invasion which did not develop. Soon Phillip was ashore again, once more the replaceable element.

Later in the year, he was sent to take over the *Blenheim*, a 90-gunner, a ship seen by the Admiralty as being in spiritual and physical disrepair, with many of its crew ill and given to revolution. At the age of nearly 60, though seemingly well-recovered from the renal problems which had plagued him in New South Wales, he was brought ashore and in 1797 made Commander of the Hampshire Sea Fencibles, a home-defence unit raised to man the Martello towers along the coast of England and to resist a French invasion. Next he was put to work inspecting the ships and hospitals where French and Spanish prisoners of war were confined. By force of seniority, he rose to be Rear Admiral of the Blue in January 1799. As a brief peace was arrived at in 1802, he was employed as an inspector into the Impress Service, the process by which men were coerced into the Royal Navy. He made no remarks in his report about the justice of such procedures, but he did suggest a central register of exemptions to save individuals in essential community services from the infamous gangs, and various methods to end corruption, the paying of bribes and so on.

In 1803, when the war began again, he became Inspector of the Sea Fencibles throughout the entire nation. He recommended that single men should not be free from impressment at this dangerous time, and that the Sea Fencibles be reduced to allow men to be freed for naval service. He travelled the coastal roads of England, Wales and Scotland, an aging man who had not yet had his due from destiny and who was acutely aware of that fact.

He therefore asked Nepean to convey to the Lords Commissioners 'that in case an enemy should attempt to land on that part of the coast where I may be . . . their Lordships are pleased to authorise me to take the command of such armed vessels, gunboats and Sea Fencibles as may be there for the defence of the coast'. Thus he cherished the daydream that his flag might be hoisted on an armed vessel or atop a tower standing between the French and the British heartland, and that his name might become a byword for grit, endurance, and good organisation. Nepean, however, chastised him for the idea: 'Applications upon subjects unconnected with the duty on which he is employed ought not to be received or transmitted by him.'

He was retired in the middle of the wars against Napoleon. Able to settle down again in Bath at 19 Bennett Street, in February 1808 he suffered a stroke, recovered, suffered another, and was now at last finally untroubled by ambition. Old New South Wales hands such as Philip Gidley King, Henry Waterhouse, who had been with him the day Willemering speared him, and John Hunter, back from his governorship of New South Wales with further tales of the intractable business intentions of Captain John Macarthur and Lieutenant-Colonel Johnston and others, came to visit him. He lived another six years, partially paralysed, and was felled by a final stroke and buried in the churchyard of St Nicholas at Bathampton on 7 September 1814.

He makes a dissatisfied ghost. But as already noted, it is in New South Wales and the ultimate Australia that his spirit is most visible, pragmatic yet thorough, caught between sparks of both authority and compassion, a bleak white icon who conducted the Sydney experiment and made it a success for the likes of Henry Kable, and a catastrophe for Bennelong and his kind.

Notes

Acknowledgements

My thanks for the research assistance of my daughter Jane, and to the staff of the State Library of New South Wales, Sydney, and the National Library of Australia, Canberra.

Abbreviations

ADB	*Australian Dictionary of Biography*
HO	Home Office
ML	Mitchell Library
OBSP	Old Bailey Session Papers
HRA	Historical Records of Australia
HRNSW	Historical Records of New South Wales
NLA	National Library of Australia

For fuller details on all books referred to in the notes, see Bibliography.

BOOK ONE

Chapter One *(Pages 1–24)*

On the journey of the First Fleet, a chief source is Hunter's journal: Captain John Hunter, Commander HMS *Sirius*, with further accounts by Governor Arthur Phillip, Lieutenant P. G. King, and Lieutenant H. L. Ball, *An Historical Journal, 1787–1792* (p. 24 quoted here). See also Arthur Phillip, *The Voyage of Governor Phillip to Botany Bay.*

As for complaints: Ralph Clark, *The Journal and Letters of Lt Ralph Clark, 1787–1792.*

For 'musty pancakes': Clark, p. 83.

Tasman and Cook: J. C. Beaglehole, *The Life of Captain James Cook*; Nicholas Thomas, *Discoveries, The Voyages of Captain Cook*, London, 2003; John Robson, *Captain Cook's World, Maps of the Life and Voyages of James Cook RN.*

Expelling convicts from Europe: A. G. L. Shaw, *Convicts & the Colonies, A Study of Penal Transportation from Great Britain and Ireland to Australia and other parts of the British Empire*, pp. 20–57; G. B. Barton, *History of New South Wales from the Records*, Vol. I, pp. 1–20; pp. 439–442.

Bacon, *Of Plantations*: 'The people wherewith you plant ought to be gardeners, ploughmen, labourers, smiths, carpenters, joiners, fishermen, fowlers, with some few apothecaries, surgeons, cooks and bakers.'

Degradados: 'Their numbers bore a greater proportion to the better settlers, and they were therefore more likely to be encouraged in iniquity than reformed by example – to communicate evil than to learn good.' – Southey, *History of Brazil*, Vol. I, p. 31, quoted by Barton, Vol. I, p. 439.

Transport to North American colonies: Shaw, p. 33.

On top of the numbers of convicts sent to the North American colonies, it was estimated by Thomas Povey, the Secretary to the Council of State and a leading London merchant with Barbadian interests, that up to 12,000 political prisoners, in addition to felons and vagabonds, had been received into Barbados by 1655. They helped to bridge the escalating demand for labour until the transition to black slavery in the 1660s: http//:iccs.arts.utas.edu.au, Andrea Button, University of the West of England.

Death rate in Virginia: Niall Ferguson, *Empire*, p. 72.

American complaints: 'The body of the English are struck with terror at the thought of coming over to us, not because they have a vast ocean to cross . . . but from the shocking ideas the mind must necessarily form of the company of inhuman savages and the most terrible herd of exiled malefactors.' – *The Independent Reflector*, quoted in Barton, p. 558; Shaw, p. 17.

Transportable offences: Barton, Vol. I, p. 218; J. M. Beattie, *Crime and the Courts in England, 1660–1800, passim*; Douglas Hay; Peter Linebaugh; E. P. Thompson; John G. Rule; Cal Winslow, *Albion's Fatal Tree, Crime and Society in Eighteenth-century England*, London, 1975, pp. 17–63.

Opposition to death sentences for theft: G. D. Woods, *A History of Criminal Law in New South Wales, The Colonial Period, 1788–1900*, p. 19.

Benefit of clergy: Beattie, pp. 88–89; Hay, p. 22.

Leniency of juries: Shaw, pp. 25–26.

Convict attitudes to hanging: Robert Holden, *Orphans of History: The Forgotten Children of the First Fleet*, p. 57; Hay, p. 66.

Executions in number and as public spectacle: Beattie, pp. 451–455; Hay *et al.*, pp. 66, 69; Roy Porter, *English Society in the Eighteenth Century*, p. 157.

Boswell attending executions: Frank Brady, *James Boswell, The Later Years, 1769–1795*, p. 282.

Pardons: Shaw, p. 28 – in the 1770s, two-thirds of the Norfolk and Midland circuits' death sentences were remitted to sentences of transportation; Beattie, pp. 430–431, 472–473, 475–479, 530–533; Hay, pp. 40–49.

Between 1770 and 1772 a number of convicts had been pardoned on condition that they join the navy. But the Lords of the Admiralty soon 'expressed their wishes that no more convicts may ordinarily be ordered on board HM's ships, as such persons may not only bring distempers and immoralities amongst their companions, but may discourage men of irreproachable character from entering HM's service.' Dr Samuel Johnson put it with more bite. 'No man will be a sailor who has contrivance enough to get himself into a gaol,' declared Johnson famously, 'for being in a ship is being in gaol, with the chance of being drowned.' Shaw, p. 28.

On prisons: Porter, p. 91; Holden, pp. 69–70; John Bonwick, *Australia's First Preacher; the Reverend Richard Johnson*, pp. 26–27; Beattie, *passim*, pp. 289–313, 560–608; Hay, *passim*.

John Howard: Beattie, pp. 288–308; 572–629; Shaw, *passim*.

On Newgate: Daniel Defoe, *Moll Flanders*, p. 28; Peter Ackroyd,

London, The Biography, p. 251; Holden, pp. 65–66; Tom Griffith (gen. ed.), *The Newgate Calendar*, 1997, pp. 3–5.

Barrington: *Australian Dictionary of Biography (ADB)*, Vol. I, alphabetical listing; and at least as far as Barrington's legend goes, Suzanne Rickard (ed.), *George Barrington's Voyage to Botany Bay, Retelling a Convict's Travel Narrative of the 1790s*.

Campbell: Shaw, pp. 34–36; The Blackheath Connection, a superbly researched website by historian Dan Byrne, is devoted to the study of activities and motivations of the men, generally Scots, of the Blackheath area and friends of Duncan Campbell's, who supplied the ships for the early penal fleets. Assembled with the help of Blackheath librarian Leo Rhind.

Hulks: Beattie, p. 567; Shaw, p. 43; Frost, p. 41; The Blackheath Connection.

Banks's testimony: HO 7/1 microfilm, ML.

Lemane settlement and opposition: Shaw, pp. 46, 48, 57.

Matra's *Proposal*: HO 7/1 microfilm, ML; Shaw, pp. 44, 45.

Lord Sydney details: Atkinson, pp. 99–100; alphabetical listing, *The Australian Encyclopaedia*; C. M. H. Clark, *A History of Australia, Volume 1, From the Earliest Times to the Age of Macquarie*, pp. 68–69.

Banks before the Commons Committee: C. M. Clark (ed. and selected), *Sources of Australian History*, pp. 61–69, from *Journals of the House of Commons*, vol. xxxvii, pp. 311–314.

Reaction to Committee, and Home Office reaction: Shaw, pp. 45–46.

Final Selection of New South Wales: Lord Sydney to the Lord Commissioners of the Treasury, August 18, 1786, *Sources*, pp. 69–72.

Jeremy Bentham and the Panopticon: J. B. Hirst, *Convict Society and Its Enemies, A History of Early New South Wales*, pp. 10–15.

Evan Nepean: *Australian Dictionary of Biography*, Vol. II, alphabetical listing.

Chapter Two *(Pages 25–39)*

Phillip's early life: Alan Frost, *Arthur Phillip, His Voyaging*; M. Barnard Eldershaw, *Phillip of Australia*; George Mackaness, *Admiral Arthur Phillip, Founder of New South Wales, 1738–1814*.

Geography of London criminals: L. L. Robson, *The Convict Settlers of Australia, An Enquiry into the Origin and Character of the Convicts Transported to New South Wales and Van Diemen's Land 1787–1852*, pp. 11–12; Thomas Beames, *The Rookeries of London*, pp. 25–27; Beattie, pp. 253–262 *et al.*

Tawny Prince and *flash* or *cant*: Captain Watkin Tench of the Marines, *Sydney's First Four Years*, being a reprint of *A Narrative of the Expedition to Botany Bay and a Complete Account of the Settlement at Port Jackson*, p. 297; Captain Grose, *1811 Dictionary of the Vulgar Tongue*.

Enclosure Acts: Porter, pp. 225–230; Hay, pp. 275–276; 313–314; digital search of Enclosure Act sites recommended.

Oliver Goldsmith, *The Deserted Village*: This version taken from Representative Poetry Online, a website of the Library of the University of Toronto.

Sarah Bellamy and her trial: Madge Gibson, *Belbroughton to Botany Bay*, booklet; PRO, Assizes 2/25; Mollie Gillen, *The Founders of Australia: A Biographical Dictionary of the First Fleet*, alphabetical listing; Arthur Bowes Smyth, *The Journal of Arthur Bowes Smyth: Surgeon, Lady Penrhyn, 1787–1789*, p. 5.

John Hudson's trials: OBSP, 1783–1784, on microfilm, ML, 10 December 1783, p. 49.

William Blake: *The Poetical Works of William Blake*, pp. 74, 104. The first continues:

> 'And because I am happy and dance and sing,
> They think they have done me no injury,
> And are gone to praise God and his priest and King
> Who make up a Heaven of our misery.'

Hudson, post-trial: Robert Holden, *Orphans of History: The Forgotten Children of the First Fleet*, p. 72.

Mary Marshall, trial: OBSP, 1783–84, p. 935.

Hippesley: OBSP, 1784–85, p. 438.

Mullins: OBSP, 1785–86, p. 525.

Peat: OBSP, 1784–85, p. 532.

Martin: OBSP, 1781–82, p. 454.

Chapter Three *(Pages 40–47)*

Howe's opinion: HRNSW, Vol. I, Pt II, p. 22.

Phillip's maritime and naval career: *ADB*, Vol. II, alphabetical listing; Frost, *Phillip*; George Mackaness, *Admiral Arthur Phillip*; M. Barnard Eldershaw, *Phillip of Australia*.

Phillip's marriage and resultant matters: *Observer of London*, 15 December 1793, *Anecdotes of Governor Phillip*.

Phillip as spy: Frost, p. 55 onwards.

Phillip's Portuguese naval career: Kenneth Gordon McIntyre, *The Rebello Transcripts, Governor Phillip's Portuguese Prelude*, especially pp. 79–161.

Phillip's return to Royal Navy: Frost; McIntyre, pp. 162–176.

Command of *Europe*: McIntyre, as above; Edward Spain, *The Journal of Edward Spain, Merchant Seaman and sometimes Warrant Officer in the Royal Navy*, especially pp. 40–49; McIntyre, pp. 162–179.

Further espionage: Frost, pp. 130–131.

Heads of a Plan: HRNSW, Vol. I, Pt II, pp. 18–19.

Chapter Four *(Pages 48–67)*

Phillip's expeditionary philosophy: HRNSW, Vol. I, Pt II, pp. 50–54.

William Richards and other contractors: The Blackheath Connection, electronic book, especially Chapter 34; Charles Bateson, *The Convict Ships, 1787–1868*, pp. 11, 20.

First Fleet vessels: Bateson, pp. 95–102; The Blackheath Connection, Chapter 34.

Security arrangements on board: Philip Gidley King, *The Journal of Philip Gidley King: Lieutenant, RN 1787–1790*, pp. 6, 7.

Phillip to Nepean: HRNSW, Vol. I, Pt II, p. 59.

Lists of convicts and first loading: Bateson, pp. 95–102.

Relationship between women and sailors: Arthur Bowes Smyth, *The Journal of Arthur Bowes Smyth: Surgeon, Lady Penrhyn, 1787–1789*, p. 25; Gibson; Gillen, alphabetical listings.

Contraceptive practice: Porter, pp. 41–42; Siân Rees, *The Floating Brothel, The Extraordinary Story of the Lady Julian and its Cargo of Female Convicts Bound for Botany Bay*, pp. 109, 110.

Phillip visits ships, and clothing of women: HRNSW, Vol. I, Pt II, pp. 58, 59.

Move to Motherbank: HRNSW, Vol. I, Pt II, pp. 33–36; 45, 46.

Henry Kable: Cobley, *Crimes*, p. 46 (under Cable); *ADB*, alphabetical listing; Gillen, ditto; *Daily Universal Register*, 15 December 1786, HRA, Vol. I, pp. 3–7.

Marines boarding: John W. Given, *First Fleet Marines of Port Jackson and Norfolk Island and in Van Diemen's Land*, pamphlet; Ralph Clark, *The Journal and Letters of Lt Ralph Clark, 1787–1792*, p. 13; *Hampshire Courier*, 12 March 1787; James H. Thomas, *Portsmouth and the First Fleet, 1786–1787*, p. 22.

Further movements of convicts: Thomas, pp. 23–25; Watkin Tench, *Sydney's First Four Years*, being a reprint of *A Narrative of the Expedition to Botany Bay and a Complete Account of the Settlement at Port Jackson*, pp. 3, 4: Bowes Smyth, p. 13.

White-washing: John White Esq., *Journal of a Voyage to New South Wales*, p. 51 (modern edition pages).

Sirius trouble: Lt Bradley's Journal, Heritage Online, website of State Library of New South Wales.

Bowes Smyth boards: Bowes Smyth, pp. 11–13.

Morale of marines: Clark, p. 19.

Infractions amongst marines: John Easty, Private Marine, *Memorandum of the Transactions of a Voyage from England to Botany Bay, 1787–1793, A First Fleet Journal*, p. 5.

Beckwith (also Beckford) and Handlyn: Bowes Smyth, p. 25; David Collins, *An Account of the English Colony in New South Wales*, Vol. I, p. 244; Gillen, alphabetical listings.

Portsmouth: Thomas, *Portsmouth*.

Opinions in press: Thomas; HRNSW, Vol. II, pp. 738–739; John Bonwick, *Australia's First Preacher; the Reverend Richard Johnson*, p. 13.

News of La Pérouse: Frost; Colin Foster, *France and Botany Bay, The Lure of a Penal Colony*, pp. 7–8.

Dawes and Astronomer Royal: *ADB*, Vol. I, alphabetical listing.

Phillip boards, clock, etc.: amongst others, Captain John Hunter, Commander HMS *Sirius*, with further accounts by Governor

Arthur Phillip, Lieutenant P. G. King, and Lieutenant H. L. Ball, *An Historical Journal, 1787–1792*, p. 3.

Hunter: Eldershaw, p. 41; *ADB*, Vol. I, alphabetical listing.

Collins: *ADB*, Vol. I, alphabetical listing; editor's introduction to Collins, *An Account . . .*, pp. xiii–xvii.

Verse, broadside: Geoffrey Ingleton, *True Patriots All*, pp. 8, 9.

Chapter Five *(Pages 68–79)*

The sources for the journey are the journals: Hunter, pp. 1–37; Collins, pp. iii–xc; White, pp. 52–101; King, pp. 5–31; Tench, pp. 11–32; Clark, pp. 11–80; Bowes Smyth, pp. 16–56; Easty pp. 5–88; James Scott, Sergeant of Marines, *Remarks on a Passage to Botany Bay, 1787–1792*, pp. 1–33; also Bradley journal, Heritage Online, State Library of New South Wales; also Bateson, pp. 95–119.

Chapter Six *(Pages 80–104)*

Approaches to landfall: King, p. 32.

Chronometer: Hunter, p. 3.

Aboriginal occupation: John Mulvaney and Johan Kamminga, *Prehistory of Australia*, pp. 69–71; Sydney region, *op. cit.*, pp. 284–89.

Firestick farming: *op. cit.*, pp. 60–62.

Reaching Botany Bay: King, p. 34.

Tribes and clans: Inga Clendinnen, *Dancing with Strangers*, pp. 290, 291; Keith Smith, *Bennelong: The Coming in of the Eora, Sydney Cove, 1788–1792, passim*; Keith Willey, *When the Sky Fell Down*, pp. 12–18.

Landings at Botany Bay: King, pp. 33–35.

Arrival of second division: Tench, pp. 34–37; Bowes Smyth, p. 57.

Shift in meaning: Paul Carter, *The Road to Botany Bay, An Exploration of Landscape and History*, p. 37.

Aboriginal resistance: King in Hunter, p. 272.

Watkin Tench: Tench, p. 32; *ADB*, Vol. II, alphabetical listing; Tench, editor's introduction, xiv–xxv.

Arrival: Tench, p. 32.

Convict women and their prospects: Portia Robinson, *Women of Botany Bay*, pp. 56–58.

Resistance to taking of fish: King, p. 34.

Natives offer women: King p. 35.

Tench's adventures ashore: Tench, pp. 36–37.

Aboriginal language: Mulvaney and Kamminga, pp. 69–77; Collins, journal, pp. 506–512.

Native lances: Bowes Smyth, pp. 57, 58.

Botany Bay: Cook's journal, original and edited, Carter, pp. 10–16; Beaglehole, pp. 230–233.

Arrival of two ships: Tench, p. 127.

Moulton: Gillen, alphabetical listing; Don Chapman, *1788, The People of the First Fleet*, ditto; Cobey, *Crimes*, p. 194, under alias *Morton*.

Decision to explore north, and subsequent discoveries: HRA, Series I, Vol. I, p. 18; Collins, pp. 2, 3.

Jacob Nagle: *The Nagle Journal, A Diary of the Life of Jacob Nagle, Sailor, from the year 1775 to 1841*, pp. 92–95.

Movements in Port Jackson, again: Phillip to Sydney, HRA, Vol. I, p. 18; Nagle, pp. 92–95.

Albion and Sydney Cove: Collins, p. 5.

Aboriginal names: Collins, p. 504 and following; reliable websites devoted to pre-European Sydney area can be accessed by typing 'Eora tribes' or 'Eora place names'.

Chapter Seven *(Pages 105–120)*

Move of the Fleet to Sydney, and arrival of La Pérouse: Hunter, pp. 29, 30; Collins, pp. 3–5.

Attitude to French: Porter, p. 21.

Clark and Tench react to Port Jackson: Clark, pp. 92, 93; Tench, p. 38.

Ross: *ADB*, Vol. II, alphabetical listing; C. M. H. Clark, Vol. I, p. 74; Alan Atkinson, *The Europeans in Australia, A History*, Vol. I, pp. 57, 58; 72–75.

Phillip as shark totem: Atkinson, p. 38.

James Ruse: *ADB*, Vol. II, alphabetical listing; Collins, pp. 75–76; Tench, pp. 197–198; Phillip in Hunter, pp. 301, 351.

Geography of Cove and settlement: Collins, pp. 4, 5.

Phillip's May 16 dispatch to Lord Sydney: HRA, Vol. I, p. 18.

Dawes and White: Collins, p. 12; White, pp. 113, 114.

Canvas Government House: Hunter, p. 53; HRA, Vol. II, pp. 666–667.

Harry Brewer: *ADB*, Vol. I, alphabetical listing; HRA, Vol. I, p. 35.

Clark and his tent: Clark, p. 93.

Native plants: White, pp. 151–158.

Building of huts, and unsuitable wood: White p. 119; Tench, pp. 38–39, 60; Collins, pp. 5, 6.

Livestock and Corbett: Collins, p. 5.

Phillip etc. and Eora: Hunter, pp. 38–46.

First farming, convicts and supervisory duty: Collins, pp. 5–7, 17; Phillip to Banks: HRA, as above.

White and Balmain: see in particular White, pp. 47–50.

Gardens: Collins, p. 13; Clark, p. 113.

Visit to La Pérouse: King, pp. 37–39.

Bradley: *ADB*, alphabetical listing; Victor Crittenden, *Naval Men of the First Fleet*, pamphlet.

French visit, Sydney Cove: amongst others, Collins, pp. 11, 12.

Death of Fr. Receveur: Collins, Vol. I, p. 16; King, *Journal*, pp. 39, 40; Tench, p. 55.

Chapter Eight *(Pages 121–132)*

Landing of women: Bowes, p. 67.

The bacchanalia: Bowes, as above.

Tench's view: Tench, p. 39.

Reading of commission, extent of claim: Collins, p. 6.

Phillip's speech: Collins, Vol. I, p. 6.

Rations: Collins, p. 7; Tench, pp. 12, 83.

Neglect of ships' captains: Bowes, p. 69.

First court-martial: Clark, p. 96.

Chapter Nine *(Pages 133–144)*

Reverend Johnson: Bonwick, pp. 62–63; Porter, pp. 63, 192–194.

Service of February 10, christening and marriages: Collins, Vol. I, p. 14; Clark, p. 97.

Smuggling: Cal Winslow, 'Sussex Smugglers', in Hay, p. 119 onwards; also Hay, pp. 260, 267; Porter, pp. 114–115.

Women's camp and expulsion of sailors: Bowes, p. 70.

Fisher and Hart: Gillen, alphabetical listings; Bowes, p. 79.

First criminal cases, judge-advocate's court: Collins, Vol. I, p. 7; Tench, pp. 44, 100–101.

Flogging: Nagle, p. 178.

Flogging of women: Easty, p. 98.

Chapter Ten (Pages 145–152)

La Pérouse and natives: Tench, p. 170; Collins, Vol. I, p. 16.

Visit by elders: Bowes, p. 69–70.

Aboriginal culture and burial: Collins, pp. 454–455; 499–505; Mulvaney and Kamminga, pp. 95–96; 359–361.

Ancient burials: Mulvaney and Kaminga, pp. 154–155; pp. 161–168.

Native tools: an excellent summation in Smith, *Bennelong*; Collins, Vol. I, pp. 486–488.

Garden Island raid: Collins, Vol. I, p. 13; Tench, pp. 215–216.

Collins laments end of good relations: as above.

Nagle and natives: p. 99.

Chapter Eleven (Pages 153–169)

King and Norfolk Island: King, *Journal*, p. 10 onwards.

Jamison and Colley: alphabetical listing *ADB*, Vol. I; for Jamison, alphabetical listings, Gillen and Chapman; King, pp. 43, 44.

Oaths of abjuration and assurance: C. M. H. Clark, Vol. I, pp. 78–81.

Tom Barrett *et al.*: Collins, p. 8; Tench, pp. 44, 101; White, p. 129.

Awesome nature of executioner: Hay, p. 66.

Bloodworth: see alphabetical listing, Gillen, Chapman; alphabetical listing, Vol. I, *ADB*; Collins, p. 115.

Unloaded ships: John Cobley, *Sydney Cove, 1788*, pp. 110–111; Collins, Vol. I, p. 18.

New rations: Tench, p. 83.

Phillip and officers: Collins, Vol. I, pp. 104, 105.

Conflict over Hunt sentence: Easty, p. 99; Cobley, *1788*, pp. 104–105.

Anti-scorbutics and venereal disease: White, pp. 113, 120, 133, 135, notes, p. 243; Collins, Vol. I, pp. 20, 373, 495–496.

Chapter Twelve (Pages 170–185)

Exploring Broken Bay: Nagle, pp. 100–102; Hunter, pp. 95–108; Phillip to Sydney: HRA, Vol. I, p. 18; Collins, p. 15.

Coo-ee: Hunter, p. 103.

Phillip's health on return: see Phillip's health in Frost, *Phillip: His Voyaging*; White, pp. 127, 131; but see also Bowes Smyth, p. 77.

Looking for land along Parramatta River: White, pp. 127–131.

Discovery of Rose Hill, Parramatta: White as above; Phillip to Sydney, HRA, Vol. I, p. 18.

Departure of ships: Collins, Vol. I, p. 18.

Killing of Ayres and Burn: Collins, Vol. I, p. 24; Tench, pp. 50, 104–105; Hunter, pp. 53–54.

Oakey and Davis: as above.

Reactions of Hunter and others: Hunter, p. 54.

Phillip's expedition and parley: Collins, pp. 24–25.

Phillip to the Marquess of Lansdown: see Arthur Phillip, *Copies and Extracts of Letters from Governor Phillip: Giving an Account* etc.

McEntire: Phillip in Hunter, p. 326; Tench, pp. 49, 105.

Henry Kable and the law: *ADB*, alphabetical listing; Gillen, Chapman, ditto; White, pp. 148, 149.

The Bryants: as for Kable; also alphabetical listing (Braund for Broad), Cobley, *Crimes*; White, p. 88; Collins, pp. 44, 45.

Corbett: as for above; then Tench, p. 61; Collins, Vol. I, pp. 26, 27, 541 n.

King's birthday: Collins, Vol. I, p. 25; Tench, p. 60; White, p. 140.

Phillip in pain: as above.

County of Cumberland: Collins, p. 25; White, p. 140, Tench, pp. 60, 112.

Sam Payton: White, p. 43; Tench, p. 61.

Earthquake: White, pp. 141–142; Collins, Vol. I, p. 27.

Sam Payton's letter: Tench, pp. 62–63.

Execution of Corbett and Payton: Tench, pp. 61–63.

Chapter Thirteen *(Pages 186–211)*

Ross to Evan Nepean: 10 July 1788, Cobley, pp. 187, 188.

Campbell to Lord Ducie: 12 July 1788, Cobley, pp. 191–193.

Phillip to Lord Sydney: July, September, HRA, Series I, Vol. 1, pp. 46–48, 73, 77–78, 86–87.

Phillip to Nepean: HRA, as above, pp. 46; 55 (private letter).

The last transports vanish: Collins, Vol. I, p. 38; Tench, p. 137; Bateson, p. 118.

The journey of the transports: Bateson, pp. 118, 119.

Aboriginal goat raid: Collins, p. 32.

Phillip asks Nepean for clothes for natives: HRA, as above, p. 46.

Failure of germination: Collins, pp. 31, 33.

Phillip orders *Sirius* to Cape Town: Hunter, p. 61; Tench, pp. 79, 120; Collins, Vol. I, pp. 33, 34, 55.

Settlement of Rose Hill/Parramatta: Hunter, pp. 94, 95; Phillip in Hunter, pp. 300–1, 303; Collins, pp. 37, 40, 42, 103; Tench, pp. 79, 136.

Augustus Alt: *ADB*, Vol. I, alphabetical listing; Collins, pp. 10, 123; White, pp. 7, 125.

Capture of Arabanoo: Hunter, pp. 132, 133; Collins, Vol. I, p. 49; Tench, p. 139.

Arabanoo in Sydney: Hunter, pp. 92, 93; Tench, pp. 142–145; Collins, Vol. I, pp. 40, 43.

Convict raid on Botany Bay: Tench, pp. 144, 145.

Ration reduction: Collins, Vol. I, p. 35.

Emergence of smallpox: Collins, pp. 496, 497; Hunter, pp. 92–94; Tench, pp. 146–149.

Surgeon White's 'variolous material': Alan Frost, *Botany Bay Mirages*, chapter entitled 'The Mark of Cain', pp. 190–210.

Finding and treatment of sufferers: Tench, pp. 146–148; Hunter, pp. 115, 116; White, pp. 19, 23; Collins, Vol. I, pp. 53, 483.

Building of storehouses: Hunter, pp. 93–94.

Discovery of crime: Hunter, p. 94; Tench, p. 145; Collins, Vol. I, p. 49.

Frazier: Tench, pp. 295, 296; also alphabetical listings Chapman, Gillen.

Trial and execution of marines: Tench, p. 145; as for discovery of crime.

Turner and Allen: Cobley, p. 18.

Continuation of smallpox and Arabanoo: Tench, pp. 147, 148.

Onset of syphilis and gonorrhoea: Collins, Vol. I, pp. 20, 295–296.

Death of Arabanoo: Tench, p. 149; Collins, p. 54; Hunter, pp. 115, 116.

Chapter Fourteen *(Pages 212–216)*
Sirius's journey: Hunter, pp. 61–76; Nagle, pp. 105–109.
Bread roll for government house dining: Tench, p. 166.

BOOK TWO

Chapter Fifteen *(Pages 219–232)*

New crowding in Britain's prisons: Byrne, The Blackheath Connection, cyber book, Chapter 34; Michael Flynn, *The Second Fleet: Britain's Grim Convict Armada of 1790*, p. 17; Siân Rees, *The Floating Brothel, The Extraordinary Story of the Lady Julian and its Cargo of Female Convicts Bound for Botany Bay*, pp. 1–23.

William Richards: Byrne, The Blackheath Connection, cyber book, especially Chapters 34 and 38; Flynn, pp. 13, 14, 127, 131; Bateson, p. 20.

Taking up and fitting of *Lady Juliana*: Bateson, pp. 120–122; John Nicol, *Life and Adventures, 1776–1801*, pp. 113–126.

Lieutenant Edgar: Bateson, pp. 120, 121; Nicol, pp. 116, 123; Rees, pp. 60, 62.

Captain Aitken: Bateson, as above; Rees, p. 60; Nicol, p. 114.

Surgeon Alley: Bateson, as above; Rees, pp. 61, 62; Flynn, p. 17.

Catherine Heyland: Flynn, *Second Fleet*, alphabetical listing; Rees, pp. 78–80.

Margaret Sullivan: Rees, pp. 80–82.

Women offered King's mercy: Rees, pp. 84, 85.

Sarah Cowden: Flynn, non-alphabetical, p. 658; Rees, pp. 85, 86, 91, 92.

Nellie Kerwin (spelled Kirvein in Second Fleet records; also Karavan): Flynn, alphabetical listing under Kirvein; Rees, pp. 51, 63, 83–89; Nicol, pp. 120, 121.

Acceptance of King's mercy: Rees as above; Flynn, alphabetical listings.

Mrs Barnsley: Flynn, alphabetical listing; Rees, pp. 70, 71; Nicol, pp. 115, 116.

Nicol in love: Nicol, pp. 121, 122.

Departure: Bateson, p. 120; Rees, pp. 96–99; Nicol, p. 121.

Nepean to Phillip: 20 June 1789, HRA, Series I, Vol. I, p. 120.

Chapter Sixteen *(Pages 233–238)*

King's birthday, 1789: Tench, p. 152; Collins, Vol. I, pp. 57, 58.

The Recruiting Officer: Collins, Vol. I, as above.

Other First Fleet books: see article (11 pp.), Colin Steele and Michael

Richards, *Bound for Botany Bay, What books did the First Fleeters read and where are they now?*, available in hard copy and online from National Library of Australia.

Time-expired convicts: Collins, Vol. I, pp. 60, 61.

Especially Cullyhorn: Gillen and Chapman, sometimes under Calleghan or Callighan, alphabetical listings; Collins, n. 548; Cobley, *1789–1790*, pp. 63–65.

Problems with supplies: Collins, Vol. I, pp. 68, 69.

John Harris and the night watch: Collins, Vol. I, pp. 63, 64, 70; Hunter, p. 140.

Collins's opinion: Collins, Vol. I, p. 70.

Chapter Seventeen *(Pages 239–254)*

Grenville: Flynn, pp. 26, 27; Atkinson, p. 78.

Camden, Calvert and King and their contract: Flynn, pp. 26–41; Bateson, pp. 32, 131, 132; Byrne, The Blackheath Connection, cyber book, Chapter 38.

The recruitment of the New South Wales Corps: Flynn, pp. 28, 29; The Blackheath Connection, Chapter 38; Michael Duffy, *Man of Honour: John Macarthur*, early chapters.

Preparations of three transports: Flynn, as previously; Bateson, pp. 126, 127; The Blackheath Connection, as previously; Duffy, early chapters.

HMS *Guardian*: Flynn, pp. 19, 24; Bateson, p. 124; Rees, pp. 72, 75.

Ruse's record: *ADB*, Vol. II, alphabetical listing; Collins, Vol. I, p. xix; Phillip in Hunter, pp. 301, 351, 364; Tench, pp. 197–98; Atkinson, pp. 169–171.

Phillip's plan: Phillip in Hunter, p. 301; the rest as above.

Major Ross's view: 10 July 1788, Ross to Nepean, Cobley, *1788*, that date.

Tench on capturing natives: Tench, pp. 158, 159.

Bradley's expedition and capture of two natives: Bradley journal, and illustration, p. 182 of journal.

Colby and Bennelong in Sydney: Tench, pp. 159, 309; Collins, Vol. I, p. 71; Hunter, pp. 116, 139–142: Bradley, Journal, online.

Banks's view: quoted, Nicholas Thomas, *Discoveries: The Voyages of Captain Cook*, pp. 80, 81.

Colby's escape: Collins, Vol. I, p. 71; Tench, p. 159; Hunter, p. 116.

Bennelong's Sydney career continued: Tench, pp. 159, 160, 167; Collins, Vol. I, p. 92; Hunter, p. 132; King in Hunter, p. 269.

Name exchange: Tench, pp. 160, 161.

Regional tribes and clans: Willey, frontispiece map and pp. 14–16; Clendinnen, frontispiece map and pp. 107, 273. Web search also recommended under 'Eora people'.

King on native borders: King in Hunter, p. 268.

Aboriginal authority system: Collins, Vol. I, pp. 452–455, 460, 461, 488–492.

Bennelong's escape: Collins, Vol. I, p. 92.

Dawes's attempt to cross the Blue Mountains: Collins, Vol. I, p. 107; Tench, p. 158.

Black Caesar: Gillen, alphabetical listing; also Chapman, alphabetical listing; Collins, Vol. I, pp. 57–59, 73, 76; Tench, p. 159.

Chapter Eighteen *(Pages 255–259)*

Ross to Norfolk Island: Tench, p. 63; King in Hunter, pp. 254, 245; Collins, Vol. I, p. 78.

Hunger in Sydney Cove: Tench, p. 166; Collins, Vol. I, pp. 97, 103.

Phillip's generosity: Collins, Vol. I, p. 88.

Sirius and *Supply* to Norfolk Island: Hunter, pp. 118–119; Collins, Vol. I, pp. 78, 80; Ralph Clark, p. 116.

Wrecking of *Sirius*: Hunter, pp. 120–123; King in Hunter, pp. 254–57; Phillip in Hunter, pp. 382, 383; Clark, *Journal*, pp. 121, 122.

Ross declares martial law: Clark, *Journal*, p. 122; King in Hunter, pp. 254, 255.

Mutton birds: Hunter, pp. 125–126; King in Hunter, p. 214; Clark, *Journal*, pp. 285, 293.

Ross's allocation of land: Atkinson, pp. 228, 229, 231.

Ross as light punisher: Clark, *Journal*, pp. 201, 219, 223.

Chapter Nineteen *(Pages 260–268)*

Riou and the *Guardian*: Bateson, pp. 124, 125; Rees, pp. 161, 162.

Lady Juliana's progress to Rio: Bateson, pp. 121, 122; Nicol, pp. 121–127; Rees, pp. 111–160.

HMS *Guardian*'s collision with ice: Bateson, pp. 124, 125; Rees, pp. 177, 178; Flynn, pp. 24, 25.

Return of *Guardian* to Cape Town and arrival of *Lady Juliana*: Nicol, p. 128.

Transfer of people and supplies to *Lady Juliana*: Rees, p. 183; Nicol, p. 128.

Sydney ration reductions: Tench, p. 166; Collins, Vol. I, pp. 97, 103.

Emancipation of Bloodworth and *Guardian* men: Collins, Vol. I, pp. 115, 160, 161.

Surprize, Scarborough, Neptune: Flynn, pp. 30, 31; Bateson, pp. 126, 127.

Arrival of soldiers: Flynn, p. 35.

Loading of transports: Flynn, pp. 32–34; Bateson, pp. 128–131.

Robert Towers: Flynn, alphabetical listing.

Trail and Shapcote: Bateson, pp. 126, 128, 130; Flynn, pp. 27, 33, 35; Tench, p. 173.

Evan Nepean to naval agent: Flynn, p. 39.

Nepean to Phillip: HRA, Pt II, Vol. I, p. 120.

Harriet Hodgetts: Flynn, alphabetical listing.

Chapter Twenty *(Pages 269–278)*

John Macarthur: For a study of Macarthur's origins, see Michael Duffy, *Man of Honour: John Macarthur*; ADB, Vol. II, alphabetical listing; Flynn, pp. 37–41; John Ritchie, *The Wentworths, Father and Son*, pp. 33, 34.

Nicholas Nepean: *ADB*, Vol. II, alphabetical listing; Flynn, pp. 13, 26, 32, 39–42.

Conflict with Gilbert: Flynn, pp. 35–41; Ritchie, pp. 32–35.

D'Arcy Wentworth's career as a highwayman: Ritchie, pp. 1–24.

Captain Trail and the *Neptune*: Ritchie, pp. 29, 32–40.

Primitive sanitation: Elizabeth Macarthur's Journal, HRNSW, Vol. II, p. 366.

The Macarthurs' discomfort: as for previous note.

Female convicts on *Neptune*: Ritchie, p. 30; Flynn, p. 33.

D'Arcy and Catherine Crowley: Ritchie, pp. 31, 34; Flynn, alphabetical listing.

Chapter Twenty-one *(Pages 279–298)*

The *Justinian*: Flynn, pp. 32, 43.

The journey of the Second Fleet proper: Bateson, pp. 126–129; Flynn, pp. 42–48.

Elizabeth Macarthur: HRNSW, Vol. II, p. 489.

Captain William Hill: 26 June 1789, HRNSW, Vol. I, Pt 2, p. 367; MSS 6821, ML.

Hill's attitude to shackles and lack of exercise: as for previous note.

The Macarthurs' transfer to *Scarborough*: Flynn, p. 48.

Arrival of *Lady Juliana* in Sydney Cove: Tench, pp. 169, 170; Collins, Vol. I, pp. 93, 96; White, pp. 20, 21; Hunter, p. 128; Phillip in Hunter, p. 299.

Arrival of *Justinian*: Tench, p. 172; Hunter, p. 128; Phillip in Hunter, p. 301.

Arrival of *Surprize*: as for previous note.

Erection of portable hospital: Collins, Vol. I, pp. 101, 103; White, p. 21.

Arrival of *Neptune* and *Scarborough*: Collins, Vol. I, pp. 99, 100, 106, 107; Tench, pp. 172, 173; Phillip in Hunter, p. 301.

The Reverend Johnson and the sick: Bonwick, pp. 91–97.

Captain Hill's estimation of the Sydney Cove area: HRNSW, Vol. I, Pt 2, p. 367; MSS 6821, ML.

And of Parramatta: as for previous note.

Convict women making clothes: Tench, p. 166.

Leasing of *Surprize* to go to Norfolk Island: Phillip in Hunter, p. 301; Ritchie, p. 52; Collins, Vol. I, p. 106.

Rations on Norfolk: Collins, Vol. I, p. 135.

Wentworth's arrival and birth of his son: Ritchie, pp. 52, 53.

Dennis Considen: *ADB*, Vol. I, alphabetical listing; Gillen, Chapman, ditto; Ritchie, pp. 54, 55.

John Irving: Tench, pp. 168, 312; Collins, Vol. I, pp. 80, 181, 360; Gillen, Chapman, alphabetical listings.

Wentworth's Norfolk Island career: Ritchie, pp. 56, 60, 61–63; Collins, Vol. I, p. 106; Ralph Clark, pp. 180, 184, 186, 191.

Ralph Clark and flogging: pp. 191, 197.

Near mutiny: Ralph Clark, p. 192.

Renewed floggings: pp. 199, 202.

Wentworth's intervention: Clark, p. 197.

Ruse's farming success: Tench, pp. 197, 198, 256; Collins, Vol. I, pp. 130, 135, 136.

Arrival of Elizabeth Perry: Tench, pp. 197, 198; Collins, Vol. I, p. 88; Flynn, alphabetical listing.

Christopher Magee: Tench, p. 256; Collins, Vol. I, pp. 314–316, 409; Atkinson, pp. 168–72; Gillen, Chapman, alphabetical listings.

Chapter Twenty-two *(Pages 299–314)*
Trail departs: Flynn, p. 52; Tench, p. 173.

Nicol and *Lady Juliana* prepare to leave: Nicol, p. 130.

Smilax and fertility: as for previous note.

The coming of the whale: Tench, p. 174; Collins, Vol. I, pp. 108–110.

The whale feast: Tench, pp. 176–178; Collins, as for previous note.

Bennelong at Manly: Tench, pp. 176–180; Collins, as for previous note.

His gift for the governor: as for previous note.

The governor visits Bennelong: Tench, p. 178; Collins, Vol. I, pp. 109–11.

Lieutenant Waterhouse: Tench pp. 178–180; Collins, Vol. I, p. 111; ADB, Vol. II, alphabetical listing.

Phillip at Manly: Phillip in Hunter, pp. 306–311; Collins, Vol. I, pp. 109–111; Tench, pp. 178–180.

Phillip's wounding: as for previous note.

Withdrawal to Sydney: Tench, p. 180; Collins, Vol. I, pp. 111–112.

Collins on Phillip's trusting nature: Collins, Vol. I, p. 111.

Bennelong not blamed: Tench, p. 184; Collins, Vol. I, p. 112; Phillip in Hunter, pp. 309, 311.

Phillip's men looking for Bennelong: as for previous note.

Bennelong, Barangaroo and others: Tench, pp. 184–186; Collins, Vol. I, pp. 311–312.

The return of stolen property: Tench, pp. 185, 186.

Bennelong's reluctance to go to Sydney: Tench, p. 187; Phillip in Hunter, p. 311.

Bennelong visits Sydney while hostages held: Tench, pp. 188, 189; Phillip in Hunter, as for previous note; Collins, Vol. I, p. 313.

Further contact with Aboriginals: Tench, pp. 187, 188; Phillip in Hunter, pp. 319–323; Collins, Vol. I, pp. 313, 317.

Pemulwuy: Collins, Vol. I, p. 118; Tench (under Pimelwi), p. 206; Phillip in Hunter, pp. 327, 328.

Karubarabulu: Collins, Vol. I, pp. 463, 464; Tench, p. 291; Phillip in Hunter, pp. 321–323.

Bennelong's tin shield, hatchets and house: Tench, p. 200; Collins, Vol. I, pp. 113, 117; Phillip in Hunter, p. 320.

Chapter Twenty-three *(Pages 315–334)*

Aboriginal women trading sex for goods: Collins, Vol. I, p. 464.

Phillip's assessment of a native woman: Phillip in Hunter, p. 327.

Bennelong's domestic brutality: Collins, Vol. I, pp. 463, 464; Tench, p. 188; Phillip in Hunter, pp. 319–321.

Bennelong's tenderness to Barangaroo: Phillip in Hunter, p. 316; Tench, p. 190; Collins, Vol. I, pp. 492, 493.

Bennelong and Karubarabulu fighting: Tench, pp. 200–203; Phillip in Hunter, pp. 319–321.

Karubarabulu in hospital: Tench, p. 203; Phillip in Hunter, as for previous note.

Bennelong's repentance: Tench, as for previous note; Phillip in Hunter, p. 321.

Bennelong's fear of Surgeon White: Tench, p. 205.

Karubarabulu hides from Barangaroo at government house: Tench, p. 203; Phillip in Hunter, pp. 321, 322.

Confusing signals from Bennelong: Tench, as for previous note; Phillip in Hunter, p. 323.

John McEntire: Tench, pp. 49, 66, 105, 116; Phillip in Hunter, pp. 326, 327.

Bennelong entertains Pemulwuy: Smith, p. 116.

Carradhys: A. P. Elkin, *Aboriginal Men of High Degree*, pp. 1–66; Collins, Vol. I, pp. 453, 493, 494.

The wounding of McEntire: Tench, pp. 207, 209; Collins, pp. 107, 108; Phillip in Hunter, pp. 326–328.

Phillip's reaction: Tench, pp. 207–209; Phillip in Hunter, p. 328.

Bennelong as distinguished visitor: Phillip in Hunter, pp. 328, 332.

Tench's reaction: Tench, p. 209.

Preparation for the expedition: Tench, p. 209.

Dawes's resistance: HRA, Series 1, Vol. I, p. 289; Hunter, p. 435 n.

Patyegarang: Smith, pp. 98, 99.

Dawes's further resistance: HRA, Series I, Vol. I, p. 292.

The first punitive expedition: Tench, pp. 209–211; Collins, Vol. I, pp. 118, 119; Phillip in Hunter, pp. 328, 329.

McEntire at hospital: Phillip in Hunter, p. 327.

Colby's intervention: Tench (under Colbee), pp. 210, 211.

The second expedition: Tench, pp. 212–215; Collins, Vol. I, pp. 118, 119.

Bennelong back in Sydney: Phillip in Hunter, p. 332.

Initiation details: Collins, Vol. I, pp. 466–489.

Corroboree: Tench pp. 277, 289, 290; Collins, Vol. I, p. 466; Hunter, p. 143; King in Hunter, p. 270; Phillip in Hunter, p. 317.

Bennelong and the two women together at Tubowgulle: Phillip in Hunter, p. 332.

Potato raid: Tench, p. 215; Collins, Vol. I, pp. 121, 122; Phillip in Hunter, p. 332.

Aboriginal found dead: Tench, pp. 215, 216; Collins, Vol. I, pp. 121, 122; Phillip in Hunter, p. 333.

Bennelong's angry response: Tench, p. 216; Phillip in Hunter, pp. 333, 334.

Port Jackson painter: Collins, p. 368.

Phillip's new rules about contact: Phillip in Hunter, p. 328.

Collins on native dispossession: Collins, Vol. I, p. 122.

Phillip refuses Bennelong entry to government house: Phillip in Hunter, p. 327.

Chapter Twenty-four (Pages 335–350)

The *Waaksamheyd*: Hunter, p. 131; King in Hunter, p. 294; Collins, Vol. I, pp. 113, 114.

Tench on Batavia: Tench, p. 217.

Waaksamheyd's cargo: Phillip in Hunter, pp. 329, 335; Collins, Vol. I, pp. 119, 120.

Detmer Smith plays games: Tench, p. 218; Collins, Vol. I, p. 123; Phillip in Hunter, pp. 335–336.

Waaksamheyd hired to return crew of *Sirius*: Collins, Vol. I, pp. 124, 127, 128; Tench, p. 218; Phillip in Hunter, p. 338.

Phillip's request to return to England: 25 March 1791, Phillip to Grenville, HRA, Series I, Vol. I, p. 377.

Phillip's wife and affairs: see Frost, *Phillip*.

His declaration of ill health: HRA, as above.

Collins to his father: 23 March 1791, Correspondence, 1775–1810, MSS 700.

Nature of Phillip's illness: G. B. Barton, *History of New South Wales from the Records*, pp. 305, 306, 368.

The request by four officers: Cobley, *1791–1792*, pp. 45, 46.

Phillip to Sir Joseph Banks: Cobley, *1791–1792*, pp. 47, 28.

Surgeon White to Grenville: Cobley, *1791–1792*, p. 50.

The journey of the *Waaksamheyd*: Tench, p. 218, Hunter, pp. 146–192.

Expedition to cross Hawkesbury River: Tench, pp. 224–234; Phillip in Hunter, pp. 340–348.

Encounters with local natives: as for previous note.

Phillip on difference between Hawkesbury language and that of coastal people: Phillip in Hunter, p. 347.

Colby and Ballooderry want to go back: Phillip in Hunter, pp. 347, 348; Tench, p. 234.

William Bryant's flogging: Collins, pp. 44, 45.

Surgeon White to the dealer in hams: White to Mr Skill, 17 April 1790, Barton, Vol. I, pp. 506–508.

John Terwood's attempted escape: Tench, pp. 181, 182; Collins, Vol. I, pp. 113, 356, 357.

The Bryants' preparations: C. H. Currey, *The Transportation, Escape and Pardoning of Mary Bryant*, pp. 12–14; Collins, Vol. I, pp. 126, 127.

Motivations: Tench, p. 162.

Fellow escapees: Currey, p. 14; Collins, Vol. I, pp. 129, 130.

Escape: Currey, pp. 19–25; *Memorandoms*, reproduced in Geoffrey Chapman Ingleton, *True Patriots All*, pp. 13–15.

Further ration reduction: Collins, Vol. I, pp. 130, 131.

Mary Morgan, Mary Whiting: Collins, Vol. I, p. 332.

Bryant's impact on colonial society: Collins, p. 131.

David Collins's opinion: as for previous note.

Tench's admiration: Tench, p. 219.

Chapter Twenty-five *(Pages 351–368)*

Bligh's interest: George Mackaness, *The Life of Vice-Admiral William Bligh RN, FRS*, pp. 298, 299.

The Memorandoms: Ingleton, pp. 13–15.

Journey to Koepang: Currey, pp. 26, 27; *Memorandoms*.

And time there: Currey, pp. 27–31; *Memorandoms*.

Pandora: Mackaness, *Bligh*, pp. 190–208; Currey, pp. 29–31.

The *Gorgon*: Bateson, p. 131.

The *Mary Ann*: as for previous note; Byrne, The Blackheath Connection.

Third Fleet and contract: Byrne, The Blackheath Connection, especially Chapter 40.

Pursuit of Captain Trail: Flynn, pp. 54–64; Ritchie, pp. 43–44.

Nelson on Trail: Flynn, p. 74.

The *Queen*: Bateson, p. 132; Flynn, pp. 60, 64, 73.

Voyage of Third Fleet proper: Bateson, pp. 131–139; Collins, Vol. I, pp. 141, 143, 145, 149, 150.

Ships' agents and short weighting: Bateson, pp. 135, 136.

The Defenders: Atkinson, pp. 178, 250.

Millennial dreams: Atkinson, pp. 249–251; Thomas Keneally, *The Great Shame*, pp. 12, 13.

Arrival of *Mary Ann*: Collins, Vol. I, pp. 140, 141; Phillip in Hunter, p. 354; Tench, p. 240.

No temptation offered to quit colony: Phillip in Hunter, p. 355.

National children: John Molony, *The Native Born, The First White Australians*, pp. 23–25.

The *Matilda*: Bateson, pp. 134, 135; Collins, Vol. I, p. 143; Phillip in Hunter, p. 356.

Bennelong in hospital: Phillip in Hunter, p. 360.

Atlantic and *Salamander*: Phillip in Hunter, pp. 357, 358; Collins, Vol. I, pp. 145, 152; Tench, p. 242.

Admiral Barrington: Phillip in Hunter, p. 368; Collins, Vol. I, pp. 151, 152.

Mrs Parker: Mary Parker, *Voyage Round the World in the Gorgon*, pp. 73–92.

Lord and Underwood: *ADB*, Vol. II, alphabetical listings.

The Reverend Bain: Phillip in Hunter, p. 366; Collins, Vol. I, pp. 148, 160, 161, 303, 334; Bonwick, pp. 114, 115.

The Reverend Johnson: as for Bonwick, previous note.

Activities of ships after delivery of convicts: Bateson, p. 139; Phillip in Hunter, pp. 368–371, 373, 375; Tench, pp. 298–300; Collins, Vol. I, pp. 151, 152, 155, 156, 258, 159.

Chapter Twenty-six *(Pages 369–379)*

The *Gorgon*'s bounty: Phillip in Hunter, p. 366; Tench, pp. 245, 248.

King and his wife: *ADB*, Vol. II, alphabetical listing.

The Great Seal: Collins, Vol. I, p. 149.

King returns to Norfolk Island: Ritchie, pp. 49, 50, 60–71; Phillip in Hunter, pp. 368, 382–384; Collins, Vol. I, pp. 148, 152, 153, 159; Clark, pp. 221–238, *passim*.

Wentworth on Norfolk Island: Ritchie, pp. 61–72.

Attitude towards his son: Ritchie, p. 68.

George Barrington: *ADB*, Vol. I, alphabetical listing; George Barrington, *George Barrington's Voyage to Botany Bay, Retelling a Convict's Travel Narrative of the 1790s* (not proven authentic, but credible and accurate on much of Barrington's personal history); Tench, pp. 242, 257, 258; Collins, Vol. I, p. 205.

Grenville replies to Phillip: 19 February 1791, Cobley, *1791–1792*, pp. 123–124.

Collins's bind: Collins to his father, 17 October 1791, Collins Papers, Vol. I, p. 62, Dixon Library, State Library of New South Wales.

Attitude towards Major Ross: as for previous note.

Loyalty to Phillip: as for Collins Papers, above.

Extra provisions on Third Fleet ships: Collins, Vol. I, p. 150.

The Bryants imprisoned on Koepang: *Memorandoms*; Currey, p. 31.

Shipped to Batavia: *Memorandoms*; Currey, pp. 31, 32.

Chapter Twenty-seven *(Pages 380–391)*

The Irish: Collins, Vol. I, p. 141; Hunter in Phillip, p. 366.

Going to China: Collins, Vol. I, pp. 154, 155; Tench, pp. 243, 244; Phillip in Hunter, pp. 333, 372; Atkinson, pp. 248–250.

Phillip addresses the Parramatta convicts: Collins, Vol. I, p. 160; Phillip in Hunter, p. 373.

Tench visits 'the Chinese Travellers': Tench, p. 246.

Demonstration outside government house, Parramatta: Atkinson, p. 248; Collins, Vol. I, p. 160.

Devereaux and Kelly: *ADB*, Vol. II, under Kelly; Portia Robinson, *The Hatch and Brood*, pp. 237, 250, 253; Molony, 73–74.

Transports go whaling: Bateson, p. 139; Phillip in Hunter, pp. 368–371, 373, 375; Tench, pp. 298–300; Collins, Vol. I, pp. 151, 152, 155, 156, 258, 159.

William Richards's dream: Byrne, The Blackheath Connection, Chapter 40.

Tench's opinion on commercial desirability of New South Wales: Tench, p. 74.

Offers to marines to remain: Collins, p. 105; Easty, pp. 134, 135.

Tench's opinion on marines' motives for staying: Tench, p. 245.

Tench's reconnaissance: Tench, pp. 246–259.

Ramsay and Leary: Tench, p. 253.

Bishop: Tench, p. 253.

Everingham: Tench, pp. 253, 254.

Rymes: Tench, p. 254.

Schaeffer: Tench, pp. 254, 255.

Magee: Tench, p. 256; Collins, Vol. I, pp. 314–316.

McCabe drowned: Collins, Vol. I, p. 243.

Tench visits Barrington: Tench, pp. 257, 258.

Populations of Sydney, Parramatta and Norfolk Island: Tench, p. 259.

Ross boards the *Gorgon*: Collins, Vol. I, p. 159; Tench, p. 259.

Duel with Captain Hill: Cobley, *1791–1792*, p. 190.

Ross's post-colonial life: *ADB*, Vol. II, alphabetical listing.

Departure of the *Gorgon*: Collins, Vol. I, pp. 159, 199; Phillip in Hunter, p. 375.

Bryant deaths in Batavia: *Memorandoms*; Currey, p. 33.

Edwards charters ships for Cape: *Memorandoms*, Currey, p. 34; Mackaness, *Bligh*, p. 208.

Chapter Twenty-eight *(Pages 392–398)*

Hatchet men (*Mogogal*): See Tench, Phillip and Collins for recurrent requests for hatchets (for example, Tench, pp. 176, 177, 188); Collins, Vol. I, p. 510.

Barangaroo: Collins, Vol. I, p. 464; Phillip in Hunter, p. 360.

Yuringa: Collins, Vol. I, p. 464.

Barangaroo gives birth: Collins, Vol. I, pp. 465, 466.

Death of Barangaroo: Collins, Vol. I, pp. 490, 499, 500.

Bennelong summons Willemering: Collins, Vol. I, p. 490.

Barangaroo's cremation: Collins, Vol. I, pp. 502, 503.

Collins observes no acts of hostility: Collins, Vol. I, p. 174.

Confrontation between Sydney and Botany Bay natives, April 1791: Collins, Vol. I, p. 490.

Corroboree at head of the stream: Collins, Vol. I, p. 491.

Ritual wounding: Collins, Vol. I, pp. 489, 490.

Killing of Noorooing: Collins, Vol. I, pp. 460, 488, 489.

Death of Yuringa: Collins, Vol. I, p. 405.

Mrs Macarthur: Elizabeth Macarthur, *The Journal and Letters of Elizabeth Macarthur, 1787–1798*, booklet.

Colby's burial of wife and child: Collins, Vol. I, p. 504.

Pemulwuy's resistance: Tench (under Pimelwi), pp. 210, 211; Collins (under Pemulwy), Vol. I, pp. 118, 371.

Lieutenant Dawes's translation of *damunalung*: Smith, p. 156; Dawes Papers, ML.

A skull for Sir Joseph Banks: Phillip to Banks, 26 March 1791, A81, ML.

Blumenbach: John Gasgoigne, *Joseph Banks and the English Enlightenment, Useful Knowledge and Polite Culture*, pp. 149–159.

Chapter Twenty-nine *(Pages 399–412)*

Pitt: Bateson, pp. 139–141.

Macaulay: Byrne, The Blackheath Connection, *passim*; Bateson, p. 139.

Women convicts on *Pitt*: p. 141; Collins, Vol. I, p. 170.

Illness on board: Collins, pp. 168–170.

Major Grose: *ADB*, Vol. I, alphabetical listing; Collins, Vol. I, pp. 96, 167.

Arrival of *Pitt*: Bateson, p. 142; Collins, p. 167.

Captain Manning sets up store ashore: Collins, Vol. I, p. 168.

Grose reacts to Sydney Cove and Parramatta: HRA, Vol. I, Pt II, pp. 2–4.

Death and burial rate: Collins, Vol. I, p. 170; Phillip in Hunter, pp. 371, 372; Cobley for March, April 1792 in *1791–1792*.

Fifty-two further land grants: Phillip in Hunter, pp. 355, 356.

Phillip to Dundas: HRA, Series I, Vol. I, p. 377.

Henry Dundas: Brady, pp. 249, 250; C. M. H. Clark, Vol. I, pp. 127, 128.

Continued death: Collins, pp. 165, 167, 168.

A teacher and a parson for Norfolk Island: Collins, Vol. I, p. 162.

Johnson's household: Bonwick, p. 88.

But lack of a glebe: Bonwick, p. 89.

Holding services in a boat shed or in the open: Bonwick, pp. 89, 90.

Further burials: Cobley, for May, June 1792, *1791–1792*; Collins, Vol. 1, p. 175.

Survivors of the Bryant party transferred to *Gorgon:* Tench, pp. 219, 220; Currey, p. 34.

Deaths of marine's children between Cape Town and England: Clark, pp. 233, 234; Scott, pp. 76–82.

Death of Charlotte Bryant: Clark, p. 234.

Arrival in Portsmouth: Currey, p. 36.

Bryant party sent to Newgate: Frederick A. Pottle, *Boswell and the Girl from Botany Bay*, p. 24.

James Boswell's involvement: Frank Brady, *James Boswell*, pp. 464–466; also Pottle, *passim*; Currey, pp. 38–46.

Other members of Bryant party released: Currey, p. 46.

John Butcher's (Samuel Broome) return to New South Wales: Currey, pp. 46, 47.

Mary Bryant goes home: Currey, p. 44.

Parsons's poem: Brady, pp. 465, 466.

Leaves from Botany Bay: Brady, pp. 572, 573.

Chapter Thirty *(Pages 413–433)*

Attempted escape on *Pitt*: Collins, Vol. I, p. 170.

Surgeon Atkins on continued hunger: Richard Atkins, *Journal, 1792–1810*, typescript copy ML, original NL.

Maize, and grinding it: Collins, Vol. I, p. 176.

Nature of Indian supplies: Collins, Vol. I, p. 191.

Shortage of rations, May 1792: Collins, Vol. I, pp. 175, 176.

New fishery for use of sick: Collins, Vol. I, p. 175.

Nature of scurvy, and thefts: Collins, Vol. I, pp. 176–178.

Atkins: *ADB*, Vol. I, alphabetical listing; Atkins, Journal, photocopy, ML MSS 737–1.

Diminishing returns: Collins, Vol. I, p. 170.

Burton: Phillip to Dundas, 5 April 1792, HRA, Series I, Vol. I, pp. 936, 937.

Burton's death: *ADB*, Vol. I, alphabetical listing; Collins, Vol. I, p. 171.

Further deaths: Cobley, *1791–1792*, for May–June 1792; Collins, Vol. I, p. 175.

Arrival of *Atlantic* and its provisions: Collins, Vol. I, pp. 184, 185.

Inadequacy of rations: Collins, Vol. I, pp. 186, 187; Atkins, Journal, ML.

Mid-winter harvest: Atkins, as for previous note.

Phillip to Nepean: 26 June 1792, Cobley, *1791–1792*, p. 275.

Discounting of bills: Cobley, *1791–1792*, pp. 275, 276, 278.

Arrival of *Britannia*, and news of Captain Trail: Collins, Vol. I, pp. 187–188.

Collins's optimism: Collins, Vol. I, p. 188.

Goods of un-merchantable condition: Collins, Vol. I, pp. 184, 185.

Emancipated convicts and Ingram: Collins, Vol. I, pp. 193, 194.

Theft of urine-steeped corn: Atkins, Journal, ML.

Phillip to Dundas: 2 October 1792, HRA, Series I, Pt I, pp. 374–381.

Chapman on Phillip: HRNSW, Vol. I, Pt I, p. 5.

Royal Admiral: Bateson, pp. 140, 141; Collins, Vol. I, p. 199.

Convicts straight to Parramatta: Phillip in Hunter, p. 371.

Thomas Watling: *ADB*, Vol. II, alphabetical listing.

Mary Reibey: *ADB*, Vol. II, alphabetical listing; Robinson, *Hatch and Brood*, pp. 69, 72.

NSW Corps 'takes up' *Britannia*: Collins, Vol. I, p. 198.

NSW Corps expect land grants: Phillip to Dundas, 4 October 1792, HRA, Series I, Vol. I, pp. 383, 384.

Shops and behaviour of settlers: Collins, Vol. I, p. 202.

Kitty: Collins, Vol. I, pp. 206, 307; Bateson, pp. 143, 144.

Phillip decides to travel on *Atlantic*: Collins, Vol. I, p. 203.

State of the colony: Phillip in Hunter, p. 372; Collins, Vol. I, p. 209.

Collins on settler morale: Collins, Vol. I, p. 210.

Bushfire and harvest: Collins, Vol. I, p. 210.

Livestock: as for previous note.

Ceremonial and departure: Collins, Vol. I, p. 211; Easty, p. 142.

Bennelong and Yemmerawanne: as for previous note.

Easty assessment of colony and journey: Easty, pp. 144, 145, 156, 157, 162, 163.

Arrival in England: Easty, p. 174; Mackaness, *Phillip*; and Frost.

Epilogue *(Pages 434–458)*

For all First Fleet convicts and personnel: see Gillen and Chapman, alphabetical listings.

For Second Fleet convicts: see Flynn, ditto.

There are *ADB* listings for the following:

ADB, Vol. I, George Barrington, Bennelong, James Bloodworth, David Collins.

ADB, Vol. II, Henry Kable, Philip Gidley King, Phillip Parker King, James Larra, Simeon Lord, Elizabeth Macarthur, John Macarthur, Mary and Thomas Reibey, James Ruse, Watkin Tench, James Underwood, Richard Johnson, Esther (Abrahams) Johnston, George Johnston, D'Arcy Wentworth, William Charles Wentworth.

For further information on Bennelong, other than sources already cited: see Isadore Brodsky, *Bennelong Profile, Dreamtime Reveries of a Native of Sydney Cove.*

For the Macarthur dynasty: see Michael Duffy, *Man of Honour: John Macarthur*; and the much earlier (by half a century) M. H. Ellis, *John Macarthur.*

For the Wentworth dynasty: see Ritchie's *The Wentworths.*

For first generation of Australians: see John Molony, *The Native-Born*, especially Chapters 1 and 2; and Portia Robinson, *The Hatch and Brood of Time*, a re-assessment of the first generation of Australian-born.

For the best study of Phillip's last days: see Frost, *Phillip*; and George Mackaness's seventy-year-old study, *Admiral Arthur Phillip.*

Bibliography

Primary Sources

A Brief Detail of Governor Phillip's Voyage to Botany Bay: With an Account of the Establishment of the Colonies at Port Jackson and Norfolk Island, Rutland, Vermont, 1795.

An Authentic and Interesting Narrative of the Late Expedition to Botany Bay as performed by Commodore Phillips, Aberdeen, 1789.

Barrington, George, *George Barrington's Voyage to Botany Bay, Retelling a Convict's Travel Narrative of the 1790s*, ed. Suzanne Rickard, London, 2001.

Blake, William, *The Poetical Works of William Blake*, ed. John Sampson, London (1913) 1949.

Bowes Smyth, Arthur, *The Journal of Arthur Bowes Smyth: Surgeon, Lady Penrhyn, 1787–1789*, eds Paul G. Fidlon and R.J. Ryan, Sydney, 1979.

Bradley, William, *A Voyage to New South Wales, 1786–1792*, Sydney 1969 but also available in transcript and original in Online Collections, State Library of New South Wales website.

Clark, Ralph, *The Journal and Letters of Lt Ralph Clark, 1787–1792*, eds Paul G. Fidlon and R.J. Ryan, Sydney, 1981.

Collins, David, *An Account of the English Colony in New South Wales, Volume 1*, ed. Brian H. Fletcher (1798), Sydney, 1975.

Easty, John, Private Marine, *Memorandum of the Transactions of a Voyage from England to Botany Bay, 1787–1793, A First Fleet Journal*, Sydney, 1965.

Fowell, Newton, *The Sirius Letters: The Complete Letters of Newton*

Fowell, Midshipman and Lieutenant aboard the Sirius Flagship, Sydney 1988.

Harris, Alexander, An Emigrant Mechanic, *Settlers and Convicts or Recollections of Sixteen Years' Labour in the Australian Backwoods,* for'd, Manning Clark, 1964 (first, London, 1847).

Historical Records of Australia, Volume 1, Series 1, ed. Frederick Watson, Sydney, 1925.

Historical Records of New South Wales, Volume 1, Part 1 and Volume 1, Part 2, ed. F.M. Bladen, Sydney, 1892–1901.

Home, Edward, *A First Fleet Letter to a Gentleman in Edinburgh,* Canberra, 1999.

Hunter, Captain John, Commander HMS Sirius, with further accounts by Governor Arthur Phillip, Lieutenant P.G. King, and Lieutenant H.L. Ball, *An Historical Journal, 1787–1792,* ed. John Bach, Sydney, 1968.

Ingleton, Geoffrey Chapman, *True Patriots All: or News from Early Australia as told in A Collection of Broadsides,* Sydney, 1952.

King, Philip Gidley, *The Journal of Philip Gidley King: Lieutenant, R.N. 1787–1790,* eds Paul G. Fidlon and R.J. Ryan, Sydney, 1980.

Macarthur, Elizabeth, *The Journal and Letters of Elizabeth Macarthur, 1789–1798,* transcribed by Joy N. Hughes, Sydney, 1984.

Nagle, Jacob, *The Nagle Journal, A Diary of the Life of Jacob Nagle, Sailor, from the year 1775 to 1841,* ed. John C. Dann, New York, USA, 1988.

Nicol, John, *Life and Adventures, 1776–1801,* ed. Tim Flannery, Melbourne, 1997.

Phillip, Arthur, *The Voyage of Governor Phillip to Botany Bay,* London, 1789, Sydney, 1970.

Phillip, Arthur, *Copies and Extracts of Letters from Governor Phillip: Giving an Account of the Fertility of the Land etc.,* London, 1792.

Scott, James, Sergeant of Marines, *Remarks on a Passage to Botany Bay, 1787–1792,* Sydney, 1963.

Sources of Australian History, ed. and selected, C.M. Clark, Melbourne, 1957.

Spain, Edward, *The Journal of Edward Spain, Merchant Seaman and sometimes Warrant Officer in the Royal Navy,* Sydney, 1989.

Tench, Captain Watkin, of the Marines, *Sydney's First Four Years*, being a reprint of *A Narrative of the Expedition to Botany Bay and a Complete Account of the Settlement at Port Jackson*, intro-annot. L.F. Fizhardinge, Sydney, 1979.

White, John Esq, Surgeon-General to the First Fleet and the Settlement at Port Jackson, *Journal of a Voyage to New South Wales*, intro. Rex Rienits, ed. Alec H. Chisholm, Sydney, 1962.

Secondary Sources

Abbie, A.A., *The Original Australians*, Sydney, n.d.

Ackroyd, Peter, *London, The Biography*, London, 2001.

Atkinson, Alan, *The Europeans in Australia, A History, Volume One*, Melbourne, 1997.

Australian Dictionary of Biography, Volumes 1 & 2, gen. ed. Douglas Pike, Victoria, 1967.

The Australian Encyclopaedia, Sixth Edition, Sydney 1996.

Barton, G.B., *History of New South Wales from the Records, Volumes 1 & 2*, Sydney, 1980.

Bateson, Charles, *The Convict Ships, 1787–1868*, Glasgow, 1959.

Beaglehole, J.C., *The Life of Captain James Cook*, Stanford, USA, 1974.

Beames, Thomas, *The Rookeries of London*, London, 1852.

Beattie, J.M., *Crime and the Courts in England, 1660–1800*, New Jersey, USA, 1986.

Blainey, Geoffrey, *The Triumph of the Nomads*, Melbourne, 1975.

Blaxell, Gregory, *The River, Sydney Cove to Parramatta*, Sydney, 2004.

Bonwick, John, *Australia's First Preacher; the Reverend Richard Johnson*, London, 1898.

Brady, Frank, *James Boswell, The Later Years, 1769–1795*, New York, 1984.

Brodsky, Isadore, *Bennelong Profile, Dreamtime Reveries of a Native of Sydney Cove*, Sydney, 1973.

Carter, Paul, *The Road to Botany Bay, An Exploration of Landscape and History*, New York, USA, 1987.

Chapman, Don, *1788, The People of the First Fleet*, Sydney, 1988.

Clark, C.M.H., *A History of Australia, Volume 1, From the Earliest Times to the Age of Macquarie*, Melbourne, 1962.

Clark, Manning, *A Short History of Australia*, Victoria, 1963.

Clark, Manning, *History of Australia*, Abridged, Michael Cathcart, Melbourne, 1993.

Clendinnen, Inga, *Dancing with Strangers*, Melbourne, 2003.

Cobley, John, *Sydney Cove, 1788*, London, 1962.

Cobley, John, *Sydney Cove, 1789–1790*, Sydney, 1963.

Cobley, John, *Sydney Cove, 1791–1792*, Sydney, 1965.

Cobley, John, *The Crimes of the First Fleet Convicts*, Sydney, 1970.

Crittenden, Victor, *Naval Men of the First Fleet*, Canberra, 1986.

Currey, C.H., *The Transportation, Escape and Pardoning of Mary Bryant*, Sydney, 1983.

Defoe, Daniel, *Moll Flanders* (1772), New York, 1961.

Dew, Sergeant William, of the Marines, *A First Fleet Family*, ed. (supposedly) Louis Becke and Walter Jeffery, London, n.d.

Duffy, Michael, *Man of Honour: John Macarthur*, Sydney, 2003.

Elder, Bruce, *Blood on the Wattle, Massacres and Maltreatment of Aboriginal Australians since 1788*, Sydney, 1988.

Eldershaw, M. Barnard, *Phillip of Australia*, Sydney, 1938.

Elkin, A.P., *Aboriginal Men of High Degree* (1945), Queensland, 1977.

Ferguson, Niall, *Empire*, London, 2003.

Flynn, Michael, *The Second Fleet, Britain's Grim Convict Armada of 1790*, Sydney, 2001.

The First Fleeters, A Comprehensive Listing of Convicts, Marines, Seamen, Officers, Wives, Children and Ships, eds Paul G. Fidlon and R.J. Ryan, Sydney, 1981.

Forster, Colin, *France and Botany Bay, The Lure of a Penal Colony*, Melbourne, 1996.

Frost, Alan, *Arthur Phillip, His Voyaging*, Melbourne, 1987.

Frost, Alan, *Botany Bay Mirages, Illusions of Australia's Convict Beginnings*, Melbourne, 1994.

Gasgoigne, John, *Joseph Banks and the English Enlightenment, Useful Knowledge and Polite Culture*, Cambridge, UK, 1994.

Gibson, Madge, *Belbroughton to Botany Bay*, Belbroughton, Worcestershire, 1987.

Gillen, Mollie, *The Founders of Australia: A Biographical Dictionary of the First Fleet*, Sydney, 1989.

Given, John W., *1787/1788 First Fleet Marines of Port Jackson and Norfolk Island and in Van Diemen's Land*, Cambridge, Tas., 2001.

Griffith, Tom (gen. ed.), *The Newgate Calendar*, Hertfordshire, UK, 1997.

Grose, Captain, *1811 Dictionary of the Vulgar Tongue*, London, 1811.

Halloran, Lawrence, *John Harris, First Fleet Emancipist*, Sydney, 1992.

Hay, Douglas; Linebaugh, Peter; Thompson, E.P.; Rule, John G.; Winslow, Cal, *Albion's Fatal Tree, Crime and Society in Eighteenth-century England*, London, 1975.

Hirst, J.B., *Convict Society and Its Enemies, A History of Early New South Wales*, Sydney, 1983.

Holden, Robert, *Orphans of History: The Forgotten Children of the First Fleet*, Sydney, 2000.

Hughes, Robert, *The Fatal Shore, The Epic of Australia's Founding*, New York, USA, 1986.

Keneally, Thomas, *The Great Shame, A Story of the Irish in the Old World and the New*, Sydney, 1998.

R.L. Kirk and A.G. Thorne, *The Origin of the Australians*, New Jersey, USA, 1976.

Langguth, A.J., *Patriots, The Men who Started the American Revolution*, New York, USA, 1988.

McIntyre, Kenneth Gordon, *The Rebello Transcripts, Governor Phillip's Portuguese Prelude*, London, 1984.

Macintyre, Stuart and Clark, Anna, *The History Wars*, Melbourne, 2003.

Mackaness, George, *The Life of Vice-Admiral William Bligh R.N., F.R.S.*, Sydney, 1931.

Mackaness, George, *Admiral Arthur Phillip, Founder of New South Wales, 1738–1814*, Sydney, 1937.

Molony, John, *The Native Born, The First White Australians*, Melbourne, 2000.

Mulvaney, John and Kamminga, Johan, *Prehistory of Australia*, Sydney, 1999.

Oldham, Wilfred, *Britain's Convicts to the Colonies*, Sydney, 1990.

Parker, Mrs Mary, *A Voyage Round the World in the Gorgon Man of War*, London, 1795.

Porter, Roy, *English Society in the Eighteenth Century*, London, 1983.

Pottle, Frederick A., *Boswell and the Girl from Botany Bay*, London, 1938.

Protos, Alec, *The Road to Botany: The Story of Frenchman's Road Randwick through the Journals of La Pérouse and the First Fleet Writers*, Sydney, 2000.

Reece, Bob (ed), *Irish Convicts, The Origins of Convicts Transported to Australia*, Dublin, 1989.

Reed, A.W., *Myths & Legends of Australia*, Sydney, 1965.

Rees, Siân, *The Floating Brothel, The Extraordinary Story of the Lady Juliana and its Cargo of Female Convicts Bound for Botany Bay*, Sydney, 2001.

Reynolds, Henry, *The Law of the Land*, Melbourne, 1987.

Ritchie, John, *The Wentworths, Father and Son*, Melbourne, 1997.

Robinson, Portia, *The Hatch and Brood of Time, A Study of the First Generation of Native-born White Australians, 1788–1828, Volume 1*, Oxford, UK, 1985.

Robinson, Portia, *The Women of Botany Bay*, Ringwood, Victoria, 1998.

Robson, John, *Captain Cook's World, Maps of the Life and Voyages of James Cook R.N.*, Sydney, 2000.

Robson, L.L., *The Convict Settlers of Australia, An Enquiry into the Origin and Character of the Convicts Transported to New South Wales and Van Diemen's Land 1787–1852*, Melbourne, 1965.

Ronayne, Jarlath, *The Irish in Australia, Rogues and Reformers. First Fleet to Federation*, Melbourne, 2003.

The Second Fleet of Convicts, A Comprehensive Listing of Convicts who Sailed in HMS Guardian, Lady Juliana, Neptune, Scarborough and Surprize, ed. R.J. Ryan, Sydney, 1982.

Shaw, A.G.L., *Convicts & the Colonies, A Study of Penal Transportation from Great Britain and Ireland to Australia and other parts of the British Empire*, London, 1966.

Smith, Keith, *Bennelong: The Coming in of the Eora, Sydney Cove, 1788–1792*, Sydney, 2001.

Thomas, James H., *Portsmouth and the First Fleet, 1786–1787*, Portsmouth, 1987.

Thomas, Nicholas, *Discoveries: The Voyages of Captain Cook*, London, 2003.

Turnbull, Lucy Hughes, *Sydney, Biography of a City*, Sydney, 1999.

Ward, Russel, *The Australian Legend*, Melbourne, 1958.

Whiteley, Gilbert, *Naturalists of the First Fleet*, Australian Museum Magazine, Jan–March 1938.

Willey, Keith, *When the Sky Fell Down, The Destruction of the Tribes of the Sydney Region, 1788–1850s*, Sydney, 1979.

Woods, G.D., *A History of Criminal Law in New South Wales, The Colonial Period, 1788–1900*, Sydney, 2002.

Electronic Sites

Dan Byrne, The Blackheath Connection (with input by Leo Rhind), available free online under that title.

Index

Weights and Measures

Linear Measure

1 inch	=	1000 mils	= 2.54	centimetres
12 inches	=	1 foot	= 0.3048	metre
3 feet	=	1 yard	= 0.9144	metre
220 yards or 660 feet	=	1 furlong	= 201.168	metres
8 furlongs or 1760 yards	=	1 (statute) mile	= 1.6093	kilometres

Square Measure

144 square inches	=	1 square foot	= 929.03	square centimetres
9 square feet	=	1 square yard	= 0.8361	square metre
4840 square yards	=	1 acre	= 0.4047	hectare
640 acres	=	1 square mile	= 259.0	hectares

Nautical Measure

6 feet = 1 fathom = 1.829 metres

100 fathoms = 1 cable's length

(In the Royal Navy, 608 feet, or 185.319 metres = 1 cable's length)

10 cables length = 1 international nautical mile = 1.852 kilometres

1 international nautical mile = 1.150 779 statute miles

(the length of a minute of longitude at the equator)

60 nautical miles = *1 degree of a great circle of the earth.*

= 69.047 statute miles

3 nautical miles = 1 marine league = 5.556 kilometres

Liquid and Dry Measure

1 gill	=	5 fluid ounces	= 0.1480	litre
4 gills	=	1 pint	= 0.568	litre
2 pints	=	1 quart	= 1.136	litres
4 quarts	=	1 gallon	= 4.546	litres
2 gallons	=	1 peck	= 9.092	litres
4 pecks	=	1 bushel	= 36.37	litres

Weights

		1 ounce	= 28.3495	grams
		1 pound	= 453.59	grams
14 pounds	=	1 stone	= 6.35	kilograms
112 pounds	=	1 hundredweight	= 50.80	kilograms
2240 pounds	=	1 (long) ton	= 1016.05	kilograms
2000 pounds	=	1 (short) ton	= 907.18	kilograms

Temperature

Fahrenheit → Celsius: $°C = \frac{5}{9} \times (°F - 32)$